ETHICS AND SOCIAL SECURITY REFORM

International Studies on Social Security

Volume 7

Ethics and Social Security Reform

Edited by
ERIK SCHOKKAERT

LONDON AND NEW YORK

First published 2001 by Ashgate Publishing

Reissued 2018 by Routledge
2 Park Square, Milton Park, Abingdon, Oxon OX14 4RN
711 Third Avenue, New York, NY 10017, USA

Routledge is an imprint of the Taylor & Francis Group, an informa business

A Library of Congress record exists under LC control number: 2001088785

ISBN 13: 978-1-138-72542-3 (hbk)
ISBN 13: 978-1-138-72539-3 (pbk)
ISBN 13: 978-1-315-19189-8 (ebk)

Contents

Preface

Stein Ringen

This volume is the seventh in a series of international studies on social security. It is published for the Foundation for International Studies on Social Security (FISS), whose Editorial Board has selected and assembled the texts from papers presented at a FISS conference in Sigtuna, Sweden in June 2000. One of its members, Erik Schokkaert, is the editor for this volume and has written an introduction.

This volume is concerned with the interaction of ethical positions and work incentives. Previous volumes have covered:

- Curing the Dutch Disease; An International Perspective on Disability Policy Reform, 1996, ed. Leo J.M. Aarts, Richard V. Burkhauser and Philip R. De Jong
- Social Policy and the Labour Market, 1997, ed. Philip R. De Jong and Theodore R. Marmor
- Ageing, Social Security and Affordability, 1998, ed. Theodore R. Marmor and Philip R. De Jong
- The State of Social Welfare, 1997, 1998, ed. Peter Flora, Philip R. De Jong, Julian Le Grand and Jun-Young Kim
- Fighting Poverty: Caring for Children, Parents, The Elderly and Health, 1999, ed. Stein Ringen and Philip R. De Jong
- Domain Linkages and Privatization in Social Security, 2000, ed. Jun-Young Kim and Per-Gunnar Svensson.

The first volume was based on papers presented at a FISS conference in Rotterdam in 1992. The other volumes derived from papers presented at small annual FISS conferences in Sigtuna, Sweden – the Sigtuna seminars. They bring together scholars and researchers from all over the world, though predominantly from Europe, Asia and North America, to present and discuss findings on economic, legal and social aspects of social security and its relationships with other aspects of society. Different academic approaches are used to address public policy issues in an international context. Social security is defined widely as transfers to households in case or in kind, be it social insurance or tax funded expenditure is meant to include related expenditure on health and education and the consequences of taxation as well as social security contributions. Young scholars are able to discuss their findings with experienced research workers. An increasing number of social security administrators and government representatives attend to listen and participate.

The papers in this series, which take an independent perspective, spell out the relevance of analytic findings to practical issues. They include reports of the consequences of specific approaches in different countries to the design and reform of welfare programmes. The papers also include a variety of intellectual approaches to social security issues. They include work in different disciplines, such as economics, law, social science and political science.

FISS would like to thank Mandy Köhlinger and Piet van Diest at the Van Diest Word Processing Office in The Hague; Jennifer Shervington in Birmingham, England and Dawn Duren at the University of Wisconsin in Madison, Wisconsin, U.S.A. for valuable assistance in formatting and typing.

Introduction and overview

Erik Schokkaert

Each and every evaluation of social policy necessarily involves value judgments. This is obviously true for the organisation of social security, which immediately raises questions on poverty, income redistribution, welfare and respect for individual privacy. Social scientists and politicians sometimes have the tendency to downplay these unavoidable ethical questions and to reduce their analysis to a purely pragmatic reasoning. This attitude does not help to clarify the debate. This volume offers a collection of papers which are more explicit in their ethical conceptions.

Ethical considerations can enter in many different guises. They first enter at the level of the definition of ethical concepts and principles (part 1). They are also relevant to understand the interaction between ethical values, social attitudes and political feasibility (part 2). They certainly are unavoidable – although sometimes hidden – for the evaluation of concrete policy measures which involve trade-offs between different values (part 3).

The first chapter by *Erik Schokkaert* gives a general overview of ethical approaches to the welfare state. The author proposes to evaluate social institutions within a broad consequentialist framework in which their goodness has to be evaluated on the basis of the level of positive and negative freedom in society. Consequentialism is a crucial feature because it opens room for the theoretical insights and empirical findings from the social sciences. Positive freedom relates to the avoidance of poverty and insecurity. The concern for negative freedom introduces considerations of personal responsibility and respect for individual privacy. However, to evaluate any concrete policy measure a careful analysis of potential consequences and of the trade-offs between different objectives is necessary. Considerations of political feasibility should also enter this analysis.

The two following chapters focus on more specific and topical questions but remain at the level of ethical concepts and principles. They illustrate how basic ethical choices get embodied in the law. *Lotta Westerhäll* raises the problem of the definition of rehabilitation and emphasizes the distinction between medical, social and employment aspects. Her careful analysis of Swedish law shows that the so-called "refinement" of the sickness insurance with a sharper focus on medical aspects has led to striking inconsistencies and to an unequal treatment of unemployed and employed people, that is difficult to justify from an ethical perspective. She argues in favour of a comprehensive view of rehabilitation leading to the respect for principles of human dignity and equality and for a functional view on the legal regulations concerning rehabilitation. *Simon Roberts* discusses another topical subject: the treatment of migrants, asylum seekers and refugees. Here also a careful analysis of the existing legal framework in different countries leads directly to deep ethical questions. What are the boundaries of equality? Or, formulated differently: how to define the constituency for which the social security system can be supposed to be relevant? When do we define someone as a "member of society"?

While legal questions about principles and concepts immediately confront us with ethical questions, one might think that this is less true for the work of social scientists on measurement issues. Chapters 4 and 5 illustrate that this is a naïve position. Both chapters treat the problem of how to measure poverty and they clearly indicate that different measures imply different ethical presuppositions. *Robert Haveman* and *Melissa Mullikin* give an overview of a wide spectrum of poverty measures. They show that the choice of measure is not a merely academic question but has immediate policy implications. Different measures lead to substantial differences in both the level and trend of poverty and in the composition of the poor population. They themselves argue in favour of a concept of self-reliance as a poverty measure where the capability to be self-reliant is linked to the family's net earnings capacity. They suggest that the philosophical roots of their approach can be found in the approach of Amartya Sen, which was also advocated in Schokkaert's introduction. *Jonathan Bradshaw* discusses the conceptual questions raised by different concepts of absolute poverty. He devotes most attention to the social assistance rates existing in different European countries and to the official USA poverty line, but also mentions subjective poverty thresholds and thresholds based on budget standards. Again, it is clear that these different approaches reflect ethically relevant differences in the weight attached to different aspects of household's living circumstances.

Attitudes of the population play a central role in the chapters in part 2 of the volume. These are relevant from at least two perspectives. Without any doubt, popular convictions and preferences codetermine the political feasibility of different policy proposals. Some would argue that they also play a more basic role in the ethical debate, because moral principles cannot be plucked from the air but should be rooted in some form of social consensus. *Peter Saunders* and *Maneerat Pinyopusarerk* explicitly take the former perspective. They review some evidence on the community acceptance of social security provisions for the unemployed in Australia and project their results against the broader background of the debate on participation and responsibility. For this purpose, they first investigate the pattern of time use for groups with a different labour force status. Their analysis of the attitudinal data suggests that public opinion distinguishes between different groups of the unemployed. While there is some support for mutual obligation for the younger unemployed, this does not apply to the older unemployed, those caring for young children and those with a disability. Moreover, most people feel that mutual obligation also implies action on the part of the government to reduce unemployment and to offer training programs and wage subsidies. Different ethical positions clearly play a role in these attitudes. "Individualist", "collectivist" and "fatalist" personal value positions have a strong influence on attitudes towards the social security treatment of the unemployed. *Andreas Cebulla* also focuses on unemployment insurance, but from a completely different perspective. He investigates the willingness to pay for private unemployment insurance in two countries (Britain and Germany). In both countries intentions to insure are strongly influenced by past experience of unemployment and subjective assessment of the unemployment risk. The latter is mainly interpreted in "global" terms. In both countries there is a concern for personal initiative and responsibility – similar to the one investigated by Saunders and Pinyopusarerk. The level of support provided by the public unemployment insurance and the availability of alternative labour market strategies – such as the activation of family members – are important factors in the explanation of the attitudes towards private insurance.

Part 3 of the volume collects a series of papers on more concrete policy issues. As in the previous parts there is a strong emphasis on labour market problems. Once we start looking at concrete questions, institutions will of course play a crucially important role in the analysis. Institutional reform is the main topic of *Jasper van den Brink* and *Esther Bergsma*. They concentrate on the transition from a state-controlled to a market-based social security system, i.e. on what they call the "pre-market phase". During this transition phase the existing institutions face a large degree of uncertainty: about the question of exactly when there will be a market, about the form that the market will take, perhaps even about the question of whether in fact a market will be introduced at all. Moreover the managing and controlling authorities face similar uncertainties concerning the redefinition of their role. All these institutions will act strategically in order to improve their "starting position" in the future market game. The authors emphasize that much more attention should be given to this pre-market phase, because it may to a large extent influence the working of the resulting market organisation – or may even lead to the abandonment of the whole market idea.

Barbara Wolfe evaluates in a detailed and informative way the incentive structure resulting from the welfare system. She focuses on Wisconsin and on the attempts to reduce dependency by moving most of those receiving cash welfare into the work force. This objective is akin to the concerns raised in the opinion surveys of Saunders and Pinyopusarerk. It turns out that it is difficult to reconcile different ethical objectives: simultaneously providing incentives to work and incentives to increase individual's labour market productivity while maintaining a minimal safety net and avoiding high marginal rates of taxation. Her careful analysis – a good example of the painstaking scientific analysis which is crucial in any consequentialist approach to ethical evaluation – leads her to advocate a second best approach consisting of a combination of a targeted earned income tax credit, a guaranteed job, child care subsidies for all those who are in the paid labour force, universal health care coverage, loans for education and training whose required payments depend on earnings and a cash transfer system for those with very young children, significant disabilities or dependents who require extensive care.

The next chapter by *Martin Rosenfeld* also treats the incentives related to active and passive labour market policies and within the latter to the combination of full-rate unemployment benefit, means-tested unemployment benefit and public welfare transfers. Yet he focuses on intergovernmental fiscal relations and on the incentives for public decision makers. His detailed analysis of the German situation leads him to propose a change in the current intergovernmental division of competences which could reduce unemployment, save on transfer payments and cut the costs associated with labour and transfer administration. Again, the chapter illustrates how scientific analysis of the trade-offs between the different objectives is necessary to clarify the difficult choices, which have to be made. As a matter of fact, Rosenfeld shows how a better institutional set up may make it easier to find an ethically attractive compromise.

Bea Cantillon, Joris Ghysels, Ninke Mussche and *Rudi van Dam* investigate the distributional impact of female labour market participation. Analysis of the LIS-data shows that highly educated women participate more in the labour market than poorly educated women and that their participation rate is about the same in different welfare state types. Participation of lower educated women is different in different welfare state types: it is lower in the conservative countries and larger in the social democratic countries, with the liberal countries in-between. Women's wages are lower than men's in all three welfare types. However, despite the large degree of educational homogamy, the correlation between the incomes of the partners is very weak and dual earnership decreases the overall income inequality. It is doubtful however whether this levelling effect will persist over time.

Chapter 3.5 by *Edward Palmer* and *Ali Tasiran* brings us back to the ethical challenges, which were raised in Lotta Westerhäll's chapter about rehabilitation. They present the results of a cross-country empirical analysis of the pattern of work resumption after a long sickness spell due to back pain. They carefully distinguish the importance of medical and vocational interventions, the work environment and economic factors. Country cohorts with good work-resumption results have better odds for improvement in the work-ability and ADL outcomes. Differences in institutional arrangements also play an important role.

The last chapter, by *Jochen Jagob* and *Werner Sesselmeier* is in a certain sense an outlier, because it does not focus on the labour market. However, it introduces another ethically crucial question: that of the intergenerational distribution. Partially funded systems must be designed in a careful way to cope with the challenge of the demographic change. The authors concentrate on Germany, but try to get some inspiration from a comparison with the Swedish system. Like the two previous chapters, this one also illustrates how revealing such international comparisons can be.

Rather than hiding value judgments behind obscure technical jargon, it is better to bring them to the open and introduce them explicitly in the social and political debate on reform measures. While social scientists sometimes are reluctant to engage in a deep ethical discussion, this volume shows that detailed empirical work and careful conceptual thinking about social security are necessary inputs in the ethical evaluation of the welfare state.

PART 1

ETHICAL CONCEPTS AND PRINCIPLES

1.1 Altruism, efficiency and justice: ethical challenges to the welfare state

Erik Schokkaert

1. Introduction

It has become fashionable to talk about the crisis of the continental European welfare states. Critics point to the sharply increasing costs and to the prospects of still further cost increases in the future. They are mainly worried about the retirement pensions in pay-as-you-go systems and about the costs of health care. At the same time, and despite these growing costs, the social security system has not been able to wipe out the remaining hard core of long run poverty. It may even have worsened the poverty problem, because the lack of flexibility on the labour market and the increasing labour costs have led to a deterioration of the employment prospects of the low-skilled. To summarize the criticism: the welfare state has not been efficient and we can no longer afford its costs. This criticism has been taken over by many political parties and one sometimes gets the impression that it is also shared by a growing part of the population. Privatisation is high on many political agendas.

These social developments have led to – or are partly caused by – developments in the sphere of social thinking. Here the criticism is not always new or original. New are the surprising coalitions which seem to form. The liberal criticism on compulsory social insurance schemes has always been there, but it has gained in popularity in an era of increasing costs and of a rise in anti-state feelings. It supports the political moves in the direction of privatisation. But this traditional 'rightist' criticism is closely related to the new position of some moderate leftists who argue for the rehabilitation of the idea of personal responsibility (Giddens, 1994,

Vandenbroucke, 1999). At the other side of the spectrum we find philosophers who are unhappy about what they see as the decline of solidarity and who look for a new foundation of the welfare state in a renewed concept of solidarity (Rosanvallon, 1995, Van Parijs, 1994). For them Bismarck is definitely out. This more 'leftist' criticism reminds us of the traditional rightist position that the increasing state intervention is detrimental to the spontaneous feelings of solidarity and has led to the loosening of important social ties.

In this chapter I investigate a possible ethical justification for the welfare state. In section 2 I will argue that the concept of distributive justice should play the dominant role in this analysis. I sketch some ethical preconceptions as a frame of reference to analyse the concepts of insurance and solidarity. I do not at all offer a balanced overview of the various ethical approaches which can be found in the literature[1]. The chapter is heavily biased towards the ethical approaches which are most often used by economists and towards my own position. This is a deliberate choice. My only purpose is to sketch a philosophical background which can underpin an analysis of the existing European welfare state institutions.

That analysis follows in section 3 I will confront my ethical framework with some facts about the outcomes of the welfare state and with survey results on its perception and evaluation by the citizens. It will turn out – and I can as well admit from the beginning – that my analysis is extremely conservative, in that I will defend the existing social security institutions. At the same time, I think that some of the challenges have to be taken seriously. Section 4 concludes.

The 'welfare state' is a broad concept, interpreted differently in different countries. I will focus mainly on income transfers such as pensions and unemployment benefits. This is not really a serious limitation: the main thrust of my argument also holds for health and disability insurance and even for systems of public education. Health care will often be mentioned in passing. I have kept my definition deliberately vague to capture the general idea of a 'large amount of government redistribution as a reaction to differences/changes in individual living standards'. Although I am well aware that the differences between different national systems are huge, I do not always make an explicit distinction between the Northern European and Scandinavian models. A second limitation is more serious. I will completely neglect in my analysis the international dimension of the ethical problems surrounding the welfare state. Given the situation in many Third World countries, there are no good ethical reasons for this choice.

Moreover, even from a pragmatic point of view, it may seem strange for a European not to say anything about the hotly debated topic of international coordination. My only excuse for this choice is my limitations of space and knowledge.

2. Liberalism, efficiency and justice

Many critics of the welfare state base their attack on one or another strand of liberalism. To many outsiders this position must seem a natural starting point for an economist. However, contrary to what one might believe when one follows day-to-day economic discussions, truly liberal ideas occupy a minority position within the world of economic science, at least when we define it as the world of scientific journals and conferences. Economists in general are much more concerned with efficiency than with freedom. I will sketch the relationship between both concepts in a first subsection and then turn to a consequentialist view about justice.

2.1 Liberalism and efficiency

There are many different strands of philosophical liberalism[2]. The strongest attack on the whole idea of the welfare state comes from what I would like to call strict liberalism or libertarianism. Rowley and Peacock (1975) – who are extremely critical of the traditional welfare economic approach – define libertarianism as being 'concerned essentially, though not exclusively, with the maintenance and extension of individual freedom, defined as that condition of mankind in which coercion of some individuals by others is reduced to the minimum possible degree' (p. 78). In this view all government intervention constitutes a violation of personal property rights: there is no basic difference between income taxation and forced labour or slavery. If freedom (defined as the lack of coercion) is the only relevant value, there obviously cannot be a role for a compulsory system of social security. For libertarians the institutions of the welfare state are ethically unacceptable and only reflect misuse of political power by specific social groups.

I think that this extreme position is consistent but unacceptable. I do not want to dwell on the basic philosophical problem of the ethical justification of the given set of property rights – a justification which is necessary to sensibly define the notion of coercion. Many people share with libertarians the strong intuition that human beings own themselves and

5

have the right to get the fruit of their own labour. But production also requires the use of natural resources. Therefore the legitimacy of existing property rights depends on the legitimacy of the initial appropriation of these natural resources, a question which has in my view not been settled convincingly by libertarians[3].

For the sake of this exposition, I will suffice with a simpler and more down-to-earth argument. It is well known that 'free' social states may involve an extremely unequal distribution of welfare, in which some people are very wealthy and others near to starvation. If the wealthy persons care sufficiently for the poor – for whatever reason – they will voluntarily help them and the worst aspects of poverty will be remedied. But this is really a statement about facts. If the rich do not care, a strict liberal will deny the starving poor any claim at all to a larger part of the resources. Only few people will accept as 'just' a distribution where human beings are starving because of circumstances which they cannot control. I am not among those few people.

It is perhaps this reluctance towards extreme poverty which explains the vague expression 'essentially though not exclusively' in Rowley and Peacock's definition. They (and some other libertarians) would accept special arrangements for the very poor. But this immediately raises the question who are the 'very poor' and what arrangements are sufficiently 'special' to be acceptable. The admission of exceptions makes a hole in the consistent fortress of freedom. As soon as one accepts some forms of coercion -in this case to avoid starvation- one is confronted with a trade-off between different values. Once one accepts the basic idea of trade-offs, one has to specify more carefully their exact range. Simple libertarianism does no longer suffice.

One possible way out is offered by the idea of the social contract. Somewhat simplistically, one could say that social contract theories legitimize coercion, if the individuals have first unanimously (mostly tacitly) accepted it. If they have freely accepted a social contract, they have to obey its rules afterwards. Depending on the exact content given to the social contract, this approach may or may not lead to a justification of welfare state institutions. I give two economic examples.

Buchanan (1986) situates the social contract in a kind of mythical constitutional stage. He argues that people in this constitutional stage will not accept inequalities following from discrimination or from different positions at birth. Therefore in his view the social contract will contain *inter alia* the acceptance of a publicly financed education system, of a large

6

tax on inheritance and of a set of rules to counteract overt discrimination in the allocation of job opportunities. At the same time, however, people at the constitutional level will be aware of the dangers resulting from an ever-growing state apparatus (Leviathan) and will formulate rules so as to constrain this coercing agency. In Buchanan's social contract there is no room for a full welfare state.

It is interesting to compare Buchanan's approach with the one of Kolm (1985). The latter goes much further in his so-called 'liberal social contract'. In his view the autonomy of individuals implies the right to give up (or exchange) rights. The legitimacy of these transactions follows from the voluntary agreement by all parties. Then comes the essential step in the reasoning. Kolm argues that some voluntary agreements or contracts will not arise spontaneously in the market place for a number of reasons which have nothing to do with the desires of the potential contractors. Examples of such reasons are the presence of transaction costs, the lack of information, the difficulty to control the free-rider problem in a situation with public goods, the problem of externalities. And here begins the role of the political process:

> 'The political process is a social process that tries to achieve what direct free exchange was unable to do.(...) The political philosophy that emanates from the liberty principle is: *any legitimate free agreement that would have been reached must be implemented*' (Kolm, 1987, p. 103).

Kolm is very explicit about the consequences of such a contract. Its implementation will require coercion: people must be forced to be free. This coercion is legitimate, however, because it increases freedom by removing the constraints impeding the actual direct agreement. How then do we know in practice the content of such liberal social contract? Here Kolm uses the insights from welfare economics but reinterprets them in the light of his freedom approach. Let me therefore first turn to welfare economic theory.

Traditional Paretian welfare economics starts from two principles. The first is consumer sovereignty: individuals are the best judges of what is good for themselves and these individual preferences have to be respected. Not doing so would involve paternalism, a pejorative notion in this approach[4]. The second is the Pareto-principle. If it is possible to find a policy measure which would not harm anybody in society and would benefit at least one individual, this measure should be implemented. Since it should gain unanimous approval, why would one not implement it?

This approach is often seen as supporting a rather unbalanced defence of the market mechanism. But it can also be used as a vehicle to study so-called market failures and then offers a convincing justification for an (extended) welfare state. To understand the argument, one can start from the generally accepted assumption that most individuals are risk averse and therefore want to insure themselves in the face of risk. In so far as this is possible through private markets, there is no need for government intervention. For some risks, however, private markets are not efficient or do not exist. The introduction of a social insurance mechanism can then be a Pareto-improvement.

It is not the place here to go deeply into the different arguments in favour of social insurance but let me nevertheless mention the most important ones[5]. Insurance activities are often characterised by increasing returns to scale: there will therefore be strong monopolistic tendencies, unless the market is regulated. Moreover, administration and other transaction costs may be lower with public (monopolistic) provision than with private provision[6]. If risks are highly correlated, private institutions will not be able to offer insurance. Typical examples of such 'collective risks' are unemployment and unexpected inflation: an argument in favour of compulsory public systems of unemployment insurance and of a pay-as-you-go system of retirement pensions. In a situation of asymmetric information, in which the insured knows better his or her own risk than the insurer, negative selection may lead to an inefficient market structure or to the complete disappearance of the private insurance market. The typical example here is health insurance, but to a certain extent the argument also holds for unemployment insurance. Each and every insurance system (whether private or public) will have to cope with moral hazard – the phenomenon that people adapt their behaviour as soon as they are insured, by being less cautious to avoid the risks or less careful in controlling the costs. In some circumstances governments are better placed to fight moral hazard, because they have the power of coercion and can use legal instruments to control the behaviour of medical providers and patients in a system of health insurance or the behaviour of firms and workers in a system of unemployment insurance.

I think that there is indeed a strong case to be made for social insurance on the basis of these efficiency arguments. We are very close here to Kolm's basic inspiration. The notions of consumer sovereignty and unanimous approval at first sight are eminently liberal and in any case bring us very far in the direction of the liberal social contract. As a matter of fact, these insights from welfare economic theory are used by Kolm to describe more concretely the content of that contract, because they indicate where we have to look for agreements which would be unanimously approved (are Pareto-improving) but do not arise spontaneously. Yet the basic underlying rationale remains different. Paretian welfare economics legitimizes social insurance institutions on the basis of efficiency and with as ultimate reference the *preferences* of the citizens. Kolm's liberal social contract legitimizes the same institutions with as ultimate reference their *freedom*. Of course, while the basic rationale is different, for all practical purposes the consequences of the argumentation are similar.

What is the ethical status of this argumentation for social insurance? Let us first return to the libertarian position. Of course, libertarians will find nothing wrong in purely private insurance. But typical for social insurance is its compulsory character: it is exactly this compulsory nature which makes it possible to address the problems of negative selection or collective risk. It is the use of political power which offers possibilities to fight moral hazard. None of these efficiency arguments will be convincing for a libertarian who is only concerned about freedom and rejects coercion almost by definition.

On the other hand one could also argue that even Kolm's liberal social contract does not go far enough. It offers a justification for social *insurance*, but not for more. To some extent, all insurance schemes implement a sort of solidarity. Ex post, i.e. at the moment the risk occurs, the unlucky or the ill are paid out of the collected resources. But ex ante, i.e. before it is known who will be lucky and will not be struck by the risk and who will be unlucky, payment of the insurance premium can be rationalized on the basis of pure self-interest. Moreover, according to the insurance principle, high risk individuals will have to pay a higher premium than low risk individuals. Most social security schemes do not follow this logic. The premia in unemployment insurance or public health insurance are not adjusted to the risks, even if these are known. Therefore, the solidarity goes much further and is also ex ante. Moreover, in many systems the premia are linked to the financial means (or the wage) of the insured. These richer forms of solidarity cannot easily be legitimized in the liberal approach.

There is, however, one possible justification (Kolm, 1985; Miller, 1988). It is a fact of life that people do care about others. It is not unreasonable to hypothesize that at least some wealthy people do care about the poor. As mentioned already before, this may lead to private charity. To get an argument for government intervention, we have to take a second step. If the welfare (or the consumption level) of the poor enters into the utility function of the donors, this welfare (or consumption level) essentially becomes a public good. Therefore, there will be a free-rider problem. Every donor wants to see the poor people become less poor, but prefers at the same time that this increase in the utility (or consumption) level of the poor is realized through the help of others. If all potential donors follow the same reasoning, the resulting transfers to the poor will be suboptimal. The welfare of the donors (and of the poor) will increase when they all are forced to give what they really want to give, but do not give spontaneously for strategic (free-rider) considerations. Therefore, compulsory redistribution through the government will lead to a Pareto-improvement. Kolm (1985) calls this phenomenon that of the 'collective gift'. It is closely related to the older idea of Pareto-optimal redistribution (Hochman and Rodgers, 1969).

While the collective gift argument goes further than private charity and offers a rationale for government intervention, the situation of the poor will still depend on the charitable feelings of the rich. Moreover, one needs a rather complex structure of altruism to justify the specific redistribution patterns within the social security system. Kolm (1985) is perfectly aware of this problem and he introduces a broader ethical view through his theory of 'fundamental insurance'. He therefore sketches a situation where people do not yet know their earning capacity, their propensity to be sick, etc. In this kind of original position, people would probably accept a system of 'fundamental insurance', i.e. a system of transfers towards the handicapped or those with lower earning capacity. This hypothetical contract is *not* a 'liberal social contract' in Kolm's terminology, however, because it is not a contract between real, existing persons. It will only become relevant within a liberal approach when real, existing persons accept the ethical argumentation behind the idea and want it to be realized. But then we are back in a variant of the altruism argumentation.

Let me summarize. The intuition that individuals in a just society have the right to the fruits of their own labour is very strong in most societies. This does not necessarily rule out the possibility of compulsory social insurance. Such insurance can be efficient and can also be rationalised within a broad theory of the social contract. However, the social insurance schemes so rationalised can only implement a weak form of ex ante-

10

solidarity. It is not even sure that they will be sufficient to avoid extreme poverty. If one considers this as unacceptable, one has to look for another approach. In the next subsection I will therefore propose a form of what can be called 'broad consequentialism'.

2.2 Justice and rights

The liberal approach (even in its social contract forms) is basically *procedural*. The ethical evaluation of policies and institutions is based on the rightness of the procedures followed. If all procedures have been respected, the outcome is just whatever the concrete consequences. Freedom and unanimous approval (be it at a social contract stage) act as constraints, which cannot be violated. One can argue that extreme poverty will not happen —or should not happen because of the phenomenon of collective gift –but if rich individuals really do not care, extreme poverty does not raise a problem of justice. As argued before, I find it difficult to accept this conclusion. This basically implies that my theory of justice has to be *consequentialist* (or at least consequence-sensitive): the goodness of institutions and social arrangements is evaluated (at least partly) on the basis of their results. Property rights are not sacrosanct and to be taken as given. Since they are part of the basic institutions of society, they must be legitimized by the conception of justice. Justice comes first.

Consequentialism is dominant in the social sciences in general and in economics in particular. It has its roots in utilitarianism, which has had such a crucial influence on economic thinking. Simply stated, utilitarians rank states of affairs on the basis of the simple sum of the utility or happiness levels of the individuals in these states. This is but one specific form of consequentialism however (Sen and Williams, 1982). First, the only characteristic of states of affairs which is considered are the utility levels of the individuals in these states. This has been called 'welfarism'. Second, to aggregate the utilities of different individuals one takes a simple sum, implying that the distribution of utilities does not matter[7]. In the broad interpretation that I follow here, consequentialism goes far beyond utilitarianism, because it uses a different metric to describe or evaluate consequences.

To a certain extent, consequentialism can even be seen as an extension of liberalism. This has most forcefully been argued by Sen (1984, 1988) who proposes to interpret 'rights as goals'. Consider the following simple example. According to liberalism, person A should not threaten the

11

personal integrity of person B (he should not black his eye), but what if he sees person C becoming aggressive towards B? Is A obliged to defend B? If we answer yes, do we then not consider the realisation of negative freedoms as a goal (instead of merely as a constraint)? Once we treat rights as goals they can be integrated in a broad consequentialist view. We can then analyse in a coherent way trade-offs between different rights and answer questions such as: what is the right action for A, should he defend B against being beaten up, even if he therefore has to break into the house of D in order to use his phone to alert the police? And, more importantly, we can still go further and also introduce so-called 'positive freedoms' (or social and economic rights) into the analysis:

> 'Why should our concern stop only at protecting negative freedoms rather than be involved with what people can actually do? Should one be under an obligation to save the person who has been pushed into the river but not the person who has fallen in it? In deciding whether one is under an obligation to help a starving person, should one say 'yes' if the person has been robbed (with his negative freedom being violated), but remain free to say 'no' if he has been fired from his job, or has lost his land to the moneylender, or has suffered from flooding or drought (without any violation of negative freedom)?' (Sen, 1984, pp. 314-315).

Of course, a libertarian will never accept this reasoning. But if one takes the consequentialist view that justice is about the goodness of social states, i.e. that consequences do matter, while at the same time having the feeling that concern for negative freedoms is important, it is reassuring that one can formulate a framework in which trade-offs between negative and positive freedoms can be explicitly articulated. This will be an important consideration as soon as we start evaluating the institutions of the welfare state.

Remains the important question: how to evaluate the level of 'positive freedoms'? How to give content to the notion of 'economic and social rights'? I take as my starting point a focus on the situation of individual human beings[8]. This does not at all imply that data at the household level are not useful or even necessary. Since information on the intra-household allocation of resources is rare and difficult to get, there is a pragmatic argument for the use of these data. There is also a more basic argument. The living standard of individuals is crucially influenced by the household in which they live, because this sociological entity determines how many material resources are pooled and how decisions about the use of these resources are taken. Therefore household decisions are crucial to understand the situation of the individuals living in the household. However, from an ethical point of view, the basic entity of the analysis in my view remains the individual. How then to describe the living standard of the individuals?

Among social security practitioners, the most popular concept is the income of the person (or the household). This is true both in policy discussions and in the largest part of the empirical research. Yet everybody will agree that income alone is only a very poor indicator of the living standard. When working at the household level, it is obvious that one has to correct for differences in household size and composition. But even if we had income information at the individual level, we still would have to correct for differences in needs. A handicapped person will reach a lower living standard than a non-handicapped person with the same income. The usual trick used by social researchers to circumvent this problem is the use of equivalence scales[9]. All practitioners know however that there is a large margin of error involved in the computations of these scales and that the choice of a specific scale often is rather arbitrary (and hidden in a footnote). This is the more serious, because there is by now plenty of empirical evidence that statements about inequality or about the incidence and the composition of poverty are sensitive to this specific choice (Buhman et al., 1988, Coulter, Cowell and Jenkins, 1992, Deaton and Paxson, 1998). Moreover, one has to think about the justification of the various methods to calculate equivalence scales. An acceptable justification will necessarily have to refer to a more 'basic' concept of living standard, which is then approximated by the 'equivalence scale corrected' income level. Income can be an instrument of social policy, but it is a very poor description of the individual's situation.

Among economic theorists another popular approach is welfarism[10]. As mentioned before, economists often stick to consumer sovereignty and to the Pareto-principle. But as soon as one wants to go beyond the Pareto-principle and to introduce distributional considerations, one needs some notion of interpersonally comparable utility[11]. The most straightforward interpretation of 'utility' or 'welfare' is then in terms of happiness. Is happiness indeed the best ethical guide as a description of an individual's situation? More and more social choice theorists answer that question negatively[12]. Utilitarians for a long time have had to make exception for

13

asocial preferences, for the psychopath who can only become happy by murdering young blonde girls. But to define what are asocial preferences, one needs a criterion which is different from 'happiness', i.e. one needs a non-welfarist frame of reference. More generally, happiness is an extremely subjective notion. Often people adjust their wants and desires to their possibilities as they learn to accept and endure terrible circumstances. What about the ethical evaluation of the living standard of a wife which is regularly beaten up by her drunken husband, but is reasonably happy because her religious conviction leads her to accept her fate patiently? And what about individuals who are unhappy because they have expensive tastes – who can only be happy if they have a red Ferrari or can consume plovers' eggs (Arrow, 1973)? There seems to be a basic difference between 'subjective tastes' on the one hand and 'needs' on the other hand:

> 'The statement "Oh Lord, I *need* a Mercedes-Benz!" is a joke. "Oh Lord, I need a coronary artery by-pass graft!" is not' (Evans, 1984, p. 53).

Most people have the intuition that needs are the responsibility of society, but subjective tastes remain the responsibility of the individual[13]. Society can only create the background conditions to make people happy. Becoming happy or not is one's own responsibility.

Given that income is too objective and happiness too subjective, it seems logical to look for a concept in between the two. The obvious candidate has already been suggested by my discussion of the weak points of the two other possibilities: a multidimensional description of people's living standard. Multidimensional approaches to poverty are already for a long time used by sociologists. The World Bank uses a kind of 'basic needs' concept for the description of the situation in Third World countries. However, this 'basic needs' terminology is perhaps too minimalist and too much geared towards the analysis of poverty. Sen (1985) has proposed similar ideas for a general description of the living standard in terms of what he calls 'functionings':

> 'A functioning is an achievement of a person: what he or she manages to do or to be. (...) It has to be distinguished from the commodities which are used to achieve those functionings. For example, bicycling has to be distinguished from possessing a bike. It has to be distinguished also from the happiness generated by the

14

functioning, for example, actually cycling around must not be identified with the pleasure obtained from that act' (Sen, 1985, pp. 10-11).

Examples of functionings are being well nourished and sheltered, being socially integrated, well educated and having the opportunity to educate one's children, etc. Of course, there remains the difficult question of how to define the vector of relevant functionings. Is happiness or utility part of it, as is sometimes suggested in Sen's writings? And how to aggregate the different functionings in one overall concept of the living standard? While the principles behind the concept are clear, it is not easy to give it an operational content. But let me for the sake of the argument neglect these operational questions and assume that we have a well-defined concept of the living standard of individuals.

Once we have defined an ethically attractive notion of the living standard (as a kind of indicator of positive freedoms), we have an important building block for the ethical evaluation of social arrangements. But some difficult questions still remain to be solved. First, how to rank social states with different distributions of individual living standards? How egalitarian should we be? Is the best possible social state one in which the living standard of all individuals is equal? To reach such an egalitarian situation would necessitate a large amount of government redistribution and, hence, of coercion, which seems hard to square with at least a minimal respect for negative freedoms. How far should 'coercion' and redistribution go? Which bring us to the second question, which was already introduced earlier: how to formalize the trade-off between negative and positive freedoms? Both these questions are related to the notion of responsibility. Let me briefly sketch two possible answers.

Sen (1985) broadens the concept of functionings to capabilities. Take the example of an ascetic, who has enough money to buy all the food he wants but deliberately chooses to fast. He may be low on the functioning 'nourishment', but it is difficult to claim that there is an ethical problem. Or take the case of a well-trained engineer who could easily find a well-remunerated job, but instead prefers to become shepherd and to live in the mountains in barren circumstances. He has the opportunity to be integrated through the labour market, but does not take that opportunity. Again, it is difficult to accept that there is an ethical problem. It seems therefore preferable to maximin an index of capabilities to function, rather than an index of functionings themselves[14]. Working with capabilities introduces a

15

notion of freedom in the analysis. By the same token it also introduces a notion of responsibility[15]. Society has to equalize (or maximin) opportunities, but individuals remain responsible for their own choices within these opportunity sets.

Fleurbaey (1995) criticizes this approach. He argues that any attempt to distinguish in a consistent way between factors for which people are responsible and factors for which they are not brings us into the morass of free choice and of the metaphysics of moral responsibility. He therefore proposes to distinguish directly two sets of outcomes irrespective of the factors influencing these outcomes. A restricted set of functionings belongs to what he calls the 'social outcomes', the primary functionings which are the responsibility of the social institutions. Examples are health, education and information, wealth, collective decision making power and social integration. All the other outcomes belong to the private sphere and in that sphere there should not be any interference by the government. He then proposes to maximin an index in which the five social outcomes and respect for the private sphere are traded-off against each other.

Neither of these two approaches gives an operational answer to the difficult questions of how to trade off different values. However, the direction in which we have to think is clear and there has been an interesting and relevant discussion of principles. Moreover, the broad consequentialist framework as sketched in this section suggests some more concrete conclusions.

First, it helps to answer the question why existing welfare states are so complicated and involve specific institutions in different spheres of life (unemployment, retirement pensions, health). Why not implement all redistribution simply through cash transfers? A possible answer is to be found in the multidimensional nature of the index of capabilities, in which health, social integration, education all directly appear. Although income is important for all these outcomes, it is definitely not sufficient. Nor is it always the most efficient instrument to improve people's position. Simple cash transfers are not sufficient and may even be counterproductive to stimulate the labour market participation of the low-skilled. Health insurance is more efficient than cash transfers to guarantee health care to the sick. Education is not only important as a way to redistribute income but should be treated as a goal in itself.

Second, is there still room for the idea of social insurance? Of course there is. Suppose we have equalized opportunities on the labour market, so that the remaining income differences are ethically legitimate and fall within the own responsibility of the citizens. Respect for negative freedom then implies that persons can use their incomes as they wish – and one possibility is of course to insure themselves. Application of the insurance principle will indeed keep existing income differences intact, but by definition these income differences were legitimate. The efficiency considerations sketched in the previous section therefore keep all their relevancy, *as soon as the earnings distribution is ethically acceptable*. This last condition of course drives a huge wedge between this consequentialist framework and the liberal approach in the previous section.

Let me now summarize. In the consequentialist setting we have to evaluate social institutions on the basis of their outcomes. Either we have to maximin a vector of capabilities, or we have to maximin an index incorporating social outcomes and respect for the private sphere. What we keep from liberalism is the basic intuition that negative freedoms are important, but they have to be traded off against social and economic rights. Without being very explicit about these trade-offs, a minimal requirement seems to be that all persons should at least reach a minimal living standard. It is well known that the results of a purely private market system may be far removed from that ideal. Government intervention is then definitely needed. Hence we have here a basic justification for redistributive policies. Solidarity is an essential component of the good society. Yet the form this solidarity has to take is not fixed *a priori*. Let me therefore now turn to a more concrete analysis of welfare state institutions. We will see that pragmatic considerations offer additional arguments for the acceptance of the principle of social insurance.

3. Challenges to the welfare state: increasing costs and remaining poverty

In principle, the task of ethically evaluating the welfare state is now easy and well-defined: we have to compare different institutional arrangements on the basis of their outcomes. However, as was already emphasized, although our concept of 'consequences' including both positive and negative freedoms is an interesting heuristic device, it is not easy to give it a concrete operational content. Moreover, to evaluate real world institutions we need a point of comparison: what would have been the situation if these concrete institutions had not been at work? It would be dangerous or at least naïve to evaluate actual outcomes with as reference point an ideal

17

situation of justice. An acceptable counterfactual reasoning requires a concrete insight into the constraints society is facing. The government is not perfect and actual institutions have to be evaluated in a realistic way. At least two elements are important in that respect.

First, government intervention is not without its costs. Each insurance system has to cope with the phenomenon of moral hazard. Even stronger behavioural reactions can be expected with more forced redistribution. The labour market will react to changes in tax rates. With an internationally integrated capital market a tax on capital (income) will lead to capital flight. In the real world the government does not have all the instruments needed to control these behavioural reactions, most importantly because the economic agents have a lot of private information which is not known to the government. One of the huge advantages of a consequentialist approach is that it becomes possible to take into account explicitly these constraints on government instruments[16].

Empirical evidence suggests that the form of the government intervention may have some influence on the magnitude of the distortions. Suppose one has the choice between two systems. One is a purely redistributive scheme, directly geared towards the poor. The other is a system of social insurance in which benefits are partially linked to contributions. At first sight, the targeting in the former system seems to allow a more far reaching distribution with a smaller amount of money transferred, and hence apparently with less severe distortions on the labour market. This 'obvious' position is indeed taken without much more argumentation by politicians who plead to break down the complicated welfare state institutions that only give 'presents to the rich'. However, one should be cautious in drawing this conclusion. A purely redistributive system imposes taxes on the middle and high income workers without there being an immediate benefit as counterpart. It can be expected that these taxes will be shifted as much as possible into the labour cost. This is not necessarily true to the same degree in an insurance system. If workers or, more importantly, trade unions see through the veil of the government budget, they may partly internalize the link between contributions and benefits and therefore accept a relative decrease in the net wage in order to get a right to larger benefits[17]. Labour market distortions may therefore be lower in an insurance system than in a purely redistributive system. The choice between the two in a second-best world cannot be made on the basis of ethical principles, but is contingent on empirical facts.

Second, one has to consider also the political feasibility of different proposals. Consider again the two benchmark examples but suppose now that the tax (or contribution) rate in both systems is fixed by majority voting. The success of the redistributive scheme will depend on the degree of altruism of the middle and high income groups. This may be a shaky basis to improve the fate of the poor. On the other hand, a social insurance scheme in the Bismarckian tradition will be in the self-interest of a larger fraction of the population. Because of its broader coverage it may attract more political support and therefore imply a higher contribution rate and possibly even a better situation for the poor[18]. Again, this is in the first place an empirical question, which cannot be settled on the basis of principles alone.

It can be argued that these considerations – of distortions on the labour market and of political support – have nothing to do with ethics, because they make concessions to unethical behaviour. Once we have defined a concept of justice, the only ethically acceptable behaviour is behaviour which follows the justice principles. This is correct. But from a pragmatic point of view, it seems clear that a naïve government could do much harm. It seems at least worthwhile to study in some detail the real-world consequences of the different systems.

While it is not easy to summarize and explain the experiences of different countries, there seem to be some reasonably undisputed stylized facts (Gottschalk and Smeeding, 1997, p. 636).

There is substantial diversity in the inequality of household disposable income across major OECD nations, with the greatest inequality in the United States and the least inequality in Nordic and Northern European countries.

Post-tax and transfer disposable income is more equally distributed than market income in all OECD nations, and there is a noticeable correlation between public cash income transfer expenditures and disposable income inequality.

Even after adjusting for real income differences across countries (using purchasing power parity) low income United States citizens have real living standards below those found in most other rich OECD countries.

With respect to income inequality Gottschalk and Smeeding (1997, p. 662) describe the following ranking on the basis of recent LIS data (mostly from the beginning of the nineties):

19

'There appears to be a clear grouping of nations. Scandinavia, Austria, and the BENELUX countries have the least inequality followed by central Europe, then the Commonwealth countries, Israel and southern Europe, with the United States, the United Kingdom, and Ireland at the bottom.'

The data about poverty in Gottschalk and Smeeding (1997) basically confirm the conclusions drawn by Förster (1994, p. 194) from a more detailed analysis of the Sen poverty index with LIS data from the mid-eighties. Förster distinguishes five groups of countries:

1. first, the European countries Austria, Belgium, Germany, Luxembourg and the Netherlands with Sen indices significantly below the average;
2. a second group of European countries (Norway, France and Italy) which have indices just below the average;
3. third, the remaining European countries (Sweden, Ireland and the United Kingdom) with indices just above the average;
4. fourth, Australia and Canada with poverty indices above the cross-country average;
5. fifth, the United States has very high low-income indicators which result in a Sen index that is more than double the average of all 14 countries.

As for the working of the tax transfer system, the magnitude of poverty reduction is the highest in the Netherlands, Belgium, the UK, Germany and Ireland. The smallest reduction is in the United States.

None of these statements is surprising. They belong to the common knowledge of everybody who is concerned with social security problems. What is surprising is the fact that the welfare state in general and the European continental social security systems in particular have come under pressure exactly at the time where they proved to be so efficient to fight the consequences of the economic depression. It is therefore important and useful to repeat again and again the same question: what would have been the living standard in Europe if we had had no social security? Moreover, it is worth emphasizing that countries with a traditional Bismarckian structure (such as Belgium or Germany) do as well as the more purely redistributive Scandinavian countries.

Can the explanation for the growing criticism be found in the feelings of dissatisfaction among the citizens? There is not much evidence to support this hypothesis either. Broad international comparison studies (Taylor-Gooby, 1993, Mossialos, 1997) show that the basic welfare state institutions have remained extremely popular. This is especially true for health care and pensions but less so for unemployment benefits.

Keeping all these results in mind, it could seem that the ethical criticism which I summarized in the introduction is completely misplaced. But this is *not* my position. Although I think that the basic institutions of the European welfare states should be defended, I think at the same time that the challenges have to be taken seriously. Let me look at them now in more detail. The first criticism is that costs are growing too rapidly. The second that, despite these growing costs, there still remains a hard core of long run poverty and, moreover, that social security may have contributed to the unemployment problem of the lower skilled.

3.1 Increasing costs and political pressure: the challenge of liberalism

The most popular criticism points to the increasing costs of the welfare state and suggests that the demographic developments and the technological progress in health care will make the present institutions unaffordable in the future. The idea is that the insurance component in the system is superfluous and could be taken over by private markets and that it would be more efficient to target all efforts towards the poor. I will return to the targeting issue in the next section. Let me first make some general remarks on the problem of costs.

Sometimes one hears the statement that 'redistribution has a high efficiency cost'. This economic jargon is highly misleading. Efficiency can only be defined meaningfully if one has first defined a set of consistent social objectives. The previous statement implicitly refers to the free market solution as the reference point. However, we rejected this reference point in the previous section on ethical grounds. In our second-best framework a system can only be called 'less efficient' if it is possible to implement another, cheaper, system with results which are at least equally good as evaluated by our consequentialist criterion. Given the empirical picture sketched before, this is not obvious. In general, 'cheaper' social protection systems yield worse justice results. It is possible that the relative cost of the welfare state in terms of GNP or GNP-growth is huge. But for an egalitarian (or maximin) ethical observer these costs can be perfectly legitimate. The simple 'efficiency' argument must therefore be used with care. The choice between different protection systems has more to do with ethics and politics than with economics.

From this perspective, a first really important challenge related to the cost problem is the possible foundering of the political support for the system, mainly among the middle and higher income groups. This point brings us right back into the heart of the discussion about the insurance principle. The welfare state is only feasible, if it remains sufficiently attractive for a sufficiently large group of voters. Going too far in the direction of targeting may make the present institutions less attractive for the middle income groups. Offering private alternatives for the wealthier groups of the population may even threaten the political support for a generous mandatory system (Casamatta et al., 2000). In fact, one of the explanations for the apparent loss of popular support in recent decades may have been the growing relative importance of unemployment insurance. Given the large negative correlation between skill level and unemployment risk, the insurance character is much lower for unemployment insurance than for pensions and health.

It is possible that future increases in the contribution rates – due to demographic or technical developments – will lead to a large increase in the GNP-cost. If this were the case, it is probable that the optimal (ethical and political) trade-off has to be reconsidered. But again we should be careful in drawing too hasty conclusions. Even in the most pessimistic scenarios of future developments of the costs of health care and retirement pensions, the working population will grow richer and richer in terms of net after tax income. Although the proportional contribution rates are increasing, what is left over after taxes and contributions also keeps growing. Then what is the problem? By focusing on proportional contribution rates, many economists have a tendency to neglect this evolution in the absolute amounts. How will people react to increasing contribution rates if they themselves get wealthier? Although it is admittedly dangerous to think that survey answers give a good prediction of actual behaviour, it is informative to look at the results in table 1.1.1, based on a representative sample of the Flemish working population (Schokkaert et al., 2000)[19]. There seems to be a real willingness to pay for higher pension contributions, i.e. there is still room for manoeuvre within the present system.

I would therefore formulate this first challenge for the welfare state as follows: look for the mix between insurance and solidarity (and possibly redefine that mix if the external constraints change) that attracts sufficient support among the higher income groups to approach the ethical ideal sketched in the previous section as closely as possible. This is a vaguely formulated challenge, whose concrete content will vary from country to country. For the countries with a Bismarckian tradition, it seems dangerous to depart drastically from this heritage.

Table 1.1.1 Willingness-to-pay for retirement pensions

The ageing of the population will make it necessary for the Belgian government to introduce some changes in the legal system of retirement pensions. In broad lines there are three categories of possible measures:
1. *increase the contributions of the working populations so as to guarantee the same pension benefits for the retired*
2. *keep the contributions unchanged but lower the pension benefits*
3. *keep contributions and pension benefits unchanged, but increase the age of retirement*

What would be your preferred measure?

According to earnings (in Belgian francs per month)					
	Global sample	-29.999	30.000-54.999	55.000-79.999	80.000+
Increase contributions	59.4	65.5	60.8	59.4	37.2
Lower pensions	30.7	20.0	30.0	32.2	46.5
Increase retirement age	9.9	14.5	9.2	8.4	16.3
According to age					
	Global sample		18-29	30-44	45+
Increase contributions	59.4		51.9	60.7	64.4
Lower pensions	30.7		35.9	29.9	27.1
Increase retirement age	9.9		12.2	9.4	8.5

All this is not to say that the cost increase has to be taken as given and unavoidable. A part of it is due to moral hazard. Privatization is often put forward as an easy solution, but this is rather shortsighted. As mentioned before, private insurers also face the moral hazard problem and they often command a weaker set of instruments than the government. In order to control for moral hazard, one should devise a good regulatory structure with sufficient attention for the finer details. While the first reason for fighting moral hazard is the desire to increase efficiency, it is important to note that such a policy also fits very well in the broad consequentialist setting with its scope for responsibility. It is not only economically meaningful, but also ethically desirable not to insure health costs for which people can be held responsible. Unemployed persons have a responsibility to look for a job – of course after opportunities have been equalized. Here is the second challenge: to devise concrete measures of cost-containment which are in line with the ethical feelings of the majority of citizens.

The third challenge is closely related – and may be conflicting – with the previous one. There is some truth in the liberal critique that welfare state institutions penetrate in people's private lives, sometimes in a rather offensive way. In a society where individual freedom and self-realisation are seen as more and more important, the opposition against this kind of state intervention will most probably grow. This implies that the regulatory structure to control for moral hazard should pay due attention to people's privacy and freedom of choice. This concern is dominant in the liberal tradition. But again, respect for the private sphere is also an important component of the broad consequentialist view that I have defended. An interesting analysis of some specific problems from an 'enlightened liberal' point of view can be found in Lindbeck (1988).

3.2 Hard core poverty and the position of the lower skilled: the challenge of altruism

While the empirical material shows that social security systems of the Bismarckian kind have performed remarkably well in the fight against poverty, it is true that despite the huge income streams which flow through the system, the poor are still with us. There remains a hard core of long term poverty even in the countries with the most generous social security system. Worse still, it has been claimed that the increase of poverty among the unskilled can partly be explained by the rise in their labour cost as a consequence of the social security contributions. Let me first briefly address the latter problem.

There has been a huge debate in the recent economic literature on the explanation of the weak labour market position of the lower skilled with skill-biased technological progress and growing international competition as the main culprits (Gottschalk and Smeeding, 1997). There is more consensus among economists on the broad lines of what would be a preferable policy. In all proposals a lowering of the labour costs of the least skilled plays a crucial role – while the challenge is to guarantee them at the same time a decent living standard[20]. Whether it is through a reduction of social security contributions, or through an earned income tax credit, or through subsidizing jobs in the private sector, or through stimulating the creation of (quasi) public jobs to address new social needs: in all cases there will be a cost for government, i.e. for the tax payers. Given that differences in skills are well known and basically uninsurable, the necessary policies will not be feasible – in the sense of getting sufficient political support – unless there is a large degree of altruistic concern among the higher skilled[21].

We can go still one step further. These labour market policies probably will not be sufficient to eradicate the hard core of long run structural poverty. It is fairly generally accepted that the traditional welfare state institutions have not been able to solve this problem, because they focus too exclusively on income transfers. To fight long run poverty other instruments are needed: housing, education and health policy (going far beyond universal and compulsory health insurance, although such insurance is a necessary condition). Again, these policies will not be costless. Again, they will only be feasible if there is a sufficient degree of altruistic concern among the wealthier citizens[22].

Note how powerful is the ethical framework in section 2 to incorporate these broader considerations. Its multidimensional nature makes it particularly suited to analyse the situation of the structural poor and to avoid income fetishism. This avoidance of income fetishism is also crucial to understand the need for policies to improve the labour market prospects of the least skilled. After all, if we do not attach a central (and independent) role to social integration and self realisation, why should it not be sufficient to transfer some income to the unemployed? The concern with job creation – which is such a crucial element in many countries – can only be ethically legitimized in a broader consequentialistic setting[23].

It should have become clear by now that one can define policies to improve the labour market opportunities of the least skilled and the fate of the structural poor. It is also clear that these policies go beyond the boundaries of the traditional social security system. They cannot be based on the idea of social insurance and require for their implementation a large degree of altruism and solidarity from the rich. The decline in solidarity which some observers claim to perceive therefore offers a real challenge. While these pessimistic feelings are not necessarily confirmed by empirical opinion surveys (see table 1.1.2 for some results for representative samples of Flemish workers[24]), in any case, altruism and solidarity are needed to attack the problem. We need 'fundamental' insurance in Kolm's terminology. Critics who argue in favour of a revival of solidarity are therefore absolutely right. Yet it is important to study carefully the role of altruism in some of these analyses.

Some critics of the welfare state tend to oppose altruism and insurance and propose altruism as a new and ethically superior basis for social security. I think that this is a dangerous position. I see no reason to think that the willingness-to-pay for insurance comes necessarily in conflict with altruism. These are two separate motivations.

Table 1.1.2 Altruism

In the system of retirement pensions
Do you think that the present pension benefits should be decreased to lower the burden on the active population?

A	According to earnings (in Belgian francs per month)				
	Global sample	-29.999	30.000-54.999	55.000-79.999	80.000+
Yes	20.2	14.5	22.2	17.1	19.0
No	79.8	85.5	77.8	82.9	81.0
B	According to age				
	Global sample		18-29	30-44	45+
Yes	20.2		25.9	21.2	13.3
No	79.8		74.1	78.8	86.7

Suppose that the actual pension system, consisting of three pillars, would be reformed into one overall system, in which the pension you will later receive is made up from the contributions you have paid on your own personal account. The pension benefit is therefore influenced by the level of your earnings and by the length of your period of employment. Would you in that case still be willing to pay an additional contribution for people who have not been able to save for a decent pension because of their low earnings or their unemployment?

C	According to earnings (in Belgian francs per month)				
	Global sample	-29.999	30.000-54.999	55.000-79.999	80.000+
Yes	52.8	36.1	48.3	66.9	74.4
No	47.2	63.9	51.7	33.1	25.6
D	According to age				
	Global sample		18-29	30-44	45+
Yes	52.8		43.5	58.3	53.0
No	47.2		56.5	41.7	47.0

Table 1.1.2 (continued)

In the system of unemployment benefits
What system of unemployment benefits would you prefer? (In the survey, the respondents were confronted with three well defined alternative systems – see Schokkaert et al., 1997, for more details.)

	Global sample	According to educational level				
		P	LS	HS	HE	U
a less generous system	11.7	10.0	4.8	10.0	16.2	20.0
the status quo	43.9	26.0	41.4	42.4	50.5	48.0
a more generous system	44.4	64.0	53.8	47.6	33.3	32.0

P = primary, LS = lower secondary, HS = higher secondary, HE = higher education, U = university

Suppose you are forced to pay for your own unemployment risk only, would you then still be willing to contribute voluntarily for people with a lower education level and working in a sector with higher unemployment probabilities?

	Global sample	According to education level				
		P	LS	HS	HE	U
Yes	70.4	62.7	65.1	67.3	76.2	81.3
No	29.6	37.3	34.9	32.7	23.8	18.7

P = primary, LS = lower secondary, HS = higher secondary, HE = higher education, U = university

As argued before, the present social insurance arrangements keep large groups of people (e.g. the retired) out of poverty. The willingness to pay for these arrangements is partly based on the risk aversion of the wealthier members of society. It would be naïve to think that the same amount of resources for redistribution could be collected in a more solidaristic, less insurance oriented system[25]. It is even possible that solidarity and insurance are complements rather than substitutes. Individuals who feel better insured, might at the same time get stronger altruistic feelings. Yes, altruism is badly needed. But no, there is not at all a conflict between insurance and solidarity. Quite the contrary: the presence of a social insurance scheme makes it easier to mobilize the necessary funds for solidarity.

Sometimes the critique of the insurance principle goes even further and gets a procedural flavour[26]. The idea then is that altruism is ethically superior over self-interest and that therefore social institutions should be based on the former rather than the latter motivation. Of course, I do agree that altruism is ethically superior. But, as should have become clear already, I think that this is largely irrelevant in this context. Only in what I have called the liberal approach is altruism needed to ethically justify social security. In my own view the welfare state – like other social institutions – should be evaluated on the basis of justice considerations. And justice is not about altruism and charity, but about how to get 'just', in the sense of ethically acceptable results. Altruism is important to realize justice. It may be necessary to reach a sufficient level of social integration. But in both cases it is in the first place a means, and *not* the ultimate touchstone of justice.

There remain at least two important questions, which I will mention only briefly. Until now, I have argued that altruism is a necessary condition to build a welfare state, but I have neglected the possible feed-back from the welfare state institutions on the degree of altruism. It has been argued that too much government intervention leads to moral atrophy, in that citizens will lose their spontaneous feelings of charity and their willingness to help. It is of course true that a part of the functions of more traditional social institutions (such as the family or the village) has been taken over by the institutionalised welfare state. There are obviously good efficiency reasons for that. Even if this has been accompanied by a decrease in spontaneous altruism, it would be extremely dangerous to think that this spontaneous altruism would rise again if one broke down these institutions. Moreover, there is not really much convincing evidence to support the hypothesis of moral atrophy. Goodin (1993) discusses some psychological and sociological evidence that suggests exactly the opposite. In a recent empirical study Jones et al. (1998) also present evidence suggesting that the severe cuts in social policy in the Thatcher years in the UK have led to a decrease in charitable giving. Their point is that welfare state institutions have a demonstration effect, inducing in the citizens the feeling that society has to be concerned about its less fortunate members.

The second question is more difficult and of more immediate relevance to social policy. In the previous section I argued that the challenge for the

28

welfare state to secure sufficient support from a sufficiently large number of voters could be seen as an argument in favour of the insurance principle. In this section I claimed that altruism is definitely needed to improve the fate of the structural poor and the least-skilled. How to combine these two requirements? One position – which I do not take – is that it will only be possible to mobilize sufficient resources for the poor by 'hiding' the redistribution in the insurance arrangements, i.e. by increasing the subsidizing and income solidarity as much as possible. Another position is that it is better to have a transparent system. If citizens understand better the insurance aspects and see the specific role for redistributive transfers, this could increase their willingness to accept solidarity – which is not low if we are willing to believe the survey results. I tend to sympathize with the latter position, but much more research is needed to be confident about it[27]. In my view, this is a crucial topic for further research on welfare state reform.

4. Conclusion

My position in this chapter has been openly conservative, in that I defend by and large the existing social security institutions. I do not think that the ethical basis on which they are built has crumbled down. The extreme liberal criticism is unacceptable. A more moderate liberal approach offers already some scope for social insurance. More importantly, I propose a form of broad consequentialism as an alternative for liberalism. In this approach the goodness of states of affairs has to be evaluated on the basis of the level of positive and negative freedom in society. Everybody has to reach at least a minimal living standard, where this living standard is seen as a multidimensional concept. When we look at the results of European welfare states from the perspective of this criterion – taking into account the economic and political constraints on government policy – they are very satisfactory. Moreover, a large majority of citizens supports the existing system.

Yet at the same time, there are real challenges which have to be taken seriously. The proposed consequentialist framework offers the possibility to interpret and structure these challenges. The increasing costs necessitate a rethinking of the mix between insurance and solidarity in order to secure sufficient political support. Moreover, new instruments have to be devised to fight the phenomenon of moral hazard. Our ethical framework suggests

29

that responsibility is a legitimate consideration and therefore supports cost containment measures to control moral hazard. At the same time it also suggests that too much government intervention in the individual's private sphere threatens negative freedom and is therefore unacceptable. The real challenge is to find a balance between these different considerations.

To fight structural poverty and to improve the labour market prospects of the least skilled will require economic sacrifices and therefore altruism from the wealthier members of society. The challenge here is how to stimulate these feelings of altruism. However, this does not require a basic rethinking of the ethical foundation of the welfare state. Charity and altruism are important, but they are not the ultimate touchstone to evaluate social institutions. The ultimate touchstone is justice.

It is clear that the ethical framework proposed in this chapter does not offer an operational answer to concrete questions about social policy. As a matter of fact, a crucial feature of the framework is that is *not* procedural and that theoretical insights and empirical findings from the social sciences are necessary to get at operational answers. The consequences of specific policy measures have to be analysed carefully. Choices have to be taken with respect to the trade-off between different objectives.

While the basic foundations of the welfare state remain firm and should be kept intact, the difficult challenges facing it require hard thinking and political courage[28]. Ethics is about choices. The only purpose of philosophical and scientific thinking can be to clarify these choices. I think that the ethical framework proposed in this chapter – largely inspired by recent developments in the economic theory of social choice – is well suited to structure the debate. It is sufficiently flexible to justify a large amount of forced redistribution, while at the same time incorporating notions of freedom and responsibility. It avoids welfarism on the one hand and income fetishism on the other hand through its multidimensional concept of the living standard. It offers scope for the introduction of new insights from the social sciences.

Notes

[1] I have given a broader overview of economic theories of justice in Schokkaert (1992).

[2] Not to mention the problem that American liberals are not European liberals. I follow the European terminology.

[3] See the discussion around Nozicks (1975) Lockean proviso. Egalitarian ideas about the distribution of these natural resources have even given rise to a school of left-libertarian thinkers.

[4] Although the possibility of myopia has always been mentioned as one of the possible justifications for a system of public pensions – see, e.g., Diamond, 1977.

[5] See Barr (1992) for a more complete and balanced treatment.

[6] This may even be true for forms of insurance which are well within the scope of private insurers. See, e.g., Von Ungern-Sternberg (1996) and Felder (1996) for an analysis of fire insurance in Switzerland and Germany.

[7] Utilitarianism may be concerned about the *income* distribution, if the marginal utility of income is declining, but it does not care about the distribution of *utilities*.

[8] I neglect the question of animal rights.

[9] See Jones and O'Donnell (1995) for an example of equivalence scales to compensate for the costs of disability.

[10] I repeat that welfarism does not coincide with utilitarianism. Both consider utility or happiness as the ultimately important variables to describe the situation of the individuals. However, welfarism allows to use non-additive aggregation functions and therefore to integrate considerations about the distribution of utility in the analysis.

[11] See Mongin and d'Aspremont (1999) for a recent overview.

[12] A detailed critical analysis can be found in Dworkin (1981).

[13] Yaari and Bar-Hillel (1984) show some empirical results suggesting that respondents in a questionnaire study choose different distribution rules in situations with different needs and in situations with different tastes.

[14] The underlying idea of egalitarianism is that once one has defined an attractive index of capabilities, incorporating notions of freedom and responsibility, there is no longer any reason why a just society would differentiate between different individuals. However, a completely egalitarian society (even if we define egalitarianism in the space of capabilities) would require much government intervention. If people react to these government measures, this might induce a loss of efficiency. To maximize the opportunities of the least well-off member of society, i.e. to maximin, is then the most egalitarian criterion which can be reconciled with a concern for Pareto efficiency.

[15] There has been a huge debate on how to give a concrete content to the idea of capabilities and personal responsibility. Important contributions were Arneson (1989, 1990), Cohen (1989, 1990) and Roemer (1996).

[16] This also explains why most social scientists are consequentialist (at least implicitly). Scientists try to predict the consequences of different institutions and policy measures on the basis of their understanding of the working of society. In a purely procedural approach – such as libertarianism – this knowledge is irrelevant. In a consequentialist approach, it becomes crucial.

[17] Some recent chapters with empirical evidence are Summers et al. (1993), Alesina and Perotti (1997), Ooghe et al. (2000).

[18] See Casamatta et al. (2000) for a nice theoretical treatment of this problem. They also investigate the consequences of allowing the possibility of private insurance for the rich.

[19] Public servants and pensioners were excluded from the sample, which is therefore representative only for the private sector workers and the unemployed, i.e. those who actually contribute to the system.

[20] An overview of the problem and a discussion of some ethical aspects can be found in Schokkaert and Sweeney (1999).

[21] To a certain extent insurance arguments can be invoked here too. Highly skilled parents may be concerned about the future fate of their possibly less gifted children.

[22] And again, there are also some self-interest arguments: even the very rich run some risk to fall into poverty (Varian, 1980) or may accept redistributive policies to minimize the danger of criminality.

[23] The relative unimportance of income for the living standard of the unemployed is one of the main findings of Schokkaert and Van Ootegem (1990) who operationalize empirically Sen's concept of basic capabilities. Note though that I do not intend this statement to be an open criticism on the idea of a basic income. Sophisticated philosophical justifications of basic income start from an inspiration which is not very different from mine (Van Parijs, 1995). More down-to-earth pleas for a basic income often emphasize its potential to improve the labour market position of the low skilled.

[24] The sample for the pensions survey has been described before. The survey about unemployment insurance was organised with a representative sample of Flemish workers, excluding the civil servants and the unemployed. More information can be found in Schokkaert et al. (1997).

[25] Taking due account of intercultural or intercountry differences. The social acceptance of pure redistribution is in Scandinavia apparently higher than in other European countries.

[26] This position is often (implicitly or explicitly) taken by thinkers in one of the Christian traditions.

[27] A similar position is also defended by Smolensky et al. (1995).

[28] I have completely neglected in this chapter what I consider to be one of the main challenges for the future welfare states: the integration of non-material values such as the environment, the family life, etc. These questions go far beyond the traditional welfare state considerations. New social arrangements will have to be found. The capabilities approach is very well suited to integrate these non-material considerations.

References

Alesina, A. and Perotti, R., 1997, The welfare state and competitiveness, *American Economic Review* 87(5), 921-939.

Arneson, R., 1989, Equality and equal opportunity for welfare, *Philosophical Studies* 56, 77-93.

Arneson, R., 1990, Liberalism, distributive subjectivism, and equal opportunity for welfare, *Philosophy and Public Affairs* 10(2), 158-194.

Arrow, K., 1973, Some ordinalist-utilitarian notes on Rawls's theory of justice, *Journal of Philosophy* 70, 245-263.

Barr, N., 1992, Economic theory and the welfare state: a survey and interpretation, *Journal of Economic Literature* 30(2), 741-803.

Buchanan, J., 1986, *Liberty, Market and State.* Brighton: Wheatsheaf Books.

Buhmann, B., Rainwater, L., Schmaus, G., and Smeeding, T., 1988, Equivalence scales, well-being, inequality and poverty: sensitivity estimates across ten countries using the LIS database, *Review of Income and Wealth* 34(2), 115-142.

Casamatta, G., Cremer, H., and Pestieau, P., 2000, Political sustainability and the design of social insurance, *Journal of Public Economics* 75(3), 341-364.

Cohen, G., 1989, On the currency of egalitarian justice, *Ethics* 99, 906-944.

Cohen, G., 1990, Equality of what? On welfare, goods and capabilities, *Recherches Economiques de Louvain* 56, 357-382.

Coulter, F., Cowell, F. and Jenkins, S., 1992, Differences in needs and assessment of income distributions, *Bulletin of Economic Research* 44(2), 77-124.

Deaton, A. and Paxson, C., 1998, Measuring poverty among the elderly, in Wise, D. (ed.), *Inquiries in the economics of ageing.* Chicago: University of Chicago Press, 169-200.

Diamond, P., 1977, A framework for social security analysis, *Journal of Public Economics* 8, 275-298.

Dworkin, R., 1981, What is equality? Part 1: Equality of welfare, *Philosophy and Public Affairs* 10, 185-246.

Evans, R., 1984, *Strained Mercy.* Toronto: Butterworths.

Felder, S., 1996, Fire insurance in Germany: a comparison of price-performance between state monopolies and competitive regions, *European Economic Review* 40, 1133-1141.

Fleurbaey, M., 1995, Equal opportunity or equal social outcome?, *Economics and Philosophy* 11, 25-55.

Förster, M., 1994, *The effects of net transfers on low incomes among non-elderly families.* OECD Economic Studies 22.

Giddens, A., 1994, *Beyond left and right?* Cambridge: Polity Press.

Goodin, R., 1993, Moral atrophy in the welfare state, *Policy Sciences* 26, 63-78.

Gottschalk, P. and Smeeding, T., 1997, Cross-national comparisons of earnings and income inequality, *Journal of Economic Literature* 35(2), 633-687.

Hochman, H. and Rodgers, J., 1969, Pareto-optimal redistribution, *American Economic Review* 59, 542-557.

Jones, A. and O'Donnell, O., 1995, Equivalence scales and the costs of disability, *Journal of Public Economics* 56, 273-289.

Jones, P., Cullis, J. and Lewis, A., 1998, Public versus private provision of altruism: can fiscal policy make individuals 'better' people?, *Kyklos* 51(1), 3-24.

Kolm, S.-Chr., 1985, *Le contrat social libéral: philosophie et pratique du libéralisme.* Paris: Presses Universitaires de France.

Kolm, S.-Chr., 1987, The freedom and consensus normative theory of the state: the liberal social contract, in Koslowski, P. (ed.), *Individual liberty and democratic decision-making.* Tübingen: Mohr: Paul Siebeck, 98-126.

Lindbeck, A., 1988, Individual freedom and welfare state policy, *European Economic Review* 32(2/3), 295-318.

Miller, D., 1988, Altruism and the welfare state, in Moon, D. (ed.), *Responsibility, rights and welfare: the theory of the welfare state.* Boulder and London: Westview Press, 163-188.

Mongin, P. and d'Aspremont, C., 1999, Utility theory and ethics, in Barbara, S., Hammond, P. and Seidl, C. (eds.), *Handbook of Utility Theory.* Dordrecht and New York: Kluwer Academic Press.

Mossialos, E., 1997, Citizens' views on health care systems in the 15 member states of the European Union, *Health Economics* 6, 109-116.

Nozick, R., 1975, *Anarchy, State and Utopia.* New York: Basic Books.

Ooghe, E., Schokkaert, E. and Fléchet, J., 2000, *The incidence of social security contributions: an empirical analysis.* Catholic University Leuven, Centre for Economic Studies: mimeo.

Roemer, J., 1996, *Theories of distributive justice.* Cambridge: Harvard University Press.

Rosanvallon, P., 1995, *La nouvelle question sociale. Repenser l'Etat-providence.* Paris: Editions du Seuil.

Rowley, C. and Peacock, A., 1975, *Welfare economics: a liberal restatement.* London: Martin Robertson.

Schokkaert, E., 1992, The economics of distributive justice, welfare and freedom, in Scherer, K. (ed.), *Justice: Interdisciplinary Perspectives.* Cambridge: Cambridge University Press, 65-113.

Schokkaert, E. and Sweeney, J., 1999, Social exclusion and ethical responsibility: solidarity with the least skilled, *Journal of Business Ethics* 21 (2-3), 251-267.

Schokkaert, E. and Van Ootegem, L., 1990, Sen's concept of the living standard applied to the Belgian unemployed, *Recherches Economiques de Louvain* 56 (3-4), 429-450.

Schokkaert, E., Verhue, M. and Omey, E., 1997, *Individual preferences concerning unemployment compensation: insurance and solidarity.* University Gent: Working Paper 97/31.

Schokkaert, E., Verhue, M., and Pepermans, G., 2000, *Vlamingen over het pensioensysteem.* Catholic University of Leuven, Centre for Economic Studies: mimeo.

Sen, A., 1984, *Resources, values and development.* Oxford: Basil Blackwell.

Sen, A., 1985, *Commodities and capabilities.* Amsterdam: North-Holland.

Sen, A., 1988, Freedom of choice: concept and content, *European Economic Review* 32, 269-294.

Sen, A. and Williams, B., 1982. *Utilitarianism and beyond.* Cambridge: Cambridge University Press.

Smolensky, E., Reilly, S. and Evenhouse, E., 1995, Should public assistance be targeted?, *Journal of Post-Keynesian Economics* 8(1), 3-28.

Summers, L., Gruber, J., and Vergara, R., 1993, Taxation and the structure of labor markets: the case of corporatism, *Quarterly Journal of Economics* 58, 385-411.

Taylor-Gooby, P., 1993, What citizens want from the state, in Jowell, R. et al. (eds.), *International Social Attitudes − the 10th BSA Report.* Dartmouth, Aldershot: Social and Community Planning Research, 81-101.

Van Parijs, P., 1994, Au delà de la solidarité. Les fondements éthiques de l'Etat-providence et de son dépassement, *Futuribles* 184, 5-29.

Van Parijs, P., 1995, *Real freedom for all.* Oxford: Clarendon Press.

Vandenbroucke, F., 1999, *De actieve welvaartsstaat: een Europees perspectief.* Dr. J. M. den Uyl-lezing.

Varian, H., 1980, Redistributive taxation as social insurance, *Journal of Public Economics* 14, 49-68.

Von-Ungern-Sternberg, T., 1996, The limits of competition: housing insurance in Switzerland, *European Economic Review* 40, 1111-1121.

Yaari, M. and Bar-Hillel, M., 1984, On dividing justly, *Social Choice and Welfare* 1, 1-24.

1.2 The ethics and the normgiving: the example of rehabilitation

Lotta Westerhäll

1. Purpose

The purpose of this chapter is to discuss the application of the regulations on rehabilitation in the Swedish National Insurance Act (AFL), chapters 3 and 22. The legal sources imply that the applicator of the law should have 'a comprehensive view' on the individual who is submitted to rehabilitation and on the overall rehabilitation situation, as well as he shall 'refine' the concepts used in the context of rehabilitation, particularly the concept of incapacity for work. The comprehensive view and the refinement are as good as each other's opposites. Theoretically, this ought to make an application of the regulations impossible. Partly, the application which takes place today is, according to several administrators whom the writer has met, not an actual application of the law, but a creation of a system of principles for the individual situation which the administrator means can give a reasonable result.

The most natural thing to do in such a situation would, of course, be to argue for a change in the legislation in order for the contradictions to disappear and the law to become applicable. However, even if the current law is to be changed, the law has to be applicable until the day when a new one is taken to practise. The main purpose here in this chapter is not to help the applicator of the law in a complicated situation, even if that would be an advantage indeed. The purpose is instead a general one, to reach different conclusions of how to apply the law by approaching it in different ways since it is so obviously contradictory. Is it possible to reach a satisfactory result from both an ethical and legal standpoint depending on which

37

perspective one has on the legal system and what norm theory that is the basic of the law?

After an introduction with a general description of rehabilitation in Sweden today, the concepts of a comprehensive view and refinement will be discussed such as they appear in the legal text and, above all, in the preparatory works. The meaning of the concept of incapacity for work is here of crucial importance. The so called 'step-by-step assessment', which is prescribed in the legal text from 1997 will be analysed and related to the concepts of comprehensive view and refinement.

The above mentioned introduction will serve as a descriptive background for a discussion about a comprehensive view and refinement in the legal application from two different legal perspectives. The first can be described as a substantial, and the second as a functional perspective. The purpose is to examine to what extent different perspectives on the legislation will confer different applications of the same. The report ends with a few comments on the legal perspective which, according to the writer, is the most reasonable due to the outcome of the legal application.

2. Generally about rehabilitation

Rehabilitation is a comprehensive term including all measures of a medical, social and employment kind helping persons back to a normal working life. The responsibility for the medical rehabilitation falls within the medical health care system, and for the social rehabilitation within the social services sector. The employer has the primary responsibility for the employment rehabilitation. In the employment rehabilitation is comprised occupational rehabilitation, for which the labour market authorities are mainly responsible. The role of the social insurance offices is to co-ordinate the entire rehabilitation process. The individual has a responsibility to co-operate actively in the rehabilitation work and to clarify his/her own goals and expectations.

Different legal regulations govern the medical, the social and the employment rehabilitation. They, in turn, are based upon various ideological evaluations. This may explain the various ways of looking upon rehabilitation within the different fields.

The medical rehabilitation has as its purpose to cure and to mitigate disabilities caused by sickness. The medical profession has a very strong professional identity. The qualification requirements for the profession are carefully regulated as are also their professional responsibility and medical management responsibility. That which shall be corrected is a medical matter. It is self-evident that the medical rehabilitation is of an utmost importance in order to restore the working capacity. Thus it forms the starting point for the so called 'working line'. It is necessary that the individual is given the possibility to medical rehabilitation in cases of sickness and disablement in order for the State to be able to demand from the individual to provide for him/herself. In order to provide for the individual during the rehabilitation process, the State has arranged an insurance system. This has resulted in the social insurance offices obtaining a central role in contexts of rehabilitation, ever since the National Insurance Act came into practise in 1962. This role has become even more important during the 1990s. The social insurance offices cannot act independently in these cases, but during the 1990s, the possibility to buy rehabilitation services has appeared. It is primarily employment rehabilitation services which have come into question and not medical rehabilitation, since the county councils (and the municipalities when it comes to medical care of elderly people) are *obliged* to provide medical care. The social insurance offices have no responsibility of its own for the care, but through their overall co-ordination responsibility for the rehabilitation, they are given the task to clarify the states of responsibilities and to facilitate and ensure that the individuals rehabilitation demands are provided for.

To sum up, it ought to be pointed out that the medical rehabilitation is provided by the medical health care system and is governed by an extensive legislation.

If the main responsibility for the medical rehabilitation falls on the medical health care system, the responsibility for the social rehabilitation falls on the social services. The work and the responsibilities of the social services are regulated in the Social Welfare Act. According to this act, the municipalities are obliged to see to that all persons who reside within the municipality, and have needs which cannot be satisfied otherwise, shall have these needs satisfied. This means that the social rehabilitation can look very different from case to case. Examples of measures which can be offered by the social services are e.g. social support of different kinds, and help in order to create a social network. In the cases which reach the social insurance office, the latter has an obligation to co-operate with the municipalities and together with them initiate, co-ordinate and realize the rehabilitation measures which are needed. As is the case for medical measures, these are not explicitly described in the legislation, but can be

39

composed of almost anything. It is the individual need which decides the contents of the social rehabilitation. To sum up, it can be pointed out that it is the social welfare board of each municipality which is responsible for, and shall see to that the rehabilitation measures are realized, and that there is a specific legislation regulating this part of the rehabilitation field.

There are many kinds of measures which together make up the employment rehabilitation. Examples are e.g. the assessment of working capacity, work training, training in a real environment etc. The rehabilitation can be supplied by the Government through e.g. the AMU (the Labour Market Training Centers), the ALI (the Institutes of Working Life and Rehabilitation) or Samhall, or it may be administered by a private rehabilitation supplier from whom the social insurance office buys services.

There is no joint perspective on the terms employment rehabilitation and medical rehabilitation, partly due to imbalance in the degree of professionalism. The knowledge about the backgrounds and the causes for disease is not turned into conscious strategies for employment rehabilitation. To a large extent, there is a lack of theoretical knowledge about the degree of success which a certain rehabilitation measure has in the individual case.

The occupational rehabilitation is the rehabilitation field which one could probably call the most central, at least when considering insurance cases where the insured person cannot return to his/her former employment. Theoretically, a rehabilitation case has really nothing to do with whether it is an insurance case or not. Neither is it necessary that a person has an employment and thus, in most cases, an employer. In reality, however, these questions are of a decisive importance. The legal regulations on rehabilitation assume that every case is an insurance case. The regulations about the employer's responsibility are based on the fact that the person in question has an employment. This can be seen clearly e.g. in chapters 3 and 22 in the National Insurance Act. Further, this is the explanation why the social insurance offices have been given the overall co-ordinating responsibility for the rehabilitation. This is also the reason why the rehabilitation has become so closely connected to the question of whether a person is entitled to allowance within the social insurance or not. Since incapacity for work is an absolute prerequisite for receiving sickness allowance, temporary disability pension, disability pension, reimbursement from the work injuries insurance or rehabilitation allowance, the demands in this prerequisite will be of great importance for the possibilities of receiving rehabilitation.

To sum up, it is true that the different kinds of rehabilitation measures often merge, on the same time as each authority has its own angles of approach on rehabilitation. Thus, the rehabilitation is founded partly on the opinions and ideas of the different actors on the contents of the concept, and partly on their interpretations of the goals. Experience points out the want for concordant goals. Presently, each authority has its own goals, and often, they do not aim in the same direction, which, in turn, leads to conflicting prioritizations. For different reasons, individuals cannot always describe their own goals and expectations. The result is that these persons will not see their needs for support fulfilled, but will instead be left in a grey-zone in between the fields of the different authorities.

3. A comprehensive view

In 1991, a new chapter on rehabilitation (no 22) was introduced in the National Insurance Act. Even though the concept of a comprehensive view is not expressed in the legal text, it nevertheless characterises it due to the fact that the Rehabilitation Committee, in the proposal SOU 1988:41 stated, that 'within the concept of rehabilitation is comprised a comprehensive view on the individual'.

Rehabilitation should be a process which is characterised by a comprehensive view on the individual, and on the individuals interplay with the environment. The rehabilitation work focuses on the needs, possibilities and resources of the individual person. From this starting point, one has to deal with difficulties which might arise.

The legal text defines rehabilitation as something which 'aims to restore the working capacity and the possibilities of supporting oneself through gainful employment, of somebody suffering from illness. The rehabilitation measures shall be planned in consultation with the insured person, and shall be based on his/her personal qualifications and needs ...'. The social insurance office shall, in consultation with the insured person, see to that his/her needs for rehabilitation are elucidated as soon as possible, and that the measures needed for an effective rehabilitation are taken. The social insurance office shall, if the insured person gives his/her consent, in the rehabilitation work co-operate with the employer and the employees union, the medical health care, the social services, the labour market authorities and other organisations which might be involved. The social insurance office shall work for that these actors, each within its own field of activities, take the measures needed in order to achieve an effective rehabilitation.

To have a comprehensive view on the concept of rehabilitation means that all aspects of human capacity have to be considered. At special so called rehabilitation clinics, this is reflected in the fact that paramedic professions such as psychologists, occupational therapists, social welfare officers and physiotherapists play an important part. The kind of teamwork which is practised at a rehabilitation clinic differs greatly from ordinary medical work at e.g. a district health care centre.

The most important quality of the comprehensive view on rehabilitation is that the application is seen from the perspective of the individual person. Thus, a comprehensive view implies that personal integrity and individuality are respected. No person should be looked upon as an object, or be treated as if the reduction of working capacity is his/her only characteristic.

A comprehensive view also implies that the supporting measures given to the person should serve to achieve a functional existence for the person as a whole. One should not provide good rehabilitation measures within one field and disregard others. Neither should the rehabilitation be planned without considering the individuals opinions on how a certain measure might work together with other kind of support. A comprehensive view shall also govern the contents and the forms of co-operation between different rehabilitation sectors, public institutions and responsible authorities. What, from their point of view, might seem as a clear picture can, from the individuals perspective be dissipated and thus result in the absence of positive effects of the rehabilitation.

The comprehensive view is closely tied to ethical values, meaning that ethical norms are of great importance in matters of rehabilitation. At its deepest, all human activity concerns man himself. The purpose is to improve conditions for human beings. Thus, the good which is to be promoted, is man and his well-being. However, in order to understand how to improve the well-being of man, it is necessary to have a conception of who man really is. Man could be described in technical terms, but could also be looked upon as something valuable as such.

Today, there are two clearly distinguishable views of man: one behaviouristic and one humanistic. The behaviourism denies that man should have freedom, personality and possibilities for self-determination. Man is supposed to be fully described and explained in behaviouristic terms.

Whereas man from a behaviouristic point of view is considered to be an object which it is possible to manipulate, the humanistic view of man is as a subject. Man is a self. He is a person with freedom, responsibility and human dignity. Kant is one of many philosophers who finds it logically necessary (however not possible to prove) to assume a self which is free and autonomous. This self is a prerequisite for all human experience. Without the self, there is no experience. Self, person and freedom are important concepts within the humanistic or personalistic view on man. One of mans characteristics is that he is creative. He is not only an individual, but is also part of a community. Man is a social being who is dependent on his environment and his social relations. Alone, he is nobody.

The idea about human dignity implies that all men are of equal value. This, in turn, means that all men have the same rights and that no man is superior to another in this matter. This principle can also be described thus: the equal value of men means that all men have exactly the same right to a dignified existence.

In the principle of equality, there is nothing to tell us what criteria are relevant. It is only a demand for equal sharing of benefits as well as disadvantages. However, the demand for equality is not absolute in the sense that everybody, regardless of circumstances, should receive exactly the same treatment. Instead it implies that alike should be treated alike. This, in turn, means that in order to apply the principle of equality, one needs criteria for what shall be considered as alike and what should not.

The principle of equality can be interpreted in several ways. One way is as a principle of equal allowance. According to this interpretation, all persons should receive the same amount of what is good, and have the same chances of realizing a good life. Everybody should have the same right to e.g. gainful employment, domestic work and social work. This will, of course, result in great inequalities between people, different persons of course having varying possibilities, e.g. due to sex roles, of making use of the gifts and opportunities they have received.

Another way in which to interpret the principle of equality is to try to obtain equality of the good which every person attains in the end. One should be able to tell approximately when two persons objectively lead equally good lives. Everybody should obtain the same degree of value in his or her lives (good or bad). This is usually called *the principle of objective equality*.

The principle of allowance according to need can be interpreted in the way that every person should be able to realize a maximal good life in relation to his/her individual properties. However, due to all inequalities between men which exist today, this will not lead to objective equality. This principle is often interpreted in the way that a certain objective minimum is stipulated. Everybody has to obtain this minimum before one is given the opportunity of realizing good in proportion to one's possibilities. In other words, the principle of need is combined with the principle of objective equality. One sometimes call it *the principle of allowance in proportion to need with the addition of objective minimal demands.* In this context arises the problem of the extent of the minimal demands. How extensive should they be? What minimal demands should there be e.g. in the relation between employed and unemployed persons?

The principle of human dignity and the principle of equality derived from the are thus fundamental ethical principles within the concept of a comprehensive view. How do they relate to the concept of refinement?

4. Refinement

4.1 Refinement in general

On the 1st of October 1995, the National Insurance Act was subjected to change. The possibility to consider factors other than purely medical ones on the evaluation of illness was decreased. The legal text was changed into the following: '...When evaluating whether sickness exists or not, one shall disregard labour market, economic, social and other circumstances' (AFL, chapter 3, 7§).

This so called *refinement* of the sickness insurance was also to cover the concept of incapacity for work through the so called *step-by-step assessment* of the right to sickness allowance and the need for rehabilitation. The latter was introduced into the National Insurance Act by the 1st of January 1997.

In the governmental directives, it was stated that 'problems which are basically not medical shall primarily be treated by labour market or social measures ...'. Hereby, we will achieve a greater degree of clarity, and costs will be entered where they arise. The Government's opinion is that such an arrangement will make political prioritizations between different areas of social welfare politics more easy.

The concept of incapacity for work is not a statistic or objective state, but a state which must be considered in relation to a certain kind of employment or certain kinds of working tasks. If the insured person cannot return to his former job, the question arises in relation to what kind of work his working capacity shall now be evaluated. Even if a legal regulation on how to answer this question did not exist before 1997, there was a possibility of considering other than medical factors, such as education, former employment, age, place of residency etc. From 1997, the incapacity for work shall, according to the legislator, be refined and assessed only from a medical point of view. The Committee for Sickness and Work Injuries asked whether the insured person's incapacity for work should be assessed strictly in relation to his ability to perform other kinds of jobs without considering the possibilities on his former place of work, or of his former employer. This kind of assessment would result in the fact that the person is not paid an allowance in cases when it is clear that he should be able to take another kind of employment available on the labour market. The Committee argued as follows.

All insured persons would have the same right to allowance. The right to allowance would not depend on the individual employment conditions, since it is only sickness and the working capacity derived thereof which govern the right to allowance. The kind of work which was performed before the person was taken ill would not influence the right to allowance. Thus, it would, in this case make no difference whether the insured person is employed by a small or a large employer, or if he is a private entrepreneur.

A consequent medical assessment of the incapacity for work results in the fact that whenever it is stated that an insured person cannot return to his former work, but has the ability to perform other kinds of work which are common on the labour market, he is not entitled to allowance. The person is considered to be fit for work, and is reduced to earn his living through other kinds of work.

4.2 Limitations of the refinement

The legislator has not, though, been consequent about the principle of refinement. However, one has omitted to point this out as an exception from the principle, even if it is evident that this is the case. In the preparatory works (Prop 1990/91:141), it is emphazised that during rehabilitation, the aim should be that the individual shall be offered a continuing employment with his old employer. Other alternatives should not be sought until the employer has done what he can in order to achieve this. The right to allowance from the social insurance office will thus become dependent upon a person's working conditions and his employer's possibilities of finding other working tasks for the person. In this way, all insured persons do not have the same right to sickness allowance and rehabilitation allowance, since this right is related not only to the sickness and the hereby caused incapacity for work, but also to the chances of the person's employer. An insured person who will be able to take another kind of employment with his former employer after rehabilitation is granted allowance even if he would be able to take another job available at the labour market without rehabilitation. An insured person who does not have the opportunity to another kind of employment with his former employer, or who has no employment at all, does not have a corresponding right to allowance as long as he is able to perform other kinds of work available at the labour market.

Every reasonable possibility for work with the employer is discussed for an insured person with an employment. The connection between the insurance and the rehabilitation responsibility of the employer is kept (as opposed to before 1997), and a person who has an employment is given the possibility to keep it. One refers to the first hand responsibility for rehabilitation which an employer has for his employees. This increases the bonds between the employer and the employee also in those cases when the employee will not be able to resume his old work due to his illness.

The Committee on Sickness and Work Injuries found that this alternative was more in harmony with the duties which are incumbent on an employer according to the Security of Employment Act. The Committee stated that the right to allowance cannot only be based on medical criteria, but that the possibilities of the employer also have to be considered. This implies an extension of the right to allowance. The advantages of this attachment to the place of work are thought to be great. According to the Committee, the combined advantages with this arrangement well motivate the resulting exception from the equal right to allowance. Therefore, the Committee suggested that the working capacity shall primarily be assessed in relation to another job with the same employer.

4.3 The step-by-step assessment

Modes of procedure. The legislator has introduced regulations on a so called step-by-step assessment as an aid for the application of the principle of refinement. What does the step-by-step assessment mean, and how is it thought to work?

The step-by-step model is meant to describe how to assess a person's working capacity with different kinds of working tasks as a ground. E.g., if the answer to the question in step 1 is 'yes', no further assessment has to be done. If the answer is 'no', one proceeds to the next step and so forth. It is presumed that it is already clarified that the person suffers from a disease, and that it is this disease which diminishes his/her working capacity. In the preparatory works, the expression 'necessary treatment and convalescence' is used to describe the period of therapeutic incapacity for work, or the period of sickness allowance which is necessary regardless of the insured person's working conditions.

In the preparatory work, the step-by-step assessment is designed thus:

Step 1: Will the insured person be able to go back to his former job after necessary treatment and convalescence? If yes: sickness allowance is paid. If no:

Step 2: Will the insured person be able to perform his former working tasks after a certain period of rehabilitation, or after adjustment of the tasks? If yes: Sickness allowance is paid during the necessary treatment and convalescence, rehabilitation allowance is paid during the necessary rehabilitation. If no:

Step 3: Will the insured person be able to perform and receive other kinds of working tasks with his former employer without special measures? If yes: sickness allowance during the necessary treatment and convalescence. No sickness allowance while waiting for the work to become accessible. If no:

Step 4: Can the insured person get other working tasks from his employer after certain education, adjustment of working tasks, or other similar rehabilitation measures? If yes: sickness allowance during the necessary treatment and convalescence. Rehabilitation allowance during the necessary rehabilitation (approximately 1 year) and, if needed, reimbursment for the costs of the adjustments made at the working place. No sickness allowance while waiting for the work to become accessible. If no:

Step 5: Will the insured person be able to perform other kinds of jobs which exist on the labour market, without extra support? If yes: Sickness allowance is not paid (the person is fit for work and is to be considered as unemployed from the point of view of the social insurance. If no:

Step 6: Will the insured person be able to take a job on the labour market after certain rehabilitation measures such as e.g. education or retraining? If yes: Sickness allowance during the necessary treatment and convalescence. Rehabilitation allowance during the necessary rehabilitation (approximately 1 year) plus, if needed, reimbursement for the costs of making adjustments at the new working place. No sickness allowance while waiting for the employment to become accessible. If no:

Step 7: Will the insured person be primarily disabled during a considerable period of time? If yes: Disability pension or temporary disability pension is paid.

In the investigation which served as a basis for the refinement principle and the step-by-step assessment, nothing is said about having a comprehensive view. The reason for this is self-evident. In this case you shall disregard all factors but one, namely the purely medical one. When applying a comprehensive view, all relevant factors should be taken into account.

Studying the rehabilitation process such as it is described in the step-by-step model, one finds that step 1, return to former employment after necessary treatment and convalescence, builds on the refinement principle. It is the medical impairment of the working capacity which determines whether the person belongs to the sickness insurance or not. Other reasons may exist, even such factors which fall outside the working situation, but they cannot be the main cause for working incapacity. Sickness must be the main reason for a possible need for rehabilitation. This rehabilitation, in turn, is a traditional medical rehabilitation, e.g. medical treatment and convalescence.

In steps 2-4, one disregards the refined concept of working capacity. The insured person's capacity for work shall not just be related to his/her possibilities of performing other kinds of work on the labour market, but one takes the possibilities of the former working place and employer into special consideration. This is a deviation from the principle of refinement and the demand for sharpened rules. The reason for this is that otherwise, the employer's rehabilitation responsibility for those able to perform different working tasks would decrease. Neither would the rules be coherent with the employer's extensive duties of replacement in the Employment Protection Act.

Thus we see a displacement of the meaning of the refined concept of working capacity. It is not used consistently in all seven steps. In steps 2-4, one deviates totally from the principle of refinement on considering factors such as the employer's possibilities for transfer to another post etc. Whether one is aware of this deviation or if one only gives the concept a new meaning is not made clear in the preparatory works.

In step 5, the refinement principle has to be applied to 100%. If the person in question is able to take another job available on the labour market, he/she is fit for work and has therefore no right to rehabilitation allowance from the insurance. This, in turn, implies that the social insurance office has no further rehabilitation responsibility for such a person. As for step 6, there are no guidelines at all as for the application.

Critical comments. In spite of the fact that the refinement principle according to the preparatory work shall be applicable on all steps in the scale, it is evident that the interpreter of the law has to consider other factors than those concerning the purely medical capacity for work. The fact that the refinement principle is disregarded here causes several questions to arise. Does one mean that a person, from a medical point of view, can be partly or fully incapacitated for work, but regain this capacity after employment rehabilitation? The absence of medical capacity for work ought not to be treatable other than through medical measures? Is not some degree of medical capacity for work a demand for employment rehabilitation to be meaningful? The probable answer to these questions is that the insured person must be sick-listed, i.e. a case of sickness has to be established. When medical treatment and convalescence are at an end and the person cannot return to his former employment, an insured person who has an employer is given the possibility of getting another job with the same employer, with or without rehabilitation. This possibility does not exist for a person who has no employer, i.e. who has no employment due to e.g. unemployment.

If the person in question is to get a new job, one cannot only consider if it is medically suitable or possible. The job also has to be possible for the insured person to perform, he/she has to be suitable for the job and have or get the required education/training. In the latter case, the person has to be able to go through such an education. Also, he/she has to have a certain amount of interest and enthusiasm about the new job, that is, he/she at least has to be able to stand the new working tasks. If the official in charge only follows the legal text and the principle of refinement, the risk for ethical principles such as the principles of human dignity and of equality to be neglected is big. Ethical considerations do not necessarily imply medical measures to be taken, but are nonetheless important in order to be able to carry through a rehabilitation process in reality. Otherwise, one could suggest e.g. that a person should be retrained from being a cleaner to becoming an engineer, since from a strictly medical point of view, he/she should be able to sit at a desk and hold a pen. Another example is the business executive with sequelae after a stroke, who is placed in a sheltered workshop with simple assembly work, since this is what he/she is medically fit for doing.

Considerations like this belong to everyday work for an officer in charge of rehabilitation. The examples given above have to be rejected since the result is absurd or unethical. The considerations done by the officers are not documented anywhere, since they are not incorporated in the current legislation. It is a serious matter for the future and the development of the rehabilitation activity that the legal rules cannot be applied without officers creating their own rules in order not to come into ethical conflicts. If, in step 5, one were only to take medical considerations, the result becomes absurd. In reality, a purely medical capacity for work involves primary physical and mental functions being intact. Whether or not the person has an education or experience which might be requested by employers is not interesting. If one is to interpret step 6 according to the refinement principle, one could say that persons with large medical reductions in their working capacity are entitled to retraining/reeducation through the social insurance. However, not taking other factors into consideration, this may result in a person with a large medical impairment and a thorough educational background receiving further education even if this is not necessary. In the same way, an uneducated person with a minor reduction in working capacity, having had the same job for his whole life and now incapable of performing that kind of work, is not entitled to a new education which would give him a chance of getting a new job.

The preparatory works thus show that the refined concept of working capacity in fact is impossible to use. In the legislative changes made in 1997, a large part of the rehabilitation responsibility which used to fall on the social insurance offices, was taken away. This change, in practise, implies a large restriction in the former insurance cover, since the important possibility for retraining has disappeared. According to the former legislation, the social insurance office, in those cases when the person was unable to remain with the former employer due to sickness, took into consideration whether or not the insured person had any education or experience which might be of value on the labour market. If that was not the case, the insured person often underwent retraining after an investigation about his talents, interests and so on. The retraining was limited to last no longer than one year. The social insurance office paid for the education and granted rehabilitation allowance for as long as it lasted. The employer also often contributed to the cost of the training, or gave a serverance pay as a help to start. This constituted a great part of what is called occupational rehabilitation.

The refinement of the concept of incapacity for work has resulted in fewer people being entitled to rehabilitation. It has never really been the legislator's purpose to decrease the number of persons entitled to rehabilitation. Instead, the legislator also confessed to the enthusiasm about rehabilitation which was characteristic of the work of the Rehabilitation Committee in the late 1980s. It is difficult to determine whether the change has resulted in any savings for society as a whole, or for the social insurance. One has not got a clear idea of the question of what authorities should take care of different problems which arise. People have regarded the strict refinement principle as incompatible with what is just and fair. Such a social insurance has not been considered as reasonable or clear, and has not gained credence with the public.

5. Discussion

It has been described above how the principle of having a comprehensive view marked the development of the rehabilitation regulations in chapter 22, whereas the principle of refinement characterized the possibility to become subject to rehabilitation in chapter 3. However, the legislator has not been able to apply the latter principle consequently in chapter 3. An analysis of the so called step-by-step assessment shows that the principle of a comprehensive view is valid here as well. If not, the concept of occupational rehabilitation would become meaningless.

Below, I will analyse if different perspectives on the law result in different legal applications. Very short, and without claiming to be complete, I will also comment on the manner in which the law is in fact applied today. The chapter will end with some comparisons between the results of the different approaches. A personal standpoint will be made in relation to the legal perspective which gives the most attractive result.

As for the application of the law, there are three possible ways to go. The first is to strictly apply the principle of refinement, which ought to result in very few people actually becoming subject to rehabilitation. In this case, one would follow the legislator's intentions of incapacity for work as a purely medical question (if ever it is possible at all to imagine such a concept). One cannot possibly make use of the rehabilitation responsibility which fall on the employer in this case. The second way of applying the law is to make use of the employer's rehabilitation responsibility, that is, with a comprehensive view, even if it is called refinement. This will result in employed persons receiving employment rehabilitation whereas unemployed persons will get no rehabilitation if they are considered to be able to take a less demanding job on the labour market. Thus, for employed persons, one makes use of the principle of a comprehensive view, whereas for unemployed persons, the principle of refinement is applied. The third possibility is to use a comprehensive view on all rehabilitation.

When applying the law according to the first possibility, the principle of equality would rule, i.e. everybody would have an equally small chance of receiving rehabilitation. However, due to this, the number of persons undergoing rehabilitation would be so small, that instead a large number of people would have no possibility to earn their own living. The working line will not be fulfilled. This means that the principle of human dignity has been given very little scope.

While applying the law according to the second possibility, the principle of equality would not be in force. Looking upon the matter from the point of view of the principle of human dignity, there is no motivation for employed and unemployed persons not to have the same possibilities to rehabilitation.

Using the third possibility, the principle of equality as well as the principle of human dignity would be applied.

The legal system can be regarded on one hand from a substantial, and on the other hand from a functional perspective. One can look upon the legal system as a beforehand given quantity making up a clearly distinguishable system of norms, thus having a substantial perspective. In this case, one thinks of all legitimate changes in the legal system as being performed outside the system, by the legislator. In this perspective, the act of legislation is the cause, and possible changes in the legal text are results, that is, there is an immediate causal connection between the legislation and the legal change.

The actual existence of the law is the basic criterion for legal positivism. This concept could be described as looking upon the validity of law as an empirical fact, since it is conditioned by certain empirically acknowledged circumstances. This is true for both the written law and the case law. It is possible to document both empirically through legislative procedures and through actual legal application.

Having a substantial perspective on legal right, one dismisses the moral and rational norms of value which exist regardless of the positive legal regulation and application, and which are included in the establishment of what is current legal practise. It does not, however, mean that one denies that the law can and should fulfill certain absolute or relative moral or rational values. These moral conceptions, however, can be regarded as explanations of why the law has developed in the way it has, not as legally relevant grounds for a legal regulation to be considered as current legal practise. The influence of moral conceptions is considered as a historical circumstance rather than an internal part of the arguing of what is current legal right. Ethical and rational values are instead looked upon as an external force governing the political decisions of the legislator. In this way, one can claim a theoretical link between current legal practise and ethical values, even if this link is dualistic.

Having a substantial perspective, one regards all legitimate changes in the legal system as being done outside the system by the legislator. Having a functional perspective, changes in the legal system are primarily considered to be caused by the system itself. The legislative mechanism is regarded as part of the system. The legislation is hereby reduced to being one of several factors through which one reaches the decision on what is to be considered as current legal right. A functional description of rights, obligations and individual legal rules creates an understanding for the conception of the legal right as an autonomous system of norms. This system develops autonomously and relates to impulses from outside with its own character as a basis. With a functional perspective on law, the interplay between law and society is visualized. An analysis of the legal system requires a conception or an idea of what the law is and how it is determined as a system. The legal system is looked upon as an open and flexible system of norms, where the law is developed continuously as an answer to different social needs.

53

If the purpose is to determine what makes up current law, in this case the possibility to undergo rehabilitation, this is a result of a composite process based on a number of legal sources, of which the legal texts and judicial decisions in the final court of appeal are, of course, central standpoints, but not the only, and not always the decisive. Among the arguments in a legal discourse are namely also opinions of the reasonableness of the regulation in question, what the Norwegian legal scientist Eckhoff calls *real considerations*. These vary from time to time, either due to the actual conditions altering or due to the change in values and attitudes. This implies that the contents of the law also change with time without there being a legislative change, or without a new, and different sentence in the Supreme Court.

The functional perspective on law is based on the construction of a useful theory of norms. This theory forms the basis of how to apprehend the law. In theoretical legal discussions, one often speaks of two theories of norms, namely the deontological and the teleological. The deontologist is primarily not interested in the consequences of a certain action, and neither is he interested in the goals of that action. The interest is in the action as such. The limitations of the deontological norm theory are that it only considers the action as such without thinking about consequences and actual circumstances. From an ethical point of view, however, one cannot only look upon the action as such. It is necessary to consider its consequences as well. If, for example, one tells you not to cause any damage, the consequences of the omission to act must also be considered. This is where the teleological norm theory comes in. It says that the action which leads to the best possible consequences is the right action. In order to determine whether the action is right or wrong, one has to know the actual consequences as well as how to evaluate them. The purpose must not justify a disgusting means. There are actions which are so wrong that they can never be justified, however beneficial the consequences. A combination of the deontology, looking at the actions as such, and the teleology, focusing on its goals or consequences, results in the best ethical norm theory. The basis will then be formed of a teleological theory, emanating from facts and values.

When a legal norm is evaluated in comparison to ethical or rational values, the evaluation is done with regard to the consequences that the norm will have for society and for the individuals. The legal regulation is then compared to the ethical values which are possible to realize in a social context. It is the quality of the general ethical norm which is estimated, the quality which is addressed to the social order and not to the individual. These values are often society-related ideas which have their origin in human relations.

That actions and their consequences are considered to be 'right' and 'just' means that they are within the frames which we find that one should keep to according to a perspective of righteousness. According to Max Weber, legitimacy is created through justifying on the basis of values. Empirical knowledge of the way things really are cannot create legitimacy, but for this is needed a yardstick or an opinion deciding how things ought to be. Legitimacy is thereby dependent on the values on which the estimation is done. Therefore, it is very important to clarify the prerequisites for this estimation.

The substantial perspective is thus not a possible way to go if one means that on one hand ethical values should be included in the legal system, but on the other hand that the legal system must be legitimate.

Before answering the question of what rehabilitation would look like if one applied a functional perspective on the law, I will say something about how the legal application has actually developed. The Supreme Administrative Court has not rendered any decisions concerning the application of the step-by-step assessment. However, there are some decisions from the administrative courts of appeal which seem to favour the refinement principle, even though this is done with great caution.

As for the application on the level of the social insurance offices, there is only the annual report of 1998 from the National Social Insurance Board, of which it is evident that the result of the rehabilitation has deteriorated. More people were taking part in the social insurance offices, purchases of rehabilitation services, but a greater part of the money was spent on investigating and establishing the work capacity, and less money was spent on education. The National Social Insurance Board sees no connection between the application of the step-by-step model and the impaired rehabilitation result, showing in the decreased number of persons regaining work capacity. It is a very likely one to presume that the fact that fewer persons are subjected to education/retraining is the cause that fewer persons regain their work capacity. The fact that the number of people admitted to education/retraining has decreased, is most likely due to a strict application of the step-by-step model.

A questionnaire and interview study shows how the legal application has been conceived by the insured persons. It is clear that persons who have had their sickness allowance withdrawn in step 5 are very disappointed on the help, or rather lack of help, that they have got during as well as after the sick-listing. The disappointment is also evident, though to a lesser extent, among the persons whose sick-listing has been concluded in step 5, but whose right to allowance has not been withdrawn. The persons in step 6 were mostly satisfied both during and after the sick-listing. The step 5-group had, to a larger extent, consulted both the employment office/employability assessment institute and the medical health care after the sick-listing. The number of persons in the study was small, but the differences are still so obvious that they ought to be taken seriously. The answers imply that the transfer of responsibility from the social insurance offices to the employment offices has not worked satisfactory. It appears that none of the interviewed persons thought that they had got any active help from the employment offices. None had received an education bought or paid for by the National Labour Market Board. What people had got was education from the so called Kunskapslyftet ('Knowledge Lift'), which is open to everyone without three years of 'gymnasium school'. A reasonable explanation for this is that the employment offices have other priorities that the social insurance offices in the context of rehabilitation.

Through the interviews merges a picture where the sudden withdrawal of all supporting measures is common to all the answers. The feeling of having been badly treated by the officer in charge of the case is also obvious. One has got along in different ways, but been subjected to hard stress. A lot of people have had a transitional period when they have not been able to get any financial support from society and have been forced to borrow money from friends or use up their savings. It is very evident in the questionnaires as well as in the interviews, that one does not think that the social insurance office has followed the existing legal regulations and that one has not felt as if one has been treated fairly. This is interesting from the aspect that people find it both fair and legally justified to receive retraining through the social insurance office in cases when they cannot remain with their former employer.

As is evident when studying the report from the Committee on Sickness and Work Injury, important presumptions which served as a ground for the argumentation on a sharpened application of the laws lacked factual material. The reason for a sharpening was to save money. The propositions for a legal change also lacked a consequential analysis. In spite of the government pointing out the importance of evaluation, up to this date only the above mentioned ten page long report, based on assessments from the National Social Insurance Board, has been published.

If one compares the statistics on rehabilitation measures taken by the employer in relation to employees, the extent of these measures was as great before as after the legislative change in 1997. This ought to imply that the comprehensive view is still present in contexts concerning rehabilitation to another job with the same employer. This means that it is the *second* possibility mentioned above which is the one that is used in reality. A comprehensive view on rehabilitation in this situation, is a natural consequence of the employer rehabilitating somebody to another job at the same place of work.

Would the application of the law look different if one had a functional view on the legal system? Above, it has been pointed out that views on the reasonability of the rules should also be a legal argument. Is it ethically defensible to put up with a unequal legal regulation, or can the legal source called 'real considerations' give another result? 'Real considerations' can be of importance both when deciding the general contents of a legal regulation and when making decisions in the individual case. Such considerations can adjust the result one would otherwise have reached having authoritative materials such as the legal text and its preparatory works as a basis. The purpose of paying attention to these considerations is to try to reach good results in terms of sense and value, but within certain frames defined by other legal sources. The 'real considerations' can be considerations of legal security, of consequence and harmony in the legal system, of purposes and interests as well as result oriented considerations of what will be possible and practical to realize. Sometimes such considerations have to give way to legal sources of a higher rank. How great an attention one should pay to 'real considerations' depends on factors such as the quality of the argument, what legal sources that points in the opposite direction etc.

With a teleological norm theory and with the working line characterizing the view on rehabilitation as a starting point, the regulations should be interpreted thus: The persons who are thought to be able to earn their own living after rehabilitation should also be subjected to such rehabilitation. There is no logical reason to shift off those lacking a gainful employment and leave them without rehabilitation, when persons in corresponding situations holding an employment will receive rehabilitation. Referring to the fact that the person in question will be capable of performing a less demanding job which is not actually available on the labour market, does not result in the working line being realized. If the person in question fulfils the prerequisites for this, he/she may be entitled

57

to unemployment compensation, but that is not the same as realizing the working line. The rehabilitation should serve to make a person fit for a job which he/she ought to have a realistic possibility of getting and making his/her living on.

A lot speaks for the fact that 'real considerations' with the contents described above ought to be attached greater importance to than an interpretation of the legal text from a refinement perspective. It has also been stated above that, even from that perspective, the comprehensive view is valid for everybody who has an employer able to offer him/her another job. The legislator has never expressed that it should be desirable that the unemployed person is not subjected to a comprehensive view. Neither has the legislator explicitly repudiated the comprehensive view described in chapter 22, and thereby not the principle of human value with its demands for equality and justice, either. On the contrary, in rehabilitation contexts, this principle has been pointed out very obviously during the last years. One example of this is the appointment of an investigation which shall design an ethical platform for rehabilitation. It is not possible to apply an ethical platform on a legal system of norms which has divided people into different groups without basic ethical values. 'Real considerations' of an evaluation character as well as a sensibility character speak against it.

As a conclusion, the reasons for interpreting the regulations on rehabilitation from a comprehensive perspective seem to be stronger than the reasons to use the principle of refinement. The confusion and the hesitation which the officer may feel in applying the regulations from 1997 would disappear if employed and unemployed persons were given the same value and the same right regardless of personal qualities and place in society. With a functional view on the legal regulations on rehabilitation, the officer can devote himself to legal application in the strict sense, and not to finding out acceptable reasons not to use the regulations. This results in rational gains as well as ethical.

References

Andersson, Jonsson, *Nekad sjukpenning i Skaraborg*, Skaraborgs läns allmänna försäkringskassa, 1998.

Benavides, Fernando G. - Benach, Joan, *Precarious Employment and Health-Related Outcomes in the European Union*, European Foundation for the Improvement of Living and Working Conditions 1999.

Berglind, Hans - Gerner, Ulla, *Motivation och återgång i arbete bland långtidssjukskrivna*, Socialmedicinsk tidskrift 1999, nr 5, s. 409 ff.

Bernt, Jan Fridthjof - Doublet, David R., *Vetenskapsfilosofi för juster - en innføring*, Fakbokforlaget 1998.

Doublet, David R., *Rett, vitenskap og fornuft. Et systemteoretisk perspektiv på den rettslige argumentasjons verdimessige forutsetninger*, Alma Mater 1995.

Eckhoff, Torstein, *Rettskildelære*, 3 udgave, Oslo 1993.

Ekblad, Susanne, *Rehabilitering med förhinder. En utvärdering av renodlingsbegreppet och de sju stegen*, uppsats vid Mitthögskolan, Institutionen för vård och omsorg och Centrum för socialförsäkringsforskning. Handledare Lotta Westerhäll, 1999.

Eliasson, Levin, Meeuwisse, Sunesson *Den värderande blicken*, Studentlitteratur, 1990.

Försäkringskassan i Stockholm län, Uppföljning av indragning/ersättning av sjukpenning och rehabiliteringsersättning, 1997.

Försäkringskasseförbundet, Socialförsäkringsguiden, 1998.

Hetzler, Hjortsberg, Eriksson, *Karriärvägar efter sjukpenningsindragning*, Malmöhus läns allmänna försäkringskassa, 1997.

Jeppson-Grassman Eva *Arbetslivets krav och människors lidande*, Stockholms universitet, Socialhögskolan, 1992.

Johannesson Conny, *Etik i förhandlingsstaten*, Högskolan i Växjö serie 2 Ekonomi och Politik nr 5:1994.

Kemi, Anita *Motstridiga roller i människovårdande arbete*, Försäkringskassan i Stockholm FoU-rapport nr 30, 1999.

Klosse, Saskia. den Uijl, Stella. Bahlman, Tineke. Schippers, Joop. *Rehabilitation of Partially Disabled People. An International Perspective*, Thesis Publishers, Amsterdam, 1998.

Lagrådsremiss med förslag till nya regler om rehabilitering och rehabiliteringserättning den 31 januari 1991.

Proposition 1996/1997:28, Kriterier för rätt till ersättning i form av sjukpenning och förtidspension.

Proposition 1996/1997:63, Samverkan, socialförsäkringens ersättningsnivåer och administration, mm.

Proposition 1999/2000:98, Förnyad arbetsmarknadspolitik för delaktighet och tillväxt.

Riksförsäkringsverket Dnr 5380/97-472.22, Redovisning av regeringsuppdrag att följa upp effekterna av nya kriterier för rätt till sjukpenning och förtidspension, mm, 1998.

Riksförsäkringsverket, Socialförsäkringen, årsredovisning budgetåret 1998.

Riksförsäkringsverket, Socialförsäkring. Lagen om allmän försäkring och andra författningar, januari 2000.

Riksförsäkringsverkets Allmänna råd 1998:2, Rätten till sjukpenning enligt lagen om allmän försäkring.

S 1999:08, Individen i centrum? En diskussionspromemoria om den framtida svenska arbetslivsinriktade rehabiliteringen. Utredningen om Den Arbetslivsinriktade Rehabiliteringen.

Schokkaert, Erik, *Altruism, Efficiency and Justice. Ethical challenges to the welfare state*, pp 3-35 in Issues in Social Security, International Studies on Social Security, this volume.

Selander, John - Marnetoft, Sven-Uno, Bergroth, Alf - Ekholm, Jan, *Arbetslivsinriktad rehabilitering - en jämförande studie av anställdas och arbetslösas arbetslivsinriktade rehabilitering*, Rapport 1997:2.

Social security & social integration. Employment & social affairs, Raising employment levels of people with disabilities. The common challenge, 1998.

Socialförsäkringsutskottets betänkande 1996/97:Sfu6, Ändrade kriterier för rätt till sjukpenning och förtidspension.

SOU 1964:43, Social omvårdnad av handikappade. En sammanställning gjord inom socialpolitiska kommittén.

SOU 1964:50, Samordnad rehabilitering. D.1. Remissyttranden över och komentarer till CRB:s PM 1962 med riktlinjer för den allmänna rehabiliteringsorganisationen. Sammanställning av centrala rehabiliteringsberedningen.

SOU 1964:51, Samordnad rehabilitering, D.2. Allmänna principer och vissa organisationsförslag. Betänkande av centrala rehabiliteringsberedningen.

SOU 1964:59, Ett socialpolitiskt utredningsinstitut. Förslag av socialpolitiska kommittén.

SOU 1988:41, Tidig och samordnad rehabilitering. Betänkande av rehabiliteringsberedningen.

SOU 1992:73, Välfärd och valfrihet - service stöd och vård för psykiskt störda. Slutbetänkande av Psykiatriutredningen.

SOU 1995:149, Försäkringsskydd vid sjukdom - Ett delbetänkande om rätten till ersättning och beräkning av inkomstunderlag under sjukpenningtid. Delbetänkande av Sjuk- och arbetsskadekommittén.

SOU 1996:113, En allmän och aktiv försäkring vid sjukdom och rehabilitering. Del I Slutbetänkande och Del 2 Bilaga av Sjuk- och arbetsskadekommittén.

SOU 1997:166, Ohälsoförsäkringen Trygghet och aktivitet. Betänkande av Förtidspensionsutredningen.

SOU 1998:104, Arbetsgivarens rehabiliteringsansvar. Betänkande av AGRA-utredningen.

Stendahl, Sara, Sick in the 80s: Unemployed in the 90s, pp 251, in Domain Linkages and Privatization in Social Security, International Studies on Social Security, FISS 2000.

Strömholm, Stig, Rätt, rättskällor och rättstillämpning. En lärobok i allmän rättslära. Institutet för rättsvetenskaplig forskning, 1981.

Töllborg, Dennis, Några reflektioner rörande relationer vetenskap/praktik inom juridiken, JT 1995-96 nr 2 s 354 ff.

Wadensjö, Eskil - Sjögren, Gabriella, Arbetslinjen för äldre i praktiken. En studie för Riksdagens revisorer. Institutet för Social Forskning, 2000.

Weber, Max, Ekonomi och samhälle. Förståendesociologins grunder. Del 1 Sociologiska begrepp och definitioner, 1983.

Westerhäll, Lotta, Rättsliga aspekter på arbetsoförmåga p g a sjukdom, Socialmedicinsk tidskrift 1997 nr 8-9, s. 356 ff.

Vinberg, Stig, Arbetsmiljö- och rehabiliteringsarbete med arbetsplatsen som utgångspunkt - en beskrivning och utvärdering av AMore-projektet i Jämtlands län, Rapport 1997:3.

1.3 Crossing frontiers: migration and social security

Simon Roberts

1. Introduction

The increasingly global characteristic of migration raises important ethical issues for social security.

The chapter analyses to what extent social security entitlements are seen as emanating from within nation states and therefore bounded by national frontiers. More specifically, it examines, firstly, how and to what extent nationality, residence and presence conditions attached to social security benefits in the member countries of the European Union exclude different categories of migrants who are not nationals of an EU member country; and secondly the theoretical justification for placing limitations on entitlement to benefit on account of nationality or residence or presence within the boundaries of a nation state.

2. Migration

People migrate for many reasons: to escape war, famine or persecution, to find better land or a better climate, or to find work or work that is better paid. The common theme is that migrants want to improve their quality of life. Some migrants travel great distances, sometimes from one side of the world to the other; others move a few dozen miles from the countryside to the city or from a declining region to a developing one.

Migration is not, of course, a recent phenomenon. The complex distribution of ethnic and linguistic groupings across Western Europe testifies to the multitude of waves of migration that has layered the European landscape since the early Iron Age (Rokkan and Unwin, 1983).

Industrial Europe has long experienced the ebb and flow of both economically and politically motivated migration. During the nineteenth and early twentieth centuries Europe was a net exporter of people. Between 1820 and 1940 an estimated 55-60 million people left Europe for overseas (King, 1990).

After the Second World War, and in particular during the 1950s, 1960s and early 1970s, there was large-scale migration from the European periphery, Mediterranean basin and former colonies into industrial north-west Europe motivated by the coincidence of people's desire to find better-paid work with the requirements of the industrial economies of north-west Europe for cheap unskilled labour (Thomas, 1982; Clout et al., 1985; King, 1990, 1993; Castles and Miller, 1993).

What is significant about 'modern' migration is that the barriers that must be crossed are not the rivers and mountains that confronted Rokkan and Unwin's early Iron Age men and women, but national frontiers.

3. The principle of state sovereignty

National frontiers border sovereign states. The principle of sovereignty, the notion that each state is a self-sufficient entity, was accepted as the foundation of international law and behaviour by the Treaty of Westphalia which brought the Thirty Years' War to an end in 1648 (Heater, 1990).

The absolute principle of state sovereignty has been eroded by the development of international measures to protect human rights, so that the power and prerogatives of the nation state are bounded.

However, international human rights instruments, by including in many cases the fact of alienage as a legitimate basis for discrimination, allow the principle of state sovereignty to compromise and dilute the principle of rights based in the person. For example, the Universal Declaration of Human Rights (1948) proclaims that 'everyone is entitled to all the rights and freedoms set forth in this Declaration, without distinction of any kind, such as race, colour, sex, language, religion, political or other opinion, national or social origin, property, birth or other status'.

However, not all of the declared rights are universal in that some require 'membership' of society. Thus when the Declaration proclaims universal rights to life, liberty and security of person and that no one shall be held in slavery or servitude or be subjected to torture or to cruel, inhuman or degrading treatment or punishment, it is clear that 'everyone' means just that – everyone. However, when the Declaration proclaims the right to social security, the universality is conditional upon being 'a member of society'. This may exclude aliens on the grounds that they may not be recognised by the host country as being a member of that country's society.

The International Convention on the Elimination of All Forms of Racial Discrimination (1966) obliges states to 'take effective measures to review governmental, national and local policies, and to amend, rescind or nullify any laws and regulations which have the effect of creating or perpetuating racial discrimination wherever it exists'. The term 'racial discrimination' is defined by the Convention to mean 'any distinction based on race, colour, descent, or national or ethnic origin which has the purpose or effect of nullifying or impairing the recognition, enjoyment or exercise, on an equal footing, of human rights and fundamental freedoms in the political, economic, social, cultural or any other field of public life' (Chapter 2).

However, this is immediately qualified by Chapter 2(1), which states that 'this Convention shall not apply to distinctions, exclusions, restrictions or preferences made by a State Party to this Convention between citizens and non-citizens'.

In other conventions, notably those of the ILO, the principle of reciprocity puts interstate relations ahead of human rights. Furthermore, member states of the UN may pick and choose which conventions they sign up to and avoid signing up without sanction. It is notable that the conventions that could be of most assistance to migrants – the International Convention for the Protection of the Rights of All Migrant Workers and Their Families, and ILO Convention No. 143 – have been signed by the fewest countries. No EU member states have signed the former, while only three have signed the latter. The effect of all this for migrants is that the principle of rights based in the fact of being human is compromised by the principle of state sovereignty.

Under the concept of state sovereignty, nation states may decide who may and who may not cross their territorial borders and the conditions under which they may do so.

4. The direct effect of immigration status on benefit entitlement

Each of the EU member countries accords different immigration statuses to newcomers, with asylum seekers and those granted exceptional leave to remain the least secure at the bottom rung of the 'ladder' and those who have been naturalised the most established at the top. The ease with which immigrants may move up the ladder to acquire settlement and/or nationality also varies from country to country (Roberts, 1998).

Immigration policies may attach conditions and penalties to the receipt of social security benefits for migrants who enter the country. There are a number of ways in which immigration policies directly affect migrants or even disqualify some of them from social security benefits (Roberts and Bolderson, 1993, unpublished; Roberts, 1998). Asylum seekers, those with short-term residence status, spouses of those with permits and those wishing to extend or renew a permit may find themselves running up against restrictive immigration rules.

4.1 Asylum seekers and refugees

Some countries permit asylum seekers restricted access to work while others do not allow them access into the labour market at all. In those countries where asylum seekers are allowed to work they may pay contributions and theoretically gain entitlement to social security benefits. However, in practice the lead times for even short-term benefits make it very unlikely that they will accrue enough contributions to gain entitlement and most will have to rely on social assistance.

In each of the EU member countries asylum seekers fall to some degree outside the main social assistance provisions. For example, some countries such as Belgium, Denmark and Sweden house asylum seekers in reception centres and provide pocket money and clothing allowances.

Other countries house a proportion of asylum seekers in reception centres while the remainder must enter the housing market. This is the case in France, Spain, Portugal and Austria. Asylum seekers in France receive a one-off payment on arrival, and those provided with accommodation in a reception centre receive free accommodation and food as well as clothing. Asylum seekers not staying in a reception centre are entitled to an Insertion Allowance paid below the normal rate.

In Ireland, the UK, Germany, Italy and Greece asylum seekers are not housed in reception centres and there are no co-ordinated reception programmes. Ireland and Germany pay cash benefits, as does Italy for a brief period. In the UK the new Immigration and Asylum Act (Home Office, 1999) replaces cash benefits for asylum seekers with a privately operated voucher scheme with reduced rates of entitlement.

In each of the countries, those granted refugee status are entitled to all the benefits under the same conditions as nationals. The status of exceptional leave to remain on humanitarian grounds in those countries where it exists is, in most cases, similar to that of those granted refugee status. In Denmark, Finland, France, Ireland, the Netherlands and Sweden, people who have left the reception centre receive full access to social security, while in Germany they have the same entitlement as asylum seekers.

4.2 Workers with a short-term permit

The effect of immigration regulations on workers who hold a short-term permit who become involuntarily unemployed either because the work permit is not extended or through loss of the job, sickness, pregnancy, industrial accident or retirement is that they would be expected to leave the country at the end of the duration of their residence permit. Exceptions are where a person has developed special links with the country (Denmark), has other sources of income (France, Luxembourg and Ireland) that may include contributory benefits in France, or is receiving benefit in connection with an occupational disease, accident or maternity in Spain. Workers who have accrued entitlement to a contributory benefit may claim that benefit for the duration of the remainder of the life of the residence permit without jeopardising their right to remain. However, should they need to make a claim for an assistance benefit this may jeopardise their residence permit.

4.3 Family reunion

Immigration policies also restrict access to benefits for spouses. A claim by the relative to social assistance before a long-term permit is granted jeopardises his or her right to remain in each of the countries (apart from those where nationality restrictions attached to social assistance make such a claim impossible).

For example, spouses may not claim social assistance in Austria until they have worked in a particular land for five years, when they may become entitled to a Permanent Residence Permit. In Belgium, Finland, the Netherlands, Sweden and the UK a claim for social assistance within the first year of arrival may result in the person being refused continuing leave to stay. In France a spouse who claims within the first three months of arrival may be expelled; and in Greece, Italy, Portugal and Spain a spouse may only claim contributory benefits. In Portugal even a long-term residence permit granted to a spouse can be withdrawn if the family cannot provide proof of their means of subsistence.

5. The effect of benefit entitlement conditions on migrants' access to social security

In addition to the direct discrimination through the operation of the immigration policies, migrants need to meet the 'normal entitlement conditions' governing benefits in the new country. These may discriminate either directly or indirectly in a number of ways.

Entitlement rules differ between countries in the extent to which they build into their benefits the need to have fulfilled contribution conditions and/or requirements about nationality, length of residence in the country or the condition that a person should be present when claiming a benefit. Entitlement conditions may therefore hinder those who are new to the country or – if there are nationality conditions attached to the benefits themselves – even those with long-term settled status (Roberts and Bolderson, 1993, unpublished; Roberts, 1998).

5.1 Nationality conditions

The countries differ in the extent to which they impose entitlement conditions which restrict benefits to nationals. None does so in relation to contributory benefits when they are claimed in the host country (with the exception of transitional benefits in the Netherlands, which serve a specific and time-limited purpose).

The main obstacle for newcomers to a country as far as contributory benefits are concerned lies in the requirement for a minimum number of contributions to have been paid in order to qualify.

This means that in practice contributory benefits may be of little use to shorter-term migrants, who may need to fall back on tax-financed and means-tested benefits. It is here that many of the countries restrict access to these benefits through nationality and residence conditions (Roberts and Bolderson, 1993).

Almost half of the fifteen EU countries require that somebody be a national of their country in order to claim at least some of their non-contributory social security benefits. Austria, Belgium, Denmark, France, Greece, Italy and Portugal all have nationality conditions attached to some of these benefits (see Footnote) (Roberts and Bolderson, 1999).

Social assistance is administered by the provinces in Austria, four of which require claimants for social assistance to have Austrian nationality. Prior to the Gaygusuz case (Council of Europe's European Court of Human Rights, case of Gaygusuz v Austria (39/1995/545/631) Judgement), Austria also confined its unemployment relief benefit, payable after the exhaustion of contributory unemployment benefit, to its nationals. In Belgium the main social assistance benefit, the Minimex, and the two non-contributory means-tested categorical benefits, the Guaranteed Income for Older People and the Disability Allowance, are confined to Belgian nationals. In France eight benefits are restricted to nationals (Allowance for Elderly Employed Persons, Allowance for Elderly Self-Employed Persons, Special Old Age Allowance, Supplementary Allowance of the National Fund of Solidarity, Income Support for Spouses of Salaried or Non-Salaried Workers, Allowance for Handicapped Adults, Mothers' Allowance and Solidarity Allowance). Italy restricts three of its benefits (Social Pension, Allowance for the Handicapped and Attendance Allowance) to nationals only. Sweden distinguishes between nationals and non-nationals when it comes to family benefits, requiring in the case of non-nationals that either the parent or the child has been resident for 180 days.

As each of these countries is a signatory of the Geneva Convention, the above benefits are open to those people who have been granted refugee status. However, Portugal requires six months' residence for refugees in order to be entitled to its non-contributory means-tested benefits.

Although there is no discrimination by nationality with respect to contributory benefits claimed domestically, there is, however, discrimination by nationality with regard to contributory benefits when it comes to exporting them (Bolderson and Gains, 1993). Some countries do not allow non-nationals to claim some of their benefits from abroad. This is the case with France, where pensions cannot be claimed from abroad by non-nationals; and Sweden, where flat-rate pensions are payable abroad for Swedish nationals entitled to income-related supplementary pensions based on previous gainful occupation in Sweden, but not for non-nationals. Other

67

countries pay higher amounts to their own nationals who are living abroad. Germany credits nationals who are going abroad with extra premiums to which non-nationals are not entitled. The Finnish contributory Old Age Pension, Survivor's Pension and Invalidity Pension can be retained and claimed abroad by Finnish nationals. Foreign nationals need the consent of the Central Pension Security Agency if they wish to have one of these pensions paid abroad.

5.2 Residence conditions

Although there are no residence conditions attached to contributory benefits, many of the countries attach residence conditions to tax-financed benefits.

To be entitled to Unemployment Benefit, Sickness Benefit, Old Age Pension and Supplementary Old Age Pension in Sweden it is necessary to have the intention and permission to reside for twelve months or more. People coming to Sweden with the intention and, where necessary, with the permission to stay in Sweden for twelve months or more are considered resident from the day they register.

In France three benefits have residence qualifications attached (Family Allowance, Allowance for Elderly Employed Persons and Allowance for Elderly Self-Employed Persons), one has a special residence qualification for non-nationals and two further benefits (Old Age Pension and Reversion Pension) have a special presence condition where non-nationals are concerned.

In the UK receipt of Income Support, Income-Based Jobseeker's Allowance, Council Tax Benefit and Housing Benefit are restricted to those who are 'habitually resident'. This term is not defined in the legislation but determined with reference to subjective criteria to do with the person's intentions, reasons for coming to the UK, employment record, length and continuity of residence in another country and 'centre of interest' (Bolderson and Roberts, 1994; Roberts, 2000). For those qualifying for Income Support the amount paid may be affected indirectly by residence conditions as additional premiums, such as the disability premium, are conditional upon entitlement to non-contributory benefits which themselves contain residence conditions (Roberts, 1997; Cox, Seddon, Mountfield, Roberts and Guild, 1997).

A number of countries require a prior period of residence as a condition for the receipt of some non-contributory benefits. For example, in

Belgium, to be eligible for the Guaranteed Family Allowance it is necessary to have lived in the country for the previous five years.

In Finland, in order to be eligible for Invalidity benefit it is necessary to have lived in the country for a total of five years. Here, Finland discriminates directly between Finnish nationals and third country nationals in that a Finnish national only has to have been resident in Finland for three years after the age of 16.

In Luxembourg, in order to qualify for the general social assistance benefit, the Revenue Minimum Garanti and two categorical benefits, Severe Disability Allowance and Heating Allowance, it is necessary to be a legal resident for ten of the past twenty years; while the Care Allowance requires residence for ten of the past fifteen years.

The non-contributory benefits in Spain – Non-Contributory Retirement Pension, Invalidity Benefit, Unemployment Assistance and the locally administered Ingreso Minimo de Insercion – all have residence conditions attached to them. It is necessary to have been a resident for ten years since the age of 16 for the Non-Contributory Retirement Pension, five years for the Non-Contributory Invalidity Benefit and to have three to five years' local residence for the Ingreso Minimo de Insercion (Roberts, 1998).

5.3 Presence

All of the EU member countries place restrictions on the payment of benefits abroad.

Short-term income replacement benefits, unemployment, sickness and maternity benefits can generally only be paid in the country in which they have been earned (Bolderson and Gains, 1993).

Dutch Incapacity Benefit and Disability Benefit can be retained if moving abroad but cannot be claimed outside the Netherlands. The residence-based benefits in Scandinavian countries have restrictions attached to taking them abroad. The Danish Old Age Pension for Persons Other than Employees and the Anticipatory Pension for Persons Other than Employees can neither be paid or claimed abroad. The Danish Early Retirement Benefit cannot be paid abroad for more than three months in any one year.

Finnish non-contributory flat rate Old Age Pension, Survivor's Pension and Invalidity Pension are payable abroad for a maximum of one year, unless the person was formerly a resident for ten years and moved abroad for reasons of health. The Finnish contributory Old Age Pension,

Survivor's Pension and Invalidity Pension can be retained and claimed abroad by Finnish nationals. Foreign nationals need the consent of the Central Pension Security Agency if they wish to have one of these pensions paid abroad. Flat-rate pensions are payable abroad for Swedish nationals entitled to income-related supplementary pensions based on previous gainful occupation in Sweden, but not for non-nationals.

The UK retirement pension is payable abroad but the annual uprating of the benefit is reserved for those who are 'ordinarily resident' in the UK (Bolderson and Gains, 1993; Roberts, 1995).

Non-contributory means-tested benefits are in general not payable abroad, or for short periods only.

The direct effect of immigration status on benefit entitlement and the effect of the benefit entitlement conditions themselves for different categories of third country migrants in the fifteen countries, create a wide diversity of entitlements between the member countries and within each country itself.

Entitlement to benefits at the different stages of settlement varies from country to country. In some countries those who have attained permanent residence status or its equivalent are eligible for all benefits. In others, migrants with established long- term residence status are, as the result of benefit entitlement conditions that restrict benefit to nationals only, not entitled to any non-contributory benefits. In others the long residence requirements attached to the conditions of entitlement to the benefit mean that someone with as long as a five-year residence permit does not qualify for any non-contributory benefit and that even with a special ten-year residence permit may not be entitled to a non-contributory retirement pension.

Shorter-term residents are not debarred from contributory benefits, the largest group of which in each country are pensions. However, such benefits are not in reality of much use to the shorter-term residents because of their long lead times, unless such residents can aggregate any contributions made, or time served, in the old country with such periods in the new, or transfer any accruements from the second country to a third. Failing these arrangements, short-term residents may need to fall back on various forms of social assistance or means-tested alternatives in the receiving country which are in most countries often localised and discretionary, carrying least clear entitlements, and in many cases not available to shorter-term residents (Roberts and Bolderson, unpublished, 1993; Roberts, 1998).

6. The boundaries of equality

The issue of exclusion of migrants from benefits raises normative and theoretical questions about who should be entitled. Should limitations be placed on entitlement on account of nationality or residence or presence within the boundaries of a nation state? What might be the theoretical justification for doing so?

The case for excluding migrants from the receiving country's social security arrangements can be made from within the communitarian tradition. The key members of this group (who do not regard themselves as a group and rarely refer to each other's work) are Sandel, MacIntyre, Miller, Taylor and Walzer. These writers, despite their professed heterogeneity, see themselves as descendants of the civic/republican tradition.

Communitarians argue that the distributive logic of the welfare state only extends to members (Freeman, 1986). For communitarians, allegiances to the community go beyond the obligations voluntarily incurred and the 'natural duties' owed to human beings as such. They allow that 'other members of the community are owed more than justice requires or even permits', not by reason of agreements made, but instead in virtue of those more or less enduring attachments and commitments which taken together partly define a person (Sandel, cited by Waldron, 1993, p. 172).

In the modern world, the 'community' is the nation state and it is the nation state that provides the boundaries of mutual support. According to communitarians people pay taxes because they feel a sense of patriotic solidarity (Taylor, 1995). It is the 'solidarities implicit in a common tax and public service system ... underpinned by the democratic solidarities of the national community' that bind the nation state together (Coughlan, 1992, p. 112).

However, this solidarity is necessarily bounded. People do not, according to communitarians, feel a sense of solidarity with the whole world, but rather only with other members of the community; 'the solidarities that exist within the nation state do not, or rarely, exist cross-nationally or between states. It is this fact above all that ties the redistributive welfare state irrevocably to the national level' (Coughlan, 1992, p. 112).

The case for including migrants in the receiving country's social security arrangements can be made from within the 'liberal' tradition. Whereas communitarians identify welfare with membership of a community, liberals assert a right of the individual to welfare independently of the community. Some rights, according to liberals, are universal in that they take moral primacy over the claims of any social collective. That men and women are entitled to make certain claims by virtue of their common humanity has a history going back to the Stoics and Roman jurists (Sabine and Thorson, 1973).

The argument for a universal right to welfare proceeds from a common human characteristic that means that needs must be provided for. That characteristic may be the 'mere' fact of being human (Vlastos, 1984; Sadurski, 1986). The argument proceeds that if human beings have a right to anything it must be to have their basic needs satisfied.

One problem with this approach is that intrinsic rights must apply everywhere and in the absence of large scale redistribution from richer to poorer countries, it may provide for only very minimal substantive social rights (Soper, 1993; Roberts and Bolderson, 1999).

A response open to liberals is to ground welfare rights in the concept of morality itself (Gewirth, 1978, 1981, 1982; Plant, Lesser and Taylor-Gooby, 1980; Plant, 1991; Doyal and Gough, 1991). Gewirth has defined human rights as the 'rights of every human being to the necessary conditions of human action, i.e. those conditions that must be fulfilled if human action is to be possible at all or with general chances of success in achieving the purposes for which humans act' (Gewirth, cited by Parry, 1991, p.73).

This gives rise to unspecified rights defined relative to the place of physical presence. It provides for a standard of social security in keeping with the established norms of the society in which a person lives (Bolderson and Roberts, 1997). According to Gewirth, 'the primary justification of governments is that they serve to secure these rights' (Gewirth, cited by Parry, 1991, p.73). The state in this view does not owe a special duty to its own citizens but an equal duty to all persons within its territory (Roberts, 1998; Roberts and Bolderson, 1999).

While the thick communitarian concept of membership makes it unhelpful in a world made up of nation states characterised by heterogeneous populations and plural values, the lack of any concept of membership in Gewirth's theory may make it unpersuasive as a motivational argument, if such an argument is sought, for including migrants in social security arrangements in a world that is composed of nation states (Roberts, 1998).

A concept of membership less exclusive than communal membership can be found within the liberal tradition. Associative membership does not require the belief among co-operators 'that they belong together' (Miller, 1992, p. 87). The bond need not be cemented by 'meanings, interests, values, sentiments, loyalties, affection and collective pride' (Parekh, 1994, p. 94). (Although it does not follow that these can be experienced by nationals only (Roberts and Bolderson, 1999).) The present need not be a moment in a long process stretching back into the past and on into the future, and members need not be marked off from other communities by their distinctive characteristics. All that is required in Oakeshott's (1990) phrase is 'a watery fidelity' on the part of those acknowledging the authority of the government and the laws of the polity (Horton, 1992, p. 169) and a value-rational belief in their own obligation and to a rational expectation that the other party will live up to it (Weber, 1978).

Migrants pay indirect taxes at least, from the moment of arrival. In placing duties on migrants to obey the law, pay taxes, etc, an implicit contract already exists between the receiving country and the migrant, but it is one-sided. It does not place a duty on the receiving state to provide benefits to all those who are present. In a social contract based on the principle of associative membership the receiving state would have to carry out these duties.

Footnote

Social security for people moving within the EU is coordinated by Regulation 1408/71. Regulation 1408/71 achieves co-ordination through four main principles: discrimination on grounds of nationality is prohibited; rules are laid down to determine which member country's legislation the person is subject to, and save for one minor exception it is provided that a person can only be subject to the legislation of one member state; rights in the course of acquisition are protected through aggregation of periods of insurance and/or residence spent in each of the respective countries; and rights already acquired are protected by allowing certain benefits to be exported (European Commission, 1995; Cox, Seddon, Mountfield, Roberts and Guild, 1997).

The Regulation applies 'to employed or self-employed persons who are or have been subject to the legislation of one or more Member States and who are nationals of one of the Member States or who are stateless persons or refugees residing within the territory of one of the Member States, as well as to the members of their families and their survivors'.

Thus, with the exception of family members, refugees and stateless persons, Regulation 1408/71 does not provide any protection for people who are not EU nationals.

References

Baldwin, T. (1992) 'The Territorial State' in Hyman, G. and Harrison, R. (eds) *Jurisprudence Cambridge Essays*, Oxford: Clarendon Press.

Bolderson, H. and Gains, F. (1993) *Crossing National Frontiers: An Examination of the Arrangements for Exporting Social Security Benefits in Twelve OECD Countries*, London: HMSO.

Bolderson, H. and Roberts, S. (1994) 'New Restrictions on Benefits for Migrants: Xenophobia or Trivial Pursuit?' *Benefits*, December.

Bolderson, H. and Roberts, S. (1997) 'Social Security Across National Frontiers' in *Social Security and Population Movement. Journal of International and Comparative Welfare: Special edition 'New Global Development'*,Vol. XIII.

Brownlie, I. (ed) (1992) *Basic Documents on Human Rights*, Oxford: Clarendon Press.

Castles, S. and Miller, M. (1993) *The Age of Migration*, London: Macmillan.

Clout, H., Blacksell, M., King, R. and Pinder, D. (eds) (1989) *Western Europe: Geographical Perspectives*, Harlow: Longman.

'Convention for the Protection of Human Rights and Fundamental Freedoms' (1950) in Brownlie, I. (ed) (1992) *Basic Documents on Human Rights*, Oxford: Clarendon Press.

Coughlan, A. (1992) 'The Limits of Solidarity: Social Policy, National and International' Chapter given to '50 Years after Beveridge'. Conference at University of York, 27-30 September. Vol 2. York, SPRU.

Cox, S., Seddon, D., Mountfield, H., Roberts, S. and Guild, E. (1997) *Migration and Social Security Handbook*, London: CPAG.

Doyal, L. and Gough, I. (1991) *A Theory of Human Need*, London, Macmillan.

Dworkin, R. (1984) 'Rights as Trumps' in Waldron, J. (ed) *Theories of Rights*, Oxford: Oxford University Press.

Freeman, G. (1986) 'Migration and the Political Economy of the Welfare State' *Annals of the American Academy of Political Science*, 485, May.

Gewirth, A. (1978) *Reason and Morality* Chicago: University of Chicago Press.

Gewirth, A. (1981) 'Are There Any Absolute Rights?' in Waldron, J. (ed) *Theories of Rights*, Oxford: Oxford University Press.

Gewirth, A. (1982) *Human Rights*, Chicago: University of Chicago Press.

Heater, D. (1990) *Citizenship*, London: Longman.

Home Office, *Immigration and Asylum Act, 1999*, London, HMSO.

Horton, J. (1992) *Political Obligation*, Basingstoke: Macmillan.

'International Covenant on Economic and Social Rights' (1966) in Brownlie, I. (ed) (1992) *Basic Documents on Human Rights*, Oxford: Clarendon Press.

'International Convention on the Elimination of All Forms of Racial Discrimination' (1966) in Brownlie, I. (ed) (1992) *Basic Documents on Human Rights*, Oxford: Clarendon Press.

'International Convention on the Protection of the Rights of All Migrant Workers and Their Families' (1990) in Brownlie, I. (ed) (1992) *Basic Documents on Human Rights*, Oxford: Clarendon Press.

International Labour Organisation (1992) *Repertoire Des Instruments Internationaux de Securite Sociale*, Geneve: Bureau International du Travail.

International Labour Organisation (1996a) *International Labour Conventions and Recommendations 1919-1951*, Geneva: International Labour Office.

International Labour Organisation (1996b) *International Labour Conventions and Recommendations 1952-1976*, Geneva: International Labour Office.

International Labour Organisation (1996c) *International Labour Conventions and Recommendations 1977-1995*, Geneva: International Labour Office.

King, R. 'The Social and Economic Geography of Labour Migration: From Guestworkers to Immigrants' in Pinder, D. (1990) (ed) *Western Europe: Challenge and Change*, London: Belhaven.

Miller, D. (1992) 'Community and Citizenship' in Avineri, S. and de-Shalit, A. (eds) *Communitarianism and Individualism*, Oxford: Oxford University Press.

Oakeshott, M. (1990) *On Human Conduct*, Oxford: Clarendon Paperbacks.

Parekh, B. (1994) 'Three Theories of Immigration' in Spencer, S. (ed) *Strangers and Citizens*, Institute for Public Policy Research. London: Rivers Oram.

Parry, G. (1991) 'Conclusion: Paths to Citizenship' in Vogel, U. and Moran, M. (eds) *The Frontiers of Citizenship*, London, Macmillan.

Plant, R. (1991) *Modern Political Theory*, Oxford, Blackwell.

Plant, R., Lesser, H. and Taylor-Gooby, P. (1980) *Political Philosophy and Social Welfare*, London, Routledge.

Roberts, S. (1995) 'Nationality and Equal Treatment: Access to Social Security Benefits and the National Health Service for Non-EEA Nationals under British Law' in von Maydell, B. and Schulte, B. *Treatment of Third-Country Nationals in the EU and EEA Member States in Terms of Social Security Law*. Max Planck Institut fur Auslandisches und Internationales Socialrecht, Munich, in collaboration with the Commission for the European Communities, Leuven: Peeters.

Roberts, S. (1997) 'Anspruchsvoraussetzungen fur Leistungen der Sozialen Sicherheit, des Sozialen Schutzes und der Gesundheitsversorgung fur Drittstaatsandgehorige in Grosbritannien' in *Sozialer Schutz von Auslandern in Deutschland*. Ed. Barwig, K., Sieveking, K., Brinkmann, G., Lorcher, K. and Roseler, S., Nomos Verlagsgesellschaft, Baden-Baden, 1997.

Roberts, S. (1998) *Not One of Us: Social Security for Third Country Nationals in the European Union*, PhD thesis, Brunel University.

Roberts, S. (2000a) 'Our view has not changed: The UK's response to the proposal to extend coordination of social security to third country nationals'. European Journal of Social Security Vol 2, issue number 2.

Roberts, S. (forthcoming 2000b) 'A Strong and Legitimate Link'. The Habitual Residence Test in the UK. Chapter presented at the conference in Helsinki 'From Citizenship to Residence. Access to Social Protection in the Nordic and EU Countries' 10-11 March 2000, Helsinki.

Roberts, S. and Bolderson, H. (unpublished 1993) 'How closed are Welfare States?' Migration, Social Security and National Frontiers: Social Security Provisions for Non-EU Nationals in Six EU Countries. Chapter given to the Annual Conference of the International Sociological Association, Oxford: September.

75

Roberts, S. and Bolderson, H. (1999) 'Inside Out: A Cross National Study of Migrants' Disentitlements to Social Security Benefits', in *Comparative Social Policy*, Ed. J. Clasen, Blackwell.

Robertson, A. and Merrills, J. (1992) *Human Rights in the World*, Manchester: Manchester University Press.

Rokkan, S. and Urwin, D. (1983) *Economy, Territory, and Identity*, London: Sage.

Sabine, G. and Thorson, T. (1973) *A History of Political Theory*, Orlando: Harcourt Brace College Publishers.

Sadurski, W. (1986) 'Economic Rights and Basic Needs' in Sampford, C. and Galligan, D. (eds) *Law, Rights and the Welfare State*, London: Croom Helm.

Soper, K. (1993) 'The Thick and Thin of Human Needing' in Drover, G. and Kerans, P. (eds) *New Approaches to Welfare Theory*, Aldershot, Edward Elgar.

Taylor, C. (1997) *Philosophical Arguments*, London: Harvard University Press.

'The United Nations Charter' in Brownlie, I. (ed) (1992) *Basic Documents on Human Rights*, Oxford: Clarendon Press.

Thomas, E-J. (ed) (1982) *Immigrant Workers in Europe: Their Legal Status*, Paris: UNESCO.

'Universal Declaration of Human Rights' (1948) in Brownlie, I. (ed) (1992) *Basic Documents on Human Rights*, Oxford: Clarendon Press.

Vlastos, G. (1984) 'Justice and Equality' in Waldron, J. (ed) *Theories of Rights*, Oxford: Oxford University Press.

Waldron, J. (1993) *Liberal Rights: Collected Papers 1981-1991*, Cambridge: Press Syndicate of the University of Cambridge.

Weber, M. (1978) *Economy and Society, Vols. 1 and 2*, Berkeley: University of California Press.

1.4 Alternative measures of national poverty: perspectives and assessment

Robert H. Haveman and Melissa Mullikin

1. Introduction

In the debate in the United States regarding the measurement of poverty, the conceptual basis of the official poverty measure has not been seriously questioned. Instead, extensive efforts have been devoted to refining the measurement of this indicator. The goal has been to improve our understanding of the level and the trend in the particular absolute, money income based concept of poverty that underlies the official United States measure.

The purpose of this chapter is to broaden the discussion of poverty and poverty measurement by introducing a few other concepts of poverty, describing their conceptual basis, and assessing the pros and cons of each. We first discuss the broad question of "what is poverty?", and describe how various poverty concepts relate to the fundamental issues that are at stake. We then summarize the official United States poverty measure, highlight its main characteristics, and note some of the criticisms that have been directed toward it. We compare this official measure to measures that rely on the level of family consumption, family potential income (or earnings capacity), and the family's own assessment of well-being, as well as a relative poverty measure that is based on a money-income concept. In the process, we provide information about what has been found regarding the level and trend of poverty which these alternative indicators reveal.

2. The concept of poverty

Although reducing poverty is a nearly universal goal among both nations and scholars, there is no commonly accepted way of identifying who is poor. Some argue for a multidimensional poverty concept that reflects the many aspects of well-being. In this context, people deprived of social contacts (with friends and families) are described as being socially isolated, and hence poor in this dimension. Similarly, people living in squalid housing are viewed as "housing poor", and people with health deficits as "health poor".

Economists tend to prefer a concept of hardship that reflects "economic position" or "economic well-being", somehow measured. This economic concept underlies the official United States poverty measure, and the proposed revision of it based on the National Research Council (NRC) Panel Report (1995)[1]. This concept also underlies several alternative measures of poverty.

The measurement of economic poverty seeks to identify those families whose economic position (or economic well-being), defined in terms of command over resources, falls below some minimally-acceptable level. In addition to requiring a precise definition of economic position or well-being, the measure must specify a minimum level of well-being (or "needs") in terms that are commensurate with "resources"[2]. Such a measure does not impose any norm on people's preferences among goods or services (e.g., necessities vs. luxuries) or between work and leisure. Moreover, it allows for differentiation according to household size and composition, and it enables intertemporal variability in access to these resources and (in principle, at least) one's ability to "enjoy" the fruits of the resources (e.g., one's health status). It does, however, link "access to resources" to "economic position" or "well-being", hence excluding many factors that may affect "utility" but are not captured by "command over resources".

Within this economic perspective, there are substantial differences regarding the specific economic well-being indicators believed to best identify those whose economic position lies below some minimally acceptable level. For example, the official United States poverty measure relies on the *annual cash income* of a family, and compares this to some minimum income standard or "poverty line". An alternative – and equally legitimate – position is that the level of *annual consumption* better reflects a family's level of living, or that some measure of a family's *capability to be self-reliant* identifies a nation's truly needy population. Indeed, one economic perspective relies on families' *own assessment of economic well-being* in measuring the level and composition of poverty. Although the poverty measures derived from each of these concepts identify the "least well-off"– the most "hard-shipped" – groups in society; acceptance of any one of them implies both a different target poverty population and a different set of anti-poverty policies[3].

Clearly, many choices are required in establishing a poverty indicator even within this narrow, "resources relative to needs" framework. However, assuming that all of these choices have been made, such poverty measures can be either *absolute* or *relative*. The indicator is absolute if the definition of "needs" is fixed, so that the poverty threshold does not change with the standard of living of the society. A relative, income-based poverty measure uses a poverty line that is in some way related to the general standard of living of the society[4].

3. The official United States poverty measure

The official United States poverty measure (including the recently proposed revisions in it) has several distinct characteristics. First, it is a measure of income poverty; the purpose is to identify those families that do not have sufficient annual cash income to meet what is judged to be their annual needs. As such, it compares two numbers for each living unit – the level of their annual cash income and the level of income that a unit of it's size and composition requires in order to secure a minimum level of consumption. By relying solely on annual cash income as the indicator of resources, this measure ignores many potential sources of utility or welfare (e.g., social inclusion, or "security") that may be weakly tied to cash income. Second, it is an absolute measure of poverty. Cash income is compared to income requirements, and that is it. As a result, even if the income of every non-poor individual in the society should increase, the prevalence of poverty in the society would not be affected.

This measure has a very particular philosophical basis. The standard here is whether or not a household, in fact, has sufficient income from either government support or their own efforts to boost them above some minimum threshold. The implied social objective is that, together, the community's efforts and those of the individual should ensure that some minimal level of living is attained. Although people may experience hardship in many dimensions – education, housing, food, social contacts, security, environmental amenities – or appear to others to be destitute in these dimensions, only a sufficiently low level of money income matters in determining who is poor. The implicit presumptions are that:

- money can buy those things whose absence makes people feel destitute,
- money income is a good proxy for welfare (or utility), and
- a particular year's income is an acceptable indicator of longer-run income[5].

The most fundamental criticisms of the official measure focus on this basic social objective on which it rests. Perhaps actual cash income is not the most salient indicator of well-being or position. Similarly, in assessing poverty trends over time, perhaps the general trend in the overall level of living should be taken into account. Other proposed poverty indicators reflect these alternative judgments.

Aside from taking exception to the social objective that underlies the official measure, most other criticisms of it focus on the adequacy of the annual cash income measure of "command over resources". While the current cash income numerator of the poverty ratio may reflect the extent to which the family has cash income available to meet its immediate needs (and hence be desirable for determining eligibility for program benefits or financial assistance), it indicates little about the level of consumption spending potentially available to the family. For many families, annual income fluctuates substantially over time. Unemployment, layoffs, the decision to undertake mid-career training or to change jobs, health considerations, and especially income flows from farming and self-employment may all cause the money income of a household to change substantially from one year to the next. As a result the consumption spending of the family in any given year may differ substantially from the family's reported income in that year (see Mayer and Jencks, 1992; Slesnick, 1993)[6]. Even as an indicator of a family's ability to meet its immediate needs, the current income measure is flawed – it reflects neither the recipient value of in-kind transfers (e.g., Food Stamps and Medicaid, both of which are major programs in the United States supporting the economic well being of low income families) nor the taxes for which the family is liable[7]. Similarly, whereas current cash income – and hence the official poverty measure – reflects financial flows in the form of interest and dividends from the assets held by individuals, the assets themselves are not counted, nor is the value of leisure (or voluntary nonwork) time reflected in the measure[8].

The United States official poverty measure is also silent on the differences in the implicit value that families place on income from various sources. Income from public transfers, market work, and returns on financial assets are treated as being equivalent in contributing to the family's well-being. As an absolute measure of poverty, the United States official measure also implicitly assumes that it is the circumstances of those at the bottom of the distribution that matters, and not income inequality per se. A growing gap between those with the least money income and the rest of society need not affect the official poverty rate[9].

Similarly, the arbitrary nature of the denominator of the poverty ratio – the minimum income needs indicator – has also been criticized. Given its conceptual basis and the crude empirical evidence on which the dollar cutoffs rest, the United States official poverty lines are essentially arbitrary constructs. Adjustments in the poverty line to account for different family sizes and structures also rest on weak conceptual and empirical foundations.

Finally, the data base on which the official United States poverty measure rests, the annual March Current Population Survey undertaken by the United States Bureau of the Census, has been faulted for failing accurately to capture true cash income, especially those components deriving from public transfers, income from assets, and illegal activities (see Rector, O'Beirne, and McLaughlin, 1990)[10].

4. Relative income poverty measures

4.1 One-half of median income

Use of a relative standard is based generally on a belief that poverty is not absolute; rather poverty is "largely a matter of *economic and social distance*". A relative poverty measure stresses the importance of how the resources of an individual can allow it to function relative to the rest of society. The use of a relative measure, it is argued, allows us to take into consideration changes in the overall economy (in terms of wages and prices), and changes in standard of living expectations (in terms of consumption, for example). As Fuchs states "Today's comfort or convenience is yesterday's luxury and tomorrow's necessity. In a dynamic society it could hardly be otherwise"[11].

One prominent relative poverty definition considers those with incomes less than one-half of median income to be in poverty, hence reflecting the view that poverty is only meaningful when compared to overall income or spending levels[12].

The choice of a standard equal to one-half of median income is admittedly arbitrary. When first offered in the 1960s, this measure approximated the level of the Orshansky measure for a family of four[13]. However, today the United States official income needs standard stands at about one-third of median income (Ruggles, 1990)[14].

This measure, of course, has other weaknesses. Critics of a relative measure point out its weakness in assessing the efficacy of antipoverty efforts. The nature of the measure ensures that the poverty threshold will rise most rapidly in periods of economic growth, during which time, those at the bottom of the distribution also experience real growth in both earnings and consumption. Hence, even though poor families may perceive themselves as better off during a prosperous period, the poverty rate may not fall, thus overstating the poverty problem. As Ruggles (1990) has stated: "poverty cannot decline under a relative poverty measure without some change in the shape of the income distribution as a whole"[15].

5. Consumption-based poverty measures

A primary criticism of income poverty measures is that the annual cash income concept on which they rest is a poor indicator of the permanent income (or, lifetime resources) of the family unit. Using such a measure, a wealthy family with a well-educated head and substantial assets, but a year of low income, would be classified as "poor".

One proposal designed to avoid this problem involves use of measured family consumption to determine poverty status [Slesnick (1993)], based on the argument that family consumption is a superior proxy for the family's permanent income, or family command over resources. Slesnick argues that poverty measures that rely on annual money income are "severely biased indicators of the level of poverty in the postwar United States"[16]. "Households in the lower tail of the income distribution are disproportionately represented by those with temporary reductions in income, and typically exhibit high ratios of consumption to income in an effort to maintain their standard of living" (p. 2). It is this classification of *temporarily* low-income families as *permanently* needy that Slesnick believes artificially drives up the poverty rate.

The consumption-based poverty indicator proposed by Slesnick uses household real consumption expenditure per equivalent adult (taken to be the quotient of real household consumption and a household-specific cost of living index and an equivalence scale) as the indicator of resources. The equivalence scales used by Slesnick are designed to reflect total household budget needs, rather than just food needs. The consumption measure is combined with a poverty threshold designed to be "conceptually consistent" with the official poverty standard[17].

The resulting consumption poverty measure suggests a much lower poverty rate than the official definition (see below). Slesnick attributes this result to the over-representation of families experiencing a transitory income reduction among any year's income poor population. Because consumption decisions are based on permanent income (and are uncorrelated with transitory income), these temporarily income-poor households will have high ratios of consumption to income, and hence are not classified as poor in a consumption-based measure[18].

Slesnick's consumption poverty measure has been criticized on several grounds. One particularly salient criticism concerns the nature of the equivalence scales that Slesnick employs. While other poverty indicators, including other consumption-based indicators (see Cutler and Katz, 1991), have shown a growing poverty rate over the last two decades, the Slesnick measure suggests that poverty in the United States has been secularly decreasing over that period. Triest (1998) attributes this result to the equivalence scales which Slesnick employs, equivalence scales which he says "take on values outside the range which many observers would consider reasonable"[19].

In addition to these criticisms specific to the Slesnick consumption poverty measure, there are other concerns associated with the use of a consumption-based measure. In general, the largest impediment to utilizing a consumption-based index is the difficulty of obtaining complete and accurate family expenditure data. Although difficult in its own right, measuring a family's income is far easier than accurately calculating the amount a household spends in a year. Furthermore, consumption may not fully reflect a family's true well-being; it is possible that simple frugality may be mistaken for poverty.

6. Self-reliance as a poverty measure

The income or consumption poverty indicators we have discussed reflect a particular social objective – that all households should have sufficient income (or consumption) from either public support or their own efforts to enable them to attain a minimum acceptable level of living.

A quite different social objective would argue that those people in society who are truly poor – who have the lowest economic position or well-being – are those who do not have the capability to make it "on their own", to be self-reliant. Two reasons – one conceptual and the other practical – suggest the need for a poverty indicator that incorporates this consideration.

The *conceptual reason* is the more basic. A self-reliant measure of poverty focuses attention on the long-term status of people, their "permanent" capabilities. As the case for a consumption-based poverty measure emphasizes, while not having income this year sufficient to cover basic needs is a matter worthy of public concern and action, being income poor is often transitory. Identifying those people who are incapable of generating sufficient income to meet basic needs may provide a more meaningful measure of long-term economic poverty.

This position has its foundations in the writings of Amartya Sen, among others. Sen has argued "that the basic failure that poverty implies is one of having minimally adequate capabilities" (p. 111) and, hence, that "poverty is better seen in terms of capability failure than in terms of the failure to meet the "basic needs" of specified commodities" (p. 109)[20]. He calls for "reorienting poverty analysis from *low incomes* to *insufficient basic capabilities*", arguing that "the reorientation from an income-centered to a capability-centered view gives us a better understanding of what is involved in the challenge of poverty" (p. 151).

There is also a *policy-related reason* for developing a "capability to be self-reliant" measure of poverty. In recent years, there has been renewed civic debate regarding appropriate norms and standards for individual responsibility and behavior, and hence the appropriate role of the state. A prominent viewpoint in this debate has emphasized the merits of individual independence (relative to reliance on government programs), the negative effects of government programs on individual behavior, and the desirability of a smaller economic and social policy role for government[21]. Through its emphasis on individual responsibility, this point of view implicitly rejects the basic income concept on which the official poverty measure rests.

Advocates of this viewpoint argue that the real problem is that the nation has substituted welfare and other public transfer income for income generated by people's own efforts, hence inducing inefficient behaviors, generating more long-term poverty as recipients come to depend on government support, and fostering the creation of a dysfunctional social class that is at the core of many of the nation's problems[22]. To those who emphasize self-reliance, then, reducing official poverty has little relevance.

It is in this context, then, that a self-reliance poverty concept and measure becomes relevant. If a nation is to base policy on the central social goal of "economic independence" – it would seem important to identify the size, composition, and growth of the population of citizens who do not have the capability to be independent in a market economy[23]. Such a concept also abstracts from taste-related choices regarding working (vs. leisure) and consuming (vs. saving), and is therefore a more accurate indicator of nontransitory family characteristics.

One capability-based poverty measure – the self-reliant poverty measure – is based on the concept of a family's net earnings capacity (NEC), which reflects a family's ability to achieve economic independence (i.e., to attain a minimum level of living) through the use of its own capabilities[24].

The NEC of a family[25] is obtained by first estimating what each adult in the family, given their capabilities and characteristics, would be able to earn in the labor market if they were to work to capacity (taken to be full-time, full-year market employment), and then summing these estimates. This value is called the family's gross earnings capacity (GEC). Then, adjustments are made to GEC for constraints on working at capacity due to health problems or disability and the expenses (mainly, child care costs) that would be required if all of a family's working-age adults did work at capacity to yield NEC. Finally, the family's NEC is compared to the official poverty line for the family. If the NEC is above the official poverty line, the family's ability to earn exceeds a necessary minimum level of consumption, and the family is considered "able to be self-reliant". Families whose NEC level falls below the official poverty line are considered "unable to be self-reliant", and are classified as being in self-reliant poverty.

Measuring "self-reliant poverty" requires several implicit conventions, norms and assumptions, and the poverty indicator based on this concept has merit only insofar they are accepted as appropriate. (A more complete description of the estimation procedure is presented in the Appendix.) To summarize the main ones:

- The NEC concept is an appropriate indicator of the capability of a family to generate an income stream that could be used for meeting needs.
- The "norm" of full time, full year work is an accepted socially-determined norm representing the full use of human capital.
- The adjustments made to GEC for health problems and disability accurately measure the effect of the factors that keep individuals from fully using their earnings capacity[26].
- The adjustment made to GEC reflecting the required costs of making full use of human capital (primarily, child care costs) accurately reflect these unavoidable work-related costs.

While the capability basis of this self-reliance poverty indicator has important and attractive features, the measure itself has drawbacks, including the following:

- The estimate of NEC reflects the application of one set of complex statistical techniques to survey data, and equally defensible procedures might lead to somewhat different results.
- Attribution of poverty status to any particular family requires prediction from statistical estimates rather than values measured in survey data (such as income), and hence is inappropriate for the purpose of, say, public benefit determination.
- Only those capabilities that are reflected in market wages are captured in the measure; the potential services of other valuable, though nonmarketed capabilities are neglected. And, any shortcomings of labor market wages in reflecting the social value of marketed services are captured in the NEC measure.

7. Subjective measures of poverty

One additional poverty indicator should be mentioned – poverty measured by the subjective responses of individuals to questions inquiring into their perception of their economic position or well-being, relative to some norm[27]. Like the official U.S. measure, these subjective measures are based on an "access to resources" concept. However, because the subjective thresholds applied by people are likely to change over time as the incomes of the respondents change, this measure tends to be a relative, rather than an absolute poverty indicator[28].

Typically, subjective poverty measures are based on surveys of households which ask the household head to stipulate the minimum level of income or consumption they consider to be "just sufficient" to allow them to live a minimally adequate lifestyle. For example, in one approach, if people have in mind some level of living that they consider "minimally adequate" (the minimum income necessary to "get along"), and if they respond that their own level of living exceeds that minimum, one could by observing their actual income obtain both a monetary poverty line (by inference), and a poverty rate[29].

Ruggles (1990) has pointed out the appeal of subjective measures: "After all, "poverty" is a socially determined state, and in the end official thresholds come down to what some collection of politicians and program administrators consider an adequate level of resources to support a life in a particular community. It seems in many ways more appropriate to ask the members of that community directly what they consider a minimally adequate income level" (pp. 21–22).

Of course, these measures are not without their drawbacks. Implicitly, subjective measures are based on individual opinions of what constitutes "minimally adequate" or "enough to get by". As such, a subjective poverty measure requires us to assume that individual perceptions of these notions reflect the same level of real welfare for all respondents. As Hagenaars (1985) indicated, this approach has merit only if "people associate a certain common, interpersonally comparable feeling of welfare with a certain verbal description". Clearly, those accustomed to having a car, a diet high in meats, and owning their own washer and dryer are more likely to consider those items "necessary" relative to those with alternative tastes or customs.

The more formal variant of this subjective approach – that relying on the normed "welfare function of income (see note 31) – is also highly dependent on both the specific functional form and parameters that are used, and on the variables (e.g., family size, education, one vs. two earner families, social reference group) assumed to be determinants of the level of the function. There is no firm basis for these choices, which implies an unattractive arbitrariness to the measure. Moreover, the choices that are made are embedded deep in a computational algorithm, making the dependence of the poverty measure on these choices opaque.

A number of subjective measures have been developed and tested, mainly in Europe. Despite rather minor differences in terminology and question phrasing among these measures, they have yielded highly diverse results. Three different methods found three different poverty thresholds, ranging from 85 percent to 229 percent of the official 1992 threshold. This wide variation with only small changes in question wording is likely attributable to differences in how respondents interpret the question.

The effectiveness of subjective measures are also limited by the nature of the data collection method. Most estimates are based on small sample sizes, yielding large standard errors. While standard errors are reduced with increasing sample size, most estimates show wide variation around the mean (National Research Council, p. 135), impeding the setting of a reliable and generally accepted poverty threshold.

8. The level and trend of the poverty rate, by various measures

Each of these alternative poverty measures reflect a somewhat different social norm or objective, and each of them encounter thorny problems of definition and, especially, empirical measurement. However, empirical estimates of poverty levels and growth rates are available for four of the five measures that we have discussed, and we present these in Table 1.4.1.

Table 1.4.1 consists of five columns, and provides some summary information on poverty levels and calculated annual growth rates for the four indicators (and variants of them) on which intertemporal estimates are available. For all of the indicators except the self-reliant poverty measure, the estimates are for the entire population; the estimates for the self-reliant measure are for the population living in families headed by a working-age person.

Column 1 shows 1991 poverty rate estimates for the measures; this is the latest date for which estimates are available for all of the measures. The estimates vary widely with the highest rate being more than twice the lowest. The official rate was 14.2 percent for the entire population. The highest rate is the relative poverty rate (based on a one-half of median income norm) estimate of 17.7 percent. Given that the poverty thresholds implicit in this measure are higher than those in the official poverty indicator, this is not surprising. The consumption poverty measure was the lowest at 8.9 percent, though it would have been 7.1 percent if the official,

Census equivalence scales were employed. The self-reliant poverty rate was 8.0 percent.

Column 2 presents the most recent poverty rate available for the two measures for which up-to-date estimates exist – the official rate in its several variants and the self-reliant poverty rate. Since the early-1990s there has been substantial convergence in the two rates. While the income-based official poverty rate (all variants) decreased from 1975 to 1997, the self-reliant rate increased by more than one percentage point over this period.

Columns 3–5 present a summary of the growth rate patterns for the four measures in the post-1974 period[30]. The growth rates in Column 3 are calculated over the longest period since 1974 for which estimates of the poverty rates are available. Because these periods differ among the measures, the differences in growth rates are difficult to interpret. Column 5 presents growth rates for the same years during this period for which estimates are available for all of the measures – 1975 to 1989. While the consumption measure indicates a downward trend over the post-1974 period, most of the other measures indicate an upward trend in United States poverty after 1974[31]. Relying on the 1975–1989 estimates, the official measure has grown at a rate of 3 percent per year over this period[32]; the relative measure by about 9 percent per year, and the self-reliant measure by 1.7 percent per year.

This pattern is not surprising. While the official measure is an absolute poverty indicator, the relative measure depends on growth in incomes at the median relative to growth in the lowest incomes. Over this period of increasing inequality, growth in incomes at the bottom has lagged behind income growth in the middle of the distribution. The rapid growth of the self-reliant measure also reflects the erosion in real potential wage rates and earnings capacity among those at the bottom of the distribution. The growth in the inequality of real wage rates (on which the self-reliant measure depends) has exceeded the growth in the inequality of family income (reflecting changes in wage rates, work hours, and income transfers) over this period. While wage rates for the least-skilled male workers deteriorated over the post-1974 period, incomes were sustained through increases in annual work hours for families (primarily, spouses), in part in response to relative (and absolute) decreases in male wages and earnings[33].

Columns 3 and 5 also indicate that the decreasing consumption poverty rate found by Slesnick depends on the particular equivalence scales that he uses. When the official, Census equivalence scales are used instead of the idiosyncratic scales developed by Slesnick, the consumption poverty rate shows a very substantial positive growth rate of about 3 percent per year during the post-1974 period – greater than that of any of the other measures.

Column 4 presents time trend estimates for the most recent 5 year period for which estimates are available for each of the measures. Since 1995, the official poverty measure has decreased by nearly 4 percent per year. By comparison, the self-reliant poverty rate remained about constant over the last five years for which it is available (from 1993–1997), again reflecting the continued increase in earnings inequality over this period.

Table 1.4.2 presents supplementary findings on rates and trends for subgroups of the population. All of the measures indicate that the poverty rate for children and for female headed families with children greatly exceed that of the overall population, while the poverty rates for the elderly are below the overall rate. Over the longer periods since 1974, the children's poverty rate has grown more rapidly than the base rate for both the official and the relative measures. However, in recent years, the children's poverty rate has fallen more rapidly than that for other groups. Over the entire period, the elderly poverty rate has fallen, while the overall rates have increased. The poverty rate pattern for female-headed families with children is of particular interest. While the levels of mother-only family poverty are from 2–3 times that of the remainder of the population, this rate has fallen over time for both the official and relative measures, especially in the latter half of the 1990s (for the official measure). Similarly, since 1974 the Self-Reliant poverty rate for female-headed families has grown more slowly than that for the overall population; over the past five years the mother-only Self-Reliant poverty rate has shown virtually no growth.

In sum, the official and the relative income poverty rates tend to be higher than either consumption or self-reliant poverty measures. While the three income/earnings capacity measures suggest an upward trend in the poverty rate over the entire post-1974 period, the Slesnick consumption-based measure indicates a slight secular decline. The upward trend in poverty indicated by the self-reliant measure persists during the last five year period for which estimates are available, the official poverty rate indicates a substantial decrease.

The official poverty rate for female-headed families with children has fallen over the entire period, and especially in the most recent period.

Table 1.4.1 Poverty rate and change using various measurement techniques

	1991 Head Count Rate	Latest Available Rate		Growth Rate—1974 to Latest Available Rate		Growth Rate—Last Five Years		Growth Rate—1975 to 1989
		Rate	Year	Growth Rate	Years	Growth Rate	Years	
Official Poverty								
Base	14.2	11.8	1999	0.21	1974–1999	-3.84	1995–1999	0.29
Working-age headed	13.1	12.1	1997	0.64	1975–1997	-3.68	1993–1997	0.73
Modified by Price Index and Demographic Groups	14.2	13.9	1995	0.36	1974–1995	-0.53	1991–1995	-0.33
Modified by NRC Equivalence Scales	14.2	13.7	1995	0.29	1974–1995	-0.89	1991–1995	-0.27
Consumption-Based Poverty								
Base	8.9*	—	—	-0.76	1974–1989	-2.81	1985–1989	-0.67
Modified by Census Equivalence Scales	7.1*	—	—	3.40	1974–1989	-1.36	1985–1989	2.99
Self-Reliant Poverty								
(Working-age headed)	8.0	9.2	1997	2.37	1975–1997	0.11	1993–1997	1.67
Relative Income Poverty—Base	17.7	—	—	0.60	1974–1991	0.00	1986–1991	0.85**

*This is the 1989 rate—the latest rate available.
**Growth rate for 1974 to 1986.

For the Self-Reliant poverty measure, the rate for mother-only families has continued to grow, but at a lower rate than for the overall population.

9. Who is poor: alternative measures and the composition of poverty

In addition to different poverty levels and time trends, the alternative measures indicate different compositions of the poor population. Because social policy choices may depend upon perceptions of which groups constitute the poor population, these differences in composition are important.

Table 1.4.3 shows the composition of the self-reliant poor population averaged over the 1995–1997 period. It also indicates the proportion of each group in self-reliant poverty relative to the proportion in official poverty.

Consider first the racial composition of poverty. In the mid-1990s, individuals living in minority headed families accounted for more than 57 percent of the self-reliant poor. The official poor population has a somewhat different racial structure, as shown by the ratios in column 2. In the mid-1990s, the share of the self-reliant poor population living in a family headed by a Black was 110 percent of that in the official poverty population. Conversely, the self-reliant poor population had a smaller proportion who were Hispanic than did the official poor.

In the mid-1990s, the self-reliant poor population was somewhat more heavily "female headed" than was the official poor population. About 66 percent of those with the lowest earnings capacity relative to needs lived in "female headed" families, which was 104 percent of the share of such families in official poverty.

In the mid-1990s, almost 21 percent of the self-reliant poor population lived in families headed by individuals with at least some college education. The share of self-reliant poor individuals living in families headed by a people with at least some college was substantially less than this group's share of the official poor population. Conversely, the self-reliant poor population is more heavily comprised of individuals with low levels of schooling than is the official poor population.

While couples without children are substantially more highly represented in the official poverty population than in the self-reliant poor population, the opposite is true for couples with children. Among families with children, single parent families are far more heavily concentrated in the self-reliant poor population than in the official poor population.

Among self-reliant poor families with children, those living in a family headed by a single mother account for about 63 percent of the population. The share of self-reliant poor individuals comprised by such families was 110 percent of the corresponding share of the official poor population in the late-1990s. Similarly, among single mothers there is a far higher concentration of those not on welfare included in self-reliant poverty than in official poverty.

In sum, the share of the self-reliant poor population comprised of individuals living in families headed by the most economically vulnerable individuals – high school dropouts, minorities, and single mothers (especially those not on welfare) – substantially exceeds their share in the official poor population[34].

10. Conclusion

Our purpose in this chapter is to extend the discussion of poverty concepts and measures beyond the confines of the absolute income position, which has come to dominate the United States discussion. We have attempted to describe a wider set of poverty concepts that have been reflected in empirical poverty indicators, and to indicate the conceptual basis on which they rest. We have also catalogued the primary concerns – both conceptual and measurement – that have been levied against all of the measures. Substantial differences in both the level and trend of poverty exist among the several measures. The composition of the poor population also varies according to the concept and measure of poverty that is adopted. These differences suggest no single poverty measure has a monopoly in the identification of the number of people in a nation who are destitute, and the growth and composition of the poor. Each measure contributes to our understanding of the nature of poverty, and hence of the consequences and costs of poverty; they are complements, not substitutes.

Table 1.4.2 Poverty rate and change using various measurement techniques

	1991 Head Count Rate	Latest Available Rate		Growth Rate—1974 to Latest Available Rate		Growth Rate—Last Five Years		Growth Rate—1975 to 1989
		Rate	Year	Growth Rate	Years	Growth Rate	Years	
Official Poverty								
Base	14.2	11.8	1999	0.21	1974–1999	-3.84	1995–1999	0.29
Working-age headed*	13.3	12.1	1997	0.64	1975–1997	-3.68	1993–1997	0.73
Children	21.8	16.3	1999	0.31	1974–1999	-5.22	1995–1999	0.88
Elderly	12.4	9.7	1999	-0.98	1974–1999	-1.96	1995–1999	-2.08
Female-headed (with children)	39.7	30.4	1999	-0.73	1974–1999	-4.47	1995–1999	-0.31
Self-Reliant Poverty								
Working-age headed	8.0	9.2	1997	2.35	1975–1997	0.11	1993–1997	1.65
Female-headed (with children)	35.0	37.0	1997	0.99	1975–1995	0.05	1993–1997	0.45
Relative Income Poverty								
Base	17.7	—	—	0.06	1974–1991	-0.0	1986–1991	0.85**
Children	24.1	—	—	1.28	1974–1991	-0.51	1986–1991	2.00**
Elderly	8.4	—	—	-0.36	1974–1991	3.93	1986–1991	-0.77**
Female-headed	42.8	—	—	-0.32	1974–1991	-0.40	1986–1991	-0.32**

*Calculated until 1997, for consistency with Self-Reliant Poverty estimates.
**Growth rate for 1974–1986.

Table 1.4.3 Composition of individuals in self-reliant poverty relative to official poverty, by characteristics of family head, 1995–1997

	Shares (percent)	Ratio of self-reliant poverty share to official poverty share
Race of Head		
Whites	42.56	0.98
Blacks	29.76	1.10
Hispanics	23.57	0.95
Other	4.11	0.71
Sex of Head		
Males	34.39	0.93
Females	65.61	1.04
Education of Head		
Less Than High School	40.83	1.03
High School Graduate	37.69	1.10
Some College	19.28	1.03
College Graduate	2.20	0.40
Families with no Children	19.89	0.75
Percent Comprised by:		
Couples	14.04	0.82
Single Men	42.66	1.15
Single Women	43.29	0.95
Families with Children	80.11	1.09
Percent Comprised by:		
Couples	29.34	0.77
Single Fathers	7.80	1.65
Single Mothers	62.87	1.10
Characteristic of Single Mother:		
On Welfare	47.00	0.88
Not on Welfare	53.00	1.14

Notes

[1] The official United States definition of poverty has played a very special role in the development of social policy in this country. A case can be – indeed, has been – made that the most important contribution of the War on Poverty era was the establishment of an official, national poverty line. Indeed, because of the official adoption of this measure, the nation made a commitment to annually chart the nation's progress toward poverty reduction by publishing and publicizing a statistical poverty index. As Professor James Tobin (1970) put it: because of this official measure "no politician will be able to...ignore the repeated solemn acknowledgments of society's obligation to its poorer members".

[2] Sen (1983) considered the needs standard (or poverty line) to have "some absolute justification of its own", it being a level below which "one cannot participate

adequately in communal activities, or be free of pubic shame from failure to satisfy conventions" (p. 167).

[3] Within each of these perspectives, there is a wide range of definitions and concepts. For example, if income is taken to be the best indicator of economic status, is annual, multi-year, or lifetime income the appropriate measure? Should we examine pre-tax, pre-transfer income or income after accounting for taxes and/or transfers? Should in-kind income be counted or not?

[4] See Kilpatrick (1973), who defines a completely relative poverty measure as having a poverty threshold that has an elasticity of 1 with respect to the general standard of living, while an absolute poverty line employs a threshold that has an elasticity of 0.

[5] This presumption is viewed by many as overly narrow. Some prefer a sociological perspective and suggest a multidimensional poverty concept that reflects the many aspects of well-being. In this context, people deprived of social contacts (with friends and families) are described as being socially isolated, and hence poor in this dimension. Similarly, people living in squalid housing are viewed as "housing poor", and people with health deficits as "health poor". The goal would be to appropriately weight these many dimensions in order to secure an index of the size of the poor population. Poverty measures derived from this approach seek to identify some aspect of "hardship", the reduction of which becomes a social objective and test of policy. However, these many possible dimensions of hardship that can serve as the basis for poverty measures complicate policy design and discussion. Indeed, each dimension implies both a different target poverty population and a different set of anti-poverty policies.

[6] This pattern is especially true for those households in the tails of the distribution of annual income in a particular year. For example, in 1994, consumer units in the Labor Department's annual Consumer Expenditure Survey reported average pretax income of about $6,800, but average consumption expenditures of about $14,000.

[7] The failure to reflect the effect of taxes is particularly troublesome in the United States context. The Earned Income Tax Credit (EITC) has expanded into a major form of income support for the low income working population. Total national "expenditures" on the credit exceed $30 billion, and low income families (of three persons) can receive up to $3800 per year in an EITC refund. However, because the refundable payments are viewed as negative taxes, they are not reflected in the definition of income used in the official poverty measure.

[8] This is less the case for the NRC-proposed revision to the official poverty measure, as it attempts to account for some in-kind benefits in assessing the relationship of resources to needs.

[9] Relative poverty measures have become the accepted measure of poverty in Europe, especially in the European Community. However, in recent years increased interest in the development of an absolute poverty measure for EC members has increased, and currently efforts are underway to develop such a measure. See Bradshaw (2001).

[10] Moreover, annual cash income may be rather ill reported to the survey interviewer. The respondent—an adult in the family, and often a nonworking adult—may not know the true income of family members, such as adult children living at home, or may not wish to reveal to the interviewer income that derives from questionable sources.

[11] Ruggles (1990), p. 94.

[12] Because the official measure is adjusted only for price level changes over time, it will decline in relation to a relative measure if there is real growth in family income.

[13] Ruggles (1990), p. 19.

[14] Eurostat, the statistical agency for the European Community, used a one-half of median income standard in its first analysis of poverty in the community; more recently, Eurostat has adopted 60 percent of the median as the threshold. See Bradshaw (2001).

[15] Ruggles (1990), p. 19. Lampman (1972) has emphasized this weakness of the relative standard as an indicator of the nation's progress in reducing poverty. "While income poverty is a relative matter, I do not think we should engage in frequent changes of the poverty lines, other than to adjust for price change. As I see it, the elimination of income poverty is usefully thought of as a one-time operation in pursuit of a goal unique to this generation."

[16] Slesnick, 1993, p. 2.

[17] The poverty threshold is simply the total expenditure required by the reference household to purchase the Economy Food Plan divided by the appropriate cost of living index and equivalence scale. In other words, those who consume above the level required to purchase the Economy Food Plan are classified as non-poor while those who consume less are considered poor.

[18] Slesnick refers to this as "the consumption-smoothing hypothesis". Slesnick supports this hypothesis by comparing the traits and characteristics of the "income poor" and the "consumption poor". The consumption poor (or, "permanent income poor") have substantially lower rates of home ownership, fewer physical assets in the form of consumer durables, higher food and necessities budget shares, and less dissaving (indicating less access to credit) than do the income poor.

[19] The equivalence scales used by Slesnick are adapted from those developed by Jorgenson and Slesnick (1987). They adjust for family size by using the age of the household head as a proxy for family size, assuming that more older children and adults would be present in households with older heads; the actual number of children in the household is not considered. While this may be a good proxy in some instances, it contains substantial measurement error, and is likely to be especially inaccurate in tracking poverty trends over time due to intertemporal changes in the age of the household head, family size, and the number of children present (Triest, 1998). Triest also finds the adjustment for gender of household head to be "very crude:" a female-headed household is estimated to need only 62 percent of what an identically situated male-headed household would need. Even though it is likely that this adjustment is meant to account for the presumption that more children are present in female headed household, Triest finds the adjustment "excessively large". Triest also notes that the adjustments made for regional differences are of "counterintuitive magnitudes". For example, the measures indicate that southern households require more than 1.5 times the expenditure needed by a similarly situated household in the western part of the U.S. to attain equivalent well-being.

[20] Sen's position is most clearly articulated in his 1992 book, *Inequality Reexamined*. (Page references in text are to this volume.) Development of the philosophical and value basis for this viewpoint is found throughout his many writings on inequality and

poverty, especially his 1979 Tanner Lecture at Stanford University (Sen, 1980), his Hennipman Lectures at the University of Amsterdam in 1982, and Sen (1997).

[21] Evidence that being "self-reliant" or "economically independent" has taken on increased weight in U.S. social policy is the provision in the 1996 welfare reform legislation, titled Temporary Assistance for Needy Families (TANF). TANF eliminated the receipt of public transfer benefits by single-parent households as an entitlement, and imposed limits on the period that eligible families could receive support. The message to single parents, irrespective of their skills, training or home demands, was that they had to learn to "get by on their own". Similarly, advocates of the privatization of the Social Security retirement program, medical savings accounts as a replacement for Medicare benefits, tighter eligibility criteria for disabled children's receipt of Supplemental Security Income benefits, the elimination of most legal immigrants from eligibility for public income support, the shift from defined benefit to defined contribution pension plans, and the substitution of loans for grants to cover the rising costs of higher education emphasize the objective of individual self-reliance.

[22] One of the earliest of the proponents of this view was Charles Murray. His influential book, *Losing Ground* (1984) was the first in a large stream of writings, speeches and political candidacies that argued that government policy – especially welfare and other income support measures – was causal to the problem of income poverty, and hence the nation should stop assisting the destitute and start emphasizing individual self-reliance.

[23] Indeed, having a self-reliance poverty measure forces the question of collective responsibility toward those incapable of being economically independent. At one extreme, one could take the position that the public sector's only responsibility is to make clear that self-reliance *is* the norm. In this world, voluntary private charity may or may not provide for families that are unable to be self-reliant, and the problem of poverty would vanish as a public issue. An alternative position would be to consider how best to increase the ability of people who are not now economically independent to become self-reliant. Here, the issue of poverty becomes recast; it does not vanish. The question now becomes: how can public policy efficiently reduce the population unable to be self-reliant; what instruments are available, and which are the most cost-effective?

[24] A related measure of family capability is Becker's (1965) concept of "full income", which includes both income realized through market work and the value of leisure time. Adjusting this measure to reflect differences in the size and composition of the consumption unit yields full income (or potential real consumption) per equivalent consumer unit. Such a comprehensive concept of economic position reflects the level of consumption a family could attain from the full use of their resources. A poverty measure that rests on the full income concept would indicate whether or not a family had the capability to support a level of real consumption in excess of needs, that is to be self-reliant.

[25] Since the emphasis is on self-reliance, the measure applies only to those families headed by an individual aged 18 to 65, that is, those individuals expected to be independent.

[26] This abstracts from short-run constraints placed on a person's earnings capacity by the demand-side of the labor market. In particular, one could argue that earnings capacities *fall* during recessions.

[27] This general approach to poverty measurement has been called the "Leyden School" approach. Bernard van Praag is the central figure in this area; see Hagenaars (1986), and van Praag, Hagenaars, and van Weeren (1982). See also Ruggles, p. 21.

[28] While this approach has been widely discussed, estimates of the level and trend of United States poverty based on it are not available.

[29] This "minimum income" question approach to poverty measurement is employed in Goedhart et al. (1977). An alternative approach involves construction of an indicator of well-being that is comparable across people (based on income levels that individuals subjectively state to be "excellent", "good", etc.), and then identifying as "poor" individuals whose indicator of well-being is less than a particular level (say, "sufficient"). This indicator of well-being has been conceptualized in a "welfare function of income", which is hypothesized to be described as a lognormal distribution function. This original concept is developed in van Praag (1968) and was used to derive a poverty measure in Hagenaars (1985).

[30] Annual estimates are used to calculate the growth rates for the official, self-reliant, and relative poverty measures; estimates approximated from published time series charts were used for the consumption measure. The self-reliant poverty rates are estimates available in Haveman and Bershadker (2000); the relative estimates are from Jantti and Danziger (1999).

[31] The Slesnick measure, in particular the downward trend that it exhibits, has been the subject of substantial controversy. The primary critiques suggest that the erosion of poverty indicated by this measure is an artifact of the questionable equivalence scales employed by Slesnick. See discussion above.

[32] However, note that when the official measure is modified so as to maintain the original demographic group specific poverty thresholds and price index or by substituting the NRC equivalence scales for the official equivalence scales, the rate of poverty growth is actually negative.

[33] There are several ways in which the self-reliance poverty measure is likely to provide information on the level and trend of poverty and, especially, its composition that are different from that provided by income or consumption poverty measures. Three factors that would account for such divergence include: 1) differences among otherwise identical families in **tastes** for income and work, 2) differences in the **disincentives** to work faced by otherwise identical families, and 3) differences in the role played by **public cash benefits**. In each case, these differences may affect differences among families in income (or consumption) but not NEC. First consider the heavy dependence of income measures on tastes, in particular, the tastes of the members of the family unit for income versus leisure. Holding all other considerations constant, a household with strong preferences for leisure (relative to income) is more likely to be counted as officially poor than is a family with weaker tastes for leisure. Differences in labour supply and earnings caused by divergent incentives to work – such as those implicit in the nation's tax and transfer systems – also affect family income. Because of labour supply responses to program incentives, the nation's official poverty count (and the age-education-race composition of the poor) will reflect both the varying structure of incentives and differential responses to them. Finally, the official poverty definition also counts public welfare and other transfer benefits in

family income. Hence, a family in a low-benefit state with positive but low earnings may be counted as income poor when a family with identical characteristics and capabilities in a high-benefit state may be classified as non-poor.[34] As a result of the divergences between family income and permanent economic capabilities, other differences are also reflected in the two measures. For example, an independent youth who chooses to remain in school may be counted as income poor, even though she has very high long-term earnings potential. As a result, the reported age distribution of the poor is younger than it would otherwise be, and more educated. Similarly, the annual net income reported by families headed by farm owners or those relying on gains from financial or real assets is notoriously unreliable, and probably lower than it is in fact; such families also tend to be over represented in income poverty measures. Again, the poor population would seem more highly educated than it really is because of the inclusion of these people. As a result, income-based poverty statistics may be providing us with a picture of a population that in many ways fails to conform with what many people consider to be poor.

References

Becker, Gary S. 1965. "A Theory of the Allocation of Time". *Economic Journal* 75: 493–517.

Bradshaw, Jonathan. 2001. "The Measurement of Absolute Poverty". In Erik Schokkaert, ed. *Ethics, Poverty and Inequality and Reform in Social Security.* Aldershot: Ashgate Publishing Company.

Cutler, David M., and Lawrence F. Katz, 1991. "Macroeconomic Performance and the Disadvantaged". *Brookings Papers on Economic Activity* 2: 1–61.

Fuchs, Victor R. 1967. "Redefining Poverty and Redistributing Income". *The Public Interest* 8: 88–95.

Goedhart, Theo, Victor Halberstadt, Arie Kapteyn, and Bernard M. S. van Praag. 1977. "The Poverty Line: Concept and Measurement". *Journal of Human Resources* 12 (4): 503–520.

Hagenaars, Aldi J. M. 1986. *The Perception of Poverty.* Amsterdam: North Holland Publishing Company.

Haveman, Robert, and Andrew Bershadker. 1999. "Self Reliance and Poverty: Net Earnings Capacity versus Income for Measuring Poverty". Public Policy Brief, The Jerome Levy Economics Institute of Bard College.

Haveman, Robert, and Andrew Bershadker. 2000. "The "Inability to be Self-Reliant" as an Indicator of Poverty: Trends for the U.S., 1975–1997".

Jantti, Markus, and Sheldon Danziger. 1999. "Income in Advanced Countries". Draft of Chapter 10 in *Handbook on Income Distribution*, edited by A.B. Atkinson and F. Bourguignon.

Jencks, Christopher, and Susan E. Mayer. 1996. "Do Official Poverty Rates Provide Useful Information about Trends in Children's Economic Welfare"? Harris Graduate School of Public Policy, University of Chicago.

Jorgenson, Dale W., and Daniel T. Slesnick, 1987. "Aggregate Consumer Behaviour and Household Equivalence Scales". *Journal of Business and Economic Statistics* 5: 219–232.

Kilpatrick, Robert W., 1973. "The Income Elasticity of the Poverty Line". *Review of Economics and Statistics* 55 (3): 327–332.

Mayer, Susan E., and Christopher Jencks 1992. "Recent Trends in Economic Inequality in the United States: Income vs. Expenditures vs. Material Well-Being". In *Poverty and Prosperity in the USA in the Late Twentieth Century*, ed. Dimitri Papadimitriou and Edward Wolff. New York: St. Martin's Press.

Murray, Charles A., 1984. *Losing Ground: American Social Policy, 1950–1980.* New York: Basic Books.

National Research Council. 1995. *Measuring Poverty: A New Approach.* Washington, D.C.: National Academy Press.

Robert, Kate, Walsh O'Beirne, and Michael McLaughlin. 1990. *How "Poor" Are America's Poor?* The Heritage Foundation, Washington, D.C.

Ruggles, Patricia. 1990. *Drawing the Line: Alternative Poverty Measures and Their Implications for Public Policy.* Washington, D.C.: Urban Institute Press.

Sen, Amartya. 1980. "Equality of What?" In *Tanner Lectures on Human Values*, ed. S. M. McMurrin. Cambridge: Cambridge University Press.

Sen, Amartya. 1992. *Inequality Reexamined.* Cambridge, MA: Russell Sage Foundation and Harvard University Press.

Sen, Amartya. 1997. *On Economic Inequality.* Oxford: Clarendon Press.

Sen, Amartya. 1983. "Poor, Relatively Speaking". *Oxford Economic Papers* 35: 153–169.

Slesnick, Daniel T. 1993. "Gaining Ground: Poverty in the Postwar United States". *Journal of Political Economy* 101 (1): 1–38.

Tobin, James. 1970. "Raising the Incomes of the Poor". In Kermit Gordon, ed., *Agenda for the Nation.* Washington, D.C.: Brookings Institution.

Triest, Robert K., 1998. "Has Poverty Gotten Worse?" *Journal of Economic Perspectives* 12 (1): 97–114.

van Praag, Bernard M.S., Aldi J.M. Hagenaars, and Hans van Weeren. 1982. "Poverty in Europe". *Review of Income and Wealth* 28 (3): 345–359.

101

Appendix: The estimation earnings capacity, data and empirical procedures

As indicated in the text, predicted values of the earnings of each working-age adult were he or she to work full-time, full-year (FTFY) are estimated using selectivity-adjusted earnings equations fit over FTFY workers. These EC values are then adjusted for health problems and disability, and shocked to reflect the effect of unmeasured variables. In the following paragraphs, we summarize the details of this procedure.

The first step is to predict the earnings capacity for each prime-aged individual in our sample. The data used in this analysis are drawn from the repeated cross sections of the U.S. population contained in the March Current Population Surveys (CPS) for 1976 to 1998[1]. From these surveys, we select a sample of 18–64 year old, noninstitutionalized, non-student, non-self-employed civilians on which to estimate the model[2]. The model which we estimate is a two-equation model of full-time, full-year labor force participation and earnings, drawing on Heckman (1976). Such a specification is appropriate, since individuals can select into the full-time, full-year labor force.

The first stage is a probit regression of FTFY labor force participation on the vector of explanatory variables assumed to influence such participation[3]. We fit four such probits for each year, one for each race/gender group (whites/non-whites, males/females). The model is identified via exclusion restrictions, including nonlabor income, participation in a health-related income support program, the state unemployment rate, veteran status (for men) and the maximum AFDC benefit for a family of four (for women), which are assumed to affect the labor force participation decision, but conditional on FTFY work, do not affect earnings.

102

The second stage is a set of selectivity corrected OLS regressions of the log of earnings on variables presumed to influence earnings. The independent variables in this equation are chosen using the human capital model as a guide, and include education, age, region of the country, rural-suburban-urban location, marital status and number of children. To correct for self-selection into FTFY labor force, we append the inverse of Mill's ratio term, derived from the coefficients in the first stage estimation, to the set of regressors.

Using the coefficient estimates and each individual's characteristics, we obtain an unconditional prediction of FTFY log earnings for each prime-aged adult in our sample[4]. Hence, we assign the same earnings capacity value to individuals with identical characteristics, regardless of their selection into or out of the FTFY labor force.

To account for unobserved human capital and labor demand characteristics and "luck" in earnings determination process, we apply a random shock to each individual's earnings capacity prediction. Specifically, we add to each FTFY log earnings prediction the standard error from the individual's race/gender earnings equation times a normal (0, 1) random variable. In making this adjustment, we assume that the distribution of FTFY earnings within a race/gender cell is normal with a standard deviation equal to the standard error of the race/gender earnings regression.

The final adjustment to the individual EC prediction is one for constraints on work due to illness and disability. We calculate an adjustment factor, $\ni$, equal to (50-WC)/50, where WC is the number of weeks the individual does not work attributed to these reasons.

To summarize, the predicted value of an individual's earnings capacity is described by multiplying equation (4) in the text by the individual adjustment factor:

$$EC_i^* = exp\,(X_i\,\exists + \Phi^* m_i) * \ni_i,$$

where X_i are the explanatory variables from the second-stage estimation, $\exists$ are the estimated coefficients, Φ is the standard error of the regression corresponding to the individual's race/gender group, m_i is a randomly distributed $N(0,1)$ variable and $\ni_i$ is the adjustment factor noted above.

Notes

[1] The March Current Population Survey is an annual survey of over 60,000 American families, containing detailed information on the income and labor market activities and outcomes of the adults in the family. Interviewers also obtain information on the size and composition of the family. It is a stratified random sample, so that using the appropriate weighting factors (provided by the U.S. Bureau of the Census) yields a picture of the economic status and labor market activities of the entire American population.

[2] We exclude the self-employed, since their earnings represent a return to both human and physical capital which cannot be disentangled using CPS data.

[3] We define FTFY labor force participation as 2000 or more hours of work in a year.

[4] We predict FTFY earnings for students and the self-employed, even though these individuals were excluded from the estimation.

1.5 The measurement of absolute poverty

Jonathan Bradshaw

1. Introduction

There appears to be renewed interest in absolute notions of poverty. For example at the Eurostat Statistical Programme Committee in November 1998, when they discussed the subject of poverty statistics, delegates requested that the subject of absolute poverty should be investigated. As a consequence Eurostat issued an invitation to tender. The objectives of the tender were 'to assess and qualify calculations of absolute poverty based on two approaches: one taking into account minimum income schemes as existing in the Member States; the other by adapting the basket of goods approach as followed principally by the United States. The general purpose will be to provide Eurostat with a framework for carrying out future work on absolute poverty, in particular by assessing methods in place in more Member States and the USA (based on minimum income schemes and the basket of goods approach).'

As a result of the tendering process Brian Nolan at ESRI, Dublin and I were commissioned to undertake the work. This chapter is based on some thinking about how one might tackle absolute poverty empirically. There are no results in this chapter. They will appear in subsequent publications.

2. Background

Before the Second World War most poverty standards were based on notions of absolute needs/minimum subsistence/basic necessities and were generally derived using budget standards, in which the food budget was commonly based on ideas of nutritional adequacy. In the post-war period poverty emerged in social scientific debates with a new conceptualisation - as relative deprivation. A variety of methods have been developed to measure relative poverty but the one most commonly employed by national governments (see *Reconciliation of Sources and Dissemination of data*, Statistics Netherlands, September 1999 – for a review of national poverty lines), and in comparative studies, has been the use of an income (and sometimes expenditure) threshold. Thus for example Eurostat in its first analysis of poverty derived from the European Community Household Panel Survey (ECHPS) estimated the proportion of households, individuals and children living below a threshold of half national average income (Eurostat 1997). More recently Eurostat has adopted 60 per cent of the median as the threshold (Eurostat 1999).

There have been a number of criticisms of this standard of poverty:

- that it is a measure of inequality not poverty,
- that it is essentially arbitrary,
- that in some countries with dispersed income distributions it produces unreasonably large poverty rates,
- that income is anyway a poor indicator of command over resources,
- and, that for these and other reasons, the measure lacks the kind of moral and political clout which had been associated with the findings of the studies based on more absolute notions of poverty.

In response a number of efforts have been made to develop other poverty standards, some of which have been based on a more absolutist notion of poverty. These have included:

- **Budget standards**: they involve drawing up a list of commodities, employing normative judgements, supported by a combination of scientific and behavioural evidence. The budget is then priced and used as an income standard – anyone living at or below that standard is in poverty. In Britain budget standards have been derived to represent a *minimum adequate standard* and a *modest but adequate standard* (Bradshaw 1993).

- The US poverty standard was developed using a related concept – what one might call a '**component-and-multiplier**' approach. Orshansky took the costs of a minimal food budget for different family sizes and derived poverty thresholds by multiplying these costs by three – that being the inverse of the share of money income spent on food by the average family (Orshansky 1965). Bradbury and Jantti (ook wel Jantii) (1999) applied the US poverty standard to Luxembourg Income Survey data using purchasing power parities.

106

- A variety of poverty standards can be derived from **expenditure data**. So for example the point of the income distribution where households spend more than a given proportion on necessities can be used (Bradshaw, Mitchell and Morgan 1987). Or the point on the income distribution where all income is spent and/or nothing spent on non necessities (Saunders, Bradshaw and Hirst 1999).
- Some countries have employed a **benefit linked income standard** to define poverty. The official social assistance scales can be used to define a threshold. A standard of this type became the official definition in the UK in a series of *Low Income Statistics (LIS)* based on the Family Expenditure Survey produced by the government until 1985. Heikkila and McCausland (1997) tried this technique using OECD data. Another technique combining expenditure and benefits has been used to estimate the budget shares spent on necessities (food, fuel and clothing) of those on Income Support and to fix an income poverty line based on that budget standard (Bradshaw and Morgan 1987).
- The main way that relative poverty has been operationalised has been using **social indicators** but there is no reason why these indicators should not also be used to measure absolute poverty. Townsend (1979) was the first to seek to operationalise this approach. For a national survey of poverty carried out in 1968/69 he built up a list of 60 indicators of styles of living. He then reduced these to 12 items to form a deprivation index, and, for each respondent, he counted the numbers lacking items on the index. Townsend's work was subject to criticisms. In the light of these criticisms Mack and Lansley developed the social indicator methodology in the Breadline Britain Surveys in 1983 (Mack and Lansley 1985) and 1990 (Gordon and Pantazis 1997). Mack and Lansley drew up a list of items and then asked a sample of the population whether they considered them to be necessities. If over 50% of the population considered an item to be a necessity then it was included as a socially perceived necessity (a 'consensual' indicator of poverty). The sample were then asked whether they possessed the item and if they did not whether they lacked it because they could not afford it. Only those items which were lacking because they could not be afforded were included in the count of items lacking. Nolan and Whelan (1996) developed the technique by using social indicators in combination with income thresholds. At present there is a *Survey of Poverty and Social Exclusion* underway in Britain which seeks to

extend the range of indicators to encompass social exclusion as well as poverty. The ECHP also has questions based on the social indicator methodology and Dirven et al. (2000) have been using them to establish a basic index of deprivation.

- **Subjective measures** where the population determine a poverty income threshold can also be used to measure absolute poverty. Thus for example after the World Summit on Social Development in Copenhagen in 1995, 117 countries adopted a declaration and programme of action which included commitments to eradicate *absolute* and reduce *overall* poverty, drawing up national poverty alleviation plans as a priority (UN 1995). *Absolute* poverty was defined by the UN as a 'condition characterised by severe deprivation of basic human needs, including food, safe drinking water, sanitation facilities, health, shelter, education and information. It depends not only on income but also on access to services'. (UN 1995, 57). Townsend and others (1997) have attempted to operationalise this notion of absolute poverty (and overall poverty) using subjective methods. Thus they employed the following questions in the *Poverty and Social Exclusion Survey of Britain 1999.*

Absolute poverty means being so poor that you are deprived of basic human needs. In order to avoid absolute poverty, you need to have enough money to cover all these things:

- How many pounds a week, after tax, do you think are necessary to keep a household such as the one you live in, out of absolute poverty?
- How far above or below that level would you say your household is?
  - a lot above that level
  - a little above
  - about the same
  - a little below
  - a lot below that level of income
  - don't know.

The 1995 ECHP used a similar question. 'In your opinion, what is the very lowest net (monthly) income that your household would have to have in order to make ends meet.' In the report (Eurostat 1999) this threshold is compared with actual net income and the proportion living below it is estimated.

In this chapter we shall explore how some of these measures of absolute poverty might be operationalised. This is work in progress and it will be seen that we have made most progress in operationalising the social assistance thresholds and the US poverty lines.

3. Using social assistance rates to fix poverty thresholds

In his book *Setting Adequacy Standards* Veit-Wilson (1998) forcefully emphasises the difference between scientific measures of poverty, the political nature of Minimum Income Standards (MIS) and social assistance scales – 'Scientific poverty lines are not MIS, and even political standards of assumed adequacy are not by that token the same as the social assistance benefit scales. They are each and all distinct in concept and practice and *there is no excuse* (emphasis added) for not distinguishing them' (111). In this project one would like to have maintained this important distinction and have used Minimum Income Standards rather than social assistance scales to fix poverty thresholds. But Veit Wilson discovered only ten countries with Minimum Income Standards and of these four countries – Finland, Norway and Sweden and Germany had MIS standards which were related to benefit levels (in the other countries they were related to earnings standards or budget standards). Many of these countries had developed their MIS in the, often, ancient past from a combination of budget standards research, minimum earnings levels, social assistance scales or a combination of the above. The rationale for a MIS had often been lost in the passage of time or as a result of adjustments made to it[1]. It appears that MIS obtained their authority as a result of government acceptance. So despite its curious origins the French SMIC retains its authority because of Government acceptance of it. The key is official recognition - however bizarre the scientific origins[2].

As for modern scientific measures of poverty, in the study undertaken for Eurostat by Statistics Netherlands (Eurostat 1999), only the Netherlands had a poverty or low income standard which was not some proportion of mean or median income[3]. It is not said how this threshold was or is derived but it gives a higher poverty rate (16.1%) for the Netherlands compared with 10.3% in that country for 60% of the median.

So given that
- most MIS schemes are related to social assistance scales
- the rationale for many are lost in the mists of time
- that government acceptability must be an important quality of an absolute poverty threshold
- that official income poverty standards which are not relative do not exist.

109

It seems to make sense to use standards that are related to social assistance norms. MIS in most EU countries means the package of social assistance and other benefits in cash and kind which provide a floor or safety net which, *inter alia*, aims to prevent people falling below it[4]. This floor may be related to notions of minimum adequacy, minimum income guarantee or social protection. So in this section one of the techniques that will be tried will be to apply social assistance scales to income data derived from the ECHP.

In order to undertake this work we need a source of social assistance scales for each country. The obvious source is MISSOC who publishes the details of social security benefits for each member of the EU on an annual basis. However the problem with the MISSOC tables is that they do not allow us to use the package of benefits and services which make up the living standards of those living on social assistance. So for example from the details published in the MISSOC tables we cannot tell whether income tax is paid on social assistance, nor whether child benefits should be added to social assistance, nor whether the family would be expected to pay any health charges out of their income, and/or whether there are any charges or benefits in respect of education to take into account. MISSOC also does not provide enough information on the scales of social assistance to calculate entitlement for the range of households that we sought to include in the analysis.

Another source is the OECD's Database on Taxation, Benefits and Incentives. Heikkila and McCausland (1997) used this source to examine the Guaranteed Minimum Income Packages in EU member countries. This source has the advantages that it takes into account taxation, child benefits and housing benefits but they were only able to produce estimates of GMIs for three family types – a single person and couple with two children and a single parent with two children. Also the GMIs covered by the OECD are in some countries not the minimum social assistance benefits but the means-tested benefit paid to the long term unemployed who have exhausted their entitlements to income related insurance benefits – and in some cases this long term unemployment assistance may be higher than general social assistance. They thought that this was the case in Austria, Belgium, Finland, Ireland and Portugal. They used these estimates to relate the GMI package to average or minimum earnings to examine the unemployment trap and the poverty thresholds in the 1994 ECHP to assess the adequacy of the GMIs. This latter comparison is a rather curious reversal of what we are intending to do – they sought to assess the adequacy of GMIs by relating them to the poverty threshold derived from the ECHP. We are using the GMIs as a poverty standard and estimating the proportion of the population below that standard using the GMIs. Nevertheless it is interesting that for all countries except the Netherlands (for singles, lone parents and couples) they found that GMI was substantially below the 1993 poverty thresholds.

Because of the weaknesses of MISSOC and the OECD sources of data on social assistance, in this study we are going to use two alternative sources of information: first the Eardley et al. (1996) study of social assistance in OECD countries will be the main source of information on the structure of the social assistance packages. In the Eardley et al. (1996) comparative study of social assistance, data on the level of the social assistance payable in 1992 was collected for a number of model families, including young singles (17), single adults (35) and childless couples (35), retired singles (68) and couples (68) and single parents with one child and couples with children one or two children. However for the analytical work using the ECHP it is proposed to use a different source. As part of the work of the European Observatory on National Family Policies, the same data on social assistance packages was collected for all EU countries for single people, childless couples and lone parents and couples with children for 1994, 1995 and 1996 (Ditch et al. 1997, 1998 and 1999). The raw data was available to use at SPRU, where we were responsible for co-ordinating the Observatory work during that period. The data for both sources was collected using the same methods. National informants were asked to provide details on the social assistance that certain model families in their countries would receive.

Table 1.5.1 shows for one family type (a couple plus three children) how the package is made up. We start with the social assistance scales and then deduct any income tax payable and social security contributions. Only Denmark, Luxembourg and Finland charge income tax on social assistance and only Finland has a social security contribution deducted. Then added are the child benefits payable to this family. All the countries have a non means-tested child benefit, except Belgium, Spain and Italy. Belgium has a generous income tested child benefit as do Germany, Spain, France, Ireland and Portugal.

Table 1.5.1 then shows the gross rent and net rent payable. Housing costs are a particularly difficult problem to deal with in this study for reasons discussed below.

Then account is taken of health costs – the base line assumption was that health care was free at the point of demand, available to all regardless

111

of means and of a similar quality in each country. National informants were asked to estimate the costs of a standard package of health care, which consisted of three visits to a general practitioner per person per year, three prescriptions for a standard antibiotic per person per year and one visit to a dentist for one filling per person per year. The costs were estimated for both adults and children annualised and then turned into a monthly charge. It can be seen that in all countries except Germany and the UK there are some health charges to be paid by families on social assistance, but they are in most countries small and only in Spain and Austria do they exceed 5 per cent of final social assistance income.

In this exercise no account was taken of the value of pre-school provision – on the grounds that parents on social assistance, not in the labour market would free to care for pre-school children at home. It was assumed as a base line that school education of an equivalent standard, including basic books, was available free of charge for all children of school age. It was assumed that the parents would have to pay for a midday meal, and that children lived near enough the school not to require public transport. Account was then taken of any charges that the parents were expected to pay for education and any other benefits (including the value of free or subsidised school meals) that they might receive. It can be seen in the table that Belgium, Luxembourg, the Netherlands and Portugal all had deductions for school costs. France, Finland and the UK all have free school meals systems for children on social assistance and the value of these meals were added.

Finally four countries Ireland, Italy, Luxembourg and Finland all had 'other' miscellaneous benefits added to their social assistance (for example in Ireland it was the electricity supplement and in Italy it was the household allowance). For the lone parent families where it was guaranteed and under-written by the state, we also added guaranteed maintenance allowance. This increased lone parent's income in Austria, France, Germany, Finland and Sweden.

The model family method is designed to enable consistent comparisons to be made between countries and the model family method provides a good deal more detail than other sources. However the method inevitably produces a description of the way the system should work rather than how it necessarily does work. This is not so serious when we are using the social assistance scales as a standard, but it should be noted that we are assuming that that standard is achieved and that people claim their rights to these benefits. The standard also looks at families at one point in time and obscures the more complex life-cycle effects of the tax/benefit system. In particular we do not take account of the future benefits that may accrue from social security contributions.

The more assumptions that we make about the model families, the less representative they are of families in the real population. This problem is an inevitable cost of achieving comparability. In order to make comparisons the families are specified quite carefully – including the adult's ages (35 for working age adults and 68 for retired adults), the children's ages (between aged 7 and 14), the size of their dwelling (and that they are tenants), and, as we have seen, what school costs are and are not included, and what health charges are and are not included. Furthermore in most countries social assistance schemes are administered at a local level and with a good deal of local discretion albeit often influenced by national guidelines. In countries like the UK and Ireland where there are national scale rates (albeit with some discretion at the margins), or Germany where there slight regional variations, this is not a problem. However in countries like Sweden and Italy the social assistance received depends not only on individual circumstances but also on the discretion of social workers operating within local guidelines. For these countries the national informants have given the best estimate they can of what benefit would be received by each family in a specific place/municipality and that estimate it may not be representative of the nation as a whole. Table 1.5.2 gives the location chosen and also indicates the degree of local discretion/national regulation.

The table also gives the name of the main general social assistance scheme. It can be seen in the table that this is not the benefit that is taken as the standard for all claimant groups. In some of the countries there is a special minimum scheme for pensioners, another scheme for lone parents and still another for unemployed claimants.

Table 1.5.3 provides some detail on how often the scales of social assistance are uprated and on the origins of the scales.

Table 1.5.1 Composition of the social assistance package for a couple plus three school age children 1994 in purchasing power parities per month

	Bel	Den	Ger	Gre	Spa	Fra	Ire	Ita	Lux	Net	Aus	Por	Fin	Swe	UK
Social assistance	631	1834	948		428	317	812	675	1436	820	844	360	1033	868	676
Income tax		-603							-36				-331		
Social security contributions													-33		
Child benefit	163		194	83		233	85		565	248	299	34	330	245	162
Income tested child benefit	473		90		68	132	15					26			
Gross rent	322	361	313	246	413	498	704	235	577	246	233	89	492	493	233
Net rent	-322	-237	-313	-246	-413	-108	-50	-235	-450	-148	-120	-89	-133		
Gross local taxes				8	17	90		10		16					62
Net local taxes				-8	-17	0		0		0					0
Health costs	-16	-5		-2	-37	-19	14	-26	-8	-36	-107	-39	-26	-36	
School costs	-28				11	142			-31	-51		-11	99		73
Other							30	183	163				82		
Total	1059	1389	1232	81	470	806	956	807	2089	980	1036	370	1153	1077	916

Source: Ditch et al., 1996

4. Housing costs

Housing costs are a particular problem in comparative research and in this project. Housing costs vary within and between countries according to tenure, and the size, age and location of a dwelling. In some countries rents may be controlled for those persons occupying a dwelling before a certain date. For owner occupiers loan structures and interest rates vary between countries, often according to the stage of the economic cycle, while the level of a mortgage will depend by the stage in the purchaser's life cycle.

There are also significant differences between countries in the tenure distribution at different income levels. However housing costs cannot be ignored partly because housing costs make up a substantial element in the out-goings of families, but particularly for this project, housing benefits are an important element of social assistance in many countries. In the model families method, national informants are asked to nominate a typical rent for the most common rental tenure in their country in the local area nominated. The size of dwellings is specified – and varies with the number of people in the family[5]. Informants provide the gross rents and the net rent – that is after the deduction of housing benefits. The nominated rents vary a good deal between countries. Also Denmark, France, Ireland, Luxembourg, the Netherlands, Austria, Finland, Sweden and the UK all have systems of housing benefit that reduce the actual rent paid. Indeed in Sweden and the UK reasonable rents are completely covered for families on social assistance. Now the particular problem for this project is that we are seeking to apply a social assistance threshold to income data derived from the ECHP. Should it be income data before or after the deduction of net housing costs? An important argument against deducting any housing costs from social assistance is that our assumed housing costs are not at all typical of actual housing costs. Yet if we do not deduct net housing costs we are not comparing like with like - some countries without housing benefit schemes will be providing an element for housing in the basic scales. Other countries do not include housing in their scales but reduce them using a housing benefit scheme and in Sweden and the UK the scales exclude an allowance for housing costs but tenants on social assistance are not expected to pay for their housing.

The solution that we have come up with for this project is that we will use as our social assistance standard the income received in the social assistance package before net housing costs and we will compare this with incomes in the ECHP before and after housing costs. This is a far from perfect solution: it has the advantage of taking into account the actual housing costs paid by each family instead of the model families housing costs; it also gives us a poverty rate before and after housing costs. However:

1. It ignores the fact that some countries social assistance allowance is higher because it includes an element for housing.
2. It assumes that in reporting net housing costs the respondents will take into account the subsidies they receive and will deduct them to establish net rent.
3. It ignores the fact that in some countries, for example the UK, social assistance rates are increased to take account of the housing costs (mortgage interest paid) of owner occupiers.

5. Family types

For this project it would have been ideal to have had the social assistance payable to all types of families. However the earlier studies of social assistance had collected details for only a standard range of families. The European Observatory had collected data for 1994 on the social assistance paid to

Single people

Couples

Couples with one, two and three children

Lone parents with one and two children.

In addition the OECD study had collected social assistance paid to single and couple pensioners for 1992. This means that we do not have information on the social assistance scales that would be received by all households in all countries.

116

Table 1.5.2 Selected characteristics of social assistance schemes (in 1992)

	Selected commune/local area	Main general social assistance scheme	Level of local discretion	Pensioners benefit	Lone parents	Unemployed	Minimum age
Belgium	Antwerp	Minimex	National regulated	Revenu garanti pour personnes agees			18 (unless pregnant or parent)
Denmark	Copenhagen	Social *bistand	Local regulated	Minimum pension guarantee			25 (youth allowance for 18-24)
Greece	Peristeri, Athens	No generalised social assistance		Non insured older person scheme			-
Spain	Barcelona					Unemployment assistance	25
Germany	Bremen	Socialhilfe	National/regional regulated				None
France	Bar le duc, Meuse	Revenu Minimum d'insertion	National regulated		Allocation pour parent isolee		25 unless parent or pregnant
Italy	Turin	Minimo vitale	Local, discretionary	Pensione sociale			18

Table 1.5.2 Selected characteristics of social assistance schemes (in 1992) (continued)

	Selected commune/ local area	Main general social assistance scheme	Level of local discretion	Pensioners benefit	Lone parents	Unemployed	Minimum age
Luxembourg	Luxembourg City	Revenu Minimum Garanti	National, regulated				30
Netherlands	*Njimegen	Algemene *bistand	National regulated	ABW	ABW or RWW	RWW/WWW	18
Austria	Salzburg	Socialhilfe	Provincial discretion	Supplementary pensions		Unemployment assistance	19
Portugal	Lisbon	Guaranteed Minimum Income	National regulated	Old age social pension			14 or 25 if in full-time education
Finland	Helsinki	Living allowance	Local, discretionary				18
Sweden	Stockholm	Social Welfare Allowance	Local, discretionary				Normally 18
UK	York	Income Support	National regulated				18

Source: Eardley et al. (1996) Tables 3.1 and 3.2

Table 1.5.3   Uprating and the origins of the social assistance scales used in this analysis

	Uprating	Origins of scales
Belgium	Annually in line with RPI (health index) but increased in real terms since 1980	Minimex rates (from 1975) were taken from the already existing guaranteed income for older people
Denmark	Annually. Since 1994, cash assistance has been linked to the level of Unemployment Benefit which *related to average earnings	For parents, social assistance is 80% of maximum unemployment benefit for others it is 60%
Germany	Generally every six months in line with price inflation but varies with political judgement	Originally set in relation to a basket of goods. Now set using expenditure patterns of households in the lower third of the income distribution
Greece	No statutory period or basis	No information
Spain	No information	No information
France	RMI can be uprated twice a year in line with prices but not automatic	No information
Ireland	Uprating within six months of a change in reference insurance benefits	Minimum rates set in line with those of disability insurance, indexed to wages.
Italy	Uprated every six months in line with the costs of living index	Social pensions are about half the *Italian poverty threshold and a quarter of the minimum *salary. Minimo vitale set locally
Luxembourg	Annually, by *decision of Parliament, in line with the costs of living according to an index used for the wages *of civil servants. Indexation can vary by 25% each way by statutory order	Rates for RMG originally set in relation to the structure of *existing social *security benefits and minimum wages

119

Table 1.5.3   Uprating and the origins of the social assistance scales used in this analysis (continued)

	Uprating	Origins of scales
Netherlands	Uprating takes *twice a year in line with changes in the minimum wage. However *benefits have been frozen for periods	The basic rate of benefit is set according to the social minimum which is a % of the net minimum wage. Benefit rates as a proportion of the social minimum vary between 60% for single people sharing dwellings and 100% for couples. The minimum wage was originally determined in relation to household expenditure surveys and the costs of a prescribed basket of goods, and then uprated by improvements in the national price index. However since 1984 the minimum wage has periodically been frozen
Austria	Annually. Increased usually in line with changes in pensions, which are linked, to earnings. However, in recent years the pension has increased faster than earnings and social assistance has fallen behind pensions	The standard rate for single people vary between 45% and 60% of the lowest net earnings and 60%-80% of the minimum pensions
Portugal	Annually by movements in prices index	No information obtained on how rates originally determined
Finland	Annually in line with flat rate pension which is linked to the consumption patterns of the lowest quintile	There are two rates depending on the cost of living in the municipality. The basic rate is set in relation to minimum flat-rate old age pensions. In the 1980s this was 80% for a single person. During the recession pensions were not indexed to the cost of living
Sweden	Standards uprated annually in line with prices and consumer patterns	Since 1985 the monetary standard was based on items included in the household budget drawn up by the National Board for Consumer Policies. The index used for assistance produces lower uprating than that for insurance
UK	Annually in November for April payments. Linked to prices since 1980 and linked to the Rossi index (RPI less housing costs)	Historically based on the former Supplementary Benefit rates, which in turn were linked to the National assistance rates recommended by Beveridge on the basis of a budget standard. Rates have not been rebased since 1948 though the structure of payments was changed substantially in 1948

Sources: Eardley et al. (1996) Table 5.1; Guibentif and Bouget (1997)

120

While these family types represent common forms throughout the countries of the EU, they are more common in some countries than others. Table 1.5.4 shows the proportion of households in the ECHP made up of these families and the proportion excluded. It can be seen that the proportion excluded varies from only 13 per cent in Denmark to 41 per cent in Spain. The characteristics of those excluded varied from country to country but they included families with children over 16, couples with more than three children and lone parents with more than two children, households with three generations and other multiunit households. The problem is that almost all the countries in the EU use the family unit as the unit of assessment for social assistance. Eardley et al. (1996) found that only Austria and Luxembourg (with exceptions) among the EU countries assessed social assistance on the income of the household - all the other countries based it on the family unit albeit with variations in the age of a dependant child. We made efforts to increase the proportion included by altering the age definition of a child from 16 to 18 but it did not add substantially to the proportion of households included. It also ran the risk of beginning to include into a single household, members who were in fact separate benefit (and/or assessment) units.

The next step was to produce social assistance standards (Table 1.5.5) for each of these households for 1994 which is the income year for the 1995 ECHP. This was straightforward for all but the pensioner households because the information had been collected for the 1994 report of the Observatory of National Family Policies (Ditch et al 1996). For the pensioner households we used the data collected for 1992 for the Eardley et al. (1996) study. These amounts were uprated to 1994 using movements in the retail price index for each country (this assumes that actual social assistance benefit has been uprated in line with the retail price index, and by not more than that over the period and that there were no changes to the structure of the benefit for other reasons). So we ended up with social assistance entitlements for nine family types.

One possible problem with the social assistance threshold is that it represents a level of income at which a substantial minority of the population might be at or about (because they are receiving social assistance). The danger of this is that a small variation in the social assistance standard may include or exclude large numbers of households. In order to test the sensitivity of the social assistance standard we will present poverty rates at 10 per cent below and 10 per cent above the threshold.

121

We shall also takes two national social assistance scales and applies them to the income of households in each country.

We have chosen Portugal to represent a social assistance threshold at the lower end of the spectrum and Denmark to represent a social assistance scale at the upper end of the spectrum.

The results that will be obtained will be influenced by the difference between the modified OECD equivalence scale used in the standard income threshold measures and the implied equivalence scale in social assistance scales. Table 1.5.6 presents the implied equivalence scales in the social assistance thresholds and compared them with the modified OECD equivalence scales. The latter makes no allowance (more or less) for a single retired person compared with a single person but it can be seen that a number of countries do. For example in Italy the implied equivalence scale in social assistance for a single retired person is 2.2 (single person=1.0), though this is mainly because the amount paid to a single person is so low. In general social assistance scales are more generous to lone parents than the modified OECD scale (assuming all children are less than 14) – Austria is comparatively the most generous country to lone parents with a scale of 2.8 compared with only 1.6 for the modified OECD scale. Only Spain, Portugal and the Netherlands are less generous than the OECD scale to lone parents. For couples with children there is a similar picture – for couples with two children the implied equivalence scale is more generous than the OECD scale for all countries except Belgium, Spain, the Netherlands and Portugal.

6. The US poverty threshold

It may seem curious to be using the official US poverty threshold in an analysis of absolute poverty in EU countries. However there are two justifications for it.

First, it is 'official' in the sense that the US government[6] uses it extensively in all sorts of ways, including as a threshold in poverty research undertaken by the US Census Bureau. Simplified versions of the poverty threshold (called poverty guidelines) are also produced each year (Fisher 1992b). These are used for administrative purposes – for instance, determining eligibility for certain federal programs such as the Head Start, the Food Stamp Program, the National School Lunch Program, and the Low-Income Home Energy Assistance program.

Second, the US poverty threshold has its origins in an absolute approach. It was developed by what Fisher calls a 'component-and-multiplier' approach. Mollie Orshansky (1965, 1969) took the costs of a minimal food budget for different family sizes and derived poverty thresholds by multiplying these costs by three – that being the inverse of the share of money income spent on food by the average family. Orshansky based her poverty thresholds on the economy food plan – the cheapest of four food plans developed by the Department of Agriculture.

Orshansky knew from the Department of Agriculture's 1955 Household Food Consumption Survey (the latest available at the time) that families of three or more persons spent about one-third of their after tax money income on food in 1955. Accordingly she calculated poverty thresholds for families of three or more persons by taking the dollar costs of the economy food plan for families of those sizes and multiplying the costs by a factor of three – the multiplier. In effect she took a hypothetical average family spending one third of its income on food, and assumed that it had to cut back on its expenditure sharply. She assumed that expenditure for food and non food would be cut back at the same rate. When the food expenditure of the hypothetical family reached the costs of the economy food plan, she assumed that the amount the family would then be spending on non-food items would also be minimal but adequate. Her procedure did not assume specific dollar amounts for any budget category besides food. She followed somewhat different procedures for deriving thresholds for one and two person units (see Fisher 1997).

The poverty threshold is up-rated every year by indexation to the Consumer Price Index but has otherwise not been changed in any major way. This means that the threshold has increasingly diverged from the living standards of the average American household. Although the poverty line is adjusted with prices, it is not adjusted to changes in price relativities. The proportion of income that the average American household spends on food has decreased overtime, indicating that the use of three as the multiplier of the food budget is inadequate (Harrington 1985, Nolan and Whelan 1996).

The US Poverty threshold has been used before as a more absolute benchmark in comparative research. Bradbury and Jantii (1999) used it in their analysis of child poverty based on the Luxembourg Income Survey.

In this project we have used the US Poverty standard for 1994. This was derived by taking the poverty thresholds published by the US Bureau of the Census (http://www.census.gov/hhes/poverty/threshld/thresh94.html)

converting these from $ to Purchasing Power Parities using 1994 OECD PPPs (OECD 1996) and standardising them using ECU PPPs (Eurostat 1999). The resulting thresholds are summarised in Table 1.5.7.

The US Poverty Standard was subject to a thorough review by the US Academy of Sciences (Citro and Michael 1995). The NAS panel identified several major weaknesses of the current poverty measure.

Table 1.5.4 Household structure: European Community Household Panel 1995

	Belg	Den	Ger	Gre	Spain	French	IRL	Italy	Lux	Ned	Ostr	Poland	UK
Single working age	11.6	20.1	17.7	7.0	5.0	14.7	9.1	7.7	14.6	16.5	15.5	3.2	10.2
Couple working age	12.2	18.5	17.0	9.1	7.3	14.5	7.8	9.0	14.8	19.6	15.3	7.8	16.3
Single pensioner	10.7	11.5	14.5	10.5	7.9	11.5	10.5	9.7	7.3	10.0	13.5	7.0	12.6
Couple pensioner	12.0	9.9	10.3	13.5	9.7	10.6	5.7	10.3	8.6	8.6	7.4	11.1	10.5
Couple + one child	11.2	10.4	8.5	9.4	10.1	10.2	6.5	10.9	11.0	7.1	7.5	13.5	7.3
Couple + two children	11.9	9.5	8.5	14.3	14.3	11.0	10.8	11.7	10.6	11.6	8.8	12.7	10.5
Couple + three children	4.1	3.1	2.4	2.1	3.4	4.2	6.6	2.8	4.2	3.8	2.4	2.2	3.7
Lone parent + one child	1.7	3.0	1.8	1.2	.5	2.3	1.6	1.0	1.8	1.5	1.6	1.0	2.4
Lone parent + two children	1.8	1.3	.7	.8	.5	1.1	.9	.8	.5	1.1	.8	1.1	2.0
Total	77.2	87.4	81.3	68.0	58.6	80.1	59.5	63.9	73.4	79.8	72.8	59.5	75.4
Other household types	22.8	12.6	18.7	32.0	41.4	19.9	40.5	36.1	26.6	20.2	27.2	40.5	24.6
	100.0	100.0	100.0	100.0	100.0	100.0	100.0	100.0	100.0	100.0	100.0	100.0	100.0
N=	3367	3223	4688	5220	6522	6722	3584	7128	707	5110	3380	4916	4548

Source: Derived by the author from original data obtained from Eurostat

Table 1.5.5   Social assistance package in ECU PPPs 1994 per month

	Single	Couple	Retired single	Retired couple	Lone parent +1	Lone parent +2	Couple+1	Couple+2	Couple+3
Belgium	470	624	471	626	743	885	723	862	1059
Denmark	497	887	485	1001	793	958	1256	1310	1389
Germany	504	758	267	510	794	986	913	1076	1232
Greece			71	119	27	54	27	54	81
Spain	271	308	211	341	334	391	365	421	470
France	276	393	424	737	445	570	519	662	806
Ireland	361	578	430	607	530	653	703	844	956
Italy	177	353	391	651	345	488	496	651	807
Luxembourg	752	1147	632	939	994	1301	1387	1687	2129
Netherlands	558	796	556	812	782	861	852	930	980
Austria	299	430	333	469	658	848	699	759	916
Portugal	244	309	129	238	323	330	315	358	370
Finland	366	568	285	682	630	987	694	945	1154
Sweden	313	516	408	718	491	669	694	872	1077
United Kingdom	283	444	380	572	497	617	626	746	916
Unweighted average	384	579	365	601	559	707	685	812	956

Sources: The data for all family types except the retired are taken from the matrix data provided by national informants for the 1994 Observatory on National Family Policy (Ditch et al. 1996). PPPs were converted from £ to ECUs. The data for the retired was computed from Eardley et al. (1996), Table 1.5.6 5a uprating from 1992-1994 using the General Index of Prices provided by Eurostat and adjusting from £PPPs to ECU PPP, using OECD (1996) for Sweden and Finland

Table 1.5.6   Implied equivalence scale in the social assistance thresholds compared with the modified OECD scale

	Single	Couple	Single retired	Couple retired	Lone parent+1	Lone parent +2	Couple +1	Couple +2	Couple +3
Belgium	1.0	1.3	1.0	1.3	1.6	1.9	1.5	1.8	2.3
Denmark	1.0	1.8	1.0	2.0	1.6	1.9	2.5	2.6	2.8
Germany	1.0	1.5	0.5	1.0	1.6	2.0	1.8	2.1	2.4
Greece	1.0								
Spain	1.0	1.1	0.8	1.3	1.2	1.4	1.3	1.6	1.7
France	1.0	1.4	1.5	2.7	1.6	2.1	1.9	2.4	2.9
Ireland	1.0	1.6	1.2	1.7	1.5	1.8	1.9	2.3	2.6
Italy	1.0	2.0	2.2	3.7	1.9	2.8	2.8	3.7	4.6
Luxembourg	1.0	1.5	0.8	1.2	1.3	1.7	1.8	2.2	2.8
Netherlands	1.0	1.4	1.0	1.5	1.4	1.5	1.5	1.7	1.8
Austria	1.0	1.4	1.1	1.6	2.2	2.8	2.3	2.5	3.1
Portugal	1.0	1.3	0.5	1.0	1.3	1.4	1.3	1.5	1.5
Finland	1.0	1.6	0.8	1.9	1.7	2.7	1.9	2.6	3.2
Sweden	1.0	1.6	1.3	2.3	1.6	2.1	2.2	2.8	3.4
United Kingdom	1.0	1.6	1.3	2.0	1.8	2.2	2.2	2.6	3.2
Modified OECD scale	1.0	1.5	1.0	1.5	1.3	1.6	1.8	2.1	2.4

Source: Calculated from data in Table 1.5.5

The current income measure does not reflect the effects of key government policies that alter the disposable income available to families and hence their poverty status. These include income taxes and benefits in kind.

- The current poverty thresholds do not adjust for rising income levels and standards of living that have occurred since 1965.
- The current measure does not take account of variations in expenses that are necessary to hold a job and earn an income – expenses that reduce disposable income.
- The current measure does not take into account variations in medical costs.
- The current poverty thresholds use family size adjustments that are anomalous and do not take into account important changes in family situations.
- The current poverty thresholds do not adjust for geographic differences in the costs of living across the nation.

They made a number of suggestions for changing the threshold. Among these were that:

- The poverty thresholds should represent a budget for food, clothing, shelter (including utilities), and a small additional amount to allow for other needs (e.g. household supplies, personal care, nonwork-related transportation).
- A threshold for a reference family type should be developed using actual Consumer Expenditure Survey data and updated annually to reflect changes in expenditures in food, clothing and shelter over the previous three years.
- The reference family threshold should be adjusted to reflect the needs of different family types and to reflect geographic differences in housing costs.
- Family resources should be redefined – consistent with the threshold concept – as the sum of money income from all sources together with the value of near money benefits (e.g. food stamps) that are available to buy goods and services in the budget, minus expenses that cannot be used to buy these goods and services.
- Such expenses included income and payroll taxes, child care expenses and other work related expenses, child support payments to another household, and out of pocket medical care costs, including health insurance premiums.

128

In response to these recommendations the US Census Bureau developed an Experimental US Poverty line (Short et al. 1999). In Table 1.5.8 we have derived the Experimental Poverty Line for EU countries using the (recommended) three parameter equivalence scale to estimate a threshold for each of our family types. These $ amounts were then converted to ECU PPPs using the same methods as for Table 1.5.7.

It can be seen in comparing table 1.5.7 and 1.5.8 that the Official Poverty Threshold and the Experimental Poverty Threshold are very similar particularly for the base case – two adults and two children $15029 per annum compared with $15166 per annum. They diverge somewhat more for other household types because the equivalence scales used are not identical (see table 1.5.9) and in particular the Experimental US poverty threshold does not have a separate equivalence for the elderly.

In comparing the standardised poverty rates obtained using the US Official and the Experimental Poverty lines Short et al. (1999) found that:

- The standardised measure results in lower standardised poverty rates for children and higher rates for the elderly compared with the official measure.
- Standardised poverty rates are lower for Blacks under the experimental measures than under the official measure.
- The experimental measures show lower standardised poverty rates for people in families with a female householder than the official measure.
- The experimental measures that take account of the costs of housing show higher standardised rates in certain areas. People with disabilities are considerable less likely to be counted as poor under the experimental measures that they are under the official measures.

As we have seen the differences between the official poverty threshold and the experimental poverty threshold are not just about the income threshold but also about the definition of income. This means that the experimental threshold are really only meaningful in connection with the Panel's specific definition of income. Thus although the experimental threshold appears to be lower than the official threshold if one only looks at the dollar figures themselves, the experimental threshold is effectively higher (in fact 14 to 33% higher in 1997) than the official threshold if one takes into account the different income definitions.

In the analysis of ECHP data this presents us with a problem – we do not have the data that enables us to get at the income definition adopted for the experimental threshold. On the income side we have data on income tax

Table 1.5.7   **US Census Bureau official poverty thresholds 1994: applied to European countries per annum incomes**

	US$ PPPs (2)	ECU PPPs (3)	Single person	Couple	Single pensioner	Couple pensioner	Lone parent +1	Lone parent+2	Couple+1	Couple+2	Couple+3
USA (1)	1		7710	9924	7108	8958	10215	11940	11929	15029	17686
Belgium	37.3	41.65	6905	8888	6366	8022	9148	10693	10683	13459	15839
Denmark	8.72	9.79	6867	8839	6331	7979	9099	10635	10625	13386	15753
Germany	2.07	2.16	7389	9510	6812	8585	9789	11442	11432	14403	16949
Greece	196	223.8	6752	8691	6225	7845	8946	10457	10447	13162	15489
Spain	121	133.1	7009	9022	6462	8144	9286	10855	10845	13663	16078
France	6.63	7.23	7070	9100	6518	8215	9367	10949	10939	13782	16218
Ireland	0.639	0.71	6939	8932	6397	8062	9194	10746	10736	13526	15917
Italy	1535	1640	7216	9289	6653	8384	9561	11176	11165	14067	16554
Luxembourg	40	39.79	7751	9976	7146	9005	10269	12003	11992	15108	17779
Netherlands	2.13	2.28	7203	9271	6640	8369	9543	11154	11144	14040	16522
Austria	13.9	14.9	7193	9258	6631	8357	9529	11139	11128	14020	16499
Poland	118	136.8	6650	8560	6131	7727	8811	10299	10290	12964	15255
Finland	6.15	6.66	7120	9164	6564	8272	9433	11026	11016	13878	16332
Sweden	9.91	10.7	7141	9191	6583	8297	9461	11058	11048	13919	16380
United Kingdom	0.646	0.7	7115	9158	6560	8267	9427	11019	11009	13870	16322
Average			7088	9123	6535	8235	9391	10977	10967	13817	16259

Sources: 1. US Bureau of the Census (http://www.census.gov/hhes/poverty/threshld/thresh94.html); 2. OECD (1996); 3.Eurostat (1999)

130

Table 1.5.8 US Census Bureau experimental poverty thresholds 1994: per annum

	US$ PPPs (2)	ECU PPPs (3)	Single person	Couple	Single pensioner	Couple pensioner	Lone parent +1	Lone parent+2	Couple +1	Couple +2	Couple +3
USA (1)	1		7022	9903	7022	9903	10601	12588	13346	15166	17289
Belgium	37.3	41.65	6289	8869	6289	8869	9494	11273	11952	13582	15483
Denmark	8.72	9.79	6255	8821	6255	8821	9442	11212	11887	13508	15399
Germany	2.07	2.16	6729	9490	6729	9490	10159	12064	12790	14534	16569
Greece	196	223.8	6150	8673	6150	8673	9284	11024	11688	13282	15141
Spain	121	133.1	6384	9003	6384	9003	9637	11444	12133	13787	15717
French	6.63	7.23	6439	9081	6439	9081	9721	11543	12238	13907	15854
Ireland	0.639	0.71	6320	8913	6320	8913	9541	11329	12011	13649	15560
Italy	1535	1640	6572	9269	6572	9269	9922	11782	12492	14195	16182
Luxembourg	40	39.79	7059	9955	7059	9955	10657	12654	13416	15246	17380
Netherlands	2.13	2.28	6560	9251	6560	9251	9904	11760	12468	14168	16152
Austria	13.9	14.9	6551	9238	6551	9238	9890	11743	12450	14148	16129
Poland	118	136.8	6057	8542	6057	8542	9144	10858	11512	13082	14913
Finland	6.15	6.66	6484	9145	6484	9145	9789	11624	12324	14005	15965
Sweden	9.91	10.7	6504	9172	6504	9172	9818	11659	12361	14046	16013
United Kingdom	0.646	0.7	6480	9139	6480	9139	9783	11617	12316	13996	15955
Average			6455	9104	6455	9104	9746	11572	12269	13942	15894

Sources: 1. Short, K. et al. (1999) Experimental Poverty measures 1990-1997 US Census Bureau, Current Population reports, Consumer Income, P60-205, US Government Printing Office, Washington DC (especially Tables C1 and C2); 2. OECD (1996); 3. Eurostat (1999)

Table 1.5.9 US poverty line equivalence scales

	Official US poverty threshold	Experimental US poverty threshold (three parameter scale)
Single	0.513	0.463
Couple	0.660	0.653
Elderly single	0.473	0.463
Elderly couple	0.596	0.653
Lone parent + 1	0.680	0.699
Lone parent +2	0.794	0.830
Couple +1	0.794	0.880
Couple +2	1.000	1.000
Couple +3	1.177	1.114

Source: Short et al. 1990

but we do not have data on child care costs, work related expenses, child support payments, medical costs and health insurance premiums (unless they are statutory social insurance contributions). On the benefit side the income definition the ECHP definition should include all cash benefits but does not include the value of food stamps like provision (for example free school meals, Common Agriculture Policy payments) which perhaps ought to be taken into account.

As for the official US poverty thresholds, the income definition conventionally used with them is before tax money income. However, the original thresholds were calculated on the basis of after-tax money income, so there is some justification for us using net income in our analysis (see http://aspe.hhs.gov/poverty/papers/hptgssiv.html).

When we come to the part of this project that uses the European Budget Survey we shall endeavour to establish an income definition closer to the US Experimental Poverty measure.

7. Subjective poverty threshold

It is arguable whether a subjective poverty threshold can genuinely be described as an absolute measure. However the ECHP question establishes the threshold with the question 'In your opinion what is the very lowest net monthly income that your household would have to have in order to make ends meet'. *Very lowest* implies something fairly absolute though *to make ends meet* may be more relative. Eurostat publish poverty rates based on this threshold plus 5% (Eurostat 1999). In the analysis we will not allow the extra 5% and will also take the proportion with net incomes not reaching their own specified threshold.

8. The poverty thresholds based on budget standards

Eurostat are keen to explore the expenditure based budget standards used in the United States. We will review the history of these, the conclusions of the Watts Committee (1980) and will apply these standards to data derived from the European Budget Survey.

However Europe has some budget standards of its own. In the UK the Family Budget Unit has undertaken sophisticated work to derive *a low cost but acceptable* standard for a variety of family types (Parker 1998). NIBUD in the Netherlands publishes a budget standard which is influential in determining its social assistance scales. The Swedish National Board for Consumer Affairs produces a budget which is influential in determining the social assistance payments made by municipalities. In Australia as part of the Department of Social Security's adequacy project the Social Policy Research Centre derived sophisticated low cost budgets (Saunders et al. 1998).

The methods employed in drawing up these standards will be critically reviewed and the standards themselves compared. We will also apply one or more of the standards to the EBS in two main ways. First to establish a point on the distribution of expenditure at which the budget standard overall is achieved in each country. Second to establish the point on the expenditure distribution at which the budget standard share of expenditure on food, domestic fuel and other necessities is achieved. Third to establish the point on the expenditure distribution at which there is no (or limited) spending on non necessities.

It can be expected that expenditure based poverty lines will vary a good deal with the standard used. Further, judging from the analysis comparing expenditure and income poverty lines (Saunders, Bradshaw and Hirst 1999) they are likely to produce very little overlap - very few poor by both measures. This is because older people tend to spend less than their incomes regardless of their income, and families with children tend to spend more than their income regardless of their income. Pensioners on the whole save for a rainy day and poor families spend in faith. We will discuss whether we decide from this that if pensioners are spending less than their income they are not in absolute poverty. Do we decide that families with children who are spending more than their income have resources that are not represented by income − and only those who spend less should be included in poverty definitions?

All we will do in this project is to undertake some sensitivity analysis. Thus we will show the composition of the income poor, the expenditure poor, the income or expenditure poor and the income and expenditure poor and those who are income poor and spend all their income. We will also do some limited analysis of those who spend little or nothing on non essentials. But this type of analysis of expenditure data needs a good deal more development work − particularly in comparative perspective before it is taken much further.

9. Conclusion

In this chapter we have derived three alternative more absolute thresholds of poverty (and variants of them). We will be applying them to income data derived from the ECHP and comparing the poverty rates and thresholds obtained with those obtained using more conventional relative measures of poverty. We will then be undertaking similar analysis of expenditure using the European Budget Survey. These conclusions are somewhat interim therefore:

There is no agreed definition of what constitutes absolute poverty.

In fact all definitions of absolute poverty are more or less relative. However Minimum Income Standards exist. Minimum Income Standards are candidates to represent a more absolute measure of poverty when they have the following characteristics:

- They are (or were originally) based on some standard budget or budget share that is related to subsistence notions.
- They are recognised and/or used by government.
- They are not relative measures.
- The most prevalent form of minimum income schemes in Europe, some of which have these characteristics are the social assistance schemes that exist in every country.

There is no routinely collected source of data on minimum income schemes or social assistance scales in EU countries. If Eurostat is to publish social assistance based poverty rates, it will be necessary to collect such data. It is lucky that thresholds were available from previous studies using the model family method.

Social assistance scales vary between countries in the income standard that they seek to provide. Not all aim to provide minimum subsistence incomes or absolute poverty. There are great variations in the implied equivalence scale between them. If instead of using national social assistance scales it was decided to adopt a single (middling) social assistance standard the implied equivalence scale would have an impact of the composition of the poor in each country.

Housing costs remain a problem. There are reasons to be anxious about how consistently respondents to ECHP record their housing costs. However even if housing costs are adequately recorded on the income side there needs to be more work done on the treatment of housing costs in social assistance in order to establish fully comparable social assistance thresholds.

The Official US poverty threshold is a much evaluated (and criticised) measure and could be adopted in comparative analysis. However the US are experimenting with an alternative measure which calls for information on income and expenditure which is not available in the ECHP.

Notes

[1] For example the French MIS (SMIC) was the statutory minimum hourly pay rate based in 1950, on a compromise between six minimum budget standards, the food share may have been influenced by Rowntree's 1937 *Human Needs of Labour* standard. Until 1970 it was uprated in line with prices, then with earnings and prices and the 'base appears to have become irrelevant'. Nevertheless we learn that SMIC is the cornerstone of economic and social policy in France and used in both wage setting and poverty measurement!

[2] So what does it take to achieve official recognition? Take Belgium for example – in Belgium a Christian Democrat Senator, Professor Herman Deleeck, chaired a committee for a like-minded Government and persuaded them to adopt an MIS based on an attitudinal poverty line produced by his own research unit.

[3] *Beleidsmatig Mimimum* Policy Determined Maximum added by editor which in 1994 was 18,149 guilders for a single person and 7,920 multiplied by an equivalence scale for multi person households.

[4] For example in Britain the social assistance scales have their origins in the absolute poverty standard that Rowntree developed especially for his 1936 survey of poverty in York. Rowntree was an adviser to the Beveridge Committee and Beveridge's 1942 estimates of the minimum subsistence income which defined the social assistance scales was derived from Rowntree's standard. The 1942 social assistance recommendations were uprated for movements in prices and began operating in 1948 as National Assistance. Over the years since then they have been uprated, more or less doubling in real terms and renamed Supplementary benefits in 1966 and Income Support in 1988. But the structure of the scales, the equivalence scale and even their relationship with average earnings are remarkably similar to what they were in 1942. No doubt this link with a standard of absolute poverty was one reason why Abel Smith and Townsend (1965) in their seminal 'rediscovery of poverty' study *The Poor and the Poorest* applied the then national assistance scales to income data derived from the Family Expenditure Survey. They not only used 100% of the NAB scales but also 120% and 140% on the grounds that the actual level of living of people dependent on national assistance was rather higher than the scales, due to the fact that some earnings and capital was disregarded in assessing social assistance and claimants were also receiving additional payments to cover the costs of heating and special diets. Following their study a standard of this type was used by the British government in what became the *Low Income Statistics (LIS)* based on the Family Expenditure Survey and produced until 1985. Note it never became an official poverty or MIS standard though it was used for that purpose. The LIS series was abandoned by the Conservative Government after 1995 on the grounds that the thresholds of 120 and 140% incorporated too many people and that increasing the real level of social assistance (in order to help the poor) had the absurd consequence of increasing the number of people defined as poor.

[5] It is assumed that one and two adult households have a one bedroom dwelling, lone parents and couples with one child a two bedroom dwelling, and lone parents and couples with two or three children a three bedroom dwelling.

[6] In this discussion I have drawn on the contents of an extensive correspondence with Gordon Fisher, US Department of Health and Human Services. He cannot be blamed for what I have said here. But only he will recognise the extent to which I have plagiarised him.

References

Abel Smith, B. and Townsend, P. (1965). *The Poor and the Poorest*. London: Bell.

Bradbury, B. and Jantti, M. (1999). 'Child poverty across industrialised countries'. Innocenti Occasional paper. Economic and Social Policy Series 71.

Bradshaw, J. R. (ed) (1993). *Budget Standards for the United Kingdom*. Studies in Cash & Care. Aldershot: Avebury.

Bradshaw, J. R. and Morgan, J. (1987). *Budgeting on Benefits: The consumption of families on supplementary benefit*. Occasional Paper No. 5. London: Family Policy Studies Centre.

Bradshaw, J. R., Mitchell, D. and Morgan, J. (1987). 'Evaluating Adequacy: The potential of budget standards'. *Journal of Social Policy* 16 (2): 165-181.

Citro, C. and Michael, R. (eds) (1995). *Measuring Poverty: A new approach*. Washington DC: National Academy Press.

Dirven H-J et al. (2000). *Income Poverty and Social Exclusion in the EU Member States: TASK 4*. Paper presented at the Working Group Statistics on Income, Social Exclusion and Poverty.

Ditch, J. and Oldfield, N. (1998). *Social Assistance in the OECD update*. Data Base. University of York.

Ditch, J., Barnes, H. and Bradshaw, J. (1996a). *Developments in National Family Policies in 1995 (Volume 2)*. European Observatory on National Family Policies, York: Social Policy Research Unit, University of York.

Ditch, J., Barnes, H. and Bradshaw, J. (1996b). *A Synthesis of National Family Policies 1995 (Volume 1)*. European Observatory on National Family Policies, York: Social Policy Research Unit, University of York.

Ditch, J., Barnes, H. and Bradshaw, J. (1998a). *A Synthesis of National Family Policies in 1996 (Volume 1)*. European Observatory on National Family Policies, European Commission. York: University of York.

Ditch, J., Barnes, H. and Bradshaw, J. (1998b). *Developments in National Family Policies in 1996 (Volume 2)*. European Observatory on National Family Policies, European Commission. York: University of York.

Ditch, J., Barnes, H., Bradshaw, J., Commaille, J. and Eardley, T. (1995). *A Synthesis of National Family Policies 1994 (Volume 1)*. European Observatory on National Family Policies. York: Social Policy Research Unit, University of York.

Ditch, J., Bradshaw, J. and Eardley, T. (1995). *Developments in National Family Policies in 1994 (Volume 2)*. European Observatory on National Family Policies, York: Social Policy Research Unit, University of York.

Eardley, T., Bradshaw, J., Ditch, J., Gough, I. and Whiteford, P. (1996a). *Social Assistance in OECD Countries: Country Reports*. Department of Social Security Research Report No. 47. London: HMSO.

Eardley, T., Bradshaw, J., Ditch, J., Gough, I. and Whiteford, P. (1996b). *Social Assistance in OECD Countries: Synthesis Report*. Department of Social Security Research Report No. 46. London: HMSO.

Eurostat (1997). 'Income distribution and poverty in the EU' in *Statistics in Focus*. Population and Social Conditions 6.

Eurostat (1999). *European Community Household Panel Survey: Selected indicators from the 1995 wave*. Luxembourg: Eurostat.

Eurostat (1999). Reconciliation of Sources and Dissemination of the Data, September 1999.

Fisher, G. (1992). 'The Development and History of the Poverty Thresholds'. *Social Security Bulletin* 55 (4): 3-14.

Fisher, G. (1997). 'The Development and History of the US Poverty Thresholds'. A Brief Overview, GSS/SSS Newsletter (Newsletter of the Government Statistics Section and the Social Statistics Section of the American Statistical Association, winter. (http://www.aspe.hhs.gov/poverty/papers/hptgssiv.html).

Gordon, D. and Pantazis, C. (eds). *Breadline Britain in the 1990s*. Department of Social Policy and Planning. Bristol: University of Bristol.

Guibentif, P. and Bouget, D. (1997). *Minimum Income Policies in the European Union*. EU.

Heikkila, M. and McCausland, D. (1997). Report on the GM! Development in EU Member Countries in 1992-1997 (photocopy).

Mack, J. and Lansley, S. (1985). *Poor Britain*. George Allen and Unwin.

Nolan, B. and Whelan, C. (1996a). 'Measuring poverty using income and deprivation indicators: alternative approaches'. *European Journal of Social Policy* 6 (3) 225-240.

Nolan, B. and Whelan, C. (1996b). *Resources, Deprivation and Poverty*. Oxford: Clarendon Press.

Orshansky, M. (1965). 'Counting the Poor: Another look at the poverty profile'. *Social Security Bulletin* June 3-29.

Orshansky, M. (1969). 'How poverty is measured'. *Monthly Labor Review* 92 37-41.

Parker, H. (ed) (1998). *Low Cost but Acceptable: A minimum income standard for the UK*. Bristol: The Policy Press.

Saunders, P. et al. (1998). *Development of Indicative Budget Standards for Australia*. Canberra: Department of Social Security.

Saunders, P., Bradshaw, J., Hirst, M. and Matheson, G. (1999). *Using household expenditure data to develop an income poverty line: experimental estimates for Australia and the United Kingdom*. Paper to the Foundation for International Studies in Social Security, Sigtuna, Sweden, June.

Short, K. et al. (1999). *Experimental Poverty Measures: 1990 to 1997*. Washington: US Census Bureau.

Townsend, P. (1979). *Poverty in the United Kingdom*. Allen Lane.

Townsend, P., Gordon, D., Bradshaw, J. and Gosschalk, B. (1997). *Absolute and Overall Poverty in Britain in 1997: What the Population Themselves Say: British Poverty Line Survey*. Bristol: Bristol Statistical Monitoring Unit, School for Policy Studies, University of Bristol.

United Nations (1995). *The Copenhagen Declaration and Programme of Action: World Summit for Social Development 6-12 March 1995*. New York: UN Department of Publications.

Veit-Wilson, J. (1998). *Setting Adequacy Standards: How governments define minimum incomes*. Bristol: Policy Press.

138

Watts, H. W. (1980). *New American Budget Standards: Report of an expert committee on family budget revisions*. Special Report Series. Wisconsin Madison: Institute for Research on Poverty.

PART 2

ETHICS AND ATTITUDES

2.1 Popularity and participation: social security reform in Australia

Peter Saunders and Maneerat Pinyopusarerk

1. Introduction[1]

'Today I want to talk to you about a great challenge: how we make the welfare state popular again. How we restore public trust and confidence in a welfare state that 50 years ago was acclaimed but today has so many wanting to bury it' (Blair, 1999, p. 7).

With these words, British Prime Minister Tony Blair began his 1999 Beveridge Lecture at University College, Oxford. He went on to argue why the British welfare state was in need of reform and to describe the main features of his 'modern vision for welfare'. His emphasis on the popularity of the welfare state was significant because it drew attention to the role and interaction between public opinion and political legitimacy – two factors crucial to the legitimacy of welfare policy.

In this chapter, we review evidence on the popularity (or community acceptance) of social security provisions in Australia in the context of the aims and methods of the contemporary reform debate. Following the work of Esping-Andersen (1990), most analysts have regarded the Australian welfare state as a classic case of a liberal welfare regime, albeit with some distinctive national characteristics (Castles and Mitchell, 1992). The Australian social security system certainly has all the hallmarks of welfare liberalism. Assistance is provided only to those who meet strict eligibility criteria, benefits are heavily means-tested and the system is financed from general revenue – the three defining features of a targeted approach (Saunders, 1991; 1999)[2]. Despite having a relatively low social security budget (less than 9 percent of GDP in 1995, compared with an OECD average of 12 percent; Whiteford, 2000), social security reform remains at the forefront of the policy and political debate.

Underlying the new approach is a set of beliefs about the activities of those receiving social security/assistance benefits, including a set of prescribed activities that constitute 'inclusion through participation' and are hence to be encouraged. There is also the idea that the welfare system must retain (or regain) its popularity with the taxpaying public if it is to survive over the longer-term. The evidence in support of both propositions is weak. Little is known about the current activities of the unemployed and even less about their views on participating, other than through getting a job. The same applies to community attitudes to the treatment of beneficiaries by the social security system; how far are people willing to support making benefits contingent upon patterns of behaviour thought to encourage participation, as opposed to increased enforcement of work and/or activity tests?

The chapter presents and analyses evidence on patterns of time use and attitudes to the requirements of the social security system, as they apply to the unemployed and sole parents in Australia. In Section 2, we analyse empirical data on time use among the unemployed and sole parents to assess the extent to which they conform to stereotypical notions of how these groups spend their time. Section 3 addresses the issue of the popularity of social security reforms designed to encourage participation, particularly through paid work, in the broader context of mutual obligation. These results reveal a complex yet sophisticated understanding of the problems confronting the unemployed and sole parents and of how policy should be addressing them. Section 4 concludes the chapter.

2. Time use patterns of the unemployed and sole parents

As indicated above, the debate over mutual obligation raises questions about what those in receipt of social security assistance are currently doing with their time, as well as what they might be doing, if required to by the social security system. This section presents evidence from the latest time use survey to explore the first of these issues; the latter issue is the subject of the next section.

Patterns of time use are intricately linked with broader changes in economic activity, social norms and the assumptions and goals of public policy. The increased prevalence of two-earner households has brought greater material prosperity to many, but the easing of income constraints has been accompanied by a more severe set of time constraints. At the same time, there is a growing divide in the distribution of work between 'work rich households' (with two earners) and 'work poor households' with no adult in paid work (Gregory, 1999). This has focused attention on the need for policy in general, and social security policy in particular, to encourage the transition from welfare to work by removing the barriers to paid work and actively encouraging those on benefit to look for work. Accompanying the increased emphasis on paid work is a growing recognition of the importance of unpaid work, particularly care provided within the home to children and older relatives. How do different groups of social security recipients currently use their time and what are the likely consequences of requiring them to undertake new activities?

Time use data provides the basis for an initial assessment of these kinds of issues. In 1997, the Australian Bureau of statistics (ABS) undertook its second national survey of time use. The Survey covered 4,059 households containing 7,260 persons aged 15 and over. Participants were required to complete a time use diary listing their main activity, its nature, timing and duration, and any secondary activity undertaken simultaneously (ABS, 1998a)[3]. The main objective of the Time Use Survey was to measure the daily activity patterns of the Australian population broken down by socio-economic and demographic characteristics. The survey findings enable the current Australian time use profile and differences in patterns of paid work and unpaid household and community work to be established.

The picture emerging from Table 2.1.1 indicates that across all labour force categories, fewer women participated in employment activities than their male counterparts. In job search activity for the unemployed, 12 percent of unemployed females reported that they were looking for work: the corresponding figure for men is 22 percent. Of those reporting that they were looking for work, unemployed women spent fewer hours than unemployed men (just over an hour a day for women and almost 2 hours a day for men). However, unemployed women participated and spent more time on education and social and community interaction than unemployed men. In contrast, more unemployed men participated in voluntary work and care activities, and spent more time participating than women.

An interesting comparison is between the time spent on education activity by men working part-time and unemployed. Over one-quarter (27 percent) of men working part-time reported spending time on education as against 14 percent of unemployed men. The average time spent in education was 376 minutes per day for men working part-time and 255 minutes per day for unemployed men.

Except for education and voluntary work and care activities, the pattern of participation for women across the labour force status categories is similar to that of men. In contrast to men, a higher proportion of unemployed women engaged in education activity than women in a part-time job (16 percent and 14 percent, respectively). The average time spent on education, however, was lower for unemployed men than for women in a part-time job (287 minutes and 330 minutes per day, respectively).

Table 2.1.1 Patterns of time use among adults (15-49) by labour force status (average time per participant in minutes per day and participation rate)[a]

| | | Labour force status | | | |
Selected activities		Employed full-time	Employed part-time	Unem-ployed	Not in the labour force
Males					
Employment related	Min/day	554	375	209	288
	Rate (%)	(73.6)	(48.3)	(26.3)	(5.6)
– Job search activity	Min/day	88	96	112	58
	Rate (%)	(0.5)	(3.7)	(21.6)	(1.2)
Education	Min/day	199	376	255	400
	Rate (%)	(2.6)	(27.0)	(14.1)	(35.2)
Voluntary work and	Min/day	106	141	149	111
care	Rate (%)	(13.1)	(18.5)	(19.4)	(13.1)
Social and community	Min/day	88	94	109	127
interaction	Rate (%)	(42.4)	(49.4)	(44.6)	(48.5)
Females					
Employment related	Min/day	510	344	192	137
	Rate (%)	(67.4)	(48.3)	(20.1)	(3.6)
– Job search activity	Min/day	48	39	73	47
	Rate (%)	(0.5)	(0.8)	(12.0)	(1.2)
Education	Min/day	187	330	287	370
	Rate (%)	(3.4)	(14.3)	(15.7)	(20.0)
Voluntary work and	Min/day	72	81	93	110
care	Rate (%)	(17.0)	(23.3)	(19.0)	(23.1)
Social and community	Min/day	84	80	121	87
interaction	Rate (%)	(50.8)	(59.3)	(58.5)	(56.9)

Note: (a) AIHW analysis of the *ABS Time Use Survey*

Source: ABS Time Use Survey, Australia, 1997 - Confidentialised Unit Record File

Table 2.1.2 explores how patterns of time use on selected activities vary for the unemployed according to the duration of unemployment. For males, there is a marked drop off in the average amount of time spent on job search after the first six months of unemployment, even though the proportion of those involved in job search activity remains almost unchanged. The percentage of the unemployed who participate in community interaction declines sharply after two years' unemployment, although the average time spent for those participating is considerable among the long-term unemployed. This evidence is consistent with the view that, for many men, long-term unemployment is associated with withdrawal from many forms of economic engagement and social participation.

Women have a greater tendency towards labour market withdrawal among women unable to find work within a relatively short period after becoming unemployed. Though fewer unemployed women engage in education than men, they spend more time on education than unemployed men. There is no evidence that women who are unemployed for more than two years engage in less social participation, as was the case for men, although voluntary work and care among women does show a decline as unemployment duration increases.

Table 2.1.3 compares time use patterns among married and sole parents by labour force status. Participation in child care (as a main activity) shows little variation with labour force status, the average time spent on child care increases markedly for mothers whose participation in the labour market is lower. This pattern is particularly strong for the time spent on 'quality child care' by sole mothers. Aside from unemployed sole parents, very few mothers spend much time on job search and only slightly more record any involvement in education. The patterns of time spent by mothers on voluntary work and social interaction by labour force status are similar to those shown in Table 2.1.1, although married mothers tend to spend more time than sole mothers in voluntary work and less time in social and community interaction.

Table 2.1.2 Patterns of time use among unemployed adults (15-49) by duration of unemployment (average time per participant in minutes per day and participation rate) [a]

Selected activities		Duration of unemployment		
		1-26 weeks	27-103 weeks	104 weeks and over
Males				
Employment related	*Min/day*	296	96	94
	Rate (%)	(26.3)	(26.8)	(25.7)
– Job search activity	*Min/day*	155	56	87
	Rate (%)	(19.1)	(24.6)	(25.1)
Education	*Min/day*	177	38	165
	Rate (%)	(26.3)	(26.8)	(25.7)
Voluntary work and care	*Min/day*	148	124	199
	Rate (%)	(18.6)	(21.7)	(18.7)
Social and community interaction	*Min/day*	107	89	177
	Rate (%)	(48.1)	(47.8)	(27.0)
Females				
Employment related	*Min/day*	221	118	89
	Rate (%)	(21.5)	(17.4)	(16.0)
– Job search activity	*Min/day*	60	122	56
	Rate (%)	(10.8)	(14.2)	(16.0)
Education	*Min/day*	239	222	118
	Rate (%)	(21.5)	(17.4)	(16.0)
Voluntary work and care	*Min/day*	100	74	66
	Rate (%)	(20.2)	(19.2)	(11.1)
Social and community interaction	*Min/day*	112	169	102
	Rate (%)	(56.5)	(60.5)	(67.2)

Note: (a) AIHW analysis of the *ABS Time Use Survey*

Source: See Table 2.1.1

Table 2.1.3 Patterns of time use among mothers aged 15-49 by labour force status (average time per participant in minutes per day and participation rate) [a]

Selected activities		Employed full-time	Employed part-time	Unem-ployed	Not in the labour force
			Labour force status		
Married mothers					
Employment related	*Min/day*	473	324	246	84
	Rate (%)	(62.8)	(46.5)	(13.4)	(2.4)
– Job search activity	*Min/day*	75	5	47	31
	Rate (%)	(0.3)	(0.1)	(8.6)	(1.0)
Education	*Min/day*	218	93	130	213
	Rate (%)	(3.2)	(2.7)	(1.3)	(5.3)
Child care	*Min/day*	107	144	151	203
	Rate (%)	(80.7)	(90.7)	(87.8)	(93.0)
– Quality child care [a]	*Min/day*	44	51	57	55
	Rate (%)	(48.9)	(58.7)	(41.9)	(63.9)
Voluntary work and care	*Min/day*	69	80	134	92
	Rate (%)	(14.9)	(20.9)	(25.4)	(25.2)
Social and community interaction	*Min/day*	69	69	138	75
	Rate (%)	(47.6)	(60.5)	(53.5)	(56.8)
Sole mothers					
Employment related	*Min/day*	513	299	73	–
	Rate (%)	(77.2)	(40.0)	(11.8)	–
– Job search activity	*Min/day*	–	–	115	–
	Rate (%)	–	–	(2.6)	–
Education	*Min/day*	74	168	60	177
	Rate (%)	(8.9)	(10.7)	(2.7)	(13.2)
Child care	*Min/day*	86	139	161	186
	Rate (%)	(80.3)	(86.6)	(87.0)	(87.9)
– Quality child care [b]	*Min/day*	39	56	85	78
	Rate (%)	(46.2)	(53.5)	(57.7)	(54.1)
Voluntary work and care	*Min/day*	52	96	49	126
	Rate (%)	(6.6)	(29.8)	(17.0)	(27.6)
Social and community interaction	*Min/day*	90	95	159	78
	Rate (%)	(33.1)	(64.8)	(60.2)	(57.0)

Note: (a) AIHW analysis of the *ABS Time Use Survey* (b) Quality child care includes teaching, helping and reprimanding children and playing, reading, and talking with children.
Source: See Table 2.1.1

3. Public opinion and mutual obligation

Australia has had rather few academic studies of public opinion to its welfare system, aside from its involvement in comparative studies such as the International Social Science Project (e.g. Bean, 1991). A notable exception is the study by Papadakis (1990) which reviewed attitudes to a range of public and private welfare provisions. In response to this, and in light of the policy emphasis on requiring mutual obligation from the unemployed and other groups receiving social security, the Social Policy Research Centre (SPRC) conducted a postal survey of a nationally representative sample drawn from the electoral rolls in the middle of 1999[4]. The survey covered over 4,000 households and achieved a response rate of 62 percent: further details of the survey methods and topics covered are provided in Saunders, Thomson and Evans (2000).

The survey includes questions about the degree of support for the level of assistance provided to the unemployed, the activity test requirements made of them, and the penalties for breaching those requirements. Most questions sought separate information about the treatment of the young unemployed (under 25), older unemployed (over 50), the long-term unemployed, unemployed people with young children (under 5) and the unemployed with a disability. There were also some separate questions about attitudes to when sole parents should be expected to look for work.

Tables 2.1.4 and 2.1.5 summarise some of the results that emerge about attitudes towards the levels and conditions attached to support for different groups of the unemployed. Table 2.1.4 shows that public opinion is divided on the adequacy of current levels of support for the unemployed, although there is clearly a widespread view that older unemployed people do not receive enough help and very few people thought that they currently receive too much support. About a quarter of respondents thought that other groups, apart from people with young children, received too much support, while nearly one-third thought that both the long-term unemployed and people with young children did not get enough support.

The survey included two questions which listed a range of activities that people might be required to do in order to receive unemployment benefits and asked which, if any, respondents thought should apply to different groups of the unemployed. The list was not related specifically to precise legislative requirements, but provided a broad summary of the kind of activities or expectations commonly referred to in discussions about mutual obligation.

Table 2.1.4 Views on levels of government support for unemployed people

Question: What do you think about the overall level of support the Government provides for the following groups of unemployed people at the moment?

	Young single unemployed (under 25)	Older unem- ployed (over 50)	Long- term unem- ployed	People constantly in and out of work	Unemployed with young children (under 5)	Unem- ployed migrants
	percent					
Too much	26.8	1.6	24.4	26.8	13.5	27.8
About right	38.2	25.9	26.6	33.3	35.4	27.3
Not enough	20.8	56.4	30.9	15.2	31.7	13.5
Don't know	14.1	14.3	18.1	24.6	19.4	31.4
Total	100.0	100.0	100.0	100.0	100.0	100.0

Unweighted n = 2,331 to 2,359

Table 2.1.5 shows the level of support for the various requirements as they applied to different categories of unemployed people. A striking feature of these results is that the variation is much greater across the rows than down the columns. This suggests that in relation to certain groups of the unemployed, people support a range of different benefit requirements, but they make a distinction between the treatment of different groups of unemployed people according to their circumstances or characteristics. There is a high level of support for the idea that young unemployed people and the long-term unemployed can reasonably be expected to fulfil certain requirements, and to take action to improve their own prospects, in return for benefits. However, people were much less likely to assume that these obligations should apply to other groups of the unemployed, especially the older group, whom many people feel receive insufficient support at present.

Table 2.1.5 Levels of support for activity test requirements

Question: Listed below are some tasks that unemployed people might be REQUIRED to do in order to get unemployment benefits. Which of these do you think different groups of unemployed people should have to do?

Requirement	Young unem-ployed (under 25)	Older unem-ployed (50+)	Long-term unemployed (of any age)	Unemployed with young children (under 5)	People affected by a disability
	Percent agreeing with each requirement				
Look for work	92.9	53.8	80.4	51.2	32.9
Complete a 'dole diary' detailing efforts to find work	79.8	41.6	70.5	42.5	25.3
Take part in a 'work for the dole' scheme	82.7	38.9	72.2	35.9	24.2
Undergo a training or re-training program	81.8	60.9	80.0	54.7	50.8
Undertake useful work in the community	78.9	63.2	76.5	47.3	45.7
Accepted any paid job offered	66.2	34.0	65.0	30.2	18.1
Move to another town or city to find work	50.2	9.9	40.7	11.5	5.3
Change appearance (e.g. get a haircut)	72.5	33.8	57.7	34.6	25.1
Improve reading and writing skills	84.2	50.0	74.0	52.9	44.3
Unweighted n = 2,373					

There was also relatively little support for extending mutual obligations to people with disabilities. Where there was more widespread support for some expectations being placed on these other groups, it was mainly in the areas of training, requiring them to undertake useful work in the community and remedial literacy[5].

Having described what the respondents thought of different obligations for the unemployed, we now summarise briefly the other side of the mutual obligation coin – what is expected of government. The first point to note is that many people think that the government should do *something* about the unemployment problem. Almost half (47.4 percent) strongly agreed or agreed that: *Solving unemployment is the Government's responsibility.* Respondents were also asked to select the three things (out of a list of thirteen) they thought that the government could do to solve unemployment. Several of the options included in the list related directly or indirectly to the mutual obligation requirements of government under the social security system.

Table 2.1.6 lists these options and the percentage of responses in each case. It is clear that there is strong support for government programs to assist the unemployed through training and wage subsidies[6]. Although providing support to the unemployed through labour market programs are not a popular option, there was high support for policies to ease the severity of the poverty trap and encourage incentives. There was also support for making unemployment benefits harder to get, though less than for the more interventionist strategies listed earlier in table 2.1.6 Many people agree that maximising the rate of economic growth is an important means of helping the unemployed, but far fewer see the solution in the creation of more public sector jobs, and almost nobody sees the solution in further deregulation of the labour market.

3.1 Attitudes to social security for the unemployed

Multiple regression analysis (OLS) has been used to explore the associations between the treatment of the unemployed and the socioeconomic characteristics of the respondents. Attitudes to treatment by the social security system have been separated into views on the overall *level of support* provided, the *activity test (or mutual obligation) requirements* upon which support should be made conditional, and the appropriate *penalties* to apply when these conditions have been breached. Although mutual obligation concerns the second of these features, the broader welfare debate also relates to the issue of benefit levels and penalties, so all three are relevant.

Respondents were asked whether, for each of the five groups of the unemployed described earlier (plus a sixth group, unemployed migrants), they thought that there is too much support, about the right amount of support or not enough support. The responses in each category have been re-coded as –1, 0 and +1 and the resulting scores aggregated to form a summary measure of overall support[7].

153

In relation to the mutual obligation requirements, respondents were asked to tick a box where they agreed that a particular requirement should apply to a particular category of the unemployed. With five categories of unemployed and nine different activity requirements (see table 2.1.5), the maximum number of ticks is 45. A summary measure of mutual obligation severity was obtained by summing the number of boxes that were ticked and deducting the resulting total from 45, so that the lower the score the greater the support for mutual obligation requirements. In relation to penalties, respondents were asked whether they thought the existing penalties for single and repeated breaches are too harsh, about right or too lenient. These responses were re-coded as $+1$, 0 and -1, respectively and summed to obtain a summary measure. The above definitions ensure that higher scores on all three summary scores imply a more lenient attitude to the treatment of the unemployed.

Table 2.1.6 Mutual obligation requirements on Government

Things the government might do to solve the unemployment problem	Percentage of responses
Give employers subsidies to take on unemployed people	11.0
Provide more training for unemployed people	11.9
Spend more on labour market programs	1.9
Improve incentives in the tax and social security systems	10.6
Make it harder to get unemployment benefits	8.3
Keep economic growth as high as possible	10.3
Create more public sector jobs	5.0
Deregulate the labour market further	1.1

Many of the independent variables included in the regression analysis are straightforward and common in studies of this kind. They include the age, sex, birthplace, education status, income and political allegiance of respondents. We also included a variable describing whether or not the respondent had direct experience of unemployment affecting a family member in the previous three years, and a variable that captured how accurately people were able to indicate (within four or five bands) the overall unemployment rate and the percentage of total unemployment that is accounted for by long-term unemployment.

In addition, three variables were constructed from a range of responses to provide an indication of the kinds of personal value systems that each respondent ascribes to. Respondents were classified by degrees as supportive of a value system that can be broadly characterised as being 'individualist', 'collectivist' or 'fatalist'. The value classification was determined in accordance with the responses given to a series of attitudinal questions. Responses to each question were scored from +2 ('strongly agree') through to –2 ('strongly disagree') and then aggregated across all questions to form a summary measure. The questions incorporated into each of the three personal value variables are shown in Table 2.1.7.

Those people who are classified as individualists are expected to adopt a harsher attitude towards the treatment of the unemployed generally, but to favour mutual obligation requirements in particular since these are intended to reinforce the need for personal responsibility in achieving financial independence. Collectivists, in contrast, are expected to show greater leniency towards the unemployed across all aspects of their treatment. The attitudes of those who are defined as resigned are less easy to predict. On the one hand, they may be sympathetic towards the unemployed, who they see as innocent victims of larger economic and social forces. Against this, they might favour a system that actively encourages people to take actions to offset the impact of these forces, particularly through the introduction of mutual obligation requirements.

Table 2.1.7 Questions used to determine personal value position

Value position	Questions used
Individualist	Economic and social change is exciting and provides new opportunities and prospects. Most people who are poor only have themselves to blame. People who are unemployed only have themselves to blame.
Collectivist	Too much emphasis is put on improving the economy and too little on creating a better society. People are poor because other people are rich. Solving unemployment is the Government's responsibility.
Fatalist	Economic and social change is inevitable and I just have to put up with it. People are poor because they have been unlucky in life. There just aren't enough jobs for all the people who want to work.

Table 2.1.8 summarises the independent variables and Table 2.1.9 presents the regression results for each of the three aspects of the system of social security support for the unemployed – the level of support provided (Support), the degree of activity testing (Mutual Obligation) and the harshness of penalties in the case of rule breaches (Penalties). In interpreting the regression results, it is important to bear in mind that a *negative* coefficient is indicative of support for *harsher* treatment of the unemployed, either through providing less overall support, requiring greater obligations on support recipients, or favouring greater penalties for rule breaches.

In terms of personal characteristics, there is a tendency for women to take a harsher line towards the unemployed than men, particularly when it comes to mutual obligation requirements. Older people, while not in favour of more support for the unemployed overall, favour fewer mutual obligation conditions and lighter penalties – possibly reflecting the conditions they themselves have become used to. Migrants from non-English-speaking countries (who represented about 16 percent of the population at the time of the 1996 Census) have a more sympathetic overall attitude to the treatment of the unemployed, favouring increased support, fewer obligations and lighter penalties. The more highly educated favour more support for the unemployed but have no strong position on increased mutual obligation or harsher penalties. There are some attitudinal differences according to previous experience of unemployment and how informed people are about the level and nature of unemployment, relating to support for mutual obligation and penalties, respectively, although these affects are rather weak. The strongest effect is for more support for lighter penalties for rule breaches among those who have a family experience of unemployment. Income is not systematically linked to attitudes, except for mutual obligation requirements, where higher income families tend to adopt a tougher line.

There are clear attitudinal differences according to political allegiance, with supporters of right of centre parties (Liberal and National Party voters) generally in favour of harsher treatment than supporters of the left-leaning parties (the Australian Labor Party and the Australian Democrats). Swinging voters (a crucial constituency in a tight electoral contest) support harsher treatment across all three categories.

However, the most interesting feature of the results in Table 2.1.9 is the strong and consistent significance of the three constructed personal value variables. Those people who are classified as supporting individualist

156

values favour harsher treatment of the unemployed in all areas, in direct contradiction to those whose value systems support a more collective view on economic and social issues. Those classified as resigned to their fate and the impact of economic and social change also favour more support for the unemployed, less activity requirements and lighter penalties. All three value variables are significant when included with the political allegiance variables, which implies that voting patterns do not capture all of the subtleties that characterise people's values and attitudes to economic and social change. Indeed, the results in Table 2.1.10 indicate that the value system variables and a small number of personal characteristics are able to explain almost as much of the variation in attitudes to treatment of the unemployed as the more complex models which include the political allegiance (and other) variables.

Table 2.1.8 Defining the independent variables

Characteristic	Definition	Identifier
Sex	Female	Female
	Male (*)	-
Age	Age in years	Age
Political allegiance	Liberal Party voter	Libvote
	Labor Party voter (*)	-
	National Party voter	Natvote
	Australian Democrat voter	Demvote
	Swinging voter	Swingvote
	Other voter	Othvote
Birthplace	Born in Australia (*)	-
	Born in another English-speaking country	Bornesc
	Born in non-English-speaking country	Bornnesc
Family income	Under $400 a week (*)	-
	$400 to $699 a week	Inc4-7
	$700 to $1,249 a week	Inc8-12
	$1,250 a week and over	Inc12+
Educated	Has a bachelor degree or higher or studying at school or university	Educ
Experienced unemployment	Family member been unemployed in last three years	Expunem
Informed	Knows the current levels of total and long-term unemployment	Inform
Individualist	See table 2.1.7	Indiv
Collectivist	See table 2.1.7	Collect
Fatalist	See table 2.1.7	Fatal

Note: (*) Indicates the category used as control in the regression equations.

3.2 Attitudes to sole parents and paid work

The Australian social security system recognises that sole parents face particular difficulties combining work and family responsibilities that warrant support. Studies show that sole parent families have far higher poverty rates than couple families with children (Saunders, 1998, Harding and Szukalska, 1999). Although based on cross-section data, these studies suggest that the two most effective routes out of poverty for sole parents are re-partnering and employment (Saunders, 1994). The Jobs, Education and Training (JET) Scheme has been successful in assisting sole parents to access training opportunities and enter (or re-enter) the labour market.

An on-going issue for policy has been trying to identify at what point it is appropriate to shift the focus away from providing income support for sole parents to allow them to care for their children towards a more active encouragement of active engagement with the labour market. Debate surrounding the appropriate point of intervention has focused on the age of the youngest child: at what point in the child's development should policy seek to encourage (or require) sole parents to join the labour force?

Community views on this issue were addressed directly in two survey questions. After noting that sole parents are currently expected to seek paid work only after their youngest child turns 16, respondents were asked at what age they thought that sole parents should be expected to undertake paid work[8]. Respondents were asked to indicate which of the following four options should apply:

- As now, once the youngest child turns 16
- Once the youngest child goes to high school (around the age of 11 or 12)
- Once the youngest child goes to primary school (around the age of 5 or 6)
- Only when the sole parent feels ready.

The same question was asked in respect of expectations about the parent undertaking part-time and full-time work. Responses to each of the four options were re-coded as 0, - 1, - 2 and + 1, so that zero indicates agreement with the current situation, negative scores imply a harsher requirement than currently and a positive score implies a more lenient attitude than currently (in the sense that the sole parent would be free to decide for themselves when to join the labour market). Table 2.1.10 summarises the responses to these questions. Despite the concerns about the wording of the question prompting a bias in the responses, most respondents support sole parents being expected to work (particularly part-time) once their youngest child first goes to school. There is considerably less support for expecting sole parents to work full-time, at least until their youngest child is in high school.

4. Concluding comments

As in many other countries, social security policy in Australia has become increasingly focused on the issue of 'welfare dependency' – prolonged reliance on benefits that can lead to exclusion characterised by disengagement from the labour force and low levels of social participation. Rather than try to address this issue by widespread cuts in benefit levels, governments have been encouraging benefit recipients back into work or into training through strategies designed to maximise the possibility of finding work. Attempts have also been made to remove the most extreme disincentives associated with high effective marginal tax rates.

In Australia, as elsewhere, more work and job search activity conditions are being imposed on working age people in receipt of social security benefits. But how far mutual obligation conditions can be imposed on the unemployed and other groups is constrained by public opinion – the basis of the political legitimacy of the welfare system. Mutual obligation also raises issues about what it is legitimate to expect of *government* in terms of providing support for the unemployed, and the terms on which such support is provided. Finally, mutual obligation policies are likely to be expensive if they are to give jobless people a realistic chance of finding work.

The time use data analysed in Section 2 indicate that, in 1997, the proportion of unemployed people engaging in job search activity was low (22 percent for men and 12 percent for women). These people spent between 1 and 2 hours a day looking for work. In addition, the proportion of unemployed participating in education was 14 percent for men and 16 percent for women, and in voluntary work and care, 19 percent for both men and women. There may be scope for an increase in participation across these activities.

Table 2.1.9   Social security treatment of the unemployed: OLS regression results

Independent variable	Support for unemployed		Mutual obligation for unemployed		Penalties for unemployed	
Constant	0.06	0.32	19.81***	15.33***	-0.17	-0.39***
	(0.14)	(1.05)	(16.94)	(19.92)	(1.13)	(4.07)
Female	-0.15	-0.21	-1.39***	-0.79*	0.11*	0.12**
	(0.81)	(1.19)	(2.83)	(1.71)	(1.81)	(2.15)
Age	-0.002	-0.009	0.079***	0.09***	0.003	0.002
	(0.26)	(1.59)	(4.54)	(6.34)	(1.22)	(1.25)
Libvote	-0.35	–	-2.27***	–	-0.26***	–
	(1.50)	–	(3.60)	–	(3.28)	–
Natvote	-1.72***	–	-3.38***	–	-0.56***	–
	(3.45)	–	(2.69)	–	(3.66)	–
Demvote	1.16**	–	0.27	–	0.28*	–
	(2.20)	–	(0.20)	–	(1.64)	–
Swingvote	-0.92***	–	-2.70***	–	-0.31***	–
	(3.56)	–	(4.06)	–	(3.68)	–
Othvote	-0.65	–	-0.32	–	-0.068	–
	(1.31)	–	(0.25)	–	(0.42)	–
Bornesc	0.42	–	1.21	–	0.100	–
	(1.45)	–	(1.59)	–	(1.06)	–
Bornnesc	0.86***	0.92***	2.15***	2.80***	0.25***	0.30***
	(2.99)	(3.39)	(2.84)	(3.91)	(2.65)	(3.44)
Inc4-7	-0.22	–	-2.52***	–	-0.13	–
	(0.83)	–	(3.56)	–	(1.43)	–
Inc8-12	-0.041	–	-2.70***	–	-0.19	–
	(0.15)	–	(3.87)	–	(2.15)	–
Inc12+	0.17	–	-3.20***	–	-0.15*	–
	(0.59)	–	(4.32)	–	(1.62)	–
Educ	0.70***	–	-0.22	–	-0.003	–
	(2.92)	–	(0.35)	–	(0.33)	–
Expunem	0.15	–	0.62	–	0.17***	–
	(0.80)	–	(1.22)	–	(2.71)	–
Inform	0.15	–	-1.00*	–	-0.026	–
	(0.69)	–	(1.76)	–	(0.39)	–
Indiv	-0.41***	-0.43***	-0.54***	-0.51***	-0.15***	-0.16***
	(8.79)	(9.63)	(4.20)	(4.28)	(9.44)	(11.13)
Fatal	0.22***	0.23***	0.78***	1.04***	0.070***	0.09***
	(4.61)	(5.34)	(6.05)	(8.97)	(4.43)	(6.16)
Resign	0.18***	0.24***	0.18	0.28**	0.060***	0.08***
	(3.58)	(5.03)	(1.34)	(2.20)	(3.67)	(4.98)
N	836	958	1,474	1,721	1,293	1,490
R^2	0.240***	0.182***	0.156***	0.119***	0.196***	0.158***

Note: */**/*** indicates that the t-statistic is significant at the 0.10/0.05/0.01 level

Table 2.1.10   When sole parents should seek paid work (percentages)

	Question: When do you think it is appropriate for a sole parent to be expected to undertake part-time/full-time work?	
	Part-time	**Full-time**
Once the youngest child reaches 16	13.0	32.9
Once the youngest child goes to high school	18.6	27.0
Once the youngest child goes to primary school	49.8	17.0
Only when the sole parent feels ready	10.1	15.1
Other/missing	8.4	8.0
Total	100.0	100.0
Unweighted n = 2,403		

The data also indicate that the intensity of job search declines as unemployment duration increases, particularly among men. Long-term unemployed men are also less likely to participate in social and community interaction. In contrast, unemployed mothers tend to devote more time to child care and social participation than mothers who are in paid work. Section 3 presents a range of evidence drawn from a survey of public opinion that addresses directly some of the issues raised in the mutual obligation debate. The data indicates that while there is support for mutual obligation, at least for some groups of the unemployed, this does not apply to the older unemployed, those caring for young children and those with a disability. While there is considerable support for expecting sole parents to work once their youngest child goes to school, this tends to extend to part-time work only rather than to full-time work.

At the same time, most people see mutual obligation as also implying action on the part of government to reduce unemployment and ease the plight of the unemployed. While few people support public sector job creation or labour market programs generally, many think that the unemployed should be assisted through training programs, wage subsidies and a tax-transfer system that encourages and rewards incentive. The high degree of public support for increased training for the unemployed is in contrast to the time use data which shows that the participation rate and average time spent by the unemployed on education are low – even lower than for people in part-time jobs.

Further research is needed on the origins, nature and consequences of attitudes to the social security system. Without this, it will be difficult to establish the legitimacy of the system and even harder to determine its popularity.

Notes

[1] The authors wish to acknowledge the statistical assistance and comments provided by Ceri Evans. The results reported in Section 3 draw on research being conducted with Tony Eardley. The usual caveats apply.

[2] In contrast, the health care system (Medicare) operates on a universal basis with funding partly provided through a special income-related contributory levy.

[3] Further details of the survey methodology and the activity classification used are provided in Appendix A.

[4] Voting is compulsory in Australia, so the electoral rolls provide a good sampling frame for the adult population.

[5] Further details of the results shown in Tables 4 and 5 are provided in Eardley, Saunders and Evans, 2000.

[6] Under a random assignment across each of the thirteen options listed in the survey instrument, each would have received 7.7 percent support.

[7] Those who responded 'Don't Know' or who did not answer the relevant questions have been excluded from the analysis. It makes little difference if these responses are all included as neutral (zero) scores.

[8] There is always a danger in providing information in the question about the current situation, respondents are encouraged to support the *status quo*. While accepting this, it was decided that the alternative would generate responses that, bearing no necessary relation to current practice, would be very difficult to interpret. Since we are primarily interested in attitudes that diverge from the *status quo*, any bias in its favour serves to strengthen the conclusions that can be drawn from the results.

References

ABS (1998b), *Time Use Survey, Australia 1997 - Confidentialised Unit Record File*, ABS Catalogue No. 4152.0, Canberra.

Australian Bureau of Statistics (ABS) (1998a), *Time Use Survey, Australia. User's Guide 1997*, ABS Catalogue No. 4150.0, ABS, Canberra.

Bean, C. (1991), 'Are Australian Attitudes to Government Different? A Comparison with Five Other Nations', in F.G. Castles (ed.) *Australia Compared. People, Policies and Politics*, Allen & Unwin, Sydney, pp.74-100.

Blair, T. (1999), 'Beveridge Revisited: A Welfare State for the 21st Century', in R. Walker (ed.), *Ending Child Poverty. Popular Welfare for the 21st Century?*, The Policy Press, Bristol, pp. 7-18.

Castles, F. and Mitchell, D. (1992), 'Three Worlds of Welfare Capitalism or Four?', *Discussion Paper No. 21*, Public Policy Program, Australian National University.

Esping-Anderson, G. (1990), *The Three Worlds of Welfare Capitalism*, Polity Press, Cambridge.

Foster, R. A. (1996), *Australian Economic Statistics 1949-50 to 1994-95*, Occasional Paper No. 8, Reserve Bank of Australia, Sydney.

Gregory, R. G. (1999), 'Children and the Changing Labour Market: Joblessness in Families With Dependent Children', presented to the conference on *Labour Market Trends and Family Policies: Implications for Children*, July 14-15, Canberra.

Harding, A. and Szukalska, A. (1999), 'Trends in Child Poverty in Australia: 1982 to 1995-96', *Discussion Paper No. 42*, National Centre for Social and Economic Modelling, University of Canberra.

Organisation for Economic Cooperation and Development (1999), *OECD Economic Surveys 1998-99. Australia*, OECD, Paris.

Papadakis, E. (1990), *Attitudes to State and Private Welfare*, SPRC Reports and Proceedings No. 88, Social Policy Research Centre, University of New South Wales.

Saunders, P. (1991), 'Selectivity and Targeting in Income Support: The Australian Experience', in *Journal of Social Policy*, Vol. 20, No. 3, pp. 299-326.

Saunders, P. (1994), *Welfare and Inequality. National and International Perspectives on the Australia Welfare State*, Cambridge University Press, Melbourne.

Saunders, P. (1998), 'The Re-emergence of Poverty as a Research and Policy Issue', in *Wealth, Work and Well-Being*, Occasional Paper 1/1998, Academy of the Social Sciences in Australia, Canberra, pp. 54-78.

Saunders, P. (1999), 'Social Security in Australia and New Zealand: Means-tested or Just Mean' in *Social Policy & Administration*, Vol. 33, No. 5, pp. 493-515.

Saunders, P., Thomson, C. and Evans, C. (2000), 'Social Change and Social Policy: Results from a National Survey of Public Opinion', *Discussion Paper No. 106*, Social Policy Research Centre, University of New South Wales.

Whiteford, P. (2000), 'The Australian System of Social Protection – An Overview' in *Policy Research Paper No. 1*, Department of Family and Community Services, Canberra.

2.2 Coping with risk: attitudes towards private unemployment insurance in Britain and Germany

Andreas Cebulla

1. Introduction

During the past two decades, public policy in Great Britain (GB) and the Federal Republic of Germany (FRG) has restricted access to and eligibility for national unemployment benefit (cf. Rosenfeld, in this volume). In both countries, responding to these changes, the private insurance market has developed new products designed to protect income during unemployment to supplement public insurance policies.

This chapter has two principal objectives. First, it records the present uptake of private unemployment insurance in the two countries. Secondly, and in greater depth, the chapter explores people's intentions to insure in the future and their reasons for considering or rejecting private unemployment insurance.

Proponents of welfare reform have argued that, as public welfare is reduced, people would behave 'rationally' and, upon consideration of their welfare needs, seek private insurance as an alternative or addition to shrinking public social security. As a result, there would be no, or only a temporary, decline in the extent of the population's cover against insurable risks. This chapter reports the findings of research that investigated the extent to which people form rational judgements as to the need for, and the benefits of, private unemployment insurance. It asks who would take out private insurance and explores the extent to which perceptions of job insecurity and the risk of unemployment affected attitudes towards unemployment insurance. The comparative element of this chapter examines whether risk perceptions and responses to risk reflect systemic differences between GB's and the FRG's labour markets and welfare systems.

2. Welfare and change in GB and the FRG

In both the FRG and GB, there is evidence of a growing disjunction between economic change on the one hand and the rigidity of the national welfare systems on the other. Benefits provisions have been criticised especially in GB – but as far as social assistance is concerned equally in the FRG – for failing to alleviate poverty and being insufficient to maintain a decent standard of living. Benefits have also been described as inadequate means for providing the extent of protection that a diversifying, more complex and 'riskier' labour market requires, where full employment and standard employment relations are no longer the norm (Shaw and Walker, 1996; White, 1996; Klammer, 1998).

In the FRG, rising unemployment during the 1980s and 1990s has moved a growing number of long-term unemployed from unemployment insurance benefit to the lower-rate unemployment assistance and, ultimately, social assistance benefit (Walker et al., 1995; Heinelt and Weck, 1998; Clasen, 1999). The same can be observed in GB, where the proportion of contributory (non-means-tested) benefit claims has decreased as the expense of a growing share of means-tested benefit claimants. The shortening of the maximum period during which contributory Jobseeker's Allowance (unemployment insurance benefit) can be claimed from 12 to six months in 1996, has added to the effect. In particular younger age cohorts fail to qualify for contributory, non-means-tested unemployment insurance, as fewer remain in employment sufficiently long to make the minimum contributions necessary to be eligible for this benefit. Labour market de-regulation in Germany in the early 1990s removed some of the employment protection that used to characterise Rheinland capitalism (Hutton, 1996) and left few substantial regulatory differences between this country and GB (Raines et al., 1999).

During the same period, there was an increase in the acquisition of private insurance. However, this rise was confined largely to GB and its impact has been small. Private social expenditure in GB accounted for over 35 percent of total welfare expenditure in 1993, up seven percentage points from 28 percent in 1980 (Adema and Einerhand, 1998, p. 25). In the FRG, the private share of total public and private social expenditure stood at just 9.13 percent in 1993, down from 10.16 percent in 1980 (ibid. 1998, p. 25).

Given these contrasting developments in private provision in the two countries, the reductions in social security and the assimilation of the two economies' regulatory systems, what evidence is there to assume that people in GB and the FRG will turn to private unemployment insurance to secure their living standards? In particular, to what extent can it be assumed that labour market changes, especially with respect to the risk of unemployment, will influence decisions about insurance as rational choice theory would suggest?

The following sections address these questions, initially by investigating the extent to which *people in employment* in GB and the FRG already possess, or would consider taking out, private unemployment insurance and what sets the insurance-seekers apart from the insurance-averse. Subsequent sections argue that assumptions of rational choice will need to be qualified to take account of the effect on attitudes and insurance behaviour of provision available under the current public insurance systems, the role and constitution of domestic households and people's exposure to financial services generally. The next section, however, briefly describes the research methodology.

3. Research methodology

The research is the result of two consecutive projects concerned with attitudes towards the welfare state and the potential of private unemployment insurance, one undertaken in GB[1] between 1996 and 1999, and the other undertaken in the FRG[2] between 1999 and 2000. Both studies employed largely identical methods and approaches, with the German study, as the second of the two, aiming carefully to replicate the surveys and analyses of the GB study. The methods included:

- a national omnibus survey of over 1,000 employed individuals each in GB and the FRG – to record perceptions of the risk of unemployment, attitudes to private unemployment insurance and willingness to pay, and test assumptions about the role of socio-economic, cultural and psychological factors affecting attitudes; and
- in-depth interviews with waged and unwaged households, including some with private unemployment insurance (totalling over 100 in GB

and over 60 in FRG) – to explore risk perceptions, insurance attitudes/behaviours and the link between the two in more detail.

For the face-to-face interviews, the GB topic guide was adapted for use in the interviews in Germany. Likewise, the German omnibus survey contained questions translated from the earlier GB omnibus survey, which allowed a complete replication of the subsequent data analyses. The analysis reported here used logistic regression to explore the characteristics of people who would consider taking out insurance.

The following explorations of the possession of private unemployment insurance and potential uptake in the two countries are based on the analysis of data collected in the two national omnibus surveys. Section 6, which is concerned with investigating in more detail factors or considerations that affect people's insurance decisions, is based on evidence collected from the face-to-face interviews.

4. Private unemployment insurance - coverage and scope

In GB and in the FRG, about one person in twenty claimed to possess insurance providing income in the case of redundancy, i.e. private unemployment insurance (GB: 5.8 percent; FRG: 5.2 percent). Determining the possession of insurance products can be a difficult exercise. There is mounting evidence of the poor knowledge people have of the insurance policies they possess. Moreover, even where people know the insurance products they have, they frequently know little or are unsure about the type and extent of cover they offer. This is particularly true for insurances that are rarely invoked and new insurance products. The market penetration of private unemployment insurance of some five percent of the population in GB and the FRG ought therefore to be treated with some caution.

4.1 Possession of insurance and intentions to insure

Higher socio-economic groups (SEGs), who were also higher earners, were most likely to claim to possess private unemployment insurance in GB (Tables 2.2.1 and 2.2.2)[3]. In the FRG, differences in the extent of insurance possession across SEGs, except for the unskilled, were less pronounced, but still apparent.

Intentions to insure also varied greatly across SEGs, but this time in both countries. In GB, proportionately twice as many survey respondents said they would seek to take out private unemployment insurance 'one day' in the future than was the case in the FRG (GB: 23.1 percent; FRG: 11.9 percent)[4]. In Britain, people from socio-economic groups, which already reported a high incidence of insurance possession were less likely to consider taking out insurance in the future than people from socio-economic groups with an as yet low level of insurance uptake. These were above all manual workers, but also low-skilled non-manual employees and – exceptionally – employers and managers. In the FRG, manual workers were also disproportionately likely to express an interest in private unemployment insurance, as were medium and low-skilled non-manual employees. The exception amongst the manual workers were semi-skilled workers, who, although claiming a disproportionately high level of insurance possession, expressed no intention to acquire further unemployment insurance policies in the future.

Summing insurance possession and intentions to insure suggests a potential coverage of private unemployment insurance of about a quarter of people in employment in GB (28.9 percent) and less than one-fifth in the FRG (17.1 percent) (Tables 2.2.1 and 2.2.2). In the FRG, semi-skilled workers were by far the least likely to have or to consider acquiring private insurance. Other SEGs showing little propensity to seeking insurance were employers and managers, professionals and the unskilled. In GB, by contrast, employers and managers, and professionals were most likely to already possess or to consider acquiring private unemployment insurance. Lower socio-economic groups, with the exception of skilled manual workers, were least likely to have or to consider acquiring private unemployment insurance.

5. Intention to insure against unemployment and other risks

This section and the one that follows explore in more detail what makes people in the two countries consider taking out private unemployment insurance. Intentions to insure appeared in both countries strongly influenced by past experience of unemployment and subjective assessments of the risk of unemployment.

In order to shed more light on the factors that swayed respondents towards private unemployment insurance, a logistic regression was conducted, using information about subjective risk assessment and a range of demographic statistics and household characteristics collected in the two surveys. The regression estimated the odds of a person expressing his or her intention to acquire this type of insurance, whilst controlling for a number of explanatory variables.

The results of the logistic regression analyses are shown in Tables 2.2.3 and 2.2.4 The tables only show the statistically significant variables, and their estimated odds and levels of significance. For each variable (e.g. age of respondent), the sub-group (e.g. aged 50 years or over) whose percentage response came closest to that of the whole population (e.g. GB survey respondents) was chosen as the reference group. The odds and statistical significance of odds of other sub-groups (18 years - 29 years etc.) were estimated in relation to the reference group.

For GB, the analysis (Table 2.2.3) revealed that, ceteris paribus, intentions to insure increased with:

- the presence in the household of a partner with a recent experience of unemployment;
- and decreased with:
- age;
- employment in the public services or the utilities and construction sectors; and
- the perception of one's risk of unemployment being lower than that of others living in the same neighbourhood as the respondent (a 'neighbourhood effect').

For the FRG, the analysis (Table 2.2.4), which followed the same methodological steps and used the same (aggregation of) variables, produced rather different results. There, the intention to insure privately increased with the respondent:

- having a temporary, fixed-term or no employment contract;
- banking for less than 10 years; and
- considering the loss of income due to an accident likely.
  Conversely, the intention to insure declined with:
- age (50 years or more);
- the absence of children; and
- the perception that unemployment of two months or more was unlikely/neither likely nor unlikely.

Table 2.2.1 Possession of, and intention to obtain, private unemployment insurance status, GB, by socio-economic group (in % of people in employment or self-employment)

Insurance	Socio-economic group							
	Employers/ managers n=197	Professional n=73	Intermediate non-manual n=159	Junior non-manual n=206	Skilled manual n=215	Semi-skilled n=182	Unskilled n=42	All (row %) n=1074
Median annual personal gross income (£) x 1,000	25 +	14-25	14-25	8-14	8-14	4-8	4-8	8-14
(a) Redundancy Income Protection	8.3	11.2	8.0	1.2	6.6	4.5	0	5.8
(b) Intent to obtain Income Protection	26.0	16.9	19.9	24.6	23.4	21.8	26.2	23.1
Sum (a + b)	34.3	28.1	27.9	25.8	30.0	26.3	26.2	28.9

Note: Column response percentages unless otherwise indicated
Source: GB Omnibus Survey November 1997

Table 2.2.2 Possession of, and intention to obtain, private unemployment insurance, FRG, by socio-economic group (in % of people in employment or self-employment)

Insurance	Socio-economic group							
	Employers/ Managers[1]	Professional[2]	Intermediate non-manual[3]	Junior Non-manual[4]	Skilled manual[5]	Semi-skilled[6]	Unskilled[7]	All (row %)
	N=61	N=273	N=487	N=114	N=140	N=46	N=12	N=1250
Median monthly household net income (DM)	6843	6000	4500	4433	4200	4800	3493	5000
(a) Redundancy Income Protection	6.4	4.9	5.7	7.1	5.3	6.2	0	5.2
(b) Intent to obtain Income Protection	5.3	9.8	15.3	12.1	15.4	0	16.7	11.9
Sum (a + b)	11.7	14.7	21.0	19.2	20.7	6.2	16.7	17.1

Note: Column response percentages unless otherwise indicated. SEG translations in omnibus survey: [1] Arbeitgeber/Manager, [2] Angestellter mit hochqualifizierter Tätigkeit, [3] Angestellter mit qualifizierter Tätigkeit, [4] Angestellter mit einfacher Tätigkeit, [5] Facharbeiter, [6] Angelernter Arbeiter, [7] Ungelernter Arbeiter; numbers do not add to total due to omission of unclassified 'others/Sonstige' (118).
Source: FRG Omnibus Survey August/September 1999

Table 2.2.3 Best fitting logistic regression model for predicting intention to obtain private unemployment insurance – GB (stepwise entered - significant variables)

	Estimated Odds	Significance
Age of Respondent		***
50 yrs or over	1.00	
18 yrs-29 yrs	7.86	***
30 yrs-39 yrs	4.03	***
40 yrs-49 yrs	3.37	***
Standard Industrial Classification		**
Private Services	1.00	
Utilities & construction	.41	**
Manufacturing	1.14	
Public Services	.63	*
Chance of unemployment compared to others in neighbourhood		*
Greater	1.00	
Equal	.57	
Lower	.36	**
Partner's unemployment record in last 5 years		**
Unemployed once	1.00	
Not unemployment	.74	
Unemployed twice or more	2.52	*
No partner	1.27	
Constant		***

Significance levels:
 * p < 0.05
 ** p < 0.01
 *** p < 0.001

Table 2.2.4 Best fitting logistic regression model for predicting intention to obtain private unemployment insurance - FRG (stepwise entered - significant variables)

	Estimated Odds	Significance
Age of respondent		**
40 yrs-49yrs	1.00	
18 yrs-29yrs	0.97	
30 yrs-39 yrs	1.02	
50 yrs or over	.31	**
Children in household		*
Yes	1.00	
No	.60	
Type of contract		**
Six or more years with same employer/self-employed	1.00	
Permanent	1.35	
Temporary/fixed-term/no contract	2.65	***
No. of years banking		**
More than 10.5 years	1.00	
Less than 4.5 years/not at all	2.26	**
Between 4.5 yrs and 10.5 yrs	2.06	**
Likelihood of 2 months or more unemployment		*
Likely	1.00	
Unlikely/neither-nor	.53	
Likelihood of income loss due to accident		**
Unlikely	1.00	
Likely	1.99	**
Neither/nor	1.06	

Significance levels:
   * $p < 0.05$, ** $p < 0.01$, *** $p < 0.001$

174

The age characteristic was the only one that affected insurance attitudes in both countries. In both GB and the FRG, younger employees were more inclined to consider private unemployment insurance than older ones. This was especially so in GB, where people aged between 18 and 29 were up to eight times more likely to contemplate taking out private cover than people aged 50 or over. In the FRG, the 18-29 years olds were as likely to consider acquiring private unemployment insurance as the reference group (40- to 49-year olds), but were three times as likely to consider insurance as those aged 50 or over. Age-related differences may reflect support for systems of national welfare that has grown and consolidated over time and is more strongly represented among older generations (Matheson and Wearing 1999). It may equally reflect structural factors, such as the prospect of retirement, which reduces incentives to take out this type of insurance, compared with concern for security of income and especially living standards early in a career, which increases them.

However, this is not the place to discuss why each of the factors identified in the analysis should affect intentions to insure. Rather, the aim must be to draw out the key events or characteristics that the analysis suggests informed insurance intentions and distinguished insurance intentions in GB and the FRG. Three are discussed here:

- subjective perceptions of the risk of unemployment;
- the role of the composition and the experience of unemployment in the household; and
- banking and banking behaviour.

The following sections discuss each of these features in turn, drawing in large part on the findings of the face-to-face interviews conducted with households in GB and the FRG.

6. Insurance and insurance attitudes – interview evidence

6.1 Subjective perceptions of the risk of unemployment

Whilst the preceding analyses produced ample evidence of a link between socio-economic status and intentions to insure, the regression analysis of the FRG data suggested that personal perceptions of the risk of unemployment had a significant, albeit mediated, effect on insurance intentions. A less direct link, based on subjective perceptions of unemployment risk relative to others (in the neighbourhood) was apparent

175

from GB data analysis[5]. Following Weinstein (1980) people tend to be overly optimistic with respect to the likelihood of a negative event happening to them rather than others they know or observe. In GB, people inclined towards a more positive or 'optimistic' view of themselves were less likely to consider private unemployment insurance.

The analysis of the face-to-face interviews in GB and the FRG showed that perceptions of the risk of unemployment were mostly perceptions of the 'global' rather than the personal risk of unemployment. In both countries, the risk of unemployment was frequently explained with reference to changes in the global economy as they affected national and regional economies and, ultimately, the employer's business. Except for the case of older workers, where age was seen as increasing the risk of unemployment and reducing the chances of re-employment, and casual labourers, the risk was not, or only rarely, presented as emanating from personal factors or characteristics. Conversely, however, personal factors were most prominent in 'explaining' a widespread optimism with respect to the re-employability of respondents.

In their current employment, many in the GB sample argued that hard work and showing commitment to work, such as working long hours, would make them less dispensable at their workplace and thus reduce the risk of unemployment. Interviews with utility and public service workers in GB suggested private unemployment insurance was rejected for different reasons. Public service workers felt generally more secure and protected by their status as civil servants. However public service workers who were not civil servants, especially to teachers, felt more vulnerable. Utility workers argued they felt securely employed because their previously nationalised industry had already undergone restructuring as part of their privatisation and was now consolidating, reducing the risk of redundancy.

There was less evidence that similar attitudes and perceptions with respect to performance at the workplace informed unemployment risk assessments in the FRG. In Germany, indispensability at work was almost exclusively 'measured', by those working in the higher-skilled, professional services sector, by the number of clients or customers one was dealing with. However, there was some concern about younger, and also more qualified, people threatening one's employment position. Conversely, the regression findings suggest that the greater regulation of temporary and fixed-term working in the FRG, which may reduce entitlement to social security increases propensities to insure. The same was true for self-employed people in both countries, because they are not covered by their national unemployment insurance schemes.

In both GB and the FRG, there was a strong belief that, following redundancy, a new job needed to be found quickly (although more quickly in GB than the FRG), which made additional private unemployment insurance redundant. This view was also shared by most of the people who had taken out insurance. However, this group also felt that having the added safety net of private insurance allowed them to take more time in finding the 'right' new job, whilst maintaining much of their previous living standard. Some of the insured, who may be described as particularly risk-averse (but possibly also more realistic), were wary that in reality job-search might prove more difficult and re-employment harder to achieve.

In both GB and the FRG, people viewed the personal risk of unemployment, where it was acknowledged to exist, with a degree of resignation and inevitability. However, people in the FRG argued more forcefully for greater independence from means-tested, though not insurance-based welfare, without proposing a dismantling of the current provision of unemployment and social assistance. In GB, a widely held view favoured greater self-provision in social security amongst higher earners and – especially amongst lower socio-economic groups – greater scrutiny of eligibility and investigation of welfare fraud. This view was much less evident in the FRG, where it was more frequently argued that greater personal initiative and responsibility should apply to all, regardless of income or status.

Many people in the FRG sample also doubted the state's ability to manage its finances and secure the current welfare system. This appeared to contribute to the greater propensity of people in the FRG who felt insecure in their employment to contemplate private cover. It was less likely in GB, where unemployment insurance and assistance benefits were thought of as too low to be considered 'earned' entitlements that properly reflected contributions made to the insurance system. Although there was also some evidence of people's mistrust of state organisations, given the low value of benefits, this was of little consequence for people's insurance attitudes. The low value of benefits increased the propensity to insure across all unemployment risk groups.

6.2 Household composition and the experience of unemployment

Concerns about the welfare of the family played an important part in shaping perceptions of the risk of unemployment, in particular fear of the event and its (financial) consequences. The risk of a fall in the family's living standard encouraged people to contemplate the benefits of private unemployment insurance. However, whereas in the FRG the presence of children was the key factor, in GB the partner's employment record proved more important, although the face-to-face interviews showed that having children was an important additional factor (for a discussion of the contribution of female earnings to household income cf. Cantillon et al., in this volume).

Encouraging the partner to take up employment or to increase the hours worked was a strategy repeatedly proposed – and recalled – in GB interviews in order to cope with the financial and material deprivations of unemployment. This was reflected in the logistic regression analysis as an increased propensity to insure where a partner's poor employment record suggested that 'activation' might not be a feasible strategy. Current levels of unemployment benefit were seen as inadequate to live on, especially where there were no savings. But having a job was also a matter of pride and status. Except for men – and women – ideologically opposed to the female partner working, both partners tended to support activation.

In the FRG, there was less evidence for activation strategies, although mutual support, more often in the context of assisting one partner to undertake training, education, re-training or finding a new job following redundancy was reported. Income protection granted under the existing German National Insurance was generally seen as adequate to compensate for either partner's loss of income due to redundancy. Higher SEGs in particular felt that at least for a limited time period, there would be little need to adjust to a lower standard of living. Again, only the presence of children increased the concern for added social security, as children add to expenses and may also impede the job-search capability of partners.

Households in the FRG were also less concerned about debt than GB households. Many were very strongly opposed to taking loans or credit, whereas in particular credit was an established means of financial management in GB. The absence of such financial liabilities and a confidence in the household's ability to manage lessened concern about the impact of unemployment on the household and its living standard in the FRG.

In both countries, saving and, where financially feasible, investment in stocks, shares or bonds, was seen as preferable to buying insurance. This was for a number of reasons. First, saving was seen as the 'natural' first measure of financial planning and building a personal and family safety net. Secondly, savings and investments were seen as offering (the potential of) a return that insurance did not, or at least not until a claim was lodged. Thirdly, savings and investments were perceived as more flexible as, unlike insurance policies, they could be accessed as need be and not only during unemployment.

Although savings rates (cf. Jupp 1997) are generally lower in GB than the FRG, it was respondents in GB who were most concerned that having put money into savings and possibly investment, there was little left to spend on insurance. This view was most frequently expressed by lower and lower-middle class respondents. This concern was, in GB, compounded by a 'hierarchy of family risk' that respondents had developed (Quilgars and Abbott, 2000). According to this hierarchy, families were most concerned about insuring risks that most directly affected other family members, i.e. death, retirement and accident or illness. Beyond this, lower income groups in particular saw little realistic opportunity, given financial constraints, to take out further insurance policies covering situations such as unemployment.

The results of the logistic regression for the German data suggest a greater affinity between banking and attitudes towards insurance than appeared to be the case in GB, especially amongst people with more recent banking experience and exposure. This may however, merely reflect a greater propensity to seek independent financial security, in the first instance through saving, and greater financial scope for investing in insurance. That said, as in GB, people in the FRG who already had acquired a number of personal accident, pension and/or home insurance policies were reluctant to consider additional insurance, such as insurance to protect income during unemployment.

7. Conclusion

This chapter explored the extent of coverage of private unemployment insurance in GB and the FRG. It showed that whilst a similarly small fraction of both populations claimed to possess private unemployment insurance, there was much greater interest in GB in acquiring such a policy in the future than there was in the FRG. Rational choice theory suggests personal risk of unemployment will be the main influence on attitudes towards this insurance, but this study showed that personal concerns for family welfare and domestic financial management are also influential.

Many of the arguments for or against private unemployment insurance took account of the level of financial support provided by the public unemployment insurance and social assistance systems. However, equally important was the consideration of alternatives that would help to avoid having to draw on welfare support. Paramount amongst them were labour market strategies, which involved the activation of family members, especially partners. In the FRG, partners were more likely seen as a resource that might help the unemployed person find a new job. Moreover, there was evidence of respondents in the FRG placing greater emphasis on careful domestic financial planning, in particular by avoiding unnecessary debt, which would exacerbate the risk to one's living standard in case of unemployment. Although attitudes towards insurance, relative to other means of assembling financial assets and thus financial security, appeared not to differ substantially between the two countries, confidence in one's ability in handling finances (and dealing with banking institutions) had a positive influence on intentions to insure in the FRG. In sum, although respondents took into account public provision when assessing the benefits of private insurance, the availability of alternative coping strategies was an equally important consideration. In doing so, they took account of the opportunities and constraints presented by labour markets and welfare systems.

These alternative strategies constitute major barriers to the expansion of the private provision of unemployment insurance, which the present analysis suggests looks unlikely to extend beyond about one-third of the working population.

Notes

[1] Funding by the Economic and Social Research Council (award reference no. L211252054) is gratefully acknowledged. The research team also included Prof. Robert Walker (formerly Loughborough University, now University of Nottingham), Prof. Janet Ford and Deborah Quilgars (both University of York), Dr Simon Roberts (Loughborough University) and David Abbott (formerly Loughborough University, now University of Bristol).

2 Funding by the Anglo-German Foundation for the Study of Industrial Society (award no. 1247) is gratefully acknowledged. The research team also included Prof. Hubert Heinelt (University of Darmstadt) and Prof. Robert Walker (formerly Loughborough University, now University of Nottingham).
3 In GB survey, socio-economic group (or status) was defined according to respondents' employment. In the FRG survey, it was self-assigned, i.e. the respondent was asked to indicate which SEG best described his or her employment.
4 The survey questions were: 'Do you think that one day, you might take out insurance against loss of income due to unemployment? (Yes/No/Don't know)'/Glauben Sie, Sie werden eines Tages eine private Versicherung gegen den Verlust von Einkommen durch Arbeitslosigkeit abschliessen? (Ja/Nein/Weiss nicht).
5 It should be noted at this point, that neither analysis included local area unemployment statistics amongst the independent variables, although regional dummies (including East and West Germany) were used, proving non-significant. However, a separate analysis of GB data, for which unemployment statistics at the level of postcode zones could be obtained, produced no different result.

References

Adema, W. and Einerhand, M. (1998) The growing role of private social benefits. Labour market and social policy - Occasional Paper No. 32, OECD.

Clasen, J. (1999) 'Beyond Social Security: the Economic Value of Giving Money to Unemployed People', in *European Journal of Social Security*, Vol. 1/2, 151-180, Netherlands: KLI.

Heinelt, H. and Weck, M. (1998) Arbeitsmarktpolitik – Vom Vereinigungskonsens zur Standortdebatte. Leske + Buderich, Opladen.

Hutton, W. (1996) *The state we're in*. Vintage, London.

Jupp, B. (1997) *Saving Sense: A new approach to encourage saving*. Demos, London.

Klammer, U. (1998) Reformbedarf und Reformoptionen der sozialen Sicherung vor dem Hintergrund der 'Erosion des Normalarbeitsverhältnisses', in K. Eicker-Wolf, R. Käpernick, T. Niechoj, S. Reiner and J. Weiss (eds.), Die arbeitslose Gesellschaft und ihr Sozialstaat, Metropolis-Verlag, Marburg, pp. 249-287.

Matheson, G. and Wearing, M. (1999) Within and Without, Labour force status and political views in four welfare states, in: S. Svallfors and P. Taylor-Gooby (eds.) *The end of the welfare state? Responses to state retrenchment*, London/New York, Routledge, pp. 135-160.

Quilgars, D. and Abbott, D. (2000) 'Working in the risk society: families perceptions of, and responses to, flexible labour markets and the restructuring of welfare', *Community, Work & Family*, 3, 1, pp. 15-36.

Raines, P., Döhrn, R., Brown, R. and Scheuer, M. (1999) *Labour Market flexibility and inward investment in Germany and GB*, Anglo-German Foundation, London.

Shaw, A. and Walker, R. (1996) 'Disjointed interaction: the labour market and the benefits system', in P. Meadows (ed.) *Work out – or work in? Contributions to the debate on the future of work*, York: YPS, pp. 87-105.

Walker, R., Shaw, A. and L. Hull (1995), 'Responding to the risk of unemployment', in *ABI, Risk Insurance and Welfare*, Association of British Insurers, London, pp. 37-52.

Weinstein, N. D. 1980, 'Unrealistic optimism about future life events', *Journal of Personality and Social Psychology*, 39, 5, 806-820.

White, M. (1996) 'The labour market and risk', in P. Meadows (ed.) *Work out - or work in? Contributions to the debate on the future of work*, York: YPS, pp. 59-86.

PART 3

ETHICS AND THE EVALUATION
OF CONCRETE INSTITUTIONS

3.1 The pre-market phase: the transition from a state-controlled to a market-based social security system

Jasper C. van den Brink and Esther N. Bergsma

1. Introduction

The public implementation of a social policy causes problems in many countries. It is often accused of being inefficient and not sufficiently customer orientated. In the Netherlands, an attempt has been made to improve this situation through the introduction of a form of market-based setting. Various studies have also explored the options for a market-based approach to the implementation of social policy. In particular, these studies examine the pros and cons of the market-based as opposed to the state-controlled implementation of social schemes. However, little has been written so far about the phase in which a state-controlled context is transformed into a market context, even though this transition phase can have a major influence on the ultimate form and effectiveness of the market. This chapter therefore discusses this transition phase and the influence it could have on competition in the market.

1.1 The implementation of employee insurance schemes in the Netherlands

In the Netherlands a distinction is made between the implementation of employee insurance schemes and public insurance schemes. This chapter only deals with the implementation of employee insurance schemes.

These schemes are divided in three important laws, the Sickness Benefits Act, the Disability Benefits Act and the Unemployment Benefits

Act. The Sickness Benefits Act used to be an insurance for the first year of an employee's sickness. However this act was almost completely privatised in 1996. The private market was to carry out both the insurance and the implementation of the insurance. Only certain vulnerable groups were excluded from this privatisation (such as pregnant women and employees on a temporary contract).

Both the Disability Benefits Act and the Unemployment Benefits Act are still in the public domain. The terms of the insurance policies are still drawn up by the state. The administration of these acts is the responsibility of five implementing bodies. These implementing bodies are part of the private domain at least from a juridical point of view. When studied from a sociological point of view it becomes clear that they are still very dependent on the state, both financially and in terms of policy. The management and control of these implementing bodies is the responsibility of (representatives) of the state. Because of this strong dependence on the state they are here viewed as state organisations[1].

All the implementing bodies are part of holdings. In these holdings the implementing bodies are in what is called the 'public division'. This is the part of the holding which is under strong government control. The other part of the holding is the 'private division', which cannot be controlled by (representatives) of the state. In these private division many activities are taking place. For example, private divisions of many holdings engage in insurance activities, as well as consulting activities on working conditions and computer support.

The size of the implementing bodies varies considerably, with one body covering over 50% of the field and the two smallest ones only 3 or 4% each. Since al employers are obliged to be connected with an implementing body these bodies have a guaranteed number of customers. Switching from one implementing body to the other is legally possible but is very difficult, so it does not happen in practice.

It is primary the Ministry of Social Affairs that makes the policy in this field. It sketches the policy in broad outlines. The National Institute for Social Security Schemes (the LISV) works out this policy in more detail. It is also responsible for the contracts with implementing bodies. The supervision of the field is in the hands of the Social Security Supervisory Board (the Ctsv).

The introduction of a market-based approach was only considered for the implementing bodies. The aim was to encourage competition between those bodies. A policy memorandum published in 1997 put forward the idea that these five implementing bodies, together with any new providers, could compete for contracts to implement the social insurance's schemes. The government would still draw up the conditions for insurance, but the various implementing bodies would have to compete on the basis of the costs and quality of implementation. How exactly such a market would be structured has been a topic of discussion for many years. The position of the LISV, the Ctsv and the precise organisation of the customer-side of the market were particularly very unclear. The main idea was that smaller employers especially should be brought together to empower their position on the market[2].

1.2 Survey

At the end of 1998 and the beginning of 1999, we carried out a survey on the way in which the five implementing bodies were preparing for the anticipated market (see Bergsma, Van den Brink, Burger and Cordia (Ctsv), 1999). At that time, the implementing bodies were to a greater or lesser extent involved in trying to make their organisations more competitive. We interviewed 20 directors and staff. Policy documents were also analysed.

The survey provides insight into the steps that the implementing bodies concerned are taking, even before the decision to adopt a market-based context has been formally taken. It therefore provides material to describe the strategies, which the providers are developing in a field that is gradually moving from a state-controlled to a market-based context. We have termed this phase the 'pre-market' phase.

1.3 Pre-market phase

The pre-market phase starts with a serious discussion concerning the introduction of a market, without official decisions having been taken, and ends with the actual introduction of a market structure. Until the actual creation of the market, the field will still largely be state-controlled, at least in theory[3].

A market cannot of course be created overnight in an existing field. In order for a market to function properly, various preconditions are necessary. Not only the *creation* of the preconditions themselves costs time, so does the *discussion* about its structure and the scope of its preconditions.

The pre-market phase is characterised by decreasing uncertainty about the precise structure of the market and an increasing amount of problems concerning existing management and control instruments. It begins with the introduction of the idea to adopt a market-based context and ends with the introduction of a fully-fledged market structure[4]. The introduction of the idea of a market-based approach can take place in the context of either a social or a political discussion. Putting forward the idea can be enough to persuade providers in the field to undertake preparatory action. The speed with which decision-making takes place and the speed with which the adjustments are made can differ depending on the field, as a result of which the duration of the pre-market phase also varies.

The developments during this period are not only influenced by the decisions made by politicians. It is an existing field consisting of various players, each of whom has their own interests. The actions of these various players can influence subsequent developments. In this chapter, we demonstrate that the actions of the implementing bodies in the pre-market phase can influence the way in which the market will ultimately function.

In the next section, we will be looking at the strategies of the implementing bodies and at the steps they have already taken. In the following section we will look at two key characteristics of the pre-market, after which we will explore the relationship between the characteristics of the pre-market and the strategies of the providers. We will devote special attention to the consequences of the action taken by the providers in order to ensure the smooth functioning of the future market. In the subsequent section, we conclude that there is an irresolvable dilemma inherent in the pre-market.

2. Preparatory work carried out by the providers[5]

While the discussion concerning the structuring of the market was still under way, the implementing bodies for the social insurance schemes had already begun taking preparatory steps. They had already developed survival strategies during the pre-market phase in anticipation of the market-based context. From our survey we conclude that these strategies strongly focus on retaining their own circle of customers.

The various strategies, which the implementing organisations have used, are examined in this section. The strategies have in common the fact that they both 'attract' and 'include' the customer. The strategy of attracting the customer is designed to win him over by making the provider appear as attractive as possible. In the case of 'inclusion', the aim is to make it difficult for the customer to leave the provider[6].

2.1 Inclusion through the product

The implementing bodies in the pre-market strive to offer a total package. This is a service package which not only involves the implementation of employee insurance schemes but also includes e.g. health and safety insurance and sickness insurance, and occasionally also banking activities. These products are offered in partnership with the private divisions of the holdings and with commercial partners. Various (holdings of) implementing bodies have sought collaboration with insurance and/or banking companies to be able to offer a total package. This total package gives the employer (the probable future customer of the implementing body) an integrated and co-ordinated package of services. He only has to deal with a single organisation and can benefit from an integrated approach to problems, such as sickness of an employee. It is more difficult for him to switch to a different implementing body, however, due to the financial 'quantum deficits' that occur when purchasing only part of the total package. Some of the services are also only offered if they are jointly purchased. Various reintegration placement agencies only accept contracts if the employer has taken out sickness insurance with the same implementing body or with a partner of that implementing body.

2.2 Inclusion through interdependency

Another strategy is the so-called one-stop shop. Here, employers can submit data for various policies. The one-stop shop then distributes this data to various organisations with which the implementing body collaborates. This saves the employer a great deal of work and is thus geared towards attracting the employer. At the same time, this strategy also has an inclusive aspect, in that the employer is asked to supply the data in a specific way. This forces the employer to adjust his administration to the requirements of the implementing body. An interdependency is thus created between the work processes of the customer and of the provider. This makes it difficult to switch to another provider, since the administration must then be adjusted once more[7].

189

2.3 Inclusion through co-optation

A final strategy (used by a number of implementing bodies) is that of co-optation (Selznick, 1966). The customer becomes the (co) owner of the provider, for example by being a member of the board. If in a market-based context the customer moves to another provider, this implies fewer customers for the organisation of which he himself is co-owner. He is thus acting against his own interests. For the customer, the strategy of co-optation also exercises an attraction, since employers can more directly influence service levels.

2.4 Offensive and defensive providers

Although the strategies of the various implementing bodies show the same tendencies, there are some differences. Some implementing bodies can be described as offensive, while others are more defensive. The difference between these two groups lies in the degree of advancement. While some speak merely of ideas, others actually have realised some of their strategies. Both groups, however, aim to retain their own circle of customers.

3. The characteristics of the pre-market

The previous section described how the providers are preparing for the forthcoming market. They are doing this within a special period, namely the pre-market phase. Two specific characteristics of this period could explain the behaviour of providers, namely constantly changing levels of uncertainty and problems relating to management and control.

3.1 Uncertainty

A key characteristic of the pre-market is *uncertainty*. This uncertainty can occur on a number of aspects.

First of all, there is uncertainty about the question of exactly *when* there will be a market. There is no doubt that during the initial stage of the pre-market – the stage at which no formal decision has yet been taken – this uncertainty plays a key role. The government has expressed its intention to introduce the market-based approach, but it is still a matter of waiting to see when exactly it happens. And even when a formal introduction date has been fixed, there is still a chance that the government may decide to postpone the introduction of the market-based system.

Secondly, there is uncertainty about the *form that* the market will ultimately take. The market will be shaped by the *formal* structure of the market (the formal limiting conditions within which the market can develop) and by the *relational* form (i.e. market relations between suppliers and demanders). For example, the following aspects are relevant concerning form: will there be hard negotiations or will relations be based more on trust? In what areas does the government wish to retain the control it currently exercises? What precisely will and will not be opened up to the market? How much freedom will the providers have to offer products outside the new market? Will new providers be created? Will the appearance of new providers constitute a threat? Will there be full competition or will there be partial monopolies? Similar uncertainties could arise concerning relations between those on the demand-side. Can or even must customers make joint purchases?

The formal preconditions defining the field will in many cases become gradually clearer during the pre-market phase. Initially, the broad outlines will be defined in plans which will then be elaborated in more detail in the form of laws and regulations. Uncertainty about the relationship structure within the field will also gradually lessen. The various players will gradually develop strategies, and new (coalitions of) demanders and providers will appear on the pre-market.

Thirdly, there may be uncertainty about the question of whether in fact *a market will be introduced at all*. Even if a formal decision is taken to introduce the market at a specific time, the pre-market will still be under the influence of politics and hence of the government. This will continue to give rise to uncertainty as to whether the market will ever be introduced. Until the market is a reality, the decision can still be reversed, postponed or weakened. Once again, the expectation is that the likelihood of backtracking on the decision to adopt a market-based approach will diminish as introduction date draws nearer.

These three forms of uncertainty will not play as great a role in all the pre-markets. In some pre-markets, it will become clear very soon what the plans are or else there will be a large measure of political consensus about need for a market, thereby creating greater certainty. The uncertainty will diminish as the market comes closer.

191

Once formal decisions are taken, the uncertainty can be reduced very suddenly; thereby each decision gives more clarity and reduces uncertainty. Progressive insight into the development of (for example) relationship structures also gradually diminish the uncertainty. The reduction of uncertainty therefore takes place both gradually and in a sudden way. However, as long as there is still a pre-market, there will be uncertainty:

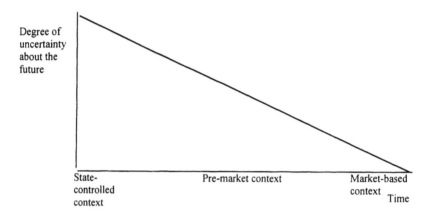

In the case, which we examined, there was uncertainty in all the areas identified. This uncertainty meant that for the providers (i.e. the implementing bodies) were not clear what was expected of them in the future. It was therefore difficult for them to chart their course for the future. This uncertainty appears to have given rise to two apparently conflicting responses. On the one hand there was a large measure of similarity in the *way* in which the providers prepared themselves, and on the other hand there were differences in the *degree* to which they did so.

It is striking to note how similarly the providers prepare themselves for the future market. The development of a form of total package for all providers is, for example, a core activity in preparations for the new market. There is consequently a high degree of isomorphy: the various providers copy each other's behaviour, thereby creating a large measure of similarity of behaviour within the field. Dimaggio and Powel (1991) have identified three causes of isomorphy – coercive isomorphism, normative isomorphism and mimetic isomorphism.

Coercive isomorphism refers to enforced isomorphic behaviour, in which coercion can be both formal and informal. Normative isomorphism refers to isomorphism influenced by the increasing professionalisation of employees and managers. The professional standards dictating the actions. In the field that we studied, there was no clear pressure to e.g. offer total package. The role of the professionals also does not appear to give any clear reason for isomorphic behaviour. What then remains is the relationship between uncertainty and isomorphic behaviour. This study cannot demonstrate that such a relationship exists, although it does appear to be arguable.

There are consequently strong similarities in the way in which the providers prepare themselves. However, the degree to which they prepare themselves differs. The providers can be divided into two groups of offensive and defensive providers respectively. The offensive providers respond to uncertainty by enthusiastically preparing themselves for the forthcoming market. The uncertainty and the associated problems of management and control, which subsequently have to be, addressed gives these providers considerable scope. The offensive providers use this scope to the full, since they see in the pre-market above all a phase in which there are opportunities. The defensive providers focus more on the threats associated with uncertainty. They have a stronger orientation on the risks attached to overly enthusiastic preparation for the market. Until there is a clear picture of the market and while it is not entirely clear even whether the market will in fact be introduced, these providers will tend to want to hold back. Until the future is certain, they feel there is too great a risk that investments for a possible market will prove to be wasted, for example because the plans for a market-based context might be withdrawn during the pre-market phase. The defensive providers see the pre-market phase mainly as one in which threats are created.

3.2 Management and control

However, uncertainty not only affects the providers but also the managing and controlling authorities. Because so little is known about the transition from a state-based to a market-based context in social policy, it is difficult for the managing authorities to anticipate the behaviour of the providers. Due to uncertainty about the future, it is also unclear how the providers will respond. In the field which we studied, management and control is carried out primarily by the National Institute for Social Insurance Schemes

(LISV) and to a lesser extent by the Ministry of Social Affairs and Employment. During the entire pre-market phase, these authorities are responsible for management and control within the field, which of course is still largely controlled by the government. However, because the state-controlled context is being increasingly exchanged for a market-based context, management and control is becoming more and more difficult.

In an interview (Vrij Nederland, 2000), the chairman of LISV, Mr. Buurmeijer, describes how he was surprised by the speed with which some providers exploited the prevailing uncertainty about the course to be adopted:

> Interviewer: 'LISV should surely be keeping an eye on this kind of thing? Doesn't that also apply to the collaborative partnerships that implementing bodies have concluded with banks or large insurance companies (...)?'

> Buurmeijer: 'I've no problem admitting that I saw these developments too late. You could call it foolish. I prefer to describe it as naive. In any case, I wasn't the only one. I was completely taken aback by the fact that the management of implementing bodies went for the rapid approach method so quickly.'

It is difficult to intervene subsequently because the management and control instruments are still geared towards the state-controlled context. Developments in the direction of a (private legal) market are therefore difficult to steer. In the case that we studied, the possibility of management and control (and supervision) was limited to the public domain. However, preparations for the market took place mainly in the private divisions of the concerns and therefore could not be steered. The influence of these private preparations in the pre-market reached further, however. They also influenced the market position of the existing public divisions of the holding as soon, since the public and private divisions will form one provider in the future market-based context.

The logical question put by the interviewer was why LISV had not intervened. The answer was:

> 'We didn't have that authority. (...) We supervise all the public elements of the implementing bodies which we still have some

control over. However, we no longer supervise commercial business units.'

The limited management and control options during the pre-market phase are however not the only problem. Above all, the question is whether management and control can in fact be exercised at all in an uncertain situation.

In the discussion concerning management and control by the government[8], it is generally assumed that management and control is based on goals which has often been determined by policy (see e.g. Braam, 1987). Management and control suggests that a specific practical content is being given as an answer to the question how to reach these goals. As outlined earlier, in a pre-market there is great uncertainty about the goals and the policy to be adopted. Without specific goals, management and control is in theory impossible.

In the field of social insurance in the Netherlands, the minister is responsible for setting the goals and formulating the policy that are then translated by the Ministry and especially by the LISV into concrete management and control activities. Due to the uncertainty concerning a fundamental choice such as 'what the transition will look like', management and control are very difficult to exercise. For example, will the transition be a 'Big Bang', a sudden changeover from a state-based to a market-based system, or will there be a gradual transition in which demanders and providers are slowly converted from state-based into commercial players? However, the political discussion only focused on the final phase, namely what will the market look like? The practical transition from state-controlled to market-based was a question of secondary importance which was postponed. This uncertainty also created an unclear role for the LISV. The management and control activities by the LISV were based on a single line in the Act in which the LISV was entrusted with the task of: *promoting competition between implementing bodies*[9]. This does not clarify the exact tasks and competence's involved. This chapter made the LISV responsible for correct implementation as well as for making preparations for the changes. However, the preparations required for the changes are very difficult to separate from the preparations which the implementing bodies are themselves making to improve their position. The large-scale IT investments made by the providers are intended to improve the existing implementation, but are also important for, and of influence on, the competitiveness of the providers on the market. This distinction is very difficult for the managing authorities to make. The distinction between the investments needed for a going concern and investments based on the creation of a competitive position can be analytically made but is very difficult to achieve on a practical basis.

Another factor is that the managing authority also has its own interests with regard to the future. The managing authority is after all trying to safeguard its own position for the future. In addition to weighing up conflicting government targets, the managing authorities must also therefore weigh up the government goals and their own goals, namely their own continuity. The separation of these roles will probably not provide a solution. As outlined earlier, regular implementation and preparation on the market can be analytically but not practically separated. As a result, management and guidance based on these two goals will be difficult to separate in practical terms.

A final problem is that the legitimacy of many of the management and control measures is reduced as the market draws closer. This affects above all management and control which is geared towards retaining state-controlled arrangements until the (legal) moment of transition. This was very clearly reflected in the sphere of social security in the open conflict between one of the implementing bodies (the Sfb) and the managing authorities (LISV and the Ministry) concerning its desire to carry out public activities on a commercial basis – in this case, the collection of premiums. One of the main reasons for not wanting to withdraw the collection of premiums from the private division to the public division of the holding, was that this would only be for a period of two years, after which there e would be a market and the collection activity could be returned again to the private arm. In short, the advent of the market was now so close that, according to the Sfb, there was no longer any point in supervising the state-controlled requirements so closely. The legitimacy of management and control as a means of upholding state-controlled goals therefore diminishes as the introduction of the market draws closer.

4. Future problems

In the previous two sections, we began by outlining the steps taken by providers in the field of social insurance during the pre-market phase. We then went on to detail the main characteristics of this phase. In this section, we will be looking at the consequences of the steps taken by the providers.

These consequences have not been empirically registered since there is still no market. Instead, we offer a risk analysis of what could go wrong in the light of the preparations made by the providers and the characteristics of the pre-market phase.

If the benefits of a market[10] are to be recognised, a number of conditions must be satisfied. In order to bring about more efficient and more effective 'production', there must be competition. The key aspect of competition is the very real threat that customers could switch to another provider (Bergsma, Van den Brink et al, 1999, p. 24). As a result, it is especially important that there are other providers and that a customer is given the opportunity to go over to that other provider (for a more detailed elaboration of the necessary conditions, see Bergsma, Van den Brink et al, 1999, p. 24 et seq.).

4.1 Freedom in the choice of provider

We concluded that different implementing organisations were involved in different ways in bringing about the 'inclusion' of customers in order to make it more difficult for them to switch to another provider. These strategies thus limit the customer's freedom in choosing a provider. The inclusion strategies can be applied in a pre-market because the customers in the state-controlled setting (which at that time still applies) cannot leave. The pre-market phase can in that sense be used more or less safely to develop strategies to bind future customers. Moreover, there is little the managing authorities can do to combat this, since the inclusive strategies such as 'the total package' and 'co-optation' are mainly implemented in the commercial divisions of the holding. The managing authorities have no control over these divisions.

4.2 Number of providers

Some of the identified strategies and actions could have consequences for the number of providers on the market. There are two ways in which it is being made more difficult for new providers to enter the market.

In the first place, the *collaborative partnerships* that have been concluded with other organisations are important. Implementing bodies have signed collaborative agreements with possible future competitors, such as e.g. insurers. As a result, the number of providers on the future market is limited, and potential future competitors are 'enclosed'. It can

197

also influence the future market-based approach due to the fact that large providers might arise, as a result of which newcomers will have to make major investments if they want to be players of any consequence[11].

In the second place, the *holding constructions* are also important. There are two ways in which these holding constructions can affect competition. To begin with, there is the risk that the providers in a pre-market might use public resources for investments in (future) commercial activities – for example by declaring investments which will give the provider a lead on the new market over new providers, e.g. when setting up large-scale ICT projects. Because it is difficult for the managing authority to draw a distinction between projects that are necessary to guarantee the existing quality of implementation (in a state-controlled context), and projects which are primarily intended to improve a provider's competitive position (see previous section), this could pose a greater risk for the management and control problems described above. The degree to which this distorts competition obviously depends on the question of whether new entrants are *allowed* to access the new market. If new providers can be created, then these investments will throw up barriers for them since they will be required to pay for these investments themselves.

In the second place, a holding construction can complicate the creation of competition due to the fact that it can give rise to a form of 'trial market'. In the private division of the holding, back-up activities such as IT support also take place alongside commercial activities. The public division of the holding administers these activities. This creates a so-called 'trial market'. The private elements can carry on developing undisturbed since they have a more or less fixed basis thanks to the fact that the public division is making the payments. These trial markets give rise to two risks. The existing providers obtain a lead over new providers since they have been able to continue on a trial basis undisturbed. Poor service or inadequate products do not, for example, lead to the rapid departure of the customer – in this case the implementing body – since he is part of the same holding. In addition, the private division of the holding could even benefit financially due to the fact that the rates that are charged are higher than they would be in a genuine market situation. As a result, public money is being channelled into private activities. New providers cannot benefit from public funding in such a way, as a result of which they will be forced to make bigger investments.

Rules have been drafted concerning the contracting out of activities by the implementing bodies, but these do not appear in practice to be able to prevent problems from arising. For example, according to the LISV it is unclear for many tariffs whether or not they are market-based (LISV, 2000). And even if the tariffs are market-based, there is still the problem that in a holding construction, the customer and the provider are so closely linked that the private divisions of the holding can prepare themselves almost with a minimum of effort for the forthcoming market. After all, both the customer and the provider are members of the same holding, so that an exit option is in fact not available.

5. Conclusion

The pre-market influences the ultimate structure of the market. Both for the purposes of scientific study and for the development of policy, it is important to take account of the influence exercised by the pre-market phase. The debate on the market-based approach should not therefore focus solely on the ideal-typical end situations that are anticipated. Much more attention must be given to the pre-market which will precede the market. The introduction of a market does not occur in a vacuum: it is necessary to work together with existing players who will want to secure their own position in the future market.

5.1 Rapid versus cautious introduction of the market

The main problem of the pre-market phase is that the existing players could behave in such a way that little may come of the original goals. This could argue for the shortest possible pre-market phase; a rapid introduction of the market would give existing providers little opportunity to sew up the market beforehand. This would reduce the problem of uncertainty during the pre-market phase. A major disadvantage of this solution is – certainly in view of the public importance of social insurance schemes – that the quality of implementation could be compromised. Without careful preparation of both the practical side (how do you implement social insurance schemes in a market-based context?) and the conditional side (what conditions must a market-based context satisfy?), a smooth implementation of social insurance schemes could be compromised.

Hence when transforming an existing publicly-controlled field into a field in a market-based context, there is a dilemma of rapid introduction versus cautious introduction. Rapid introduction could provide a solution to the problem of uncertainty, and also to some extent to the management and control problem. However, it also creates the risk of the structure of the new market being flawed.

5.2 Epilogue

The uncertainty felt by the providers which we studied appeared to be justified. However, political consensus now seems to have been reached on something that was previously predicted by very few players; namely, that there will be no market in the implementation of social insurance schemes in the Netherlands. The pre-market phase will ultimately not evolve into a genuine market, and the state-controlled context will be retained. Competitors will be expected to work together in a single extended public organisation. How precisely this will be structured is still unclear. Little thought has so far been given to the way in which the 5 rival providers will be merged into a single government-controlled organisation. To be continued.

Notes

[1] In this chapter, we refer to a state-controlled context and a market-based context. It is not our intention to analyse these two terms here in detail. For this chapter, we will simply apply a 'working definition'. The differences between the state-controlled context and the market-based context are primarily determined by the relationship of dependency between the provider and the other players in the field and the associated (un)certainty concerning the availability of resources (Lane, 1987). In the (ideal-typical) state-controlled context, the provider is in a situation in which one dominant player (the state or a representative of the state) manages the organisation without that organisation having to compete with other organisations for the provider's role and the for associated resources. In other words, each provider has his own area of operations. The provider in a market-based context, on the other hand, is operating in a situation in which several players (customers) are sharing resources and in which several providers are having to compete for these resources (see also in 't Veld, 1995). This competitive situation dictates the behaviour of providers.

[2] The market-based context described here has some of the characteristics of a quasi-market instead of a classical market, with the main quasi-market characteristic being the use of intermediary organisations (Bartlett and Le Grand, 1993), i.e. organisations that make purchases for groups of customers. However, quasi-markets are also based on the premise that competition is an important, if not the most important driver.

[3] Clearly the state continues to have responsibilities in a commercial market, even if it is only to guarantee the upholding of e.g. contracts. This role is far more limited than it is in a state-controlled environment, however.

[4] Both delimitations are in many cases vague. When, for example, can we speak of a serious discussion about a market-based context and when does the market proper 'begin'?

[5] Parts of the following sections are based on 'Op weg naar concurrentie in de uitvoering' Towards competition in implementation, Bergsma, Van den Brink, Burger and Cordia, Ctsv (1999).

[6] Many of these strategies have also been in other fields like public housing or hospital care (Brandsen, van den Brink and Putters, 1999).

[7] Or vice versa the competitive provider can decide to adjust his own administration to that of the employer, but even then this pushes up the costs of a transfer (and the higher the transfer costs, the less likely a transfer is made).

[8] The definition used here appears to relate to *state* management and control. Over the past 10 years, the government has decided to change the way it manages social security schemes, and to reduce its management activities, for example by only drafting preconditions and subsequently 'allowing the market to get on with its work'. Management and control activities must then to some extent be left to the invisible hand of Adam Smith; this 'management and control by the market' however is of an entirely different order to that described in this chapter.

[9] Social Insurance Schemes Organisation Act 97, Articles 38i.

[10] This also applies to a quasi-market which will probably occur in this field (see note 5).

[11] Although newcomers can also exploit a niche in the market.

References

Bartlett, W. and LeGrand, J. 'Theory of quasi-markets' in LeGrand, J. and Bartlett, W. (ed.) *Quasimarkets and social policy*, pp. 13-34, London, 1993.

Bergsma, E.N., van den Brink, J.C., Burger, J.C. and Cordia, L.A.J. (Ctsv) *'Op weg naar concurrentie in de uitvoering'*, Ctsv, Zoetermeer, The Netherlands, 1999.

Braam, A. van *'leerboek bestuurskunde'*, Muiderberg, 1987.

Brandsen, T., van den Brink, J.C. and Putters, K. 'De klant beklemd: concurrentie in de uitvoering van sociaal beleid' in *beleidswetenschap*, vol. 14, nr. 1, pp. 52-71, 2000.

DiMaggio, P.J. and Powell, W.W. 'The iron cage revisited: Institutional isomorphism and collective rationality in organization fields' in *The new institutionalism in organizational analysis* ed. Powell, W.W. and DiMaggio, P.J. (ed.), University of Chicago Press, Chicago/London, 1991.

Lane, J.E. 'Public and private leadership' in Kooiman, J. en Eliassen, K.A. *Managing public organizations; lessons from contemporary European experience*, Sage, Beverly Hills, 1987.

LISV, LISV informatie, vol. 2, nr. 3, p. 13, Amstelveen, The Netherlands, 2000.

Selznick, P. *'TVA and the Grass Roots'*, New York, 1966.

Veld, R.J. in 't *Spelen met vuur, over hybride organisaties*', VUGA, Den Haag, 1995.

Vrij Nederland 'de klamme deken moet eraf, chaos in uitkeringsland', pp. 23-25, 29 January 2000.

3.2 Public programs create private incentives and disincentives toward work

Barbara L. Wolfe[1]

Abstract

The Personal Responsibility and Work Opportunity Reconciliation Act of 1996 changed the U.S. welfare system dramatically. Its primary goal was to reduce dependency by moving most of those receiving cash welfare into the work force. One tool to accomplish this objective was a change in the incentives facing actual and potential recipients. States were granted flexibility in how to accomplish this objective. This chapter evaluates the program in one state, Wisconsin, in terms of efficiency and equity. It looks briefly at resulting labor force participation and incomes of those most directly affected by welfare reforms. The analysis highlights the difficulty of simultaneously providing incentives to work and incentives to increase individuals' labor market productivity while maintaining a minimal safety net and avoiding high marginal rates of taxation. The need to coordinate the benefit and withdrawal schedule of programs designed to help this population flows from the analysis.

The welfare system in the United States changed dramatically in 1996 with passage of the Personal Responsibility and Work Opportunity Reconciliation Act. The primary goal of the reform enacted then was to reduce dependency on the system by moving those on the rolls into the work force[2]. The reform eliminated the cash assistance component of the welfare system, Aid to Families with Dependent Children (AFDC), and expanded the employee-based subsidy for work. It also encouraged states to establish programs providing assistance to enable parents to work. As a result, the incentives facing low-skilled individuals have been altered. This chapter evaluates the resulting efficiency and equity consequences for welfare recipients and those who would have been recipients. It then looks briefly at the labor force participation and incomes of those directly affected by the welfare reform and concludes by identifying a few programs that states and perhaps other countries may wish to consider in rethinking their social welfare programs. The emphasis is on programs that attempt to defy the traditional equity-efficiency trade-off.

To evaluate the success of welfare reform in changing incentives toward work, I first discuss the incentives of the "old" system, described in detail in Appendix a. I then compare these incentives to those of the new system; because each state has its own version of the program, Temporary Assistance for Needy Families (TANF), I use one state, Wisconsin. This state is selected as it is the state that many see as a model for welfare reform in the United States. Whether the new programs can avoid a "poverty trap," the point at which marginal tax rates are so high that they discourage work effort, is a focus of the discussion.

1. The old system

The old welfare system was a cash assistance program primarily for single parents with dependent children, and benefits were based on family size.[3] Figure 3.2.1 provides an illustration for a typical state.[4] A 45-degree line is used to compare family income which is measured on the vertical axis to earnings which are measured on the horizontal axis, for a family consisting of a single parent and two children, one of whom is assumed to be younger than school age and the other to be of school age (6 or older). All dollar values are inflated to 1999 dollars; the parameters are for the system in place in 1996. The lowest line, showing cash benefits (AFDC) plus earnings (squares), demonstrates how income changes as earnings increase. (If income exactly mirrored earnings, all points on the graph would be on the 45-degree line.) In this typical state, a three-person family on AFDC and without any earnings would receive approximately $5,400 a year. (Note that larger families would get more, because cash benefits were conditional on family size.) As a single parent started to work, she could keep the first $30 of earnings per month and then her AFDC grant was reduced by two-thirds (67 cents) for every dollar, so that she soon faced a marginal tax rate of more than 69 percent, since the payroll tax also reduced take-home pay[5]. Soon, however, that rate rises to 93 percent, meaning that she loses nearly a dollar in her grant for each dollar earned. Beyond about $8,500, income depends solely on earnings, because she is no longer eligible for cash benefits.

The typical welfare family would be eligible for other non-cash benefits, including Food Stamps (vouchers to buy food, which depend on income and family size); public health insurance (Medicaid) for all members of the family, another categorical program; and a housing benefit (available to about 30 percent of this population)[6].

This combination of programs (excluding the Earned Income Tax Credit, discussed below, and housing assistance) is captured by the middle line of Figure 3.2.1 (circles), showing the result of a set of programs that were income-conditioned[7]. As a woman begins to work, she at first faces a marginal tax rate of about 63 percent (which includes the payroll tax), but this quickly increases to more than 100 percent as benefits are reduced. As her earnings increase and the AFDC benefit is reduced, she soon loses eligibility for Medicaid[8]; then, as her earnings increase further, her older child also loses Medicaid coverage and, as family income reaches the poverty line, Food Stamps are reduced substantially. By the time the woman's earnings reach $15,000 she faces a marginal tax rate of more than 125 percent, as she begins to pay federal income taxes, loses eligibility for Food Stamps, and the youngest child loses Medicaid coverage. This line portrays the poverty trap-as a woman earns more, her family income (including the value of benefits in kind) increases very gradually, if at all[9]. Once all benefits have been eliminated and the woman's earnings are at about 160 percent of the poverty line, she faces a much lower marginal tax rate, 27 percent.

An exception to this set of incentives, one which increases the gain to work, is the Earned Income Tax Credit (EITC)[10]. This credit is paid only to those with children and with earnings. The top line of Figure 3.2.1 illustrates the effect of including the EITC as earnings increase. Over much of the range the EITC lowers the marginal tax rates, but as the EITC is reduced, marginal tax rates increase. As of 1996, as a result of changes passed in 1993, the EITC rewarded earnings of individuals with two or more dependent children at a 40 percent rate, reaching a maximum of $3,556 ($3,816 in 1999 dollars) when a family with two or more children received wages of $8,890, then remained flat until earnings reached $11,610, just below the poverty line. After this the EITC was "clawed back" at a rate of about 21 percent, and was fully phased out at earnings of

205

$28,490[11]. (Appendix Figures 3.2.A1 and 3.2.A2 show the parameters of the EITC in 1993 and 1999.) The top line of Figure 3.2.1 shows the budget constraint of an AFDC recipient with two children including the EITC, as of 1996.[12] The EITC provided a substantial increase in income among low-earning families with children. It made work pay, over a limited range.

Even with the EITC, this recipient family faced substantial marginal tax rates as earnings increased. After an initial range in which the marginal tax rate was a relatively low 24 percent, the rate increased to nearly 100 percent as the mother lost Medicaid coverage. All three points (see Figure 3.2.1) at which eligibility for Medicaid is lost have extremely high rates[13]. And just beyond the poverty line (again see Figure 3.2.1), the marginal tax rates facing this family are increased as the EITC is clawed back, in addition to a reduction in Food Stamps and loss of Medicaid for the youngest child. It is not difficult to see why the program was disliked. It provided clear incentives to forgo work; its benefits were primarily paid to single parents and were thought to increase family break-up and illegitimacy. The program also did not eliminate poverty.

2. The new system

Recognition of these negative incentives, combined with continued poverty, led to frustration and attempts to modify the system. Substantial changes resulted from the Family Support Act of 1988, which provided an entitlement to child care subsidies for AFDC recipients who entered the work force, required about 10 percent of recipients to enter a program of work or training, and offered a one-year extension of Medicaid (health insurance) for those who left AFDC because of increased earnings. In subsequent years states requested waivers from the federal government to experiment with alternative policies[14], and various research groups evaluated these demonstrations. Wisconsin made significant changes under its waivers, and ultimately eliminated AFDC altogether. In early 1996 the state set up programs in a number of counties that attempted to move welfare recipients into employment and divert new applicants directly to work[15]. Under the state's current TANF program, Wisconsin Works (W-2), cash assistance is eliminated and all who receive assistance must work.

The general emphasis of the 1996 federal reform legislation is on getting recipients and would-be recipients into the work force. The message is that individuals must ultimately be self-reliant. The 1996 federal law:

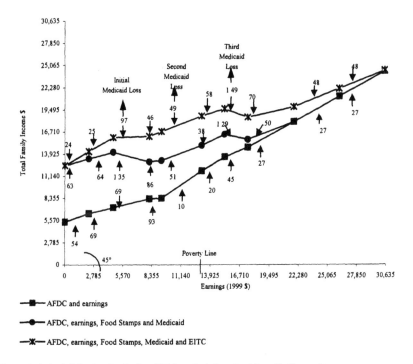

Figure 3.2.1   Welfare, earnings, and income of a single parent with two children: AFDC 1996

- ended entitlement to AFDC.
- allowed each state to determine how it would treat its low-income population, subject to certain constraints. Funding was through block grants, whose amounts were based on historical expenditures.

- established an expectation that most heads of families were to work within two years.
- established a federal five-year limit for the receipt of cash assistance; states were permitted to impose shorter time limits[16].
- prohibited states from providing cash assistance to unmarried teens (under age 18) unless the mother stayed in school and lived with an adult.
- required mothers of children older than 12 months to work, while allowing states to set stricter requirements.
- prohibited the use of federal funds for assistance to immigrants, and set tighter eligibility requirements for the program for disabled individuals (SSI).
- set limits on counting participation in vocational education as meeting work requirements.

Over time, states are required to meet certain reductions in their caseloads. Within these limits, states are given a great deal of flexibility.

Associated with, but not a direct part of, the welfare policy change was the expansion of the EITC, especially for families with two or more children, and an increase in the minimum wage. A comparison of the generosity of minimum wages and the EITC is presented in Table 3.2.1 The last row of the table sums up the potential impact of these changes for a three-person family headed by a single parent. If the parent worked full-time, full-year at a minimum-wage job, paid payroll taxes, and received the EITC, her income from these sources would have increased from 78 percent to 96 percent of the three-person poverty line. These changes are consistent with the goals of welfare reform and should work to further the work-not-welfare policy.

Did the changes substantially alter incentives? Does work *pay* under the new system? Figure 3.2.2 provides a picture of the effects of these changes. Dollars are in 1999 values.

3. The Wisconsin system

We focus on a state that offers no cash benefits unless an individual works, Wisconsin. Wisconsin Works, or W-2, requires *all recipients* of welfare assistance to engage in work or a work-like activity. In order to do so, the state developed a self-sufficiency ladder, which establishes four levels of work or work-related activity. In essence the ladder is set up to guarantee a work opportunity. The highest level is unsubsidized employment, in which the recipient works in the private sector and receives a market wage greater than or equal to the minimum wage, plus the federal and state EITC and Food Stamps, as long as the parent is income- and asset-eligible[17]. The next level is Trial Jobs, in which the state pays a subsidy to employers to hire a TANF participant and the individual receives at least the minimum wage, plus the federal and state EITC and Food Stamps. Forty hours of work per week are required. The third tier is Community Service Jobs, for those not yet able to hold a private sector job. These individuals are required to work 30 hours per week and may obtain training or work an additional 10 hours per week. In this tier the individual is not eligible for the EITC, because she receives a grant rather than earnings, but is eligible for Food Stamps. Finally, for those least able to work, the bottom tier is W-2 Transitions, which requires 28 hours per week of productive activity and 12 hours of training. This also involves a grant, permitting receipt of Food Stamps but not the EITC. Activities in this tier may include care of a disabled child or parent. Thus *all* W-2 participants are required to work, and Tiers 3 and 4 ensure that there is a "job" for everyone. Trial jobs and subsidized jobs are for limited periods of time and viewed as transitional although they can be renewed. Mothers of newborn infants are exempt from these work requirements until the infant is 12 weeks old. Everyone in W-2 has an opportunity for gainful employment and nearly everyone faces pressure to work. Those who do not fully participate are sanctioned at a rate of $5.15 per hour (the minimum wage) of missed required activity. Beyond wages, EITC, and Food Stamps, the state offers assistance in the form of subsidized health insurance to families with incomes below 185 percent of the poverty line, child care assistance, and transportation assistance. There is an attempt to provide tailor-made management in the form of job center assistance that helps co-ordinate benefits, obtain child support from absentee parents, and obtain health insurance, and that offers relevant referrals and provides short-term loans.

Figure 3.2.2 illustrates the incentives of the Wisconsin program for an individual starting in Tier 3, Community Service Jobs. This job provides the mother and her family with $8,076 per year in cash income. The line with squares shows what would happen if she moved up to Tier 2 and received the minimum wage. Her cash income would increase only modestly if she worked 20 hours per week – to $9,345, or by 15.8 percent.

Table 3.2.1   Potential impact of raising the minimum wage and EITC on income and poverty of three-person, single-parent families (1999 dollars)

	1993	1997	1999
Minimum wage	$4.89	$5.33	$5.15
Maximum EITC, two-child family	$1,738	$3,786	$3,816
Minimum wage earnings, FTFY	$9,780	$10,660	$10,300
Minimum wage + EITC	$11,518	$14,446	$14,116
Minimum wage + EITC payroll tax	$10,777	$13,636	$13,328
Ratio to three-person poverty line	0.776	0.98	0.96

This woman and her family are able to keep only 24 cents of every dollar earned in Tier 2; or, in other words, the woman faces a marginal tax rate of 76 percent due to the loss of her TANF grant. Then, as she completely moves out of Tier 3 and loses her Tier 3 cash grant, and works 35 hours per week at $5.15, her income declines to $9.300; she faces a marginal tax rate of more than 100 percent! (Also see column 2 of Table 3.2.2.) However, she would receive the EITC, so her income would increase more dramatically. The top line shows her full income as she moves from Tier 3 to Tier 2 and then Tier 1 (see discussion below). The starred line shows what happens to the woman's family income once taxes are imposed. These taxes include payroll taxes, which begin with the first dollar earned, as well as state and local and federal income taxes[18]. Federal income taxes begin at about the federal poverty line for this family of three. The imposition of these taxes leaves the family with less income and imposes even higher marginal tax rates. As the woman shifts from Tier 3 to Tier 2 she first faces a marginal tax rate of 88 percent followed by a marginal tax rate of 113 percent (or a decline in family income of 13

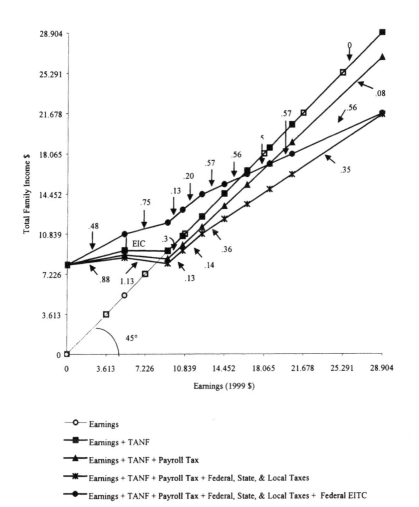

Legend:
- —○— Earnings
- —■— Earnings + TANF
- —▲— Earnings + TANF + Payroll Tax
- —✳— Earnings + TANF + Payroll Tax + Federal, State, & Local Taxes
- —●— Earnings + TANF + Payroll Tax + Federal, State, & Local Taxes + Federal EITC

Figure 3.2.2   **Welfare, earnings, taxes, and EITC of a single parent (for a woman who is initially in Tier 3 with a Community Service Job) with two children: TANF (W-2) in Wisconsin, 1999 renewed; mothers of new-born infants are exempt from these work requirements until the infant is 12 weeks old**

211

percent as she increases her work effort from 20 hours per week to 35 hours per week). Beyond this point (when she no longer receives any TANF cash grant) she faces much lower marginal tax rates of 13-14 per cent up to a full-time job at $6.00 per hour and then a marginal rate of 36 per cent once federal income taxes are imposed. (See column 3 of Table 3.2.2.)

The earned income tax credit is designed to encourage work and it does clearly decrease the marginal tax rates of low wage earners. The line with circles shows how the work incentives change with the introduction of the EITC. With the receipt of EITC, a program that the woman would be eligible for as she shifts from Tier 3 to Tier 2, the marginal tax rate she faces falls from 88 to 48 percent as she begins to work in Tier 2, then as she increases her work effort in Tier 2 (and moves to Tier 1) she faces a marginal rate of 75 percent, still very high but far below the 113 percent rate without the EITC. At this point working 40 hours per week at the minimum wage, she maintains the maximum level of the EITC and her marginal tax rate is at 13 percent. However, beyond this level of earnings, the EITC begins to be clawed back and hence the marginal tax rates she faces are increased. Her family income remains higher than without the EITC through out the range of earnings shown, which goes up to $14 per hour full time. At this point the EITC for which she is eligible is only $96. This figure then captures the role of an earnings subsidy program: at very low levels of earnings, the subsidy makes work pay far better than without the EITC. However, as a targeted program, it is also clawed back and as it is clawed back, it increases family income at a declining rate and raises marginal tax rates. So, while the EITC encourages work among very low earners, it may well discourage work as it is clawed back. (See column 4 of Table 3.2.2 for more detail on the marginal tax rates[19].)

Figure 3.2.3 shows the impact of benefits in kind and the cost of work for this mother of two children. Again we compare income on the vertical axis with earnings on the horizontal. The first program considered is Food Stamps. The value of Food Stamps that a family receives is based on family size and income. However source of income matters as earnings are treated more generously than other sources of income, again in an attempt to encourage work[20]. The addition of Food Stamps adds to the families' economic resources and we include the value of Food Stamps at its cash value. The maximum amount of Food Stamps this family is eligible for is $3480 when they are only receiving the grant from Tier 3. This amount steadily declines although slowly so that adding in the value of Food Stamps adds to the marginal tax rate the family faces nearly across all of the categories we model. (See the line with triangles. See also column 6 of Table 3.2.2.)

If this mother with a child under two and an 11-year-old is to work, she requires child care. The TANF program in most states, including Wisconsin, subsidies child care but the subsidy is income conditioned. We take child care into account by assuming that the state subsidy is accepted by all eligible families and that when the family is no longer eligible, it will pay the state average cost for one preschool-age child and one school-age child, requiring only after school and vacation child care. Among families

Table 3.2.2   Wisconsin, marginal tax effects at various income levels

	Marginal Tax Rates on Income from			
	(1)	(2)	(3)	(4)
Earnings	TANF and earnings	TANF, earnings, and payroll taxes	TANF, earnings, payroll, and income taxes	TANF, earnings, federal EIC, and taxes
0	—	—	—	—
5,316	0.76	(+) 0.84	(+) 0.88	(-) 0.48
9,300	1.01	(+) 1.09	(+) 1.13	(-) 0.75
10,632	nd	(+) 0.08	(+) 0.13	(nd) 0.13
12,384	nd	(+) 0.08	(+) 0.14	(+) 0.20
14,448	nd	(+) 0.08	(+) 0.36	(+) 0.57
16,512	nd	(+) 0.08	(+) 0.35	(+) 0.56
18,576	nd	(+) 0.08	(+) 0.35	(+) 0.56
20,640	nd	(+) 0.08	(+) 0.36	(+) 0.57
28,896	nd	(+) 0.08	(+) 0.35	(+) 0.56

Note: Sign in parenthesis refers to the direction of change of the marginal tax rate as we move across each row and add each additional component of tax or benefit. nd = no difference

ith an infant the cost of care is far greater, so that losing the state subsidy ould raise the marginal tax rate considerably. For example, among

213

Wisconsin low-income families with a child under age 2 receiving subsidies, the monthly cost of child care in spring 1999 was about $535. Families receiving state subsidies paid $42 on average, and the state paid $494. Families with incomes below 165 percent of the poverty line are eligible for the subsidy, and eligibility can continue up to 200 percent of the poverty line. The maximum required co-payment is limited to 16 percent of gross income under the subsidy program. Loss of the subsidy would require this family to pay an annual amount for infant care equal to nearly 50 percent of the three-person poverty line.[21] In Figure 3.2.3 we subtract the cost of required child care (see the line with diamonds).

The mother does not pay any child care while earning the minimum wage but then as her wage goes up, she begins to pay a share.

Table 3.2.2   **Wisconsin, marginal tax effects at various income levels (continued)**

(5)	(6)	(7)	(8)	(9)
TANF, earnings, federal and state EIC, and taxes	TANF, earnings, federal and state EIC, food stamps, and taxes	TANF, earnings, federal and state EIC, food stamps, childcare, and taxes	TANF, earnings, federal and state EIC, food stamps, childcare, homestead, and taxes	TANF, earnings, federal and state EIC, food stamps, childcare, homestead, MC, and taxes
—	—	—	—	—
(-) 0.43	(+) 0.48	(nd) 0 48	(-) 0.39	(nd) 0.39
(-) 0.69	(nd) 0.69	(nd) 0.69	(-) 0.59	(nd) 0.59
(nd) 0.13	(+) 0.36	(+) 0.52	(+) 0.62	(nd) 0.62
(nd) 0.20	(+) 0.45	(+) 0.60	(+) 0.70	(nd) 0.70
(+) 0.60	(+) 0.83	(+) 0.98	(+) 1.09	(nd) 1.09
(+) 0.59	(+) 0.83	(+) 0.96	(+) 1.06	(nd) 1.06
(+) 0 59	(+) 0 82	(+) 1.25	(+) 1.31	(nd) 1.31
(+) 0.60	(+) 0.84	(-) 0.69	(nd) 0 69	(nd) 0.69
(+) 0.59	(+) 0.64	(+) 1.07	(nd) 1.07	(+) 1.16

By the time her earnings are at $28,800, she is paying $5,150 per year if she uses the licensed care for which she is subsidized at lower earnings. Hence subtracting the required cost of child care from her income increases the marginal tax rate she faces beginning at about $10,000 of earnings. (See also column 7, Table 3.2.2). Wisconsin has a program to help lower income households with housing. It is in the form of a Homestead credit[22], which is a refundable credit that works through the state income tax. A household income must have been less than $20,290 as of 1999 in order for the household to be eligible for the credit. Since the credit is targeted on those with low income, it both adds to resources and to incentives to work at very low levels of income but then as with all other income conditioned programs, once the credit is clawed back, incentives to work harder are reduced by the increase in marginal tax rates over the interval of about $9,000 to $19,000. (See column 8 of Table 3.2.2.)

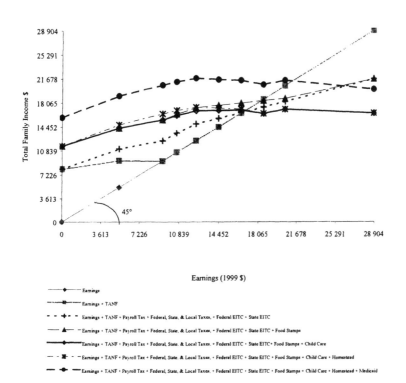

Figure 3.2.3   **Welfare, earnings, taxes, EITC, Food Stamps, child care, homestead, and Medicaid of a single parent (for a woman is initially in Tier 3 with a Community Service Job) with two children: TANF (W-2) in Wisconsin, 1999**

Finally we add the value of medical assistance to the resources of this three-person family. We do so using the average value of medical services received in Wisconsin for non-aged, non-elderly adults and two times the average value of non-disabled children. Wisconsin is unusually generous in terms of medical assistance, as it is the only state that offers publicly subsidized coverage to adults[23]. Adding in the cash value of the average amount of care increases family income. Since in this state, medical assistance is continued up to 185 percent of the poverty line, only the incentives of the highest earners included in our analysis are negatively affected. For them, the required contribution for coverage adds to the already very high rates facing this group as their earnings increase from $10 to $14 per hour. (See column 9 of Table 3.2.2.)

Clearly, the system has a "poverty trap," though it does not fully hit until earnings are close to the poverty line. The trap is postponed, but not eliminated. The inclusion of child care costs accentuates the poverty trap and increases the trap as the subsidy is significantly withdrawn at an income about 165 percent of the poverty line.

3.1 Time limits

What happens if an individual in Wisconsin reaches the time limit and is no longer eligible for jobs in Tiers 3 or 4? This can be viewed as the long-run situation facing current recipients in Wisconsin. The combination of TANF grants and earnings, would begin at zero for those without earnings. Food Stamps, child care subsidies, and Medicaid would continue. But the important points here are (1) that it is far easier to set up a program with very low marginal tax rates if there are no (or very low) cash grants, and (2) that eventually the marginal tax rates become very high and create a "poverty trap". Time limits increase the pro-work incentives of the EITC, as there is no reduction of an income-conditional cash grant. Rather, the full impact of the EITC for an individual is that a head of family would face a negative marginal tax rate as she begins to work. The -28 percent means that for every dollar the woman earns, her family income increases by $1.28. Beyond this initial level, the rate she faces remains negative at 7–8 percent up to an earnings level of about $9,300. After this, her marginal tax rate increases so that by the time her earnings reach about $12,500, or about $6.00 per hour working full-time, full-year, she faces very high rates. This illustrates the "iron law": A program that provides targeted cash benefits

216

must reduce these benefits as income rises, leading to high marginal tax rates, which discourage work effort.

Thus we see that a system of multiple assistance programs targeted on the poor reduces the incentive to work longer hours. This is so even in the face of an expanded EITC, which is specifically designed to make work pay, is targeted on families with children, and has a rather low claw-back rate of 21 percent that begins at an hourly wage rate of about $6.23 (full-time, full-year) and continues to an hourly rate of $15.29 (full-time, full-year), or about 220 percent of the poverty line for a three-person family[24]. (See Figure 3.2.A2 for the exact 1999 parameters of the EITC program.) More coordination of benefits might reduce the intensity of the poverty trap, but only more universal benefits are likely to significantly reduce the very high marginal tax rates facing the poor. It is possible to reduce these very high rates if we were to modify some of the benefit schemes of TANF. For example, a state could provide health insurance, either on a universal basis, by subsidizing it for all persons, or by withdrawing the subsidy after withdrawal of the EITC. The latter might be accomplished using a tax-refundable credit. Figure 3.2.A3 show how incentives would change in Wisconsin if all persons (at least up to earnings of $28,000) were provided with health care insurance coverage without having to pay a premium or additional taxes. (Note that in most states adults are not eligible for subsidized coverage and so the work disincentives are fare stronger. See Wolfe, 2000, and Table 3.2.3 below which shows eligibility for a selected set of states.) The work disincentives resulting from high marginal tax rates are clearly reduced and, while high rates remain, they are not even close to the much higher rates that result from income-conditioned medical care. A similar result could be achieved if all individuals and their families were provided health insurance at their place of employment with little or no cost-sharing required.[25] The children's health insurance programs (CHIP) change the income level at which children lose eligibility for subsidized insurance. CHIP does not change eligibility for adults.

3.2 Child care

One of the most difficult issues in moving families off welfare and into work concerns child care. Child care is expensive and, unless subsidized, greatly reduces the take-home income of poor single-parent families, potentially making them worse off financially than if they did not work at all. In the figure above, the starred line represents income minus child care

217

costs, after taking account of state subsidies to offset those costs[26]. This is for a family with one pre-school-age child and one school-age child. Without child care subsidies the families would gain little from working[27]. Under child care subsidy programs, most families must pay a share of the cost, and the subsidy is income-conditioned. This means that child care adds to already high marginal tax rates. Those families with younger children (infants) are likely to face even higher marginal tax rates as the higher subsidies are withdrawn. Requiring labor market participation of single parents with infants, when the costs of such care are equal to about two-thirds of a full-year, full-time job, raises questions of efficiency and further complicates the design of work incentives for the low-income population.

Recent evidence suggests that the picture presented in the diagrams may be more positive than is actually the case for many of the families eligible for assistance. According to an October 1999 news release by the U.S. Department of Health and Human Services, only 10 percent of children eligible for federal child care assistance in 1998 received it. The percentage ranged from a low of 4 percent in Mississippi to a high of 24 percent in West Virginia. Most states set limits below the federal maximums. The report found that "There were approximately 10 million children eligible under state-set limits in 1998, of whom only 15 percent were served. At the federal maximum limit, 27 states are serving less than 10 percent of eligible children, with the remaining states serving between 10 and 25 percent" (see http://www.acf.dhhs. gov/news/cc98.htm).

4. Early results under the new system

To learn how recipients are faring under this new system, the traditional evaluation approach would be to use a national data set, such as the Current Population Survey or the Survey of Income and Program Participation, to model the parameters of the state rules in which the family resides and analyze whether these parameters influence outcomes. Unfortunately, the TANF programs are so new that such work is in the early stages[28]. We instead use state administrative data, which have the virtue of being more rapidly accessible and avoiding certain selection problems in data reporting.

• Receipt of cash assistance is down dramatically. Figure 3.2.4 provides an overview of the AFDC/TANF caseloads over the period since 1987, using 1987 caseloads as the basis of the normalization. The caseload decreased dramatically after 1996, when the federal welfare reform was passed[29]. Wisconsin's reforms prior to the federal legislation appear to be reflected in the earlier and more dramatic decrease in that state.

- State studies of former AFDC/TANF recipients ("leavers" studies)suggest that 55–65 percent of former recipients have jobs about a year after exiting from AFDC/TANF; 35–40 percent are working full-time; perhaps 85 percent held a paying job at some time during the first year, but about a quarter returned to AFDC/TANF cash assistance within the first year[30].
- Among those who are working, average quarterly earnings are about $2,500, and earnings drift up at about 8–10 percent a year for those who remain employed. This is consistent with the poverty trap noted above. However, this average masks large differences in quarterly earnings. For example, the most common industries of employment among former welfare recipients in Wisconsin are retail trade, health services, restaurants, and temporary agencies.

Table 3.2.3   Medicaid eligibility levels and CHIP coverage in selected states, 1999

State	Medicaid Eligibility (pre-CHIP)				CHIP Coverage by Age			
	0–1	1–6	6–14	14–18	0–1	1–6	6–14	15–18
Pennsylvania[a]	185%	133%	100%	39%	235%	235%	235%	235%
Indiana[b]	185%	133%	100%	100%		150%	150%	150%
California[c]	200%	133%	100%	85%	250%	200%	200%	200%
Wisconsin[d]	185%	185%	100%		185%	185%	185%	185%

Notes:

[a]Families with incomes between 200 and 235 percent of the poverty line pay half the cost of premium for children.

[b]No premium imposed currently, but that will change if proposed expansion is approved.

[c]Ages 0–1: premiums 2% of family income; ages 1–19: 100–150% of poverty line, $7/month for one child, $14/month for two children; 150–200% of poverty line, $9/month for one child, $18/month for two children. Copayments: $5 for most services with a $250 annual cap.

[d]Parents of children covered by CHIP also covered; families can remain in program until incomes reach 200% of poverty line, at 150%+ of poverty line, premiums 3–3.5% of family income.

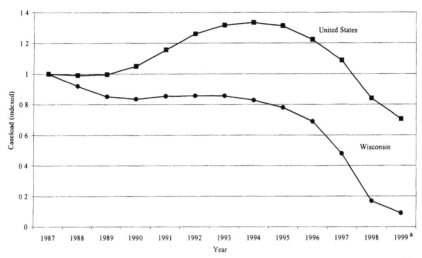

Notes: Wisconsin data: calendar year monthly average. Wisconsin Department of Workforce Development, Economic Support Division; U S
data: federal fiscal year monthly average: Health and Human Services, Administration for Children and Families
a March 1999 data

**Figure 3.2.4   AFDC/TANF caseloads, 1987-1999, as a multiple of the
1987**

- According to Unemployment Insurance (UI) records, average first-quarter earnings in these sectors were, respectively, $1,960, $2,947, $1,630, and $1,782 (Cancian, Kaplan, and Meyer, 1999). Women who began employment in temporary agencies tended to move to higher-paying jobs, especially among those with limited education and little or no prior work experience.
- The majority of former recipients still have at least one family member covered by Medicaid. This program provides either full coverage or no coverage. In contrast, fewer than half of these families receive Food Stamps, a program whose benefit is reduced as family income increases. Families that are eligible may only be eligible for small amounts, and requirements for recertification of eligibility at frequent intervals may deter claiming the benefit[31].
- In terms of income, early evidence suggests that about 60 percent of former recipients have lower total income than they did while receiving AFDC/TANF. This analysis uses the combination of AFDC/TANF, the purchase value of Food Stamps, and the EITC with

221

an adjustment for taxes. Perhaps 75 percent of these families live below the poverty line in their first year off of welfare. Poverty is higher among larger families, who are more likely to have experienced an income loss, because the cash assistance and Food Stamps they received under AFDC/TANF are conditioned on family size, while earnings are not[32].

In most states cash benefit levels have been reduced, and those remaining on the rolls have less income than prior to reform. Some studies suggest that recipients continuing to receive aid are less able to work than are those who left the rolls in terms of education, mental health, a history of abuse, and the presence of disabled children[33].

TANF programs can be expensive. Their costs include direct benefit payments, administrative costs, and costs of case management. A recent estimate in Wisconsin of the cost per family receiving benefits, excluding case management, was $13,500 (verbal communication, John Tuohy, Wisconsin Workforce Development). This reflects high administrative costs in areas with few recipients, and also reflects the high costs of a program designed to bring individuals who have limited if any job market experience into the work force.

An additional issue concerns spillover to others in the labor market; that is, has the rise in labor force participation of former and potential welfare recipients had negative consequences on other low-skilled workers? Figure 3.2.5 indicates that it has not, owing to the creation of jobs, low unemployment rates, and increases in earnings among those in the lowest decile.

What then can be concluded from a review of the incentives of the new system and preliminary evidence concerning the new system? The current U.S. programs, as designed by states and constrained by the federal government, have not been successful in combining strong incentives to work with a safety net that can eliminate extreme poverty and provide an adequate income for those who will never succeed in the labor market. Federal law does permit states to allow up to 20 percent of their base-year caseload to waive many work requirements. One difficulty facing states is how to distinguish those who truly cannot succeed in the labor market from those who prefer not to work or to work only limited hours. States have not found a way to discourage cash assistance while encouraging full use of such in-kind benefits as Food Stamps. By deciding not to adopt a universal health insurance system, the United States lessened the incentives to work under TANF. The need to reduce health insurance benefits as income rises adds to high marginal tax rates. The decision to exempt from work requirements mothers who have children less than 12 months old greatly increases the public cost of the 'welfare' system and adds to the difficulty of designing a system in which it pays to work[34]. Is it likely that a TANF recipient will have earnings over the long run that keep her in the area of high marginal tax rates? Evidence from multiple sources all suggests yes. Table 3.2.4 indicates that white non-Hispanic and black non-Hispanic women aged 18–24 who had 9–12 years of education and who worked full-time, full-year had earnings of just under $12,000 in 1989. These earnings increased to only just over $14,000 among those aged 30–34. Women with a high school degree fared somewhat better: among white women aged 30–34, mean earnings were nearly $18,000. The full-time, full-year earnings of black women with a high school education were $16,269. In 1998 dollars, this is $23,443 among white women aged 30–34, but only $21,385 among their black counterparts, $19,742 among those aged 25–29. For those with 9–12 years of education, average earnings in 1998 dollars would be $18,986 among white women aged 30–34. Women working fewer hours have far lower average incomes, as can be seen in the table; these are the majority of working women with 9–12 years of education.

Median usual weekly earnings of full-time wage and salary workers for the third quarter of 1999, as reported by the Bureau of Labor Statistics (BLS), are $287 per week, or about $14,500 per year, for women aged 25 and over with less than a high school diploma, and $409 per week, or about $20,000 per year, for women of the same age group who are high school graduates (http://stats.bls.gov/news.release/wkyeng.t04.htm). The BLS also has reported annual growth rates in real hourly earnings over the years 1978–1995 among women aged 31–38 in 1998. For those lacking a high school diploma, these rates were 2.9 percent at ages 23–27 and 0.9 percent at ages 28–32. For women with a high school diploma, the rates were 3.3 and 2.9 percent, respectively (http://stats.bls.gov/news.release/nlsoy.t05.html).

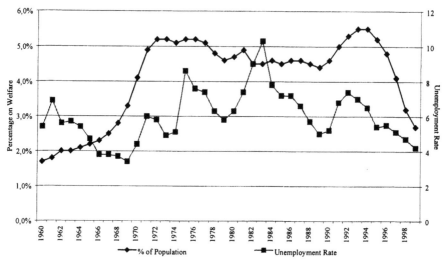

Source U S Department of Health and Human Services, January 1999 <http://www acf DHHS gov/news/stats/6090_ch2 htm> and U S Department of Labor, 1999, Labor Force Statistics from the Current Population Survey <http://stats bls gov/cpset bs htm>

Figure 3.2.5   **Percentage of the U.S. population on welfare and unemployment rate since 1960**

We conclude that the majority of single women with children can expect to continue to face high marginal tax rates even when they work full-time, full-year and increase their labor market experience. To avoid high marginal tax rates, they must earn more than $10 per hour, work full-time, full-year and receive medical insurance coverage from their employer at little or no cost to themselves. When children requiring child care are present, most women need a wage rate of at least $15 per hour and must work full-time, full-year to avoid these rates. The incentives now are clearly to work, but working more or harder does not seem to pay.

Table 3.2.4   Selected labor force and earnings profiles of white and black women, 1989

	9 to 12 Years of Education		High School Graduate[a]	
	White Non-Hispanic Women	Black Non-Hispanic Women	White Non-Hispanic Women	Black Non-Hispanic Women
Ages 18-24				
% of those who worked < FTFY[b]	80%	79%	57%	65%
Average annual earnings in $	3,848	3,784	5,725	5,310
If work FTFY[b] in $	11,974	12,099	13,272	12,837
Average hourly wage in $	5.62	5.68	6.26	6.07
Ages 25-29				
% of those who worked less < FTFY[b]	56%	58%	42%	47%
Average annual earnings in $	6,690	6,166	8,240	7,906
If work FTFY[b] in $	14,331	13,565	16,476	15,019
Average hourly wage in $	6.64	6.32	7.68	7.08
Ages 30-34				
% of those who worked less < FTFY[b]	51%	52%	43%	42%
Average annual earnings in $	7,166	6,970	8,330	8,900
If work FTFY in $	14,444	14,091	17,834	16,269
Average hourly wage in $	6.97	6.60	8.27	7.65

Source: 1990 Census of Population and Housing, Subject Summary Tape File (SSTF) 22 Earnings by Occupation and Education <http://govinfo.library.orst.edu/earn-stateis.html>
Notes: [a] includes GED. [b] Full Time Full Year.

Are there aspects of these programs conducive to achieving the goals of welfare reform? Several components of state TANF programs seem to achieve efficiency with equity. These include the federal EITC, which is supplemented in several states. (The data for Wisconsin incorporated its state EITC.) One advantage of the EITC is that it is (or can be) targeted on a particular group, such as parents of dependent children. A second advantage is that because it is an earnings supplement, it encourages work. A disadvantage of its current form is that because it is targeted on lower-income groups, it must be reduced as income rises, discouraging additional work effort.

The welfare reform policies in a number of states, including Wisconsin, provide a guaranteed job opportunity for everyone in the program. This is likely to require public service jobs as a backup or safety net for any system in which work is required. Any program that requires work as the basis of earning the right to benefits must provide a job for all those who request a job. Public service jobs, especially at times of high unemployment, may be the key to the success of work requirements.

Another positive component of state welfare systems is the use of skilled case workers to develop a plan to help low-skilled individuals achieve job preparedness, to act as job placement agents, to help arrange child care, and to assist recipients in applying for other assistance programs. This is part of the design of the Wisconsin program. Finding and training case workers who can do this is not an easy task, yet such a system can greatly improve the outcomes of the policy and the lives of the clients.

An aspect needing careful consideration is the provision of targeted child care subsidies. In addition to subsidies, some regulation of the quality of care statewide and an information network to facilitate locating care may improve the functioning of the system and the well-being of children. Combining direct subsidies with refundable child care tax credits may make care affordable and reduce the disincentives associated with increased earnings. Expanding the current exemption beyond the first 12 months of a child's life deserves consideration.

Table 3.2.5   Earnings and work experience of Wisconsin leavers in three years after exit (1998 Dollars)

All Leavers (4th Quarter 1995 N=8042)	First year after exit	Second year after exit	Third year after exit
Percentage with earnings	81.1	78.5	76.9
Among those working in year			
Mean earnings	$9,108	$10,294	$11450
Median earnings	$8,608	$9,627	$10,924
Mean number of quarters worked	3.0	3.2	3.3
Percentage continuously employed	66.2	69.7	71.1
Percentage continuously employed by same employer	42.4	44.7	45.3

Source: Cancian, Haveman, Meyer, and Wolfe (1999), from Table 3.2.3

Another lesson to be learned from Wisconsin's welfare reform is that temporary jobs may be a useful transition into the work force for individuals without prior work experience. In temporary placements individuals receive training in the world of employment and learn about the expectations of employers. The experience of leavers in Wisconsin suggests that most move from temporary employment into higher-paying positions within one year.

The major message from this analysis is that it is very difficult to design a program that encourages work among those with limited earnings capacity, provides an adequate safety net so that no family is in severe poverty and is not so expensive that it requires high tax rates on all earners

227

creating significant work disincentives. Universal programs such as universal health insurance coverage would reduce some of the very high marginal tax rates. However, universal programs also reduce the incentive to work. Perhaps the second best approach, in a world that seems without a first best approach is a combination of a targeted earned income tax credit, a guaranteed job, child care subsidies for all those who are in the paid labor force, universal health care coverage, loans for education and training whose required payments depend on earnings and a cash transfer system for those with very young children, significant disabilities or dependents who require extensive care.

Notes

[1] The author wishes to thank Dawn Duren, Ingrid Rothe, Jan Blakeslee, Betty Evanson, Daryl Glaser, Sandra Barone, and Elisabeth Boehnen for skillful assistance, and Derek Neal, Robert Haveman, Tom Kaplan, and members of the Policy Analysis Workshop Series at the LaFollette Institute for Public Affairs, University of Wisconsin–Madison, for very helpful suggestions.

[2] Other goals included making both parents responsible for their children, decreasing teen pregnancy and births, and shifting responsibility for welfare to the states.

[3] The vast majority of cases on AFDC were single-parent families with a dependent child under age 18. A much smaller program, AFDC-UP, existed for two-parent families in which the principal breadwinner was unemployed.

[4] The example used is Pennsylvania since it is the state used most often in federal government publications such as the Green Book.

[5] This is calculated for an earnings disregard of $30 plus one-third of earnings. In addition, the employee's share of payroll taxes is subtracted from earnings, so that the marginal tax rate equals .69.

[6] In 1995, expenditures on AFDC, Food Stamps, Medicaid, and the Earned Income Tax Credit (EITC) on behalf of non-disabled working-age families were more than $100 billion, or about 1.4 percent of the U.S. GDP. Of this, AFDC accounted for $22 billion, Food Stamps for $18.5 billion, Medicaid for $36 billion, and the EITC for about $25 billion.

[7] Food Stamps are valued at their cash value and Medicaid at two times the average expenditure per child and one times the average expenditure per non-elderly, non-disabled adult in this state. This understates the value of Medicaid for some families and overvalues it for others, as it captures average spending, which might be greater or less than the amount this family consumes – greater than the family would consume if it were not fully subsidized. It does not capture the insurance value of health care coverage.

[8] Rather than model the budget constraint as one with "sharp edges", in which the exact dollar of earnings at which an individual loses Medicaid eligibility is shown, the budget constraint here is smoothed. This is the author's preferred approach, because

eligibility is determined on a monthly basis and individuals are likely to know, in general, about eligibility rather than know that if they work one more hour they will lose benefits.

[9] If the family received housing assistance, the marginal tax rates would be even higher, as housing accounts for 30 cents for every dollar increase in earnings.

[10] The EITC was initially enacted in 1975 as a means of tax relief; it has been expanded three times, in 1986, 1990, and 1993.

[11] For a family with one child, the EITC supplemented earnings at a 34 percent rate up to a maximum credit of $2,152 and was fully phased out at about $25,000 of earnings.

[12] As of 1993 the EITC was less generous. Earnings up to $7,750 were subsidized at a rate of 20 percent for families with one or more children. After earnings reached $12,200, the subsidy was gradually clawed back. By $23,050, the EITC was entirely clawed back.

[13] One could view the incomes at which each family member loses Medicaid as "notches", marking an immediate shift to lower family income.

[14] In order to change the parameters of the state AFDC program, states had to obtain a federal waiver under the cost-sharing arrangement for AFDC.

[15] Wisconsin's waiver programs were Self-Sufficiency First and Pay for Performance.

[16] States can use their own funds to provide assistance beyond 60 months. Michigan and Rhode Island plan to do so. Illinois will do so for families with earned income from working a minimum of 20 hours per week.

[17] Wisconsin is one of seven states that offer a refundable credit.

[18] In this analysis only the employee's share of FICA is subtracted from the employee's wages.

[19] Some states, including Wisconsin, have a supplementary EITC. In the case of Wisconsin, the maximum value of its EITC for a family with two children is $512. It essentially follows the schedule of the federal EITC and so adds to the incentives of the federal EITC, encouraging work for lowest wage workers and potentially discouraging work effort at higher, though still low, levels of earnings.

[20] The deductions allowed include 20 percent of earned income and the actual costs of childcare. All households get a standard deduction of $134 per month.

[21] Estimates in this paragraph are based on Wisconsin administrative data for April and May 1999. In California, the average monthly cost of infant day care in 1998 was $585, more than 50 percent of the three-person poverty line (see Adams, Schulman, and Ebb, 1998, for more on the challenge posed by child care).

[22] A homestead is defined as the home occupied, whether owned or rented. For more on the credit see http://www.dor.state.wi.us/faqs/home.html.

[23] Wisconsin has a waiver from the US government to offer subsidized coverage to adults under the Children's Health Insurance Program (CHIP) which otherwise is offered only to children. In most states children up to 185 percent of the poverty line are eligible for coverage. Wisconsin's program is called Badger Care. See Table 3 for some sense of eligibility parameters for Wisconsin. Three other states are included to give the reader some idea of the diversity in eligibility across states.

[24] For a family with one child the claw-back rate is below 16 percent. The lower tax rate on their credit is tied to the lower maximum credit. The maximum credit for a family with one child is about 60 percent of that of a two-child family.

[25] Working, including working full-time, does not assure that individuals will have coverage. It is even less likely that their families will have employer-based coverage. Over all poor families in 1998, 47.5 percent of full-time workers were without coverage for the entire year (http://www.census.gov/prod/99pubs/p60-208.pdf). There are many reasons for low coverage: working for firms that do not offer coverage, not being eligible for a firm's coverage, or declining a firm's coverage due to substantial cost-sharing requirements. Lower-wage workers receive lower tax subsidies for private employer-based coverage, as the subsidy depends on one's marginal tax rate. (See Wolfe and Vanness, 1999, for more on employer-based coverage and coverage of low-skilled workers.) Those working part-time rarely receive health benefits. In 1994, the Bureau of Labor Statistics reported that only 5 percent of part-time workers in firms of 100 or fewer employees received health benefits (U.S. Bureau of Labor Statistics, 1994).

[26] Under the 1996 welfare law, the federal government estimates that 14.7 million children would be eligible at the federal limit of 85 percent of the state median income level. However, most states have set their income caps well below the federal ceiling (http://www.acf.dhhs.gov/news/cc98.htm).

[27] The Child Care and Development Fund is the major source of federal child care assistance for low- and moderate-income families. The program provides funding to states to subsidize care of the parent's choice, whether in a family child care home, with a relative, or in a child care center.

[28] Some recent work has used state waivers as the basis of analyzing the labor force response to welfare reform. See, for example, Moffitt (1999) and Figlio and Ziliak (1999). The potential endogeneity of state policy limits the usefulness of such studies for understanding the impact of the federal reform, however.

[29] The strong performance of the economy and the increase in the minimum wage are also likely to have contributed to the observed decline in caseloads. See, for example, a report by the Council of Economic Advisers, attributing about 35 percent of the decline to welfare reform, 10 percent to the macro economy, and 10–15 percent to the increase in the minimum wage (Council of Economic Advisers, 1999).

[30] For more detail, see Cancian, Kaplan, and Meyer (1999) and U.S. Department of Health and Human Services (1999).

[31] Recent newspaper articles suggest another reason for low enrollment – reluctance by intake workers to provide information to potential beneficiaries on where or how to apply.

[32] These families may have additional income from a variety of sources such as earned and unearned income of other adult family members, earnings not subject to UI reporting and income from unreported activities (underground economy activities).

[33] A study by Primus (1999) using Current Population Survey data for 1993–1997 suggests that the bottom decile of the population has experienced a significant drop in income. For a description of those remaining on cash assistance see, Danziger et al. (1999).

[34] Single individuals do not face these high rates, because they are eligible for only limited forms of assistance, such as Food Stamps and a small EITC. Figure 3.2.A4 shows the relationship between earnings and income for such individuals. It shows that the marginal tax rate facing them ranged from .18 to .27; alternatively, their incomes were considerably lower than the three-person single-parent family that received all assistance for which the family was eligible.

References

Adams, Gina, Schulman, Karen, and Ebb, Nancy. 1998. *Locked Doors: States Struggling to Meet the Child Care Needs of Low-Income Working Families.* Washington, DC: Children's Defense Fund, March.

Cancian, Maria, Haveman, Robert, Meyer, Daniel R. and Wolfe, Barbara. 1999. 'Before and After TANF: The Economic Well-Being of Women Leaving Welfare.' Unpublished report, Institute for Research on Poverty, University of Wisconsin–Madison, December.

Cancian, Maria, Kaplan, Tom, and Meyer, Daniel. 1999. 'Outcomes for Low-Income Families under the Wisconsin AFDC Program: Understanding the Baseline So That We Can Estimate the Effects of Welfare Reform.' Special Report no. 76, Institute for Research on Poverty, University of Wisconsin–Madison, July.

Council of Economic Advisers. 1999. 'The Effects of Welfare Policy and the Economic Expansion on Welfare Caseloads: An Update.' Technical Report. August 3, 1999.

Danziger, Sandra, et al. 1999. 'Barriers to the Employment of Welfare Recipients.' Discussion Paper no. 1193-99, Institute for Research on Poverty, University of Wisconsin–Madison.

Dickert-Conlin, Stacy, and Houser, Scott. 1999. 'EITC, AFDC, and the Female Headship Decision.' Discussion Paper no. 1192-99, Institute for Research on Poverty, University of Wisconsin–Madison.

Figlio, David, and Ziliak, James. 1999. 'Welfare Reform, the Business Cycle and the Decline in AFDC Caseloads.' In *Economic Conditions and Welfare Reform,* edited by S. Danziger. Kalamazoo, MI: Upjohn.

Green Book. 1998. U.S. House of Representatives, Committee on Ways and Means. *Background Material and Data on Programs within the Jurisdiction of the Committee on Ways and Means.* Washington, DC: Government Printing Office.

Moffitt, Robert. 1999. *The Effects of Pre-PRWORA Waivers on AFDC Caseloads and Female Earnings, Income and Labor Force Behavior.* Mimeo, Johns Hopkins University.

Primus, Wendell. 1999. 'Recent Changes in the Impact of the Safety Net on Child Poverty.' Center on Budget and Policy Priorities, December 23.

U.S. Bureau of Labor Statistics. 1994. 'Employee Benefits in Small Private Establishments, 1992.' Bulletin 2441. Washington, DC: Government Printing Office.

U.S. Department of Health and Human Services, Office of the Assistant Secretary for Planning and Evaluation. 1999, June. 'Interim Status Report on Research on the Outcomes of Welfare Reform'.
<http://aspe.hhs.gov/hsp/welf-ref-outcomes99/outcomes99-interim.htm>

Wolfe, Barbara L. 2000. 'Incentives, Challenges, and Dilemmas of TANF.' Discussion Paper no. 1209-00, Institute for Research on Poverty, University of Wisconsin–Madison.

Wolfe, Barbara, and Vanness, David. 1999. 'Government Mandates and Employer-Based Health Insurance: Who Is Still Not Covered?' Discussion Paper no. 1198-99, Institute for Research on Poverty, University of Wisconsin–Madison.

Appendix

a. The welfare system until 1996:

The core of pre-reform assistance policy consisted of four awkwardly integrated programs targeted at poor working-age families with children.

1. *Aid to families with dependent children (AFDC)* (discontinued under welfare reform, replaced by Temporary Assistance for Needy Families, TANF):
   - Cash assistance to poor families with children headed by a single parent or guardian.
   - AFDC provided family-size-conditioned cash income support to about 14 million people in 5.1 million families, or about 5.5 percent of the nation's population. The support ranged from $740 per month in Connecticut to less than $150 per month in Mississippi. Average benefits had eroded over time from $704 per month in 1970 (1995 dollars) to $377 in 1995.
   - AFDC penalised earnings. For every $1 increase in earned income over allowable deductions, benefits were reduced by 67 cents initially. After four months, benefits were reduced dollar-for-dollar with an increase in earnings. Thus the statutory tax rate on earned income, or benefit reduction rate, for AFDC recipients was 67 or 100 percent, clearly discouraging work.
   - AFDC was an entitlement program; that is, if a family satisfied the eligibility condition(s) for AFDC, then it received benefits according to the appropriate benefit formula.
   - On average 55 percent of the cost of AFDC was financed by the national government.
   - States administered the program, set benefit levels, and shared costs.

2. *Food stamp program* (continues under welfare reform, although changes were made to require work and reduce eligibility, described below):

   - Poor families are eligible for Food Stamps, which entitle the holder to purchases at authorized food stores, depending on their income.
   - The federal government pays for the Food Stamp Program, but the local offices administering the AFDC/TANF program determine eligibility and amounts.
   - In 1998, the Food Stamp Program provided about $16.9 billion in benefits or $170 per month to the average recipient family. In that year, about 20 million of the nation's population received Food Stamp benefits. This is down from 25.5 million two years earlier (pre-reform).
   - To be eligible, a family must pass an asset test and a net and gross income test. Net income must not exceed the poverty line, equal to $13,880 in 1999 for a single parent with two children, and gross income must not exceed 1.3 times the poverty line. A household is limited to $2,000 in assets plus a car worth less than $4,650.
   - Maximum Food Stamp benefits vary by family size and are reduced as family net income increases. Net income includes AFDC/TANF benefits, and there are deductions for work expenses, child care expenses, and shelter expenses.
   - States generally require Food Stamp households to have their eligibility recertified every three to 12 months.
   - TANF Modifications to Food Stamp Program.
   - Under TANF, states may disqualify individuals from participation in the Food Stamp Program for TANF violations.
   - Under TANF, able-bodied adults without dependents who, during the preceding 36-month period, received Food Stamp benefits for at least three months but worked less than 20 hours per week are disqualified. Similarly, the act required the states to remove most permanent resident aliens, who were previously eligible to receive Food Stamps.

3. *Medicaid program* (continues under welfare reform, expanded to cover more children):

- Provides health care benefits to poor children (even those in two-parent families), single mothers who receive AFDC/TANF benefits, and pregnant women.
- The benefit package is quite generous, roughly equal to a private comprehensive package of health insurance.
- Medicaid is administered by the states (again, largely through the local welfare offices), which also bear some of the costs of the program, according to a matching formula.
- AFDC/TANF recipients losing eligibility because of increased earnings receive Medicaid for an additional 12 months. However, after this period the adults lose all benefits unless income remains below the cut-offs in effect in the state under AFDC.
- All states are now required to cover all children less than 6 years old with family income below 133 percent of the poverty line, and all children born after September 1, 1993, with family income below the poverty line. This change, which was made under AFDC, was designed to reduce the negative work incentive effects of the tie between Medicaid and AFDC.

4. *Earned income tax credit (EITC) (continues under welfare reform)*:
    - EITC works through the federal income tax. It is available to all low-income working taxpayers but is targeted on those with dependent children. It is a refundable credit: If the amount of a family's credit exceeds its tax liability, the family receives from the Internal Revenue Service a refund check for the difference. If a working family earns too little to owe federal income tax but qualifies for the EITC, the IRS sends the family a check.
    - Only those who work can qualify for the EITC. For families with very low earnings, the value of the credit increases as earnings rise. The EITC operates effectively as a wage supplement, lifting low-wage working families with children closer to, or in some cases above, the poverty line.
    - The benefit subsidises annual earnings at a 40 percent rate up to about $9,500 for a family with two children (for a credit of more than $3,000 per year). This maximum credit is reduced as family earnings rise above about $11,500; no EITC is available for families with income in excess of about $29,500.
    - Increases in the EITC enacted in 1990 and 1993 provided a larger credit each year from 1991 through 1996 to qualifying families with children.

- A number of states enacted EITCs that supplement the federal plan.
- The federal EITC was established in 1975 to offset the adverse effects of Social Security and Medicare payroll taxes on working poor families and to strengthen work incentives.

b. The major provisions of welfare reform in the U.S. include:

- Eliminating the Aid to Families with Dependent Children (AFDC) program, thereby eliminating the right to public financial support when destitute.
- Reassigning fiscal and regulatory responsibilities for assisting the nation's poor families from the federal government to state and local governments.
- Providing a 'block grant' to each state, paid for with money saved by eliminating AFDC, and giving states wide discretion in the use of these funds.
- Imposing responsibilities on states for enforcing work – often full-time, year-round work – by poor, often single-parent, families.
- Creating a new and less supportive environment in which poor families have to cope.

c. Federal requirements imposed on states by welfare reform:

- States must meet stiff goals in terms of the proportion of assisted families that have full-time workers; for example, by 2002, 50 percent of all assisted one-parent families must have a worker employed at least 30 hours per week.
- States are required to collect child support payments from non-custodial parents.
- States must impose rules that eliminate the provision of income support to any family after it has received a total of five years of help.
- States must require that unmarried teen parents who receive help attend school and live with their parents (or other adult supervisors).
- States must deny income support to anyone convicted of a drug-related crime, to mothers who won't identify the fathers of their children, and to legal immigrants admitted to the country after August 1996.

d. Definition:

MOE – Maintenance of Effort: In enacting TANF, the U.S. Congress imposed an MOE obligation on states, providing that a state would be penalized if it failed to maintain spending of at least 80 percent (or 75 percent if the state met TANF participation rates) of a 'historic state spending' level each year.

e. Forms of subsidy for child care:

1. Non-refundable tax credit for taxpayers who incur work-related child care expenses. Maximum amount goes to those at 140 to 160 percent of poverty line; $2.8 billion in 1998.
2. Block grants to states that can be used to subsidize child care for low-income parents who are working or participating in work-related activities or education programs. Average federal subsidy is $66 per week; total expenditure $2.9 billion in 1997.
3. Employers may exclude the provision of child and dependent care or employee contributions to such care accounts from employees' taxable income and Social Security earnings. Worth most to those in high marginal brackets.

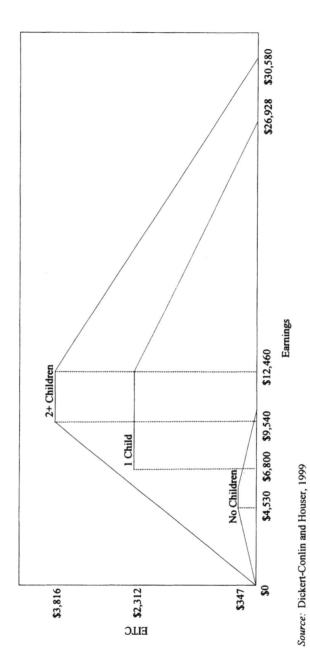

Source: Dickert-Conlin and Houser, 1999

Figure 3.2.A1 Federal EITC parameters 1999

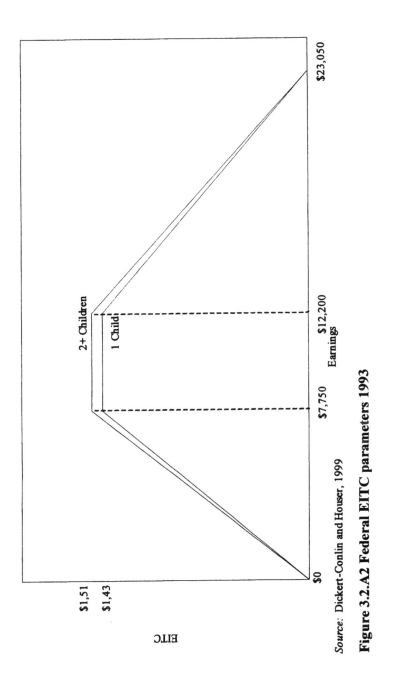

Source: Dickert-Conlin and Houser, 1999

Figure 3.2.A2 Federal EITC parameters 1993

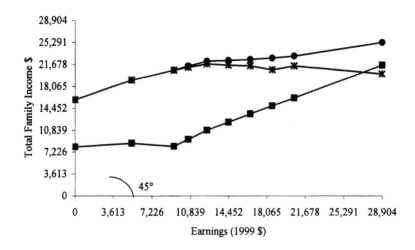

Figure 3.2.A3 Wisconsin - TANF parameters with universal health coverage

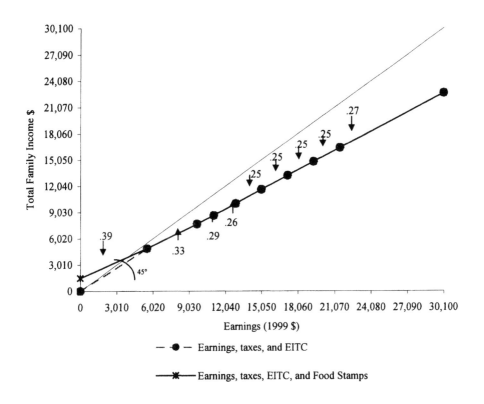

Figure 3.2.A4   Earnings and income of a single individual, Pennsylvania, 1996

3.3 Social security, intergovernmental fiscal relations and efficiency: the case of the two systems of public assistance for the unemployed in Germany

Martin T.W. Rosenfeld

1. Introduction

Over the last 10-15 years, the future of the welfare state and the various options for reforming social security systems have become permanent features of academic and political debate in practically all western industrialised countries. In Germany, high and persistent unemployment means that the reform of the social security system for the unemployed is of particular interest. Along with a wide range of active labour market policies this system at present chiefly comprises three types of wage substitution payments (= passive labour market policies): full-rate unemployment benefit (*Arbeitslosengeld*), means-tested unemployment benefit (*Arbeitslosenhilfe*) and public welfare transfers (*Sozialhilfe*) to the unemployed[1].

The debate on the German social security system for the unemployed is primarily based on the consequences that the structure of the various active labour market policies as well as the three types of monetary transfers to the unemployed have for the (re)integration of the latter into the regular labour market and for public expenditure. Ways of improving the structure of active labour market policies and monetary transfers to the unemployed are also considered. However, up to now there has been little

243

discussion of the *intergovernmental set-up* for active and passive labour market policies[2]. This above all involves the division of competences for structuring, executing and financing the various types of active and passive labour market policies between the public authorities. This chapter aims to show the impact of the present intergovernmental set-up on the effectiveness and efficiency of social security for the unemployed in Germany and to describe ways in which the division of competences could be reformed, using the example of means-tested unemployment benefit and public welfare transfers together with the associated active labour market policies.

The proposal to integrate these two systems of means-tested transfers to the unemployed into one system has recently attracted widespread interest and support[3]. There is little difference between those out of work and claiming means-tested unemployment benefit and those out of work and claiming public welfare, and there are various overlaps and points of comparison between the two transfer systems. However, public welfare and means-tested unemployment benefit are financed and administered separately and the content of the two systems is very different. The following section will give an overview of the current regulatory structure of means-tested unemployment benefit and public welfare as well as the intergovernmental division of competences for these transfers. The third section of the chapter will discuss the extent to which the present intergovernmental set-up for means-tested unemployment benefit and public welfare may impair the effectiveness and efficiency of social security for the unemployed[4]. Against the background of the shortfalls in the institutional status quo, the fourth section will examine how these could be eliminated by a reallocation of competences. In this context, the consequences of integrating means-tested unemployment benefit and public welfare will be considered in the framework of both the current and an amended division of responsibilities.

2. The institutional status quo

Differences between the structure of means-tested unemployment benefit and the public welfare system.

Both means-tested unemployment benefit and public welfare transfers are based on the *need* of the claimant. A pre-condition for these transfers is a 'means test' or 'income test', which establishes whether a claimant can cover necessary living costs using his own resources (including other state payments)[5]. The award of means-tested unemployment benefit is however bound up with further conditions and the two forms of benefit differ considerably when it comes to the definition of 'need'.

Means-tested unemployment benefit is nowadays only paid to needy long-term unemployed persons who paid unemployment insurance contributions when in work but have been unemployed for a long time; therefore, they are no longer eligible for full-rate unemployment benefit.[6] As eligibility for means-tested unemployment benefit is dependent on the individual having previously received full-rate unemployment benefit the former is sometimes referred to as 'follow-up benefit' (*Anschluss-Arbeitslosenhilfe*)[7]. Those out of work but ineligible for means-tested unemployment benefit are above all former self-employed workers, persons who had live-in positions with a family and those who were out of work in the period before they registered themselves unemployed (this group primarily concerns school leavers, former students and women who have stayed at home to look after their children for an extended period). This group is reliant on public welfare which, unlike means-tested unemployment benefit, is paid to *all* persons deemed eligible, irrespective of whether they are unemployed or have ever paid unemployment insurance contributions. Accordingly, the unemployed represent only a part of the group of those receiving public welfare.

It is uncertain how many unemployed persons there are receiving public welfare. The basic premise is that all public welfare claimants aged between 15 and 65 are fit for work. On 31 December 1998 there were around 1.8 million such persons in Germany[8]. Of these 148,627 were in work and 709,326 were registered unemployed. This figure also includes those receiving public welfare as a supplement to means-tested unemployment benefit as the latter amount was below the minimum living income. The remaining public welfare claimants of working age (908,461 persons) were neither in work nor registered unemployed as they were taking part in training schemes, granted permission to stay at home to take care of their young children after a separation or divorce, or classed into the group of those considered unsuitable for work by the public welfare administration on account of their age[9]. Those belonging to this group of public welfare claimants could also in part be counted as unemployed as many would make real efforts to obtain work in a favourable labour market[10]. It should therefore be assumed that there are considerably more

245

unemployed persons claiming public welfare than the number of registered unemployed would suggest.

With regard to the calculation of 'need', considerably more income elements are excluded from the income taken into account by means-tested unemployment benefit than in the case of public welfare. With means-tested unemployment benefit, an additional income of at least DM 315 per month is allowed. Public welfare claimants may have an additional income of up to half of the amount corresponding to the normal consumer goods requirements of the main breadwinner of the household *(Regelsatz eines Haushaltsvorstandes*, around DM 250) before there income is taken into account in the rate of benefit awarded[11].

There are also considerable differences in the *scope* of means-tested unemployment benefit and public welfare. These are most evident in terms of how these benefits are *aligned with the consumer goods requirements of the recipients*. Whilst means-tested unemployment benefit is purely a substitute for the income that the unemployed previously received whilst in work, public welfare is available to all, irrespective of whether they have ever or recently been employed. It is not intended as a substitute for any previous income but rather to cover the minimum requirements for a 'humane existence'. Claimants unable to cover the minimum requirements for a 'humane existence' are thus always entitled to public welfare. This would be the case, for example, if the consumer durables of a claimant needed replacing. By contrast, means-tested unemployment benefit does not take such requirements into account[12]: those on this type of benefit basically receive as few or as many payments as determined by their former income from employment and the current rate of transfers (according to the regulations of the system of means-tested unemployment benefit)[13]. Whilst means-tested unemployment benefit barely takes into account the family circumstances of a claimant, in the case of public welfare all family members are individually considered with the intention of providing a minimum standard of living for the entire household. Moreover, in the framework of public welfare, certain persons such as the severely handicapped are considered to have more consumer goods requirements. In addition, public welfare claimants can obtain one-off assistance for living costs[14] as well as assistance in particular circumstances[15]. Whilst public welfare does not pay old age insurance contributions and only pays health insurance contributions for certain claimants, means-tested unemployment benefit usually covers both.

In that means-tested unemployment benefit is linked to the individual's former income from employment, many claimants are also reliant on supplementary public welfare transfers as the amount of unemployment benefit awarded often lies below the (gross) amount of public welfare that can be claimed, which is basically intended to always guarantee a minimum living income. Those claiming means-tested unemployment benefit who also obtain supplementary public welfare can be termed *combined benefit claimants*[16]. Those only drawing one or the other of the two forms of benefit can be termed *sole claimants of public welfare* and *sole claimants of means-tested unemployment benefit* respectively. When looking at quantitative figures for these three categories, it should be noted that in the framework of the German public welfare system reference is often made to so-called *Bedarfsgemeinschaften*, private households with members who are eligible for benefit and whose collective need should be covered by public welfare. Consequently, public welfare statistics often only contain data on the *Bedarfsgemeinschaften* and not on individuals. Data on the combined benefit claimants is only available at the level of the *Bedarfsgemeinschaften*. On 31 December 1997 (1998) there were 1,486,019 (1,469,739) claimants of means-tested unemployment benefit, 1,285,746 (1,286,900) *Bedarfsgemeinschaften* receiving public welfare (comprising a total of 2,893,178 [2,879,322] persons) and 128,139 (132,738) *Bedarfsgemeinschaften* receiving supplementary public welfare together with means-tested unemployment benefit in Germany[17].

Regulations on the definition of 'reasonable' employment for those on benefit also vary considerably, as do the penalties if claimants show unwilling to work and the active labour market policies targeted specifically at the respective benefit claimants. It should be stressed that if an unemployed person keeps rejecting offers of work he may risk losing his means-tested unemployment benefit completely but will continue to receive public welfare, which is intended to guard against total poverty.

Intergovernmental division of competences for the provision of means-tested unemployment benefit and public welfare transfers.

In the context of the allocation of *legal competences for determining the structure of public goods and services*, it should be noted that both means-tested unemployment benefit and public welfare are nowadays largely governed by federal law. The legal basis for this is the Social Security Statute, Book III (*Sozialgesetzbuch, Buch III* or *SGB III*); public welfare transfers are regulated by the Federal Law on Public Welfare (*Bundessozialhilfegesetz* or *BSHG*). However, federal law allows the local authorities considerable freedom in how they arrange the details of the public welfare system[18]. Accordingly, the local authorities can basically establish their own active labour market policies (in the framework of the so-called 'assistance for employment' *[Hilfe zur Arbeit]* provisions of the Federal Law on Public Welfare) and they also have scope to organise the allocation of transfers beyond the regular public welfare payments to cover the basic cost of living (*laufende Hilfe zum Lebensunterhalt* or *HLU*). By contrast, the only area where the employment offices (*Arbeitsämter*) remain largely independent from the federal government is in structuring active labour market policies for claimants of means-tested unemployment benefit.

The employment offices have the *executive responsibility* for means-tested unemployment benefit (in the sense of awarding payments). The local authorities (comprising counties *[Kreise]* and 'free' towns independent of the county administration *[Kreisfreie Städte]*) hold the main executive responsibility for public welfare. The employment offices are the lowest administrative level of the Federal Employment Agency. They are responsible to the regional employment administration (at Land level) and the central administration of the Federal Employment Agency.

The federal government is responsible for *financing* means-tested unemployment benefit. However, this only stretches to the payment of transfers: the *administrative costs* are borne by the employment offices, which also meet most of the costs of their active labour market policies for means-tested unemployment benefit claimants from their own resources. The main source of revenue for the employment offices is unemployment insurance contributions, which are regulated at the federal level. There is also a federal subsidy to cover the financial deficits of the employment offices or the Federal Employment Agency as a whole. The local authorities have almost exclusive financial responsibility for public welfare[19]. This applies to transfer and administrative expenditure as well as their active labour market policies for public welfare claimants.

Seen from an economic perspective, the outlined division of competences for public welfare transfers (structure determined at federal level, financial commitment at local authority level) represents a break in the so-called principle of connexity (*Konnexitätsprinzip*), according to which an authority that stipulates financial expenditure should also have to pay for it[20]. This has been subject to criticism for a long time.

3. Consequences of the current intergovernmental division of competences

The institutions responsible for paying wage substitutes to the unemployed and the associated active labour market policies must firstly be judged according to whether and, if so, to what extent they aid the integration of the unemployed into the regular labour market. If these measures do not have a suitable effect on the labour market, transfer payments will represent a greater burden for public budgets than if the institutional status quo were better equipped to combat unemployment. The current regulations on the intergovernmental division of competences can however be bound up with cost advantages or disadvantages irrespective of their impact on the labour market.

3.1 Effects on the labour market

From a theoretical perspective, if one assumes the rational economic behaviour of the actors responsible for labour market policy, one can anticipate an insufficient integration of the unemployed into the regular labour market on account of the current division of competences.

Do the employment offices deliberately shift their burdens onto the local authorities and vice versa? The most familiar consequence of the current division of competences, and already a subject for public and academic debate, is that the allocation of financial responsibilities encourages the federal government, the employment offices and the local authorities to shift their financial burdens and the responsibility for measures to combat unemployment onto other authorities. Up to now this tendency has however mainly been discussed with relation to the local authorities. The terms 'shunting yard' or 'revolving door effect' are often applied in this context. Shifting burdens in this way impairs efforts to combat employment for the groups concerned[21].

It is in the interest of the local authorities to carry out as many job creation measures – in the sense of creating jobs subsidised by the local authorities and subject to social insurance contributions - for as many sole claimants of public welfare as possible, so that these will qualify for unemployment insurance and can thus be exempted from public welfare (if they lose their job again they will firstly obtain full-rate unemployment benefit followed by means-tested unemployment benefit). Transferring the financial burden onto health insurance also plays a role which already has an effect in the course of these measures[22]. The federal government has an interest in relieving itself of its financial commitments associated with means-tested unemployment benefit through restricting eligibility for claims (qua a change in the law), with the result that public welfare offices *(Sozialämter)* at the local level increasingly assume the responsibility for unemployed persons who had the right to means-tested unemployment benefit before the changes. For the employment offices, no additional financial costs from paying means-tested unemployment benefit (which is financed by the federal government) are incurred, but neither do they gain anything from the reintegration of recipients of means-tested unemployment benefit into the labour market. As a result, the employment offices are mainly interested in those on full-rate unemployment benefit. Considering that recipients of means-tested unemployment benefit present an administrative burden for the employment offices and eat into their resources for labour market measures, one could expect the employment offices to seek to resolve this by looking for opportunities to shift these persons onto the local authorities. The question is whether these hypotheses are borne out in reality.

The strategy whereby the local authorities shift their burdens onto the employment offices has been pursued with a vengeance for years by most public welfare offices at local level, without any attempt to veil their motives. As far as the local authorities are concerned, any method of reducing the burden of public welfare is to be seen as a success. It is certainly possible to reintegrate some of the unemployed persons into the labour market by providing them with an occupation subsidised by the local authorities and subject to social insurance contributions. However, as the local authorities have a vested interest in providing posts for the unemployed of at least (only) one year, it cannot be expected that such measures will be structured to allow as many as possible to gain a foothold in the regular labour market. (After having paid contributions to the unemployment insurance system for one year, an employee qualifies for full-rate unemployment benefit.)

There is evidence that the federal level does act as suggested[23], although the motives cited by the politicians for restricting eligibility for means-tested unemployment benefit are almost always different to those outlined here. As it is possible for the federal government to keep reducing its costs by restricting the conditions for eligibility for means-tested unemployment benefit, it only has a limited interest in reintegrating the long-term unemployed into the labour market. Up to now there has been little research into the scale of the negative effects that ensue.

If it is presumed that the employment offices deliberately shift their burdens onto the local authorities, the question is how they manage to do so. Measures to reduce means-tested unemployment benefit in the event that claimants refuse to take on reasonable employment would be one alternative. However, there is no empirical evidence to suggest that the employment offices deliberately employ such measures in the attempt to pass their burdens on elsewhere. It is true that those on means-tested unemployment benefit often become increasingly reliant on public welfare. This may be more a consequence of the current legislation under the Social Security Statute, Book III than a conscious move on the part of the employment offices or their staff, but as long as the employment offices are not doing enough to reintegrate the long-termed unemployed into the labour market the result will be a transfer of burdens onto the local authorities. Claimants of means-tested unemployment benefit have to accept a wage corresponding to their benefit (Social Security Statute, Book III, § 121). If those who take on a post according to these terms lose their job again their full-rate unemployment benefit will thus be much lower than it was the first time they were unemployed. Correspondingly, over the course of time it is more and more likely that unemployed persons will have to draw on supplementary public welfare transfers in order to support themselves. Moreover, means-tested unemployment benefit is recalculated every year. If, for example, an unemployed person's health has deteriorated, it may be the case that after recalculation he will receive less benefit than during the previous year as in the view of the employment office his state of health means that he would not be able to achieve the same wage on the labour market as before[24].

Do the employment offices and public welfare offices focus exclusively on their own clients? As a result of the above division of competences the employment offices and local authorities will both tend to focus on their 'own' unemployed clients. In the framework of their active labour market policies, they will exclude or pay insufficient attention to those unemployed persons for whom the other authority has financial and administrative responsibility. Hence, the employment offices will tend to neglect those on public welfare and the public welfare offices those on means-tested unemployment benefit. Provided that the labour market instruments applied by the employment offices and the public welfare offices have their own specific advantages, this focus on one's 'own' clients means that not all unemployed persons can benefit from measures which could help their (re)integration into the labour market. When it comes to combined benefit claimants, it is to be expected that neither the employment offices nor the local authorities feel responsible for reintegrating these persons into the labour market. Moreover, as the employment offices are only responsible for the administration and not the financing of means-tested unemployment benefit, one can expect them to neglect those receiving this kind of benefit (compared to those on full-rate unemployment benefit). Even if the employment offices were to regard the federal funds earmarked for means-tested unemployment benefit as their own resources, one could expect them to exclude those on this form of benefit from their labour market policies as these persons cost less than equivalent persons receiving full-rate unemployment benefit.

For the above hypotheses to be borne out in practice would firstly require proof that both the employment offices and the public welfare offices were particularly capable of implementing specific labour market instruments. This largely depends on the institutional links between the employment offices and the Federal Employment Agency on the one hand and the links between the public welfare offices and the local authorities on the other. Links between the employment offices and the Federal Employment Agency mean that vacancies can be filled on a national basis. The local authorities could also try to establish a network of public welfare offices and thereby make it possible to find work for public welfare claimants nationwide. However such a network would be costly and only benefit a small percentage of those on public welfare, that is those who would in any case be candidates for vacancies on the regular labour market. It is, after all, unlikely that inter-authority arrangements would be established to place public welfare claimants in the second (subsidised) labour market or the third labour market (subsidised labour market in combination with specific arrangements for disadvantaged persons who need the special care of social workers in order to be able to engage in regular employment[25]) or on (re)training schemes. A local authority in which suitable positions or measures were available to benefit claimants from other local authorities would only agree to take on these persons if the local authorities from which they came were prepared to finance these positions or measures, which would lead to high negotiation costs. In addition, inter-authority job placements could be an incentive for some local authorities to rid themselves of the burden of some of their public welfare claimants by passing them on to other authorities with exaggerated information about their knowledge and abilities.

Through their links with the Federal Employment Agency, the employment offices are also relatively well-informed as to which jobs and career sectors tend to offer stable employment in the medium term, the profile which job seekers need to match if they wish to obtain a certain position, and the quality of the active labour market measures carried out by private entrepreneurs. This information can enhance the quality of their own active labour market policies. The local authorities would only be able to draw on such information if they were to seek vacancies and scan the labour market as intensively as the Federal Employment Agency or if the latter were to make all of its labour market information available to the local authorities. Even if this were the case, each local authority would require at least one qualified official able to gather and apply the information provided by the Federal Employment Agency.

The employment offices have a further advantage over the public welfare offices in the field of arranging employment, because whilst the latter generally seek to provide work for low-skilled and poorly educated clients the former deal more with the short-term unemployed and never with persons lacking any professional experience. In this respect, there is a certain 'stigma' attached to those on public welfare. This could mean that employers will, where possible, approach the employment office rather than the public welfare office in order to fill their vacancies. Yet the employment offices themselves often tend to suggest unsuitable candidates to potential employers as in this way they can test whether these unemployed persons are willing to work. Precisely because they are mainly dealing with 'difficult' clients, the public welfare offices only tend to place persons who are really suitable for the posts offered by the employers. There is thus little justification for the view of employers that welfare recipients are always less suitable for a job than those on means-tested unemployment benefit.

The specific role of the public welfare offices in labour market policy lies in the fact that they are able to articulate additional public demand and create jobs for the unemployed within the local authority, sometimes in the framework of special businesses or firms set up by the local authority. By creating jobs for the unemployed at local level it is possible to ascertain their knowledge and skills by assessing their performance in a job lasting several weeks and in turn to provide better guidance or a more suitable position for them (these measures are known in practice as 'measures to

253

evaluate the unemployed' ['Feststellungsmassnahmen'])[26]. Moreover, if they gain work in a local authority rather than in the private sector, 'difficult' cases may receive social-pedagogical and expert guidance at work which enables them to practice a certain line of work in the longer term (these measures are known as *'third labour market'* measures[27]). Finally, the local authorities can also provide work for the unemployed through classic job creation schemes (known in Germany as *'Arbeitsbeschaffungsmassnahmen'* or *'ABM'*), which may be regarded as *'second labour market'* measures. The benefits of the subsidised second labour market are however very much contested, particularly as jobs provided for the unemployed by the local authorities almost always imply the crowding-out of private enterprises or regular workers. If there are a good number of people within a local authority district working as part of measures to evaluate the unemployed or in the second or third labour markets, the best solution may often be to set up a special local authority body (enterprise or firm) for this purpose.

The public welfare offices are able to articulate additional public requirements as their links with other local public offices keep them well informed about the need for 'supplementary'[28] local services (e.g. the upkeep of green areas and sports grounds, waste clearance from dilapidated houses or ruins, helping the socially disadvantaged to move house, positions as school caretakers, redeveloping industrial wasteland) than the employment offices. In principle, the local authorities can of course make this information available to the employment offices. This is indeed the case with the second labour market: If the employment offices wish to place their own clients in jobs offered by the local authorities, they have to ask the local authorities for possible jobs and pay them a subsidy. However, it is not enough just to be informed about local public requirements. The employment offices could create their own enterprises to provide the unemployed with work in line with local demand. However, in many cases these enterprises would have to come to an agreement with the local authorities, which would lead to higher transaction costs than if the persons concerned were directly employed by these authorities. Moreover, the employment offices could run the risk of being exploited by the local authorities if these act in an opportunistic manner by exaggerating local public requirements[29].

The intensive job searches carried out by many local authorities – often using private enterprises such as the Dutch firm Maatwerk – are often also seen to give the public welfare offices an advantage over the employment offices, for as the recruiters work closely with the public welfare claimants it is certain that only really suitable candidates will be recommended to the employer. However, the employment offices could of course also make such intensive efforts to find work for their clients.

The above has shown that both the local authorities and the employment offices have their own specific potential for labour market policies. The question arises as to whether the supposed exclusion of means-tested unemployment benefit recipients from local authority measures and of unemployed persons claiming public welfare from the measures conducted by the employment offices really has negative consequences. For this assumption to be valid, there would firstly have to be equivalent persons in the two categories of benefit claimants. The group of those drawing public welfare often contains 'difficult cases' who are generally unable to gain a foothold in the first labour market without social-pedagogical guidance. Many public welfare claimants have become completely unaccustomed to regular employment and have become afraid of the demands of work. However, whether they are really always more 'difficult' than recipients of means-tested unemployment benefit is a matter for debate. It is true that – unlike many of those on public welfare – all those claiming means-tested unemployment benefit have the advantage of being able to prove that they have worked before. Moreover, they have often already taken part in various job creation measures and have not completely got out of the habit of working. They can thus better judge their capabilities than those who have been out of work for years and have an unrealistic perception of their abilities. Nonetheless, many of those on means-tested unemployment benefit have been 'out of the habit' of regular work for a long time, and so may have similarly complex problems to those unemployed persons on public welfare.

There is as yet no data on the involvement of unemployed persons claiming public welfare in the labour market policies of the employment offices nor on how available the labour market policies of the public welfare offices are to those on means-tested unemployment benefit. Neither side would deny that it focuses its respective labour market policies on its own clients. However, representatives from the employment offices assert that they treat sole claimants of public welfare the same as those on means-tested unemployment benefit, at least when it comes to advice and placement. Moreover, some of the employment offices also offer other labour market measures such as job creation schemes or professional training to sole claimants of public welfare – although only when the clients (of the employment offices) intended for these measures do not take up their places. The local authorities stress that those claiming means-tested unemployment benefit hardly ever participate in local job creation measures. All of this indicates that at present both persons on means-tested unemployment benefit and those claiming public welfare continue to be excluded from services that could really help their (re)integration into the regular labour market.

The fact that the employment offices concentrate on their 'most expensive' clients – those on full-rate unemployment benefit – is probably not just down to the incentives they receive from the current division of competences. The officials responsible for placing unemployed persons wish to show that they have succeeded in filling vacancies, which is most likely with candidates who are 'safe bets'. Moreover, from the perspective of these officials, those on means-tested unemployment benefit and most of those on public welfare have little chance on the labour market. As a result, efforts are concentrated on those receiving full-rate employment benefit. This view is backed up by the fact that claimants of means-tested unemployment benefit will presumably have sought work via the employment office whilst drawing full-rate unemployment benefit and it is unlikely that their success in finding work will have improved over the course of time. Finally, it should be noted that the employment offices should focus at least in part on the 'safe bets' or those who are easy to employ, as only in this way can professional links be made with employers who may then be prepared to take on some of the 'risky cases' from the employment offices if necessary. Another reason for public welfare claimants to be neglected by those in the employment offices responsible for placements is that they have frequently got used to being unemployed and adapted themselves to a life on benefit. They must regularly sign on at the employment office but really only want the necessary proof to present at the public welfare office so that their benefit will not be cut. In such cases the officials responsible for job placements will often 'just stamp the papers' of the public welfare claimants 'to be left in peace' instead of making any real efforts to find work for them.

Is there a general tendency to neglect combined benefit claimants? Up to now there has been no data on the involvement of the combined benefit claimants in the labour market schemes of the employment offices and public welfare offices. Representatives from the employment offices deny that they treat sole claimants of means-tested unemployment benefit any differently to combined benefit claimants when it comes to labour market measures. By contrast, the local authorities concede that they neglect combined benefit claimants as these persons are 'inexpensive' for the public welfare offices. In addition, the local authorities are largely of the opinion that labour market policy for combined benefit claimants primarily falls within the remit of the employment offices. Moreover, current regulations according to the Social Security Statute, Book III also encourage local authorities to neglect combined benefit claimants in their labour market policies. In this respect, as soon as a combined benefit claimant obtains employment of more than 15 hours a week via a local authority he loses his right to means-tested unemployment benefit[30] and from then on would have to be financed to 100% by the local level.

In various cities and counties, the attempt has been made to stop the marginalisation of combined benefit claimants by establishing cooperation between the employment offices and the public welfare offices. Such cooperation is organised in different ways, but the following example can be used by way of illustration. The employment office and public welfare office co-finance a project (to 80% by the employment office and 20% by the public welfare office), in the framework of which combined benefit claimants (75%) and sole claimants of public welfare (25%) can take on a three-year post subject to social insurance contributions within a sector of public interest. This institutional arrangement avoids the following: 1) that the local authorities merely pass the unemployed persons on to the employment offices (as is generally the case with the one-year placements, which are mainly selected by the local authorities); and 2) that combined benefit claimants are not helped at all. However, one can presume that the local authorities will only have an interest in such an arrangement if the employment office provides most of the funding – as in the case considered – or also cooperates in the framework of other job creation measures, for example by considering sole claimants of public welfare in its job creation schemes. The commitment of the employment office to the combined benefit claimants can only be partly attributed to the advantage that – at least in the short term – the practice of shifting burdens from the local authorities onto the employment office is being halted or delayed. In the above example the management of the employment office concerned would also probably make particular efforts for the long-term unemployed out of a personal feeling of responsibility. However, one cannot take such personal commitment as read in every employment office.

Do the employment offices and public welfare offices hinder each other's active labour market policies? Over the last 20 years, the insufficient labour market policies of the employment offices for sole claimants of public welfare have induced the local authorities, as those responsible for this form of benefit, to develop their own labour market policy instruments, as detailed above. On account of the differing legal principles and the fact that the labour market policies of the employment offices and the local authorities are governed by the aim of saving own resources, it can be assumed that the two sides will hinder – or at least not complement – each other's measures.

When it comes to filling vacancies with their own clients, there is indeed competition between the public welfare offices and the employment offices. This competition is fierce, not least because the clients are often only able to carry out low-skilled work which is in any case in short supply and also in demand for handicapped persons and young offenders. Moreover, potential employers often receive requests for vacancies from the employment offices and the public welfare offices at the same time. As a result they feel overburdened and are less willing to cooperate.

3.2 Consequences for public expenditure

As it stands, the intergovernmental division of competences influences the volume of public transfers but also the administrative costs incurred by the employment offices or the public welfare offices. However, there is not enough information at present to quantify these additional costs. Excessive public expenditure results firstly from the fact that – as demonstrated above – current regulations represent a partial hindrance to the effective implementation of labour market instruments. Consequently, there are probably more unemployed persons today than there would be if the employment offices and the public welfare offices were to run coordinated policies.

The dual administration required for combined benefit claimants also leads to excessive administrative costs. In the status quo there is hardly any formal cooperation between the employment offices and the public welfare offices when it comes to calculating transfers, with the result that the public welfare offices have to record various details about welfare claimants that have already been taken down by the employment offices. However, informal contacts are sometimes made, for example when a public welfare office checks the details of a new client who asserts that he has not made a claim with the employment office as well.

Another reason for increased administrative costs is that at present the public welfare offices often have to make payments due from the employment offices if combined benefit claimants do not immediately register their claim for means-tested unemployment benefit with the employment office and thus initially have to be completely supported by the public welfare office. In this case, the employment office must reimburse these payments at a later date, which increases personnel costs. All those on full-rate unemployment benefit automatically receive an application form for means-tested unemployment benefit from the central administration of the Federal Employment Agency about 7 weeks before their claim expires. However, it is to be expected that many unemployed persons will not follow this up straight away.

Additional administration costs also arise from the fact that dissatisfied clients can be referred from one office to another. An employment office may, for example, refer persons who are frequently discontented with the services it provides to the public welfare office just to get rid of persistent 'moaners', even though it is obvious that these persons will not get anything from the public welfare office either.

When it comes to transfer payments, the current division of competences also occasions certain cost reductions which are, however, not foreseen in the relevant legislation and should therefore on the whole be seen in a negative light. Claimants of means-tested unemployment benefit sometimes do not apply for supplementary public welfare even though they are eligible for it[31]. This above all concerns persons who would only receive a very small amount and do not bother applying so as to avoid the hassle of additional bureaucracy.

4. Possibilities and consequences of reform

4.1 Overview of the alternatives

The previous section of this chapter showed that the division of competences for the transfers under consideration is one reason for the shortfalls in measures to combat unemployment as well as for excessive transfer and administrative costs. A reallocation of competences could then enable more effective measures to combat unemployment and reduce the burden on public expenditure. Nonetheless, the negative as well as the positive effects of reform should be borne in mind. The negative aspects would be mainly associated with the costs of administrative reorganisation.

The following subsections will firstly discuss the possibility of eliminating the current shortfalls purely by reallocating competences, assuming that the systems for means-tested unemployment benefit and public welfare remain separate. Possible changes in the administration of transfers as well as in financial competences will be examined[32]. Next it will be considered to what extent the current deficiencies could also be eliminated by integrating the two welfare systems whilst retaining the given competences. The final subsection will assess the option of combining a reform of competences with an integration of the two forms of transfer.

4.2 Reforming competences whilst maintaining the distinction between the two forms of benefit

Changes in executive responsibilities The current deficiencies in the systems for allocating means-tested unemployment benefit and public welfare will not be eliminated by altering the competences for the award of transfers (the executive responsibilities) if the financial competences are not reformed as well. This particularly applies to the consequences of the present division of competences for active labour market policy. Nevertheless, it may be useful to consider how the structure of executive competences could best be organised under the (heroic) assumption that the allocation of financial competences would have no consequences for the efficient provision of the two forms of benefit[33]:

- One would firstly have to establish whether it would be efficient to shift the responsibility for the award of supplementary public welfare for combined benefit claimants to the employment offices. Those concerned would then only have to apply to one authority and administrative costs would be reduced as there would be no more dual administration or reimbursement claims to be processed between the employment offices and public welfare offices[34]. However, within each city or county transfers governed by similar rules would be dealt with by two different bodies, which would hardly be efficient. One advantage would be that through no longer having contact with the public welfare office, combined benefit claimants would lose their 'stigma' and potential employers would not be reluctant to offer them work because of them being on public welfare. Yet it is questionable

260

whether today's potential employers are really going to find out about the supplementary public welfare received by combined benefit claimants. It should also be borne in mind that the employment offices would not only need more staff but also more space to cope with the increased workload involved in the allocation of transfers. At present, they lack the relevant experts who would be needed if the public welfare law in force were to be largely extended to the current recipients of means-tested unemployment benefit.

- If the employment offices were to assume the responsibility for the award of *all* public welfare benefits, the aforementioned disadvantage of matters being dealt with by two separate administrations (which are, however, responsible for the same region) according to the same rules would no longer apply. Moreover, there would be the advantage of public welfare recipients losing their 'stigma'. Yet it may also be the case that following such a reform the employment offices have a worse image than they have now so that the 'stigma' would indeed not disappear. It would not necessarily be a good thing for public welfare claimants to lose their 'stigma' anyway as they may increasingly take their benefits for granted and not make as much of an effort to find work. A further downside of this alternative is that by extending the transfers dealt with by the employment offices passive labour market policy may encroach upon active labour market policy, which may in turn prove an obstacle to the effectiveness of labour market policy. Finally, the costs for reorganisation may be higher than those associated with the previous reform option.

- Concentrating all of the administration for means-tested employment benefit and public welfare in the public welfare offices would also imply high reorganisation costs. As with the above-mentioned option, dual administration could be eliminated. It is possible that as a result of such a reform a 'stigma' would be attached not just to those on public welfare, as at present, but to all those drawing means-tested unemployment benefit, which may hinder their chances of integration into the labour market.

- Finally, there is the option of only transferring the responsibility for the award of means-tested unemployment benefit for combined welfare recipients to the public welfare offices. As with the first option (transferring the responsibility for supplementary public welfare benefits for combined welfare recipients to the employment offices)

261

this alternative would seem to have little to commend it (parallel award of one type of transfer by two neighbouring bodies).

To sum up – under the assumption that the competences for the award of benefits can be reallocated independently from financial competences – the option of giving either the employment offices or the public welfare offices the full responsibility for all transfers would seem better than the two other alternatives. It is not however possible to say which of the two bodies would be best suited to assume this responsibility.

Reforming financial competences alone This section will examine the consequences of only reforming financial competences, assuming that the distribution of the other competences remained the same.

With regard to transfer payments, if the federal government were to assume some of the local authorities' public welfare burden, it would perhaps increase its efforts in terms of labour market policies for those on this form of benefit and exert its influence within the Federal Employment Agency so that the employment offices would also do more for this group. Nonetheless, unless it were to finance public welfare to practically 100%, the federal government would still be encouraged to shift the burden of means-tested unemployment benefit onto the public welfare system. Yet it would not be advisable for it to finance public welfare to 100% as the local authorities would then lose the incentive to be economical with their resources for public welfare payments (which they would presumably still be responsible for administering) and to implement labour market instruments for those on benefit. It would thus be better if the local authorities and the federal government were both to finance means-tested unemployment benefit and public welfare to the same extent. Such combined funding is however frequently bound up with the problem that neither of the funding bodies considers itself responsible for the task in hand, which hampers its effectiveness and efficiency. If the federal government had too much of a financial say in a certain task then this would turn into a kind of government scheme and stricter rules would be required on the allocation of government resources in order to prevent them being squandered by the local authorities. As a result, the scope for action of the local authorities would be severely limited which in turn would impair the quality of the tasks executed. It follows that the local authorities should instead have a greater financial stake in the services in question (and thereby hold the main responsibility for means-tested unemployment benefit as well as public welfare). This would not exclude them from receiving additional general financial resources (for example increased tax shares) by way of compensation for the increased burden associated with these responsibilities.

It remains unclear how the financial interest of the employment offices in claimants of public welfare and means-tested unemployment benefit could also be increased. A financial involvement of the employment offices in the transfers is out of the question as this would *ceteris paribus* inevitably lead to higher unemployment insurance contributions, whereas at present there seems to be general political consensus in Germany that these contributions should decrease. One alternative could be for the employment offices to obtain premiums from the local authorities and the federal government if they succeed in finding work in the regular labour market for those on means-tested unemployment benefit or public welfare. At the moment this would not be much use as the employment offices already receive a general subsidy from the federal government. Premiums would reduce this subsidy and could not be passed on to those paying unemployment insurance through a reduction in contributions. A reallocation of the financial competences would not then in itself be enough to make the employment offices increase their labour market efforts for the unemployed.

The proposed involvement of the local authorities in financing means-tested unemployment benefit would slightly discourage them from passing on the burden of public welfare. Having been 'successfully' transferred to the employment offices, unemployed claimants of public welfare would after a limited period start to (re)claim means-tested unemployment benefit and therefore be (partly) funded by the local authorities. The temptation for the local authorities to shift the burden of public welfare onto the employment offices would decrease further if they were also to have a general financial responsibility for full-rate unemployment benefit or, even better, if those authorities guilty of such behaviour (that is shifting their burdens onto the employment offices) had to assume the entire costs for the full-rate unemployment benefit due to former public welfare recipients.

In sum, an isolated change in the financial competences for the transfer payments could eliminate major problems in stimulating public efforts to find work on the regular labour market for unemployed persons on benefit. However, similar incentives would not be achieved for the employment offices.

An isolated change in the financial competences for the costs of administration would not reduce costs and/or unemployment or give the federal level, the employment offices or the public welfare offices greater incentives to achieve efficient and effective labour market policies. The exclusive responsibility of the local authorities for financing their own active labour market policy measures does not produce any negative incentives as long as they have to finance the major part of the transfer payments for public welfare (and, if appropriate, for means-tested unemployment benefit); this should then basically remain as it is. It is a different story for the active labour market policy of the employment offices, which is currently chiefly financed from their general resources. If the federal government (or the federal government together with the local level) were to assume the responsibility for financing labour market policy for unemployed persons eligible for means-tested unemployment benefit, the employment offices would no longer have a real reason for not doing enough for these persons. However, as the employment offices still do not share in the success of their active market policy for these persons, if they were to be relieved of the costs of active labour market policy one could expect them to waste the external resources.

Combined changes in the competences for the execution and financing of transfers It is not possible to state which of the two options for a 'well-organised' system of executive competences (i.e. where both means-tested unemployment benefit and public welfare are administered either by the employment offices or the public welfare offices) is best: both would have a similar effect. When it comes to financial competences, the above section showed that the best solution would be to divide the financial responsibility for the transfer expenditure for public welfare and means-tested unemployment benefit between the federal and local levels. No way was found to raise the incentive for the employment offices to implement labour policy instruments for those unemployed persons eligible for means-tested unemployment benefit and public welfare. If the local authorities bore the responsibility for the full-rate unemployment benefit paid to former recipients of public welfare, they may be prevented from shifting their burdens onto the employment offices.

In principle, both alternatives for reforming the system of competences for the execution of transfers are compatible with the proposed changes in the financing of benefits. However, the preferred option of financing transfers by the federal government (less than 50%) and the local authorities (over 50%) would not encourage the employment offices to be more economical with the award of transfers. Giving the local authorities and federal government greater control over the employment offices would be one way of preventing resources from being wasted, but expensive to maintain. If the responsibility for the transfer of benefits were given to the public welfare offices, such control would be much less expensive to administer as the local authorities would have a major interest in an economical allocation of transfers on account of their financial involvement in them. When reforming financial competences, it would thus seem advisable to reform the system for the execution of transfers at the same time by switching it to local level.

Ways of eliminating the differences in the systems for means-tested unemployment benefit and public welfare.

This section will examine whether and to what extent the problems arising from the current division of competences for means-tested unemployment benefit and public welfare can be eliminated simply by *integrating* both transfer systems, an issue which is currently under debate. The two ways of doing this will be discussed, but first there will be an excursion giving reasons to support an integration of the two transfer systems irrespective of the disadvantages bound up with the present division of competences.

Excursion: Reasons for integrating the transfer systems (irrespective of the current distribution of competences). The negative effects of the status quo mentioned above stem from the current division of competences for means-tested unemployment benefit and public welfare, which ultimately arises from the 'institutional choice' made in Germany to keep means-tested unemployment benefit and public welfare separate. The current distinction between means-tested unemployment benefit (formerly known as crisis welfare [*Krisenfürsorge*]) and public welfare (formerly known as poor persons' welfare [*Armenfürsorge*]) is primarily based on decisions taken in 1926/27 in connection with the introduction of an unemployment insurance system financed by contributions and the separation of the employment offices from the local authorities[35]. Besides the aforementioned disadvantages resulting from the current division of competences, there are a range of further negative aspects caused *exclusively* by this split between the two transfer systems.

Current regulations mean that the various categories of unemployed persons are not treated equally. Correspondingly, there are *two classes of*

265

unemployed persons[36]. Only those claiming means-tested unemployment benefit – not, however, sole claimants of public welfare – have a right to take part in the labour market schemes run by the Federal Employment Agency. Claimants of means-tested unemployment benefit are also treated more generously than those on public welfare (including combined welfare claimants) when it comes to the award of transfers. Moreover, from the perspective of *horizontal justice* it seems unjust that persons who do or did not have to pay unemployment insurance contributions but are in an identical economic situation to those for whom these are or were compulsory are excluded from certain state benefits.

The *principle of equivalence* is the main argument cited to justify keeping the status quo. According to this principle, those on means-tested unemployment benefit have a right to unemployment insurance on account of the contributions they have previously paid. In the longer term, these contributions may no longer justify the award of full-rate unemployment benefit, but are seen as enough to legitimate more generous transfers and for the persons concerned to be treated preferentially to non-contributors when it comes to labour market policies. If an individual has, for example, paid unemployment insurance contributions for 30 years and is out of work for the first time at age 50, he may consider the restricted duration of the award of full-rate unemployment benefit and his subsequent transfer to means-tested unemployment benefit as well as, if appropriate, the supplementary payment of public welfare to be unjust on account of the high contributions he has paid in the past. On the other hand, a young person who has not yet had the chance to work on account of the general labour market situation would also regard it as unfair that he receives a lower amount of public welfare than someone who has perhaps just been lucky to have had a job for a while and whose only advantage is having some practical work experience. One alternative would be to increase the duration of eligibility for *full-rate unemployment benefit* according to how long unemployment insurance contributions have been paid[37]. If this aspect were taken more into account, the different levels of financial assistance awarded to claimants of means-tested unemployment benefit and public welfare would hardly appear justified from the perspective of the principle of equivalence. It should also be noted that according to the status quo means-tested unemployment benefit is financed by all taxpayers but – in the case of long-term unemployment – only awarded to those who have previously contributed to the unemployment insurance system. The

266

subsequent exclusion of, for example, the self-employed from benefits which they help to finance seems unjust under the principle of equivalence[38]. Similarly, the labour market policies of the Federal Employment Agency and the employment offices are largely reserved for contributors despite being financed in part by general tax income.

Moreover, it is possible that the current institutional division between means-tested unemployment benefit and public welfare may result in recipients of the former not having an *incentive to find work*. As a result of the current separation between the two transfer systems, it is necessary to align the amount of means-tested unemployment benefit awarded with previous income from employment. Under the current wage agreements, persons who previously had quite a high working income will not wish to take on a job which pays a salary less than the amount they can claim in means-tested unemployment benefit. A (further) reduction in the means-tested benefit awarded to the unemployed may provide more of an incentive for them to find work[39] but in this case, means-tested unemployment benefit would be rendered obsolete in practice if virtually all claimants were to start receiving combined welfare.

There are but few advantages to offset the negative aspects of the current split between the two transfer systems. On account of the comparatively simple system of administering means-tested unemployment benefit, there are savings in administrative costs compared to the current regulations on public welfare. A further advantage is that the conceptual difference between means-tested unemployment benefit and public welfare as well as the fact that means-tested unemployment benefit is aligned with previous income can give current claimants of the latter the impression that they have not yet been 'written off' from the labour market. However there is no reason why those persons fit for work and only claiming public welfare should not share this view.

Impact of integrating the two transfer systems on the status quo of the division of competences The following alternatives could above all be applied to integrate the two benefit systems under consideration[40]:
1. Increasing means-tested unemployment benefit to at least the level of public welfare by integrating the consumer goods requirements of the unemployed into the benefit formula. Supplementary public welfare for claimants of means-tested unemployment benefit would then no longer exist.

267

2. Abolishing means-tested unemployment benefit. This would mean that all long-term unemployed persons (those previously claiming full-rate unemployment benefit) would cease to receive means-tested unemployment benefit and instead obtain public welfare transfers based on their individual needs.

Alternative (1) would do nothing to change the unfairness inherent in the present systems for awarding benefits. Nor would it give benefit claimants any more or less of an incentive to find work as the total volume of the respective unemployment benefits would remain constant. It can be expected that combined welfare claimants would not be as 'stigmatised' as today. However, this 'stigma' is probably not very widespread in any case as potential employers do not know whether a recipient of means-tested unemployment benefit is also on supplementary public welfare.

The effect on administrative costs would most probably be the same as if the responsibility for the award of supplementary public welfare for combined welfare claimants were transferred to the employment offices. There would no longer be dual administration for those on combined welfare, but the transfer system in the employment offices would be more complicated and costly than at present. These additional burdens on the employment offices would probably outweigh the benefits of eliminating the dual administration for combined welfare claimants. By implementing alternative (1) the employment offices would to a certain extent be turned into a kind of second public welfare office. For each local unit there would be two administrative bodies dealing with the award of benefits according to (or based on) the Federal Law on Public Welfare. One-off assistance for living costs as well as benefits awarded in particular circumstances would also have to be dealt with by the employment offices to avoid the public welfare offices also being involved in the provision of assistance to those on means-tested unemployment benefit. Many people now have other problems in addition to being unemployed. The unemployed should therefore be offered assistance beyond the measures to help them get back to work.

Implementing alternative (1) would slightly increase the cost of benefits for the total economy as claimants of means-tested unemployment benefit would no longer refrain from claiming supplementary public welfare (something that the legislators do not want them to anyway).

Alternative (1) would *ceteris paribus* only bring about changes in labour market policy for combined welfare claimants. Assuming that financial competences remained the same, there would be increased costs for the federal level whilst the local authorities would be relieved of their financial burden. As a result, the federal level would have more of an incentive than at present to promote the re-integration of combined welfare recipients into the labour market. However, the employment offices and public welfare offices would remain separate with regard to labour market policy and continue to shift burdens onto each other. In sum, this alternative would then not appear very wise in the absence of complementary changes in financial competences.

Alternative (2) focuses more on the basic shortfalls in the status quo than alternative (1)[41]. It could serve to eliminate the unfairness of the system and increase the benefit claimants' incentive to seek work. However, former claimants of means-tested unemployment benefit would have more of a 'stigma' attached to them than at present, which could hinder their chances on the labour market.

Assuming that the current division of competences still applied, that is, for example, that the extended public welfare were financed by the local authorities, there would also be negative consequences for the reintegration of the long-term unemployed as the employment offices or the Federal Employment Agency, to which they are responsible, would no longer have an incentive to implement labour market instruments for these persons. *Ceteris paribus* this would imply an increase in the cost of transfers.

On the other hand, alternative (2) would *ceteris paribus* reduce public transfer costs as the public welfare awarded is less generous than means-tested unemployment benefit at present. However, one could reckon with an increase in administrative expenses. Although there would no longer be dual administration for combined welfare claimants, the administration of public welfare is much more costly than that for means-tested unemployment benefit. Extending public welfare claims to current recipients of the latter would thereby *ceteris paribus* almost turn into an employment programme for public welfare officials.

To prevent administrative costs from rising too dramatically, the extension of eligibility for public welfare to include all those currently on means-tested unemployment benefit could be accompanied by a simplification of the public welfare regulations in force. One-off assistance for living costs could, for example, be standardised to a much greater extent. The problem would be that this would require an increase in monthly transfer payments to ensure that benefit claimants were armed for all eventualities (in other words there would be a trade-off between the volume of administrative expenditure and the volume of transfer expenditure). Public welfare would thereby start to resemble the proposals for a general 'guaranteed minimum income'. In addition, when a benefit claimant has spent all of his – perhaps increased – benefit and then gets into financial difficulties, under the current regulations the public welfare office responsible for awarding benefit cannot simply leave him to his own devices but has to offer additional assistance. This regulation could of course be changed and the problem countered by adopting a system based more on vouchers such as food vouchers (like the 'food-stamp' programme in the US). In this way, claimants would be discouraged from squandering their benefits and from making unnecessary purchases. If the decision were taken to introduce a more standard level of public welfare, it would be necessary to ascertain whether the average or the maximum of the welfare claimant's needs should be taken as the basis. Many claimants would be worse off compared to today if average needs were taken as the basis. Yet even such standardisation may mean that the principle of keeping the amount of benefit awarded to the unemployed under the level earned by those employed on a low income *(Lohnabstandsgebot)* could no longer be retained. Consequently, benefit claimants would have less of an incentive to find work than they do at present. If the maximum need were chosen there would be more negative consequences and the total transfer costs would rise.

To reduce the additional expense associated with a more standardised rate one could – in line with the regulations in the US – consider dividing the public welfare claimants (increased according to alternative [2]) into the so-called 'worthy poor' and 'unworthy poor' and creating two separate public welfare programmes ('Programme A' and 'Programme B')[42]. Programme A would be designed for those who are basically fit for work (in any case all those currently drawing means-tested unemployment benefit) whilst Programme B would be targeted at the current recipients of public welfare who are considered unfit for work as they are too young or too old or have a long-term illness or handicap. Programme B could comprise relatively generous provisions and also include further standardised one-off payments to assist with living costs, whilst Programme A could award less than the current public welfare transfers as those claiming this form of benefit can basically expect to be able to support themselves through employment. Programme A could also be given a new name that seems less discriminatory than 'public welfare' and would not be associated with any 'stigma'. Dividing up the integrated systems for public welfare and means-tested employment benefit would be problematic in that the boundaries between those 'fit' and those 'unfit' for work are fluid and change over the course of time. It is always difficult to specify exactly what 'fit for work' means. Someone who is an alcoholic today may be cured (and able to work) tomorrow but relapse the day after. However, the group of public welfare claimants who are basically unfit to enter the labour market can at least be relatively clearly defined. One could raise the objection that the proposed division of public welfare would breach the principle of equality assuming that an individual fit for work and, for example, a severely handicapped person basically has the same needs, despite the special problems resulting from the handicap. However, this argument does not carry much weight as there are considerable differences between 'unemployed persons who are fit for work' and 'handicapped persons'.

Possibilities of both integrating the transfer systems and reforming the division of competences.

Looking at the two alternatives for integrating the benefit systems together with the proposed changes in the division of competences it can be seen that both would be compatible with a reorganised division of competences. However, the arguments cited in the excursus above would suggest alternative (2) to be the better option.

5. Conclusion

This chapter has shown that a change in the current intergovernmental division of competences can help reduce unemployment, save on transfer payments and cut the costs associated with labour and transfer administration. By contrast, integrating the means-tested unemployment benefit and public welfare systems would not in itself have any comparably positive effects. There are, however, other arguments to support an integrated means-tested unemployment benefit and public welfare system, which should be structured in such a way that all current claimants of means-tested unemployment benefit would be provided with assistance according to the rules of public welfare. At the same time, a division of the extended public welfare system into two sub-programmes (Programme A for those claimants who are fit for work and Programme B for those who are basically unfit for work) would have some advantages.

Whilst the local authorities would assume the responsibility for the award of transfers in the framework of both sub-programmes, it would seem necessary for the transfer payments to be financed mainly by the local authorities and to a lesser extent by the federal government.

However, three problems remain, which will require analysis in future research. First, there is the question as to how the financial involvement of the federal government in the extended public welfare system should be organised at institutional level[43]. Second, the possibility of providing the local authorities with extra resources to compensate their increased financial burdens should be examined. Third, there is the issue of how to deal with the continued lack of interest on the part of the employment offices in promoting active labour market policies for those receiving benefit in the framework of the extended public welfare system. A further reform in the distribution of competences could be proposed as a solution to the latter problem. A 'Federal Agency for Active Labour Market Policy', financed to 100% by the federal government, would on the one hand ensure that the advantages of the present employment offices for the active labour market remain but on the other hand also provide greater incentives than the present Federal Employment Agency to implement active labour market policy instruments as efficiently and effectively as possible for those claiming benefit according to the extended public welfare system[44].

Notes

[1] Public welfare is not in fact designed specifically for the unemployed but for various reasons it has over the course of time increasingly become a wage substitute for those unemployed persons who do not (or no longer) qualify for unemployment benefit.

[2] For the general debate on intergovernmental relations in the area of social security, often defined as 'functional federalism' (*funktionaler Föderalismus*) see, for example: Klaus Mackscheidt; Geert Böttger; Klaus Gretschmann: Der Finanzausgleich zwischen dem Bund und der Rentenversicherung, in: Finanzarchiv, N.F. Vol. 19 (1981), pp. 383-407; Klaus-Dirk Henke: Der parafiskalische Finanzausgleich, dargestellt am Beispiel der Gesetzlichen Krankenversicherung, in: Finanzwissenschaft im Dienste der Wirtschaftspolitik (Festschrift Pohmer), Franz Xaver Bea und Wolfgang Kitterer (eds.), Tübingen 1990, pp. 357-373; Klaus Mackscheidt: Finanzausgleichsmaßnahmen zwischen dem Bund und den Trägern der Sozialen Sicherung und zwischen den Trägern der Sozialen Sicherung untereinander, in: Finanzierungsprobleme der sozialen Sicherung, Vol. I, Kurt Schmidt (ed.), Berlin 1990, pp. 145-180; and Holger Feist; Ronnie Schöb: Workfare in Germany and the Problem of Vertical Fiscal Externalities, in: Finanzarchiv, N.F., Vol. 55 (1998), pp. 461-480.

[3] For the current debate on this issue, see: Deutscher Bundestag, Drs. 14/1347, July 28, 1999. Previous research into welfare reform by the author of the present chapter also points out the advantages of combining means-tested unemployment benefit and public welfare. See Martin T.W. Rosenfeld, Arbeit für Sozialhilfeempfänger: Zwischen welchen Wegen können wir heute wählen?, in: Wirtschaftsdienst, Jg. 77 (1997), pp.

505-512, here p. 512; and Arbeit statt/und Sozialhilfe?, in: Jahrbuch für Wirtschaftswissenschaften, Vol. 48 (1997), pp. 241-268, here p. 266.

[4] Researchers have up to now paid little attention to the effect of the intergovernmental distribution of competences on active and passive labour market policies. Consequently, this section is based in part on interviews with experts conducted in autumn 1999 in the framework of a research project commissioned by the German government. The project dealt with the various possibilities of increasing the effectiveness and efficiency of labour market policy in Germany.

[5] In so far as these have to be taken into account in the unemployment benefit awarded.

[6] For details of current regulations, see the Social Security Statute, Book III, (Sozialgesetzbuch, Buch III or SGB III), § 127.

[7] Up to the end of 1999, certain categories of unemployed persons (e.g. civil servants without a lifetime contract) who had not paid taxes to the unemployment insurance system could still claim means-tested unemployment benefit. This was known as originäre Arbeitslosenhilfe.

[8] This figure and those that follow are from the German Federal Office for Statistics (Statistisches Bundesamt).

[9] In public welfare administration it is often general practice to class the over 55s as no longer fit for the labour market.

[10] See Lutz Bellmann, Struktur der Arbeitslosigkeit und Sozialhilfebedürftigkeit, in:Sozialer Fortschritt, Jg. 1998, pp. 207-209, especially p. 208.

[11] The basis for this can be found in § 76 para. II a of the Federal Law on Public Welfare (Bundessozialhilfegesetz or BSHG).

[12] Except that those out of work with children qualify for higher means-tested unemployment transfers than those without children.

[13] Means-tested unemployment benefit comprises 57% (for persons with children or a spouse with children) or 53% of the so-called flat-rate net remuneration (pauschaliertes Nettoentgelt), minus the income taken into account by the means test. See Social Security Statute, Book III, § 195.

[14] See Federal Law on Public Welfare, § 21.

[15] See Federal Law on Public Welfare, §§ 27-75.

[16] Many persons on full-rate unemployment benefit also receive supplementary public welfare transfers. The associated problems lie beyond the scope of this chapter.

[17] Source: Federal Employment Agency (Bundesanstalt für Arbeit) and the Federal Office for Statistics. All data on public welfare is based on the regular public welfare payments to cover the basic cost of living (laufende Hilfe zum Lebensunterhalt or HLU) paid to persons who are not housed in institutions such as old people's homes or hospitals.

[18] The Länder are additionally involved in structuring the public welfare system, for example through setting the so-called standard public welfare rate, which should correspond to the continuous basic needs of the claimant.

[19] On this see also Frank Klanberg; Alois Prinz: Sozialhilfe im Spannungsfeld gesellschafts- und haushaltspolitischer Interessen, in: Wirtschaftsdienst, Jg. 64 (1984), pp. 237-244.

[20] By contrast, in the field of jurisprudence the term 'connexity' (Konnexität) usually means the link between executive and funding competences (see Heinz Großekettler, Die deutsche Finanzverfassung nach der Finanzausgleichsreform, in: Hamburger Jahrbuch für Wirtschafts- und Gesellschaftspolitik, Jg. 39 [1994], pp. 83-113, here: p. 104).

[21] See for example Holger Feist and Ronnie Schöb, ibid.

[22] When public welfare claimants start a job subject to social insurance contributions, they are immediately entitled to benefits from the statutory health insurance. The local authorities must generally pay the medical costs for the other benefit claimants.

[23] The most recent example of this tendency at federal level is the abolition of the so-called *originäre Arbeitslosenhilfe* defined in footnote 8.

[24] See Social Security Statute, Book III, § 200, para. I.

[25] The terms 'second labour market' and 'third labour market' are not applied uniformly in literature or practice. This chapter will take the second labour market to mean positions found for unemployed persons to produce 'supplementary' goods and services. These positions are (co)financed by public resources and generally subject to social insurance contributions. The unemployed persons concerned do not usually require long-term social-pedagogical guidance and already have enough knowledge and skills to carry out certain tasks in the longer term following an initiation period. By contrast, positions in the third labour market are only partly liable to social insurance contributions and always involve intensive social-pedagogical and expert guidance for the unemployed persons who take them on.

[26] It is of course just as possible for corresponding positions to be created with non-public bodies of common interest, although this would require public subsidies.

[27] See above, footnote 26.

[28] Pursuant to the Federal Law on Public Welfare, but also the Social Security Statute, Book III, unemployed persons may only be given publicly financed work if it fulfils the criteria of what is considered 'supplementary'. In principle, almost every publicly financed 'supplementary' position could of course also be carried out by regular employees. Correspondingly, the publicly financed positions granted to the unemployed almost always imply the crowding-out of such regular employees.

[29] Such behaviour could however be prevented if the local authorities were to be involved in financing such measures.

[30] See Social Security Statute, Book III, § 141.

[31] The same could also apply to those on full-rate unemployment benefit.

[32] Following the above consideration of the special advantages of the employment offices and the public welfare offices in terms of active labour market policy, the premise here is that the current division of competences for active labour market policies should remain on account of the particular advantages this brings.

[33] This chapter will not discuss the option of setting up completely new authorities for social transfers (on this see Gutachten der Experten-Kommission 'Alternative Steuer-Transfer-Systeme' [report of the expert committee on alternative tax transfer systems] in BMF (*Bundesministerium der Finanzen* [Federal Ministry of Finance]): Probleme einer Integration von Einkommensbesteuerung und steuerfinanzierten Transfers, Bonn 1996, especially pp. 110 ff.). These would only be worthwhile if they dealt with other types of transfer besides means-tested unemployment benefit and public welfare.

[34] On the possible synergy effects of combining the organisation involved in transfers paid to one and the same claimant, see the report of the expert committee on alternative tax transfer systems in BMF: Probleme einer Integration von Einkommensbesteuerung und steuerfinanzierten Transfers, pp. 110-111.

[35] On this, see Martin T. W. Rosenfeld, Evolution öffentlicher Aufgaben und Ökonomische Theorie des Institutionellen Wandels, Berlin (Volkswirtschaftliche Schriften, Heft 466) 1996, especially pp. 198-204.

[36] If the differences between persons on full-rate unemployment benefit, those on means-tested unemployment benefit, sole claimants of public welfare and combined welfare claimants are taken into account, there are even four classes of unemployed persons at present.

[37] In the status quo (§ 127 Social Security Statute, Book III, para. II). The length of time for which contributions have been paid is taken into account when calculating the length of eligibility for full-rate unemployment benefit but the grading system is quite limited, beginning with duration of 12 months and ending with duration of 64 months.

[38] On this view, see ASU (Arbeitsgemeinschaft Selbständiger Unternehmer e.V. [association of self-employed workers]): Eine marktwirtschaftliche Reform der Arbeitslosenversicherung, np, 1984, pp.11-14.

[39] However, such measures should not be seen as a universal solution. On the conditions which can provide a greater incentive for benefit claimants to seek work if the amount of benefit is reduced, see Martin T.W. Rosenfeld, Arbeit statt/und Sozialhilfe?, in: Jahrbuch für Wirtschaftswissenschaften, vol. 48 (1997), pp. 241-268, here: pp. 254 ff.

[40] The further option of introducing a 'guaranteed minimum income' or a 'negative income tax' will not be discussed in this section as it would, in principle, only represent an amended version of alternative (2).

[41] In the framework of alternative (2) it could be considered whether the principle of equivalence should be abandoned altogether for persons who have paid contributions to the unemployment insurance system, or some of its aspects integrated into public welfare. Public welfare for previous recipients of full-rate unemployment benefit could, for example, be aligned with the previous income from employment for a limited period of time. Alternatively, the means test could be more liberally interpreted for previously employed persons than for those who have never worked. If the (extended) public welfare were partly aligned with the principle of equivalence, according to which the volume of state benefit awarded depends on the amount of contributions previously paid, those concerned could see it as protecting their standard of living (a guarantee of their property rights). Another option would be to compensate current contributors against the loss of property rights resulting from an abolition of means-tested unemployment benefit by extending the duration of eligibility for full-rate unemployment benefit, for example to 15 instead of the 12 months at present. However, such amendments would not completely eliminate the aforementioned unfairness in the systems for awarding benefit.

[42] On related proposals, see Martin T. W. Rosenfeld, Arbeit für Sozialhilfeempfänger: Zwischen welchen Wegen können wir heute wählen?, in: Wirtschaftsdienst, Jg. 77 (1997), pp. 505-512, here: p. 512.

[43] A number of proposals for this kind of reform can be found, for example, in Martin Junkernheinrich, Reform der Sozialhilfefinanzierung, Bochum (Diskussionspapier Nr. 23 der Gesellschaft für interdisziplinäre Forschung) 1990, pp. 12-16.

[44] The Federal Employment Agency or the unemployment insurance system would thereby only retain the responsibility for awarding insurance payments of full-rate unemployment benefit. The German National Association of Employers proposed such

a development as long ago as 1993. On this, see Stefan Sell, Polarisierung der Arbeitsverwaltung, in: Sozialer Fortschritt, Jg. 43 (1994), pp. 296-304, here: p. 299.

References

ASU (Arbeitsgemeinschaft Selbständiger Unternehmer e.V.): Eine marktwirtschaftliche Reform der Arbeitslosenversicherung, np, 1984.

Bellmann, Lutz: Struktur der Arbeitslosigkeit und Sozialhilfebedürftigkeit, in *Sozialer Fortschritt*, Jg. 1998, pp. 207-209, especially p. 208.

Deutscher Bundestag: Drs. 14/1347 of July 28, 1999.

Feist, Holger; Schöb, Ronnie: Workfare in Germany and the Problem of Vertical Fiscal Externalities, in *Finanzarchiv, N.F.*, Vol. 55 (1998), pp. 461-480.

Großekettler, Heinz: Die deutsche Finanzverfassung nach der Finanzausgleichsreform, in *Hamburger Jahrbuch für Wirtschafts- und Gesellschaftspolitik*, Jg. 39 (1994), pp. 83-113.

Gutachten der Experten-Kommission 'Alternative Steuer-Transfer-Systeme' beim BMF: Probleme einer Integration von Einkommensbesteuerung und steuerfinanzierten Transfers, Bonn 1996.

Henke, Klaus-Dirk: Der parafiskalische Finanzausgleich, dargestellt am Beispiel der Gesetzlichen Krankenversicherung, in *Finanzwissenschaft im Dienste der Wirtschaftspolitik (Festschrift Pohmer)*, Franz Xaver Bea und Wolfgang Kitterer (eds.), Tübingen 1990, pp. 357-373.

Junkernheinrich, Martin: Reform der Sozialhilfefinanzierung, Bochum (Diskussionspapier Nr. 23 der Gesellschaft für interdisziplinäre Forschung), 1990.

Klanberg, Franz; Prinz, Alois: Sozialhilfe im Spannungsfeld gesellschafts- und haushalts-politischer Interessen, in *Wirtschaftsdienst*, Jg. 64 (1984), pp. 237-244.

Mackscheidt, Klaus: Finanzausgleichsmaßnahmen zwischen dem Bund und den Trägern der Sozialen Sicherung und zwischen den Trägern der Sozialen Sicherung untereinander, in *Finanzierungsprobleme der sozialen Sicherung*, Bd. I, Kurt Schmidt (ed.), Berlin 1990, pp. 145-180.

Mackscheidt, Klaus; Böttger, Geert; Gretschmann, Klaus: Der Finanzausgleich zwischen dem Bund und der Rentenversicherung, in *Finanzarchiv, N.F.*, Vol. 19 (1981), pp. 383-407.

Rosenfeld, Martin T. W.: Evolution öffentlicher Aufgaben und Ökonomische Theorie des Institutionellen Wandels, Berlin (Volkswirtschaftliche Schriften, Heft 466), 1996.

Rosenfeld, Martin T. W.: Arbeit für Sozialhilfeempfänger: Zwischen welchen Wegen können wir heute wählen?, in *Wirtschaftsdienst*, Jg. 77 (1997), pp. 505-512.

Rosenfeld, Martin T. W.: Arbeit statt/und Sozialhilfe?, in *Jahrbuch für Wirtschaftswissen-schaften*, Vol. 48 (1997), pp. 241-268.

Sell, Stefan: Polarisierung der Arbeitsverwaltung, in *Sozialer Fortschritt*, Jg. 43 (1994), pp. 296-304.

3.4 Skills, gender equality and the distributional impact of female labour market participation in the three worlds of welfare capitalism

Bea Cantillon, Joris Ghysels, Ninke Mussche and Rudi van Dam

1. Introduction

'Gender ideology is no help. How can culture and socialisation explain sex roles in mammals lacking language and symbolic thought? There must be evolved emotional differences between males and females, differences that go beyond the two major physical differences, birth and lactation. What besides ideology produces this seemingly unbridgeable chasm of difference between aloof fathers and 'instinctively' caring mothers? Initial differences turn out to be surprisingly minor – tiny compared with the magnitude of the eventual dichotomy.' (Sarah Blaffer Hardy, in Mother Nature. A History of Mothers, Infants and Natural Selection, 1999.)

Sarah Blaffer Hardy's evolutionary statement strikes as generally explanatory for differences between men and women. Nonetheless, after about thirty years of women's emancipation, we are still faced with the blatant fact that equality between women and men has not reached completion. The rich literature on the Welfare State demonstrates vast differences between various regimes, according to the institutional context. It is hard not to recognise the influence of social policy and societal organisation on differences/inequality between women and men. Thus

Sarah Blaffer Hardy's statement could be complemented with arguments originating from these fields, such as the ones elaborated upon in this chapter.

Esping-Andersen (1990) hypothesised that each welfare state model would shape a different female employment pattern and more specifically would result in different female employment levels. He argued that women's employment rates would be highest in the social democratic countries, as a consequence of an elaborate public services sector. Somewhat lower levels of female employment would be found in the liberal countries, where workers – including women – are more dependent on waged labour, as alternatives to labour market income are limited. The conservative countries would present the lowest levels of women's employment and the largest gender gap, resulting from a slow-growth service sector and policies encouraging mothers to remain in the home. Empirical research largely confirms these predictions.

The question can be raised whether this general hypothesis is still valid when women are divided into groups according to levels of education. Do poorly, moderately and highly educated women have different employment and earnings patterns? Is the size of the gender gap different when poorly skilled men and women are compared? Does Esping-Andersen's welfare state typology apply similarly to women of different levels of education? What are the consequences for the distributional impact of female labour income?

2. Methodological note

Empirical data on which the analysis is based, originate from the Luxembourg Income Study (LIS), an archive of micro-data sets from numerous industrialised countries. The LIS data sets are primarily based on household surveys and hold demographic, labour market, and income data at the individual- and household-level. For this analysis, we use fifteen data sets from the third, and most recent wave (1992-1995/Spain 1990) of LIS data. Each country's sample includes adults aged 20-59 from all occupations excluding the agricultural and mining sectors. These individuals include persons from all family types (married or single, with or without children). A separate analysis is made for married women and men, who are parents of children under age six.

278

Individuals were qualified as employed if they reported current employment, including self-employment, at the time of the survey. In the ten LIS countries for which data on hours was available, part-time employment was examined. Part-time employment is distinguished from full-time employment, using a 35-hour working week as cut-off.

To make international comparison possible, we developed a three-level indicator of educational levels (low, medium and high) based on the national codes of educational level (i.e. highest educational qualification achieved). Unfortunately, there is no straightforward way of achieving this classification. While in some countries the educational system is clearly stratified in primary, secondary and third level education, this is not the case in many other countries. Additionally, several types of training are considered to belong to secondary school in some countries, while being classified as higher education in other countries. Therefore, we opted for a classification that reflects the internal rank of the respondent's educational level. In the age group of 20 to 59, we classified all respondents according to whether they belonged to the upper, middle or lower third part of their country's whole population's educational distribution[1]. This way, all respondents were positioned relative to the current distribution of formal educational qualification in the active population of their own country.

3. Multi-speed emancipation

3.1 Introduction

Janet C. Gornick (1999) suggests that women's employment levels vary according to the three welfare state models. Women work more in social democratic countries (except Norwegian women) than they do in the liberal countries. Women in liberal countries have a higher employment level than they do in the conservative countries. Women's part-time employment on the other hand does not reveal a clear pattern along the lines of welfare state models. Moreover, Gornick observes that married women with children younger than six years of age have a significantly lower employment level in all countries.

Gornick also examines the earnings differentials between men and women, and concludes that differential earnings ratios cut across welfare state types. Countries belonging to the three welfare state types are represented in the higher and lower earnings ranks (Australia, Belgium,

279

Finland and Sweden), that Gornick explains through the variation of the overall degree of earnings dispersion, and other economy-wide factors. A clearer picture – more along the Esping-Andersen lines – is presented when listing women's share in total labour market earnings. In the social democratic countries, except Norway, women's share in the total earnings is highest (approximately 40%). These countries are followed by the liberal countries, except the U.K., and Norway, Belgium and France (more than 30%). In the rest of the conservative countries women's share in total earnings is less than 30%. However, married women with young children have even lower earnings levels, never bringing home more than one third of total household earnings.

Within the framework of Esping-Andersen's hypothesised welfare-state models, one can assume that the labour market participation and financial independence of poorly and highly educated women are divergently influenced by the three following factors: the differential offer (and price) of 'care' services, the differential alternatives to labour income (especially social transfers) and the general shift in demand away from unskilled jobs.

First, traditional unpaid care work in the household is more easily transferred to paid market or public services by women who can afford to pay for it, i.e. highly educated women. Indeed, the relative benefits and burdens of paid labour vary according to level of education. Combining family and work is probably more problematic for poorly educated women, who are part of the lower social strata, and lead more often to a choice not to enter the labour market. For high-skilled women with high earnings and great(er) job satisfaction, the benefits outweigh the burdens, even if there are many children. This will lead them to combine work in and outside the household. Poorly skilled women, to the contrary, will experience more burdens than benefits of paid labour, and consequently, there is a greater likelihood that they will remain at home.

Second, this different level of labour participation and economic independence according to women's educational level, is influenced by the availability and use of alternatives to labour income. These alternatives to labour market participation, predominantly in the form of social benefits, have little or no effect on highly educated women's labour market participation, who generally enjoy quality employment and remuneration which makes employment worth taking up. Contrary to highly educated women, poorly educated women do enjoy social benefits to a much greater extent; for them, the advantages of social benefits are significantly higher than for highly educated women. The difference between low-skilled wages and social benefits are not large enough for a poorly educated woman to conclude that taking up a job in the labour market would make up for the disadvantages it entails. Poorly educated women's poor labour market situation leads them to decide not to exchange relatively generous social benefits for low-quality, low-paid jobs.

Third, the decline of demand for unskilled jobs is a consequence of the post-fordian transition of the economy, which implied a shift away from an industrial economy. In the post-industrial era the economy is less in need of unskilled labour, but rather demands intellectually skilled workers. As a consequence, the majority of new jobs are professional or administrative functions.

Moreover, the differentiated birth rate between poorly and highly educated women also predicts considerable differences in gender equity, according to level of education. A link exists between a woman's educational level and motherhood. The Fertility and Family Surveys (FFS) depict a decline of the number of children over the last decades. This decline is more important as the educational level rises. Beets (1998) shows that the differences are sometimes quite considerable: the average number of children of low-skilled Dutch women is 1.9, compared to 0.5 among more educated women. The educationally grounded difference is partly due to the fact that a higher proportion of highly skilled women are childless. At the age of 35, there are significantly more childless women among the highly educated than among those with a secondary or a lower education.

3.2 Gender inequalities in employment

Men and women compared. In the early nineties women's employment rates (Gornick, 1999) diverged to a large extent among the fifteen countries, ranging from 85% for Sweden to 31% for Spain, which comes down to a range of more than 50 percentage points. A parallel contrast between the countries can be noticed when comparing the female/male employment ratio. Whereas Sweden has a 0.98 ratio at the top of the social democratic countries, the ratio diminishes gradually for the liberal countries (in the 0.80 points, except for Australia at 0.73), to drop below 0.70 for the conservative countries (except France with 0.72) with Spain at the bottom with a 0.39 ratio. This significant variation indicates gender specific elements in the employment structure.

According to educational level: highly-educated women. However, this general picture hides sharp contrasts between the different employment levels of poorly, moderately and highly educated women. Comparing highly educated women's employment levels within the different countries belonging to the three welfare state types, one notices much smaller differences between employment levels than the general picture indicates.

The range is limited to about 32 percentage points, ranging from Sweden with a female employment rate of 82.7% to Spain with an employment rate of about 50.2%. Omitting Spain and Italy from this picture, the spread diminishes even to less than 20 percentage points. This brings us to conclude that, with some reservations towards the Southern European countries, the distinction between the different welfare state types disappears almost completely when it comes to employment levels of highly educated women.

Table 3.4.1 Female employment rates and employment ratios in thirteen countries, according to educational level

Educational level	Female employment rate			Female/male ratio		
	Low	Middle	High	Low	Middle	High
Denmark (1992)	62.1	70.6	82.1	0.90	0.90	0.97
Norway (1995)	65.1	72.0	80.4	0.79	0.85	0.92
Sweden (1995)	68.2	84.9	82.7	0.85	0.997	0.998
UK (1995)	59.1	61.7	77.9	0.89	0.75	0.90
USA (1994)	59.4	68.8	78.7	0.76	0.85	0.87
Canada (1994)	43.4	66.3	77.4	0.67	0.87	0.93
Belgium (1992)	29.1	59.0	82.0	0.45	0.69	0.92
France (1994)	49.9	68.9	77.7	0.70	0.77	0.85
Luxembourg (1994)	39.1	51.7	63.9	0.51	0.56	0.67
Germany (1994)	48.3	60.8	69.8	0.71	0.75	0.86
The Netherlands (1994)	46.2	65.2	78.9	0.62	0.74	0.86
Spain (1990)	20.4	37.2	50.2	0.27	0.45	0.68
Italy (1995)	22.2	46.0	56.5	0.35	0.58	0.81

Note: Prime age individuals i.e. persons aged 20 to 59. This population was split into three roughly proportional, groups according to the national educational qualifications.
Employment does not include vocational training (Germany).
Source: LIS

The female/male ratio for highly educated men and women remains slightly higher for the social democratic countries, scoring higher than 90 per cent. Nonetheless, the difference between the ratios of both the liberal and conservative countries disappears completely, situated above 0.84 (with exception of Spain, Italy and Luxembourg). Overall, it is correct to say that the differences between the countries are very small.

Two preliminary conclusions can be drawn from these findings. First, it becomes clear that in all welfare states highly educated women's labour market participation reaches completion. This is certainly true if one takes into account the generational factor (age ranging from 20 to 59) present in the analysed tables. Second, it becomes clear that policies such as breadwinner modelled policies, the availability of care services or alternatives to labour market participation in the form of social benefits, have little or no effect on highly educated women's labour market participation. Indeed, Dutch, American or Norwegian highly educated women participate to about the same degree in the labour market.

According to educational level: poorly educated women. In contrast to highly educated women's labour market situation, poorly educated women's predicament is remarkably different. In all fifteen countries poorly educated women participate much less in the labour market than do highly educated women. The difference between these two groups of women ranges from a low of about 15 to 20 percentage points in the social democratic countries, up to a difference of about 35 percentage points for Spain.

Moreover, the contrast between poorly educated women and men is also bigger than it is for highly educated women and men. The female/male ratio is indeed generally much lower for poorly educated women and men. The tables point to increasing gender inequalities in all countries, as a woman's level of education diminishes (gradually from high to middle to low).

Also, the disparity between the distinct welfare state types regarding the female/male ratio for poorly educated women and men is substantial. The social democratic countries have very high ratios (up to 0.90 for Denmark), followed by the liberal countries (with ratios between 0.67 for Canada and 0.89 for the U.K.), with the conservative countries achieving ratios as low as 0.27 for Spain. Furthermore, the countries *within* each welfare state model show a fairly sizeable degree of homogeneity. The range between the countries is only 0.11 for the Scandinavian countries, up

283

to 0.26 for the conservative countries (disregarding Spain and Italy with exceptionally low employment ratios). The Esping-Andersen framework of welfare state regimes and employment outcomes is thus largely consistent with the labour market situation of poorly educated women.

Preliminary conclusion. From these findings the following conclusions can be deduced.

In all welfare states, education is a determining factor for female labour market participation and gender equity. The lower women's educational level is, the higher the inequalities become.

Gornick's fairly clear image on women's employment levels is sharply obfuscated when women with a high, middle or low educational level are observed separately. Regarding highly educated women's employment situation there is hardly any difference between the various regime types. For poorly educated women, the differences between countries is very big. Denmark and the UK have the smallest differences in the female/male ratio between poorly and highly educated women (less than 8 percentage points). There are somehow more considerable differences in Sweden, the US and Norway, and large arrears (of 15 percentage points and more) in Canada, France, Luxembourg, Germany and the Netherlands. In Belgium, Spain and Italy, the differences are larger than 40 percentage points.

The effect of schooling on women's labour market participation is smaller in the social democratic and liberal countries (with exception of Canada) and larger in the continental conservative countries. Indeed, the difference between Female/Male employment ratios of highly and poorly educated women (Table 3.4.1) is significantly smaller in social democratic and liberal countries than in conservative countries. Whereas the first two welfare models never demonstrate a difference higher than 15 percentage points (with the exception of Canada), the conservative welfare states never indicate a difference *less* than 15 percentage points, even crossing 40 percentage points for Belgium, Spain and Italy.

3.3 The impact of young children

To start with, it is important to note that the group of women and men with children younger than six years of age, form a more homogeneous group to compare the two sexes than the population of prime age people we have been studying so far. This group is quite homogeneous regarding age and the effect of the 'child burden' is counted in.

Overall, the presence of young children is a powerful source of gender differentiation. The female/male employment ratio diminishes in all countries, meanwhile keeping up the pattern of the three welfare state types (Gornick, 1999). Except for Norway, the social democratic countries still have a relatively high employment ratio (with Sweden at 0.93). The liberal countries float between 0.54 for Australia and 0.61 for USA and UK. The conservative countries, with the exception of France and Belgium, do not reach a ratio higher than 0.45. The range between these countries is considerable, namely 0.64.

When differentiating between educational levels (Table 3.4.2), the labour market participation drops, parallel to a decreasing female/male ratio as the educational level goes down. This drop is much stronger for the group of mothers with young children than it is for all women taken together. Particularly for poorly educated women the presence of young children is a powerful source of gender differentiation. Indeed, the drop in percentage points of the employment ratios of all women taken together compared to mothers taken separately, is generally higher for poorly educated mothers than for highly educated mothers (compare Table 3.4.1 with Table 3.4.2).

Moreover, the different patterns proper to each welfare state type are clearly discernible for the group of poorly educated young mothers. The social democratic countries still boast a relatively high employment ratio, ranging from 0.61 for Norway to 0.77 for Denmark. The liberal countries have a ratio of about 0.50, with the exception of the USA (0.67). No conservative country has a higher female/male ratio for young mothers than 0.40. Germany, Luxembourg, Spain and Italy drop even below 0.25, resulting in less than a quarter of low-educated mothers working compared to low educated men.

These findings result in a huge contrast between the ratios of the different welfare state types. It is clear that the effect of child burden as well as the effect of education is stronger in the liberal and conservative countries than it is in social democratic countries. For poorly educated mothers with young children Esping-Andersen's typology has an extensive predictive power. This is much less so for highly educated women – with or without children.

As a preliminary conclusion, we can state that education is a determining factor in gender equity through labour market participation in all welfare states, especially if young children are in play. This is more so in the conservative countries than in the liberal countries and certainly in the social democratic countries. A convincing indication of that conclusion is found when comparing the diffuse image of highly educated women's

Table 3.4.2   Female employment rates and employment ratios for women with a child under age six, in thirteen countries, according to educational level

| | Female employment | | | Female/male ratio | | |
Educational level	Low	Middle	High	Low	Middle	High
Denmark (1992)	69.1	81.8	87.6	0.77	0.88	0.97
Norway (1995)	55.8	73.7	84.7	0.61	0.76	0.87
Sweden (1995)	61.8	87.7	86.1	0.72	0.94	0.96
UK (1995)	37.2	46.9	61	0.51	0.56	0.67
USA (1994)	55.7	65.4	73.7	0.67	0.75	0.80
Canada (1994)	36.9	58.1	70.4	0.53	0.69	0.78
Belgium (1992)	28.7	50.7	80.2	0.39	0.58	0.85
France (1994)	30.3	58.5	73.3	0.37	0.63	0.77
Luxembourg (1994)	23.6	34.0	45.7	0.24	0.36	0.45
Germany (1994)	19.5	38.7	53.4	0.24	0.44	0.56
The Netherlands (1994)	34.2	47.8	66.1	0.39	0.54	0.72
Spain (1990)	14.7	26.2	53.8	0.19	0.29	0.57
Italy (1995)	15.1	39.3	63.1	0.19	0.43	0.65

Note: Prime age individuals are persons aged 20 to 59. The population was split into three, roughly proportional, groups according to the national educational qualifications.
Source: LIS

situation in Table 3.4.1 and the clearly ordered image of poorly educated women's situation in Table 3.4.2.

This empirical observation can be interpreted as a confirmation of Esping-Andersen's hypothesis. Indeed, one can conclude that both the possible alternatives for labour income (whether or not in the form of policies directed to keep mothers at home) and (the cost of) household care services are especially important for poorly educated women. These women, moreover, face potentially low levels of remuneration, substandard labour conditions, less job satisfaction and less labour law inspection/protection. Accordingly, contrary to highly educated women,

286

poorly educated women weigh the advantages and disadvantages of outdoor work more negatively.

3.4 Gender inequality in earnings

Inequality men/women. Comparing women and men's average labour income (Table 3.4.3), it is clear that women still earn considerably less than men do. Taking only into consideration the *full-time* labour market, women's average wage is at least 15% less than men's, in all three welfare state types, irrespective of women's educational level. In most countries the difference between the wages floats between 40% and 25%, with a low peak for poorly educated women in Spain (0.55 ratio).

In view of the fact that many women take up part-time employment, a significantly larger group can be compared when calculating the female/male earnings ratios for the *Complete* Labour Force. There, women's average earnings drop even more. Irrespective of their educational level, women's earnings are everywhere at least 25% less than men's[2]. In most countries the difference between the wages floats between about 40% and 45%, with a low peak for poorly educated women in Spain (0.53 ratio).

Mothers' average wages in the full-time labour force (Table 3.4.4) are generally lower compared to wages of women coming from all family types[3] (except for poorly educated Italian women, earning even more than men: 1.02 ratio). The differences between mothers and women from all family types are nowhere higher than 0.15 (except for poorly and highly educated German mothers with earnings ratios of respectively 0.35 and 0.31). There is no clear pattern arising along the lines of the three welfare state types. The social democratic, the liberal and conservative countries' ratios mostly lie between 0.45 and 0.70, a range of only 0.25. Mothers' earnings levels in the Complete Labour Force show the same pattern, however on a lower level.

Remarkable about these findings are the small contrasts between women of different educational levels. Highly educated women's higher employment level is not reflected in a higher earnings ratio. On the contrary, *poorly* educated women working have higher earnings ratios than *highly* educated women do, in the social democratic countries, the USA, France, Germany, and Italy. The difference is limited however to a maximum of 0.17 (for France, full-time labour force). In the other countries, such as Canada, Belgium, Luxembourg and Spain, highly educated women's earnings ratios are higher, but there the differences compared with poorly educated women's ratio is also no more than 0.15 (except for Spain 0.18, complete labour force).

Table 3.4.3   Gender earnings differentials in the full-time and complete labour force, in thirteen countries, according to educational level

Educational level	Female/male earnings ratio full-time labour force			Female/male earnings ratio complete labour force		
	Low	*Middle*	*High*	*Low*	*Middle*	*High*
Denmark (1992)	-	-	-	0.73	0.74	0.66
Norway (1995)	-	-	-	-0.70	0.67	0.67
Sweden (1995)	0.83	0.80	0.68	0.70	0.69	0.63
UK (1995)	0.69	0.70	0.69	0.48	0.52	0.57
USA (1994)	0.72	0.71	0.68	0.66	0.64	0.63
Canada (1994)	0.66	0.73	0.71	0.58	0.65	0.64
Belgium (1992)	0.66	0.76	0.74	0.52	0.66	0.67
France (1994)	0.86	0.80	0.69	0.71	0.69	0.64
Luxembourg (1994)	0.69	0.78	0.76	0.54	0.71	0.69
Germany (1994)	0.61	0.78	0.60	0.55	0.62	0.52
The Netherlands (1994)	0.75	0.76	0.68	0.47	0.54	0.55
Spain (1990)	0.55	0.65	0.71	0.53	0.63	0.71
Italy (1995)	0.84	0.82	0.74	0.77	0.75	0.72

Note: Female/male earnings ratio is defined as the unadjusted ratio of female by male mean gross labour income (net labour income for France, Italy, Luxembourg and Spain). Included individuals are manual workers and employees aged 20 to 59. Part-time employment is employment of less than 35 hours a week (except Spain). This population was split into three roughly proportional, groups according to the national educational qualifications. Employment does not include vocational training (Germany).
Source: LIS

This image is largely upheld when calculating the earnings ratios for married/cohabiting women.

Women's share of total earnings. While the comparison of average wages between men and women does not lead to a picture of equality of remuneration between the sexes, the study of women's share in total earnings leads to an even more unequal picture (Table 3.4.5). In not one of the thirteen countries women's share is more than half of the earnings. The three welfare state types offer parallel results with ratios around 0.40 for Denmark and Norway (all educational levels), UK, US, Canada, Belgium, France, and Italy (highly educated women).

Table 3.4.4   Gender earnings differentials in the full-time and complete labour force, for married women with a child under age six, in thirteen countries, according to educational level

	Female/male earnings ratio full-time labour force			Female/male earnings ratio complete labour force		
Educational level	*Low*	*Middle*	*High*	*Low*	*Middle*	*High*
Denmark (1992)	-	-	-	0.62	0.67	0.59
Norway (1995)	-	-	-	0.52	0.61	0.64
Sweden (1995)	0.66	0.50	0.47	0.56	0.42	0.45
UK (1995)	0.77	0.65	0.69	0.47	0.37	0.44
USA (1994)	0.68	0.64	0.65	0.60	0.57	0.59
Canada (1994)	0.59	0.65	0.65	0.51	0.52	0.54
Belgium (1992)	0.68	0.74	0.69	0.53	0.64	0.62
France (1994)	0.71	0.75	0.66	0.57	0.66	0.60
Luxembourg (1994)	0.56	0.76	0.80	0.51	0.56	0.57
Germany (1994)	0.35	0.64	0.31	0.57	0.66	0.60
The Netherlands (1994)	0.96	0.99	0.82	0.33	0.46	0.46
Spain (1990)	0.49	0.69	0.65	0.47	0.67	0.64
Italy (1995)	1.02	0.81	0.73	0.88	0.69	0.63

Note: Female/male earnings ratio is defined as the unadjusted ratio of female by male mean gross labour income (net labour income for France, Italy, Luxembourg and Spain). Included individuals are manual workers and employees aged 20 to 59. Part-time employment is employment of less than 35 hours a week (except Spain). * The population was split into three, roughly proportional, groups according to the national educational qualifications. Employment does not include vocational training (Germany).
Source: LIS

When looking at women's share in total earnings, the difference between educational levels becomes clear. Except for poorly educated women from Norway and Denmark, poorly educated women's ratios never exceed 0.36 (USA). They bring home only around one third (UK, USA, France, Germany and the Netherlands) or about a quarter or less (Canada, Sweden, Belgium, Luxembourg, Spain and Italy). The conservative countries are overall doing worse than the social democratic and liberal countries.

Table 3.4.5   Share of total earnings of women in all family types and of married women with a child under age six, in thirteen countries, according to educational level

Educational level	Women's share of total earnings all family types			Women's share of total earnings married women with a child under age six		
	Low	Middle	High	Low	Middle	High
Denmark (1992)	0.46	0.37	0.41	0.38	0.39	0.39
Norway (1995)	0.43	0.30	0.39	0.30	0.28	0.32
Sweden (1995)	0.28	0.28	0.27	0.15	0.17	0.22
UK (1995)	0.35	0.31	0.39	0.17	0.17	0.30
USA (1994)	0.36	0.40	0.37	0.31	0.34	0.33
Canada (1994)	0.28	0.39	0.38	0.21	0.30	0.30
Belgium (1992)	0.18	0.34	0.41	0.18	0.29	0.36
France (1994)	0.35	0.34	0.40	0.20	0.26	0.37
Luxembourg (1994)	0.24	0.24	0.32	0.12	0.13	0.26
Germany (1994)	0.30	0.34	0.26	0.08	0.15	0.11
The Netherlands (1994)	0.30	0.28	0.28	0.15	0.20	0.19
Spain (1990)	0.14	0.22	0.30	0.09	0.18	0.23
Italy (1995)	0.25	0.28	0.40	0.05	0.21	0.32

Note: Included individuals are manual workers and employees, aged 20 to 59, working both full-time and part-time. * The population was split into three, roughly proportional, groups according to the national educational qualifications. Employment does not include vocational training (Germany).
Source: LIS

Regarding the mothers' share of total earnings, the situation looks even grimmer, especially for the poorly educated mothers. Indeed, except for Denmark, Norway and the USA, poorly educated mothers bring home less than one fifth of the total earnings. Especially Germany, Spain and Italy rank low with less than 10% of total earnings earned by women. But also highly educated mothers never bring home more than 40% of the total earnings, and often much less (Germany 0.11, the Netherlands 0.19). Interesting is the same diffuse image of the three welfare state types for the highly educated women, where – except for Germany and the Netherlands – the range between the countries is not more than 0.17.

Earnings inequalities among women. The fact that poorly educated women's share in total earnings is significantly less than highly educated women's share is due to their previously noted lower participation rates and higher part-time employment rate. The various employment patterns that women take up, such as part-time employment, full-time employment, career interruption, also result into a less equal income distribution between women. The GINI Coefficient (Table 3.4.6) for women's labour income indicates less equality among women's income than men's labour income or than the family income as a whole. However, these findings may not lead us to conclude that women's labour has a desexualising effect on the overall income distribution, rather to the contrary. As Table 3.4.6 indicates, *families' income become less equal when omitting women' labour income* (cfr. infra).

3.5 Conclusion

From our findings on women's employment and earnings levels, it becomes clear that in all welfare states, education is a determining factor for gender equity, through the means of female labour market participation and labour income, especially if young children are in play. The lower women's educational level is, the higher the inequalities. Poorly educated women participate significantly less than highly educated women. The differences between welfare state types are much larger for poorly educated women's labour market situation, with practically no difference for highly educated women. Mothers with young children overall have a lower participation rate, decreasing as the educational level goes down.

Irrespective of their educational level, women's earnings are everywhere much lower then men's, with women's share in the total earnings being ever smaller. Making a distinction between educational levels, *poorly* educated mothers earnings ratios are slightly higher than highly educated women, especially for women working full time. The favourable situation of poorly educated women in overturned in some countries, especially when examining the complete labour force. Generally, highly educated women's share in total earnings – related to their higher labour market participation – is slightly larger than poorly educated women's share.

4. The distributional impact of female labour market participation

4.1 Introduction

In most countries – including highly employment generating countries – the increase in female employment has not been uniform in its impact. Among the low skilled women, participation rates are much lower, gender gaps are much wider and the differentiation among countries is much more marked.

Table 3.4.6   GINI coefficient based on family income, family income without labour income women, labour income women, labour income men, in twelve countries

	Total family income*	Family income – labour income women	Difference 1 and 2 in %	Labour income women	Labour income men
Denmark (1992)	.2212	.2685	+21.4	.2767	.2681
Norway (1995)	.2296	.2724	+18.6	.3196	.2842
Sweden (1995)	.2048	.2383	+16.4	.3236	.3025
UK (1995)	.3413	.3724	+9.1	.3782	.2868
USA (1994)	.3579	.3935	+9.9	.4294	.3831
Canada (1994)	.2987	.3280	+9.8	.3914	.3288
Belgium (1992)	.2212	.2445	+10.5	.2345	.2197
France (1994)	.2711	.3026	+11.6	.3526	.3186
Germany (1994)	.2564	.2923	+14.0	.3852	.3082
The Netherlands (1994)	.2627	.2967	+12.9	.3660	.2354
Spain (1990)	.3006	.2960	-1.5	.3677	.2666
Italy (1995)	.3450	.3630	+5.2	.2494	.2374

Note: Belgium, France, Italy, Spain: net income. Canada, Denmark, Finland, Germany, the Netherlands, Norway, Sweden, UK, US: gross income.
Source: LIS

As poorly educated women tend to live together with a poorly educated partner (as a consequence of educational homogamy) there is thus an accumulation of labour market (dis)advantages at the household level: work-rich households, consisting of well-qualified members, accumulating the advantages of stable, well-paying jobs on the one hand, and work-poor households, consisting of one or more unskilled members on the other. *It can therefore be expected that female earnings have a dis-equalising effect on income distribution.* Does empiricism confirm this hypothesis?

4.2 Educational homogamy and activity rates

Even though there are many differences between the fifteen countries regarding educational partner choice, more than half the couples are homogamous in about all of them. The level of homogamy is even almost higher or higher than 70 per cent in Germany and Spain (Table 3.4.7).

Moreover, in most countries the heterogamy remains 'male-dominated'. Only in Sweden, UK, France, Belgium and Italy, there is a (small) prevalence of female dominated heterogamy.

Table 3.4.7 Homogamy/heterogamy in thirteen countries

	Homogamous	*Male dominated*	*Female dominated*
Denmark (1992)	53.1	26.8	20.1
Norway (1995)	52.8	25.1	22.1
Sweden (1995)	53.6	21.2	25.2
UK (1995)	58.7	16.5	24.8
USA (1994)	63.2	18.7	18.1
Canada (1994)	56.2	21.9	21.8
Belgium (1992)	59.0	18.9	22.1
France (1994)	57.1	21.2	21.6
Luxembourg (1994)	51.9	24.8	23.3
Germany (1994)	76.9	13.9	9.2
The Netherlands (1994)	50.6	30.0	19.5
Spain (1990)	69.3	19.0	11.7
Italy (1995)	65.1	15.9	19.0

Note: Included individuals are married/cohabiting partners, with the head of the household aged 20 to 44.
Source: LIS

Not surprisingly then, Table 3.4.8, indicating the Activity Rates of the female spouse according to the educational level of their male partners, shows that female employment is significantly higher among women whose partner is high skilled.

Full-time employment rates of poorly educated men's spouses, for example drop below 30 per cent for all countries, whereas these rates are all over 30 per cent (with the exception of Luxembourg) for highly educated men's spouses.

4.3 Skills and dual earnership

The share of dual earners with children contrasts sharply along the lines of the welfare state models (Table 3.4.9). These rates range from almost 80 per cent in the social democratic countries, over about 60 per cent in the liberal countries (with the exception of UK, 37.2 per cent), to about 40 per cent in the conservative countries (with the exception of France, 78.5 per cent).

In the Scandinavian countries dual earnership has practically become a fact. This cannot be said of the 'conservative countries', of which many still have a long road ahead of them. Nevertheless it is clear that the 'two earners era' is making its way.

Again a difference can be perceived between highly and poorly educated families (Table 3.4.10). For highly educated mothers and women originating from all family types (Table 3.4.10), dual earnership is quasi universal. With some exceptions (UK, Luxembourg, Germany, Italy and Spain) dual earners rates easily cross 60 per cent. This is not the case for poorly educated mothers. Even in the social democratic countries their share of dual earners is much more limited. In the liberal and conservative countries less than half of the poorly educated women belong to dual earner-families.

Irrespective of the educational level moreover, the prevalence of dual earnership fades away with the increasing presence of young children. In some countries a continuous decrease of dual earnership is apparent (e.g. the U.K., France), in others the decrease is only significant as soon as the third child comes into the picture, with a drop in the dual earners rate at that point (e.g. Norway, the US, Luxembourg). The effect of children is the smallest for the social democratic countries, much smaller than in Continental Europe and the U.K.

The negative effect of children on the dual earners rates, is most felt by the poorly educated families. Only in the social democratic countries, a little more than half of the poorly educated mothers with three or more children belong to dual earning families. In the other countries, the apparent incompatibility between two working parents and the care of three or more young children is such that more than half and up to 80 per cent of poorly educated families (can) only count on one labour income.

294

Table 3.4.8 Activity rate of female spouse, according to educational level of male partner, in thirteen countries

	Educational Level Male Partner	Low	Middle	High
Denmark (1992)	Not Employed	32.6	25.4	20.4
	Part-time	-	-	-
	Full-time	-	-	-
Norway (1995)	Not Employed	26.3	25.6	22.1
	Part-time	-	-	-
	Full-time	-	-	-
Sweden (1995)	Not Employed	30.1	22.9	23.5
	Part-time	39.4	46.0	38.5
	Full-time	30.6	31.1	38.0
UK (1995)	Not Employed	41.1	39.3	40.3
	Part-time	32.2	28.6	23.5
	Full-time	26.7	32.1	36.2
USA (1994)	Not Employed	25.8	17.8	20.9
	Part-time	20.7	23.6	25.5
	Full-time	53.3	58.6	53.6
Canada (1994)	Not Employed	39.3	29.4	25.9
	Part-time	20.9	23.7	26.4
	Full-time	39.8	47.0	47.7
Belgium (1992)	Not Employed	54.4	31.8	28.8
	Part-time	16.3	27.3	29.3
	Full-time	29.3	40.9	42.0
France (1994)	Not Employed	42.5	32.8	33.4
	Part-time	20.5	22.4	24.2
	Full-time	37.0	44.8	42.4
Luxembourg (1994)	Not Employed	54.6	56.0	46.5
	Part-time	16.7	17.8	28.3
	Full-time	28.7	26.1	25.2
Germany (1994)	Not Employed	54.4	38.8	40.7
	Part-time	16.9	23.1	27.6
	Full-time	28.8	38.1	31.7
The Netherlands (1994)	Not Employed	39.7	31.2	28.8
	Part-time	43.8	47.8	48.4
	Full-time	16.5	21.0	22.8
Spain (1990)	Not Employed	76.4	69.1	54.7
	Part-time (<13 hrs.)	1.8	1.5	1.2
	Full-time (>13 hrs.)	21.8	29.4	44.1
Italy (1995)	Not Employed	64.6	51.9	32.7
	Part-time	14.4	13.2	24.3
	Full-time	21.1	34.8	43.0

Note: Included individuals are married/cohabiting female partners, with spouse younger than 45; Education was coded as to create three, roughly proportional, groups according to the national educational qualifications.
Source: LIS

Table 3.4.9 **Rate of dual earners with a child below age twelve, with two children of which the youngest is below age twelve, with more than two children of which the youngest is below age twelve, in thirteen countries**

	Dual earners with one child below twelve	Dual earners with two children of which the youngest is below twelve	Dual earners with more than two children of which the youngest is below twelve	Total dual earners with at least one child below twelve
Denmark (1992)	78.7	81.7	68.4	78.5
Norway (1995)	83.5	79.8	69.8	78.3
Sweden (1995)	78.0	70.0	74.7	78.1
UK (1995)	42.6	38.2	28.7	37.2
USA (1994)	63.0	61.8	52.3	59.6
Canada (1994)	76.5	60.9	51.3	60.2
Belgium (1992)	66.8	65.0	40.9	59.3
France (1994)	79.9	80.0	72.9	78.5
Luxembourg (1994)	47.5	30.7	34.2	37.0
Germany (1994)	54.6	45.5	27.3	46.0
The Netherlands (1994)	65.6	42.8	37.5	47.1
Spain (1990)	25.9	19.6	16.2	20.6
Italy (1995)	39.2	30.0	18.9	31.5

Note: Included individuals are married/cohabiting partners, aged 20 to 59. * The population was split into three roughly proportional, groups according to the national educational qualifications.
Source: LIS

4.4 Impact of female earnings on income distribution

Dual earnership generates a new income distribution. For a variety of reasons mentioned earlier in this text (e.g. educational homogamy, greater inequality in female earnings than in male earnings), it could be expected that this new income distribution would be more unequal than the hypothetical distribution that would have resulted from a lack of dual earnership. This is not the case, however. Our findings (Table 3.4.6) make clear that in all countries (except Spain) the income distribution is more equal when women's and men's incomes are cumulated (i.e. the actual income distribution) than it would be in the hypothesis of an income distribution in which women's earnings are excluded. It should be noted

Table 3.4.10 Rate of dual earners a with child below age twelve, with two children of which the youngest is below age twelve, with more than two children of which the youngest is below age twelve, in thirteen countries, according to educational level of female partner

Educational level female partner	Dual earners with one child below twelve			Dual earners with two children of which the youngest is below twelve			Dual earners with more than two children of which the youngest is below twelve		
	Low	Middle	High	Low	Middle	High	Low	Middle	High
Denmark (1992)	68.4	80.9	86.4	73.6	82.6	89.3	54.5	67.5	88.6
Norway (1995)	70.4	87.1	92.1	74.8	74.7	91.8	59.5	69.5	83.3
Sweden (1995)	58.4	80.4	80.7	63.9	83	81.8	51.0	79.4	82.8
UK (1995)	36.9	32.5	51.8	34.7	35.5	41.9	30.7	24.7	33.1
USA (1994)	57.1	63.9	69.9	56.7	63.8	66.9	47.9	55.6	57.7
Canada (1994)	48.6	62.9	73.3	48.9	59.0	66.4	32.6	55.5	56.7
Belgium (1992)	56.3	62.0	80.9	48.1	62.9	77.3	17.8	35.9	66.7
France (1994)	76.1	77.6	83.0	77.2	79.4	81.8	75.4	74.8	69.5
Luxembourg (1994)	38.9	37.3	67.4	37.5	22.1	34.4	23.1	17.6	51.5
Germany (1994)	31.9	55.0	62.4	32.4	47.0	49.1	27.5	27.5	26.5
The Netherlands (1994)	50.0	66.7	82.4	33.3	46.2	56.0	25.0	42.4	47.6
Spain (1990)	12.2	26.5	44.5	11.7	19.4	42.0	12.5	16.4	39.8
Italy (1995)	10.9	36.1	49.2	7.9	22.8	44.3	5.6	3.6	49.4

Note: Included individuals are married/cohabiting partners, aged 20 to 59. The population was split into three, roughly proportional, groups according to the national educational qualifications.
Source: LIS

that we thus perform a preliminary and static comparison, because we simply excluded women's earnings, without making behavioural assumptions about compensations through social security income.

The levelling effect of double income is most significant in the social democratic countries, where the inequality decreases considerably with 15 to 20 per cent and in the conservative countries with a decrease inequality between 10 and 15 per cent. In the liberal countries the double income decreases inequality with about 10 per cent. In this last group of countries, the inequality between the hypothetical family income excluding women's earnings is the biggest.

This (counter-intuitive) observation is the final result of various levelling and disequalising effects. First, educational homogamy has not (yet) the strong disequalising effect one would expect. We previously documented that there exists a rather strong relationship between the labour force status of wives and husbands, but there is no such link between the labour income of both partners. Indeed, the (positive) correlation between the income of partners is very weak (Table 3.4.11). Most countries have a correlation coefficient no higher than .25 (except for the UK, France, Italy and Spain, crossing .30). The contrast between countries however, is very big, without there being a clear pattern along the welfare state types. The correlations range from .044 for the Netherlands to .437 for Spain.

This result offers a crucial explanation for the observed levelling effect of female earnings. At an earlier stage of our analysis we noted that female earnings are more unequally distributed than male earnings and we related this observation to the larger heterogeneity of female labour with (among others) more part-time work and irregular job patterns than men. The weak earnings correlations, however, indicate that the earnings distributions of men and women run not parallel to each other. Therefore, the average amount of female earnings in the lower parts of the overall income distribution are not so different from the average amount in the highest parts of this distribution. Hence, female earnings are proportionally more important in the lower parts than in the higher parts and, consequently, Gini coefficients record an improvement of the income distribution through the addition of female earnings.

The weak correlation between partners' income can be explained through the working of two mechanisms. The first mechanism relates to the generational aspect of dual earnership. As female labour is still a relatively recent phenomenon, it is still the case that especially young women are economically active. This is related to men's low life-time income, i.e. a low income level in view of their entire career.

Secondly, 'compensatory factors' probably play a role in the levelling effect of dual earnings as well. The classical economic reasoning would predict partners to weight the individual income and in order to decide on whether or not to take a labour market job, on the working time and the kind of work, to take into account the presence of labour income by the other partner. In this respect, men with high earnings can be expected to be married to women with low earnings, who can afford to work part time and/or to have an irregular job pattern. Women married to men with low earnings, would then have higher earnings.

Table 3.4.11 Correlation between income for spouses, in 12 countries

	Correlation
Denmark (1992)	.190
Norway (1995)	.178
Sweden (1995)	.246
UK (1995)	.311
USA (1994)	.208
Canada (1994)	.216
Belgium (1992)	.174
France (1994)	.329
Germany (1994)	.140
The Netherlands (1994)	.044
Spain (1990)	.437
Italy (1995)	.383

Note: Belgium, France, Italy, Spain: net income. Canada, Denmark, Finland, Germany, the Netherlands, Norway, Sweden, UK, US: gross income.
Source: LIS

Additionally, arbitration effects cannot be generalised irrespective of the welfare state type. This text previously documented the higher prevalence of dual earnership for highly educated women, particularly in conservative and liberal welfare states, but also – be it to a lesser degree – in the social democratic countries. We explained this prevalence through arbitration effects, namely the balancing of the costs and gains of female outdoor labour. This arbitration differs according to the remuneration level, the job satisfaction and the working conditions on the one hand, and the child burden (care costs) on the other hand. The arbitration leads to different choices for women with different educational levels, such as the poorly educated women's 'choice' for single earnership. In countries where care services are widely available (such as the social democratic welfare states) or where no alternatives for labour income exist (such as the liberal welfare states) is the arbitration effect less significant than in countries where alternatives exist in the form of social benefits (such as the conservative welfare states). The desexualising effect of the 'arbitration' is therefore smaller in social democratic and liberal countries than in conservative welfare countries.

From these findings the following could be deduced. To the extent that through the generalisation of dual earnership, the 'generational' and 'compensatory' character of female labour income will disappear, the levelling effect of dual earnership on the income distribution is bound to disappear in time. If in the future women will have an educational profile equal to men and will participate permanently in the labour market, equally to men, their income distribution will become comparable to men's. Due to social endogamy the correlation between women and men's income will become very high. As a consequence, income distribution of couples will run the same, parallel unequal course as men's income distribution. To the degree that some categories of families would not follow the trend of the generalisation of dual earnership (such as poorly educated women with children), this trend could lead to a dis-equalising effect on the income distribution and (especially) on the distribution of well-being: the concentration in the top-category of wages would increase and the income share at the bottom would become smaller.

Up to this point, this hypothesis has not been materialised. Even though poorly educated women still work less than highly educated women do and even though homogamy is widespread, the findings in this chapter indicate that poorly educated women's higher labour market participation has/will have equalising effects on the overall income distribution.

Indeed, countries which have high dual earnership rates, indicate a high levelling effect of labour women's income on the total family income. The Scandinavian countries, boasting the highest dual earners rates (over 75 per cent), also represent the highest levelling effect by women's labour income (15 to 20 per cent). France, Germany (with respectively levelling effects of 11.6 per cent and 14 per cent) have dual earners rates of respectively 75.4 per cent and 53.8 per cent. But also the liberal countries' dual earners rates are relatively high (USA and Canada – over 60 per cent), and indicate a levelling effect of women's wages of almost 10 per cent.

In light of the fact that women's labour income has an overall levelling effect on income distribution, and in light of the fact that poorly educated women participate less to the labour market, but have slightly higher earnings ratios than highly educated women do in the majority of countries, it is highly likely that a higher degree of participation by poorly educated women to the labour market will stimulate a positive, equalising evolution of income distribution. In any case, rising inequality as a consequence of female labour is not a compulsory consequence and can be avoided by stimulating employment for poorly educated women.

Table 3.4.12 Rate of dual earners, all family types, according to educational level, in thirteen countries

Educational level female partner	Dual earners all family types			
	Low	Middle	High	Total
Denmark (1992)	66.2	76.3	85.5	74.7
Norway (1995)	69.8	79.4	89.8	77.6
Sweden (1995)	68.2	82.3	84.1	80.2
UK (1995)	38.9	40.6	51.4	44.3
USA (1994)	55.4	63.5	69.3	61.7
Canada (1994)	46.6	63.1	70.2	63.0
Belgium (1992)	30.2	53.1	73.6	51.1
France (1994)	69.3	75.6	79.4	75.4
Luxembourg (1994)	29.1	29.0	50.4	35.1
Germany (1994)	44.1	54.4	57.8	53.8
The Netherlands (1994)	37.7	54.7	67.3	49.7
Spain (1990)	10.1	21.2	44.9	18.2
Italy (1995)	8.4	24.7	44.2	26.6

Note: The population was split into three, roughly proportional, groups according to the national educational qualifications.
Source: LIS

5. Conclusion

This chapter clarifies how women's educational level matters with regard to their labour market participation, their earnings, and subsequently its distributional impact. It becomes clear that highly educated women participate more in the labour market than poorly educated women do. Their employment patterns are not significantly different in the three welfare state types. Next to their lower participation rates, poorly educated women's participation rates show considerable differences between the three welfare state types. Moreover, mothers generally have lower participation rates than women originating from all family types.

Women still earn considerably less than men do. Poorly educated women, especially in the full time labour force, earn – relative to their male counter-parts from the same educational level – slightly more than highly educated women do.

In all countries, more than half of the couples are homogamous, indicating limited differences between the different welfare state types. Those couples that are not homogamous, are generally male dominated.

Poorly educated women's lower activity rates have not been translated into a less equal income distribution. Overall women's income increases equality among family incomes. Countries with the highest rate of dual earners have the highest levelling effect of women's labour income. The further generalisation of dual earnership, through poorly educated women's higher participation to the labour market, presents itself as an instrument to safeguard an equal income distribution.

Notes

[1] The classification was based on simple frequency tables. Logically, the discrete nature of the educational codes made it impossible to delineate three parts of the population with exactly the same size. In some cases, certain groups may account for 40 to 45% of the population.

[2] Except for poorly educated Italian women, earning 'only' 23% less than their male counterparts.

[3] This is not true for the full-time working mothers in the Netherlands. This group has ratios between 0.82 (for highly educated women) and 0.96 (for poorly educated women). However, taking into account the small amount of Dutch women belonging to this group (very high part-time employment rate, fairly small overall employment rate), these findings do not point to a significant trend.

References

Allaer, R. (1982). Les instances de l'inégalité sociale des revenus, Thèse de doctorat, Louvain-la-Neuve.

Bakhoven, A., Schaayk, M. (1985). Inkomenseffecten van arbeidstijdsverkorting. Economisch en Statistische Berichten.

Beets (1998). Onderwijs en de geboorte van het eerste kind in Europa: FFS gegevens. Bevolking en gezin (27): 99-121.

Bergmann, B., Devine, J., Gordon, P., Reedy, D., Save, L., Wise, C. (1980). The effects of wives labor force participation on inequality in the distribution of family income. *The Journal of Human Resources*, 3, 1980, pp. 452-455.

Blau, D. (1984). Family earnings and wage inequality early in the life cycle. *Review of Economics and Statistics* 66, pp. 200-207.

Cantillon, B. (1984). Tweeverdieners, inkomensverdeling en bestaanszekerheid. Tijdschrift voor Sociologie, pp. 87-106.

De Kam, C., Pommer, E., Wiebrens, C. (1982). Dubbel en dwars: over dubbele inkomens in 1979. Economisch en Statistische Berichten, 29 september, pp. 1040-1047.

302

Esping-Andersen G. (1990). *The Three Worlds of Welfare Capitalism* (Princeton).

Gornick, J.C. (1999). Gender Equality in the Labour Market: Women's Employment and Earnings. Luxembourg Income Study Working Paper No. 206, 38.

Gronau, R. (1982). Inequality of family income: do wives' earnings matter. In Ben Porath, Y. (ed.) *Income distribution and the family*, Population and Development Review, Suppl. to Vol. 8, 119 e.v.

Grubben, B. (1987). Dubbele inkomens en ongelijkheid, een paradox. Economisch en Statistische Berichten, pp. 736-739.

Hagenaars, A., Homan, M., Van Praag, B. (1984). Draagkrachtverschillen tussen huishoudens met één resp. tweekostwinners. Economisch en Statistische Berichten, pp. 552-559.

Harris, R., Hedderson, J. (1981). Effects of wife's income on family income inequality. Sociological Methods and Research, pp. 211-232.

Larmuseau, H. (1976). De personele inkomensverdeling in België: statistische analyse. Financiële Statistieken nr. 10.

Larmuseau, H., Lauwaert J., Spinnewijn F. (1979). Determinanten van de personele inkomensverdeling, Vlaams Wetenschappelijk Economisch Congres, Referaten Inkomens- en vermogensverdeling, Vereniging voor Economie, Brussels, I.1-26-27.

Layard, R., Piachaud D., Stewart M. (1978). The causes of poverty, Background Paper nr. 5 en 6, Royal Commission on the Distribution of Income and Wealth, London.

Layard, R., Zabalza A. (1979). Family income distribution: explanation and policy evaluation. *Journal of Political Economy* 5, pp. 133-161.

Lehrer, E., Nerlove M. (1981). The impact of female work on family income distribution: Black-White Differentials. The Review of Income and Wealth, pp. 423-432.

Morgan, J. (1962). The anatomy of income distribution. *The Review of Economics and Statistics* 3, pp. 270-283.

Nelissen, J. (1987). De invloed van het inkomen van de gehuwde vrouw op de inkomensverdeling van echtparen. *Maandschrift Economie* 51, pp. 97-107.

Odink, J., Pott-Buter H. (1981). Echtparen met dubbele inkomens. Economisch en Statistische Berichten, pp. 774-777.

Renaud, P., Siegers J. (1984). Welvaartsverschillen tussen echtparen met éénverdiener en echtparen met tweeverdieners. *Beleid en Maatschappij* 3, pp. 66-70.

Royal Commission on the Distribution of Income and Wealth (1977). Lower incomes. Report nr. 6. HMSO.

Sweet, J. (1971). The employment of wives and inequality of family income. Proceedings of the American Statistical Association, pp. 1-5.

Swidinsky, R. (1983). Working wives, income distribution and poverty. Canadian Public Policy, IX.

Winegarden, C. (1987). Women's labour force participation and the distribution of household incomes: evidence from cross-national date. *Economica* 214, pp. 223-236.

Wolfson, M. (1986). Stasis amid change. Income inequality in Canada 1965-1983. *The Review of Income and Wealth*, pp. 337-369.

303

3.5 What determines work resumption from long sickness spells? – an analysis of six countries

Edward Palmer and Ali Tasiran

In many countries, back pain is the most frequent diagnosis behind long-term absence from the workplace due to sickness and disability take-up. In fact, disability originating from back pain accounts for around 30 per cent of total disability benefit costs in many countries, and these costs have been increasing persistently for the past three decades. The economic side of this involves the exit of human capital resources from the labor market, with consequent costs for benefit systems. With low birth rates, especially for European workforce will begin to shrink within the next two decades. At the same time old-age pensioners will increase by around 50 per cent. Confronted with this prospect, countries can no longer afford to ignore the mechanisms leading to early exit from the labor force due to back pain. Something will have to happen to change the trend.

The costs of long-term sickness and disability constitute a difficult challenge for policy. It is important that people who cannot work have access to benefits. On the other hand, in many countries disability benefits provide a convenient path for exit from the labor force for older workers. In the worst case disability has been used as a convenient means for employers, with the support of unions, to rationalize the workforces of larger firms – which is a clear case of moral hazard. This practice also undoubtedly affects the motivation of older workers to seek new tasks – and for employers to encourage them – when successful return to work might call for this.

Long-term sick-listing is the step before disability, and the way to reduce the number who go on to disability take-up is to work towards returning people to their workplaces or the workforce in general instead of letting them make this final transition. This is easier said than done. It is well recognized that a large number of factors determine whether or not an individual resumes work after a long spell of sickness. The aim of this study is to shed light on how background factors and interventions affect the odds of work resumption of a group of people from different countries who have been away from the workplace with back pain 90 days or more.

The data analyzed in the study were collected by a group of international researchers participating in the Work Incapacity and Reintegration Project (WIR project) under the umbrella of the International Social Security Association. The same study design and questionnaires were used to collect data in all six participating countries. The WIR project design is described in Bloch, Prins and Veerman (1993) and Bloch and Prins (2000). Bloch and Prins (2000) is the main report from the WIR project and provides a wealth of information and analysis about the country cohorts making up the database.

This chapter follows a different approach to that employed in the analysis in the WIR study, but using the same database. In the WIR study, work resumption outcomes are analyzed at the end of one and two years using a standard logit analysis. In this study we use a discrete-time hazard model and take advantage of the fact that many people reported work resumption already between 90 days and the time when they answered the first questionnaire after 90 days. Our study focuses on the connection between work resumption, work ability, and four measures of health for which data were collected in the WIR study: ADL, pain intensity, vitality and mental health. We examine whether work resumption, work ability and health outcomes are driven by the same factors, and the importance of improved work ability and health in determining work resumption. Our aim is to gain new insights into the processes determining the outcomes of improved health, work ability and work resumption.

1. The work integration study (WIR) inclusion criteria and follow-up period

Cohorts were gathered from 6 countries: Denmark, Germany, Israel, the Netherlands, Sweden and the US. In most countries only regions participated, and the sample is not a random sample for the whole country. Employees (and not self-employed and unemployed) away from work 90 days with lower back pain and between the ages of 18 and 59 could be drawn randomly for the study.

Cases satisfying the criteria were chosen during 1994-1995 and followed for two years. All countries were finished with follow-ups by the end of 1998.

2. Work resumption and work capacity

All the individuals in this study were chosen for their country cohorts because they fulfilled the criteria that they were away from a place of employment for 90 days with a medical diagnosis of lower back pain and with their sick leave covered by social insurance. For people to have the right to compensated sick leave, *work capacity* must be reduced by poor health. Work capacity – which we will use interchangeably with work ability - is a key term, then, for this study. Health status is one of the crucial factors to be considered in explaining changes in work capacity and return to work, but the model we will test postulates that there are many other factors as well.

Our conceptual point of departure is the general model of work ability formulated by Ilmarinen (1999). In this model, human resources, or human capital, rest on a foundation of skills acquired through education, training and experience at the work place, and at any given time on the health status of the individual. Human resources and health, together with general societal attitudes and individual motivation and the workplace environment determine work ability. For persons away from work for health reasons, medical interventions, vocational interventions and interventions affecting the work environment can be used to facilitate work resumption. These are the policy variables that governments, social insurance and medical organizations and employers have at their disposal. These are also the policy variables we hope to learn something about in this study. Let us discuss these briefly.

2.1 Medical interventions

Medical interventions were documented by the participations of individuals in the WIR study. The kinds and frequency of medical interventions in the WIR data set are presented and discussed in Hansson and Hansson (2000).

A recent Swedish review of studies (SBU 2000) concludes that there is little evidence-based support in the medical literature for specific treatment effects for back pain, in spite of the fact that there are many treatments available and used. The exceptions are treatments based on manual medicine and involve manipulation according to specific techniques. Although the WIR study identified a large number of specific interventions, the study does not include a separate category for those measures that according to SBU 2000 prove to have evidence-based effects. For this reason, we have chosen to examine a widely used and broader category of 'active' measures, encompassing mainly physical therapy to determine whether an effect can be identified at this level of aggregation.

2.2 Vocational interventions

As cases become longer, the social insurance administration will begin to consider the need for some form of vocational intervention. Vocational interventions include education or training to acquire new skills, measures designed to adapt the physical workplace environment or the workplace demands placed on individuals and their control over these, hours worked, and other arrangements that can facilitate return to work.

Previous studies have not been successful in showing that vocational training shortens the duration of spells of sickness. On the other hand, vocational interventions have been shown to increase the earnings of those who do return after participating in a program, e.g. Berkowitz (1988) and Dean and Dolan (1991). These studies confirm that education and/or training yield a positive return to human capital, but provide no evidence that vocational measures shorten the length of sickness spells.

In the WIR study individuals were asked to document interventions, including the month in which they began. The frequency and use of various forms of interventions varies considerably among the countries making up the database for this study (Bergendorff and Gordon (2000)). For the purposes of the present study, interventions are grouped as training and education, workplace adaptation measures (changing the physical workplace, adapting hours and/or tasks, etc.) and other measures. These are tested as possible determinants of work resumption, improved work ability, but also improved health status.

2.3 The work environment

It is well documented that the physical demands of the workplace play an important role (e.g. Aarts and de Jong (1992) and Johnson, Baldwin and

Butler (1998)). For persons suffering chronic back pain, it may be difficult to return to the same work environment if it involves heavy lifts or repetitive movements, whereas work resumption can be easier for persons working in less physically demanding environments. This would also be true for workplaces where the workplace demands or control over the work process are not matched well to the capacity of the individual.

Heavy lifts and repetitive movements, but also noise, dust particles in the air and extreme heat or cold are among the factors that create more difficult work environments. As we age our physical strength eventually diminishes, although there is considerable evidence that this 'natural' process can be counteracted with training. Our willingness to put up with extreme heat and cold at the workplace may also change as we age, even though the remuneration may be good for this sort of work.

Research has also shown how mental demands can affect work ability. This research is mainly associated with the initial work of Karasek (1979), and more recently explored by Karasek and Theorell (1990). The major thesis and findings are that healthy work consists of a situation where individuals feel that what is demanded of them challenges them in a positive sense and that they have control over the situation. The greater the demands and the lesser the control, the more likely it is that negative stress will arise. We construct a variable to capture this effect by using the ratio of demand to control, as measured by answers to standard questions developed by Karasek and Theorell.

2.4 Some of the main features of the WIR database

A general overview of the main characteristics of the WIR data[1] with respect to the Ilmarinen model of factors affecting work capacity, and thereby work resumption show the following.

Health – A larger percent of those reporting good functional capacity at 90 days had returned in two years, compared with those with only moderate or poor functional capacity. A larger percent of those with no or only mild pain had returned to work compared to those with moderate or severe pain.

Education and skill levels – In all countries a higher level of education is associated with a higher rate of work resumption.

Motivation – This is measured in this study with questions about why one works and a personal forecast on return-to-work prospects. Specifically, people were asked whether they were just working for money;

or whether work is the most important thing in their life. This variable is examined in the present study. They were also asked in the first questionnaire at 90 days to predict whether they could return to work. The Dutch cohort was the most optimistic and the German cohort the most pessimistic, and work resumption tended to follow these predictions (Bloch and Prins 2000).

Work environment – The work resumption rate is highest among persons with the lowest physical job demands and the jobs that provide the best balance between job demands and control over these demands.

The data also indicate that with increasing age the frequency of work resumption is lower at the end of two years in all countries but the Netherlands, where, on the other hand, the cohort is younger than those from the other countries. Sickness duration and disability take-up are generally observed to increase with age. Why is age so important? Age can be a proxy for any of a number of processes that can determine work capacity and work resumption. Among these are reduced physical capacity, knowledge or skills that are not up to date, a change in attitudes about what is important as people age, and decreased ability and/or willingness to cope with job demands.

2.5 Economic factors

Ilmarinen's model focuses on factors that are important for occupational health and work capacity: health status, skills, motivation and work environment. However we expect also that the economic situation of individuals may be important. What are the hypotheses usually put forward and examined?

First, if higher education and earnings are linked to workplaces with low physical demands (the absence of heavy lifts, monotonous and repetitive work, etc.) and a healthy combination of job demands and individual control over these, return to work will be positively correlated with earnings. Second, low-income earners may not be able to afford to remain away from the workplace as long as high-income earners, which suggests that absenteeism will be longer for persons with higher earnings. (On the other hand, persons with very high earnings are notorious workaholics.) Third, however, it is probable that other income including the income of other family members, rather than individual earnings, is important for the household's evaluation of what is affordable. High family income (e.g. where there are spouse's earnings or other sources of income) may have a negative effect on work resumption.

Most studies examining the earnings or income effect on return to work have examined disability take-up, rather than exit from long-term sickness into work, as in this study. For example, using Dutch data, Aarts and de Jong (1992) found no effect of individual earnings in determining disability grants. This may be attributable to the high degree of earnings replacement in the Dutch social insurance system, although the latter study revealed evidence that other sources of household income may reduce return to work.

For Sweden, Skogman-Thoursie (1999) has shown that less restrictive criteria for take-up of disability benefits have a positive effect on the probability of receiving a benefit, i.e. of not returning to work after a long spell of sickness. As in the Netherlands, earnings replacement for sickness spells in Sweden is high, and it is not likely that people are affected much by the after tax loss if they have other sources of income than their own earnings. Butler and Worall (1985) find that higher benefit levels and lower wages are correlated with longer spell duration. Meyer and Viscusi (1995) find that higher benefit levels have a significant positive effect on benefit duration and Johnson, Baldwin and Butler (1998) find that low replacement rates promote return to work. In sum, what evidence there is suggests that there is an element of moral hazard built into insurance systems covering earnings lost due to sickness. The more people can afford to be away, the longer spells can be expected to be, with disability benefits being the likely end result as time goes on.

Economic theory has a paradigm that explains aging and work. As people get older poorer health, weaker motivation and an expectation that future earnings are likely to stagnate or fall together mean that a permanent benefit may provide almost as high a level of lifetime welfare expected earnings from additional work. The perceived value of non-work may be greatest and as a result influence individual labor supply. The tendency of employers to use disability as a path out of the labor force in the rationalization process is a demand effect. According to economic theory this effect arises because the productivity of older workers falls below a level needed to justify their current wage. Instead of accepting a flexible wage downward, it may even be in the interests of the individual to accept a disability outcome based on a higher (current or previous) wage.

This suggests yet another explanation of the age effect in the equation for work resumption as we come closer to the 'normal' age for claiming an old age benefit, the more likely it becomes for many of us that the combination of benefit systems and taxes will make it more advantageous to accept available avenues for leaving the labor force. Evidence examined recently from eleven OECD countries in a study edited by Gruber and Wise (1998) indicates that in countries where the tax-benefit system is more generous for older workers the more likely it is that they will exit the labor force early. In OECD countries the major path of exit of older workers is through long-term sickness and disability. Palme and Svensson (2000) are demonstrated this for Sweden in a recent study.

Work capacity in the insurance sense depends also on the gatekeepers, generally the doctors and insurance administrators. Different administrative process can also affect the outcome for work resumption. Wadensjö and Palmer (1996), Berkowitz and Burkhauser (1996), Frick and Sadowski (1996) and Aarts and de Jong (1996) discuss this aspect of the problem for Sweden, the US, Germany and the Netherlands. Although there is no general consensus about what is the right thing to do, factors such as early contact and screening seem to be important for prompt work resumption.

Finally, the rules regarding earnings replacement and job security during sickness are also important. Among the countries studied, Germany, the Netherlands and Sweden have good job security during sickness, whereas in Denmark, Israel and the US is easier to lose your job. The tougher regimes might be expected to lead more likely to more successful results, if economic factors are among the most important. Without job security but with generous benefits, as in Denmark, one might expect to find poor work resumption results and that people are on benefits to a greater extent. With good job security and high replacement rates, other factors, such as work environment at the present workplace may be the most important.

In sum, health, education and skill levels, motivation and the work environment, as well as individual economic considerations affecting individual labor supply and/or employer demand for older workers can all influence the outcomes of work ability and return to work. So can gate-keeping procedures and practices and the system of rules surrounding sickness.

3. Overview of the country cohorts[2]

The cohorts recruited in the six countries differ considerably, and in ways that should be expected to affect the country outcomes and that should be taken into account in evaluating the results. A number of important characteristics describing work capacity are brought together in Table 3.5.1. What does the table indicate?

The German cohort is the oldest with an average age of 49. Over 60 per cent of the cohort is 50-59 years old. The Swedish cohort is next oldest, with an average age of 44, and with 36 per cent of the cohort between the ages of 50 and 59. The cohorts from the Netherlands and Israel are the youngest. The German cohort had by far the lowest educational level, followed by the cohort from the Netherlands.

The Dutch cohort was the most optimistic about its chances of returning to work when asked at the outset at 90 days. Only 2% thought they could not return to work – compared to for example 32% in Germany. In addition 75% of the Dutch cohort predicted at 90 days that they could return to the same job. In contrast, only 25% of the Danish and 28% of the Israeli cohort predicted that they could return to the same job.

There were no large differences in country cohorts in perceived pain as measured at 90 days. On a scale of 0 to 10, where 0 is no pain, countries started at 5.6 (Denmark) to 6.3 (Israel). ADL scores, which can range from 0 (bad) to 100 (good) were between 47 and 53 in all countries but Israel, for which it was much lower. Whereas five of the six countries began with approximately the same ADL average at 90 days (scores ranging from 47 to 53), the Dutch cohort was the only one to dramatically improve its average ADL score, which went from 48 to 65.

The Dutch cohort was the only cohort reporting substantial improvement – on average – in the Sciatica score, which measures pain radiating out into the legs. The Dutch scored much higher on the vitality score at 90 days than the other countries and (together with Denmark and Sweden) scored high at the outset on mental health. This indicates that the Dutch cohort, although scoring similarly on pain and ADL functions, nevertheless may have been in better overall health at the outset than the cohorts from the other countries.

Summing up by country, the German cohort was 'old' and poorly educated, and for this reason, the least likely to succeed in terms of the work ability model presented at the outset. This was also the outcome. A large percentage – 56% – of the Danish cohort indicated that they needed to

313

**Table 3.5.1 Outcomes at two years and baseline indicators of the work
capacity of the country cohorts**

	Denmark	Germany	Israel	Nether-lands	Sweden	United States
Work resumption % at 2 years	40	35	60	72	63	62
Average age	41	49	39	40	44	42
Age, % of pop 50-59	14	61	18	18	36	-
Educ., % with low	45	95	-	67	36	-
Mother lang, % 'no'	8	3	34	2	18	18
ADL score at 90 days	48	47	34	47	53	52
Pain score at 90 days	5.6	6.5	6.3	5.8	5.9	5.9
Work resumption prognosis at 90 days:						
Yes, same job	25	38	28	75	61	57
Yes, new job	56	31	58	24	23	30
No, can't work	19	32	14	2	16	14

Source: Veerman and Palmer (2000)

change jobs to resume work; Denmark does not differ greatly from key
baseline characteristics of the other countries. The Danish cohort does not
stand out in terms of health, age or education. Nevertheless the Danes show
a poor work-resumption outcome.

The remaining four countries show the best outcomes, with the Netherlands ending up on top. The Israeli cohort was drawn from a population with work injury, and, like the Danes, 58% indicated that they would need to change jobs. In addition, 34% of the Israeli cohort had another mother tongue. The Dutch cohort was in the middle of the cohorts in terms of age, but had the second lowest educational level. On the other hand, all but 2% had Dutch as their mother language. The Swedish cohort was the second oldest – on average 44 years old and, for example, 5 years older than the Israeli cohort, the youngest. As many as 18% did not have Swedish as their mother language, but the percentage of persons with a low level of education was lower than in other countries.

The US age structure was in the middle, but 18% of the cohort had some other language than English as their mother language. The US cohort does not stand out from the others in any other respect, with one exception. Together with Israel the US stands out with regard to benefit rules. Of the non-resumers, 51% of the Israelis and 73% of the Americans had no benefit at the end of two years – compared to 11% in Denmark, 13% in the Netherlands and 17% in Sweden. In other words, a larger percent of the Americans and Israelis left benefit status without returning to work.

4. Estimation of the effects of individual factors with a discrete-time transition model

We will use discrete-time transition models to study the events of work resumption, improvements in health and work ability. Although the events of resuming work or experiencing improved health occur on a daily basis, i.e. in small discrete steps that can be viewed as occurring in continuous time, in the database information is gathered in response-time intervals *after* 90 days, one and two years. For this reason it is appropriate to use a discrete-time model in estimating the probability that a person will begin to work on these occasions.

We are interested in estimating the probability that a person will resume work at the measuring occasions of shortly after 90 days, between 90 days and one year and between one and two years. The first measurement period is of particular interest. People included in the study because they fulfilled the 90-day inclusion criterion may have already returned to work by the time they filled in the first questionnaire (between 90 days and up to several weeks thereafter).

Technically speaking persons who are still sick-listed are 'at risk' to resume work at the measurement time. The *hazard rate* for work resumption is the probability that the sick-listed person will begin to work. It is an unobserved variable that controls both the occurrence and the timing of transitions. It is the dependent variable in the model. In our modeling, by necessity, it is assumed that the hazard rate varies at measurement occasions, but is the same for all persons at each measurement occasion.

The model we have chosen to work with is well known in the literature, so we will simply summarize it here. Let P_{it} denote the conditional probability that an individual (i) has a transition from one state to another at time t, given that the individual is still at risk, e.g. has not already resumed work, at this time. By taking the logit transformation of P, where P_{it} varies between 0 and 1, we have the familiar logit expression:

$$\log\left[\frac{P_{it}}{1-P_{it}}\right] = \alpha(t) + \beta_1 x_{it1} + \beta_2 x_{it2} + \dots + \beta_k x_{itk}$$

This is the model that will be employed in our statistical analysis of the data. We allow for variation in the hazard over time with the time-variant constant, α. The explanatory variables relate to measures of education and experience, health, earnings, motivation, workplace characteristics and interventions. The coefficients β give the changes in the log odds for a unit increase in a variable x.

The results are derived from estimation of multivariate (joint effect) logit models. The entire database includes a great number of variables, and many have been tested but did not perform well and are not reported here[3].

5. The hazard analysis

Outcomes have been measured at three points in time. These were when the 90-day, first and second year questionnaires were answered. Work resumers have been defined for the purposes of this study as persons who have resumed work, but also persons who answered that they will resume work within a month after filling in the questionnaire. Once again, people could have already resumed work when they filled in the 90-day questionnaire, even though they had to be sick-listed 90 days to be included in the study. Observations classified as work resumption are uncensored observations in the hazard analysis. This group plus the respondents still not working, together with non-respondents at the measurement time, constitute the total *risk set* (stock) at 90 days. For each later period, the risk set consists of censored and uncensored persons and *new* dropouts. (Dropouts from the previous measurement time are excluded from the current risk set.)

Table 3.5.2 illustrates the procedure, based on the data for work resumption for all the countries together.

Table 3.5.2   **Work resumption 90 days sickness due to lower back pain**

Measurement time	Censored	Uncensored	Lost	Total
0 days 90 days	1734	372	500	2606
1 year	1122	99	513	1734
2 years	604	518	0	1122
Total	3460	989	1013	5462

The observed hazard rates are:

$h(1) = (372/2606) = 0.143$ (The 500 'lost' persons – who did not answer the questionnaire but dropped out instead - are included in the risk set.)

$h(2) = (99/1734) = 0.057$, (The 500 dropouts at 90 days are not in the risk set at one year, but the 513 who dropped out at one year are.)

$h(3) = (518/1122) = 0.462$ (The 513 dropouts at one year are not in the risk set at two years.)

The observed odds are:

$$o(1) = (372/1734) = 0.215$$
$$o(2) = (99/1122) = 0.088$$
$$o(3) = (518/604) = 0.858$$

Note that a drawback of the model employed here is that people can make more than one transition *within* a time interval. For example, people can have a long relapse between one and two years, but still be recorded as working at two years.

5.1 Variables

The variables used are defined in Table 3.5.3 For the most part, the definitions are straightforward. The health intervention variables need some more explanation, however. We construct and employ a variable for active interventions, defined as physical training and physical therapy. In principle, everyone in the database has had at least one visit to the doctor (which itself can entail many different things depending on whether the doctor is a general practitioner, specialist, etc.). Visits to the doctor and, implicitly, other 'passive therapy' (massage, traction, mud baths, etc.) constitute the basis of comparison in the analysis, called passive therapy.

Age is defined as a non-linear variable by including both age and age-squared. If the estimated effect of age-squared is negative, the negative effect will increase with increasing age.

The logistic regressions test whether there is a significant difference between groups. Comparisons are made between women and men; between native and non-native speaking persons; between persons living alone versus together with someone; between persons with different levels of education; between persons with a previous health history and/or comorbidity and those without; between persons who say they have social support and those who say they do not; between those whose who say their work is and those who say it is not characterized by repetitive movements, heavy lifts and a disproportion between work demands and control over one's own work situation; as well as two questions reflecting individual attitudes towards work, information on individual earnings and work history.

6. The results of estimation

Separate equations have been run for six outcome variables: work resumption, work ability, ADL, pain, vitality and mental health. Since the dependent and explanatory variables have the same definition in all countries, it seems reasonable to pool the countries into a single group. The results of estimation for all six countries together are reported in the following tables. Table 3.5.4 reports the results of regressions run for work resumption and Table 3.5.5 reports the results for the work ability and health equations.

318

7. Work resumption

Three models have been estimated for work resumption. First, we have examined the effects of work ability and the health variables, excluding all other variables. Second, we have examined the effects of work ability, the health variables and all the background variables. Finally, in the third model, we have examined the effects of the background variables alone. The third model is used for comparison with the regressions explaining work ability and health. The results of the third model are discussed and compared with the work ability and health results separately, below. Here, we focus on the results for work resumption.

The first model shows that work ability and all four health variables have a significant effect on work resumption. The most important of these is no pain, followed by no ADL limitations, perceived work ability and vitality. Mental health did not play a significant role.

In Model 2 we add all the background and time variables, and still obtain approximately the same results. According to these estimates, reduced pain and ADL limitations are important for work resumption, as is a feeling of vitality. Work ability still has a significant effect, but this is not as strong as the pain and ADL effects.

Comparison of Models 2 and 3 show that the background variables exert roughly the same effects with or without the health and work ability variables. Increasing age, being a woman, and being a foreigner reduce the odds of work resumption, while higher having a background with education improves the odds. Living alone has a negative effect and being a non-smoker and having a higher Height/Weight index have positive effects. A previous history of sickness and even more so comorbidity has negative effect on work resumption. Active medical interventions by 90 days have a positive effect compared to inactive measures. The intervention with the strongest effect is workplace adaptation.

7.1 Work resumption, work ability and health

The time variables at one year in the work resumption, work ability, ADL, mental health and vitality equations are all significant.

Table 3.5.3   Definition of variables

Gender and age

Age/10 – age at 90 days/10

Age squared – age*age/10

Female – compared to males

Health, physical capacity, social functioning

Physical capacity indicators:

Non-smoker – the individual does not smoke

Height/weight index

Health history:

Sickness – number of weeks sick-listed with back pain the previous 12 months

Comorbidity – other illness/injury that interferes with work resumption

Social functioning indicator:

Living alone – the individual lives alone (compared to living with someone)

Support – the individual receives support from family, friends

Education, skills and knowledge

Educational capital:

Education – completion of primary, secondary, tertiary or university education

Experience:

Proportion of years of work – ratio of years worked to total years from age 20

Language skills:

Foreigner – the country's language is not the individual's mother tongue (compared to native-born)

Initial capital, experience and language skills combined:

Earnings – the level of the individual's own earnings prior to the sickness spell

Workplace characteristics
Repetitive work – work involves repetitive movements
Heavy work – work involves heavy lifts, according to individual judgments
Strain – Index relating self-perceived job demands to control over job tasks

Attitude towards work
Working only for money – 'I'm only working for the money'
Work most important – 'Working is the most important thing in my life'

Medical interventions
Active medical treatment (training, physical therapy) prior to 90 days
Active medical treatment (training, physical therapy) between 90 days and one year
Active medical treatment (training, physical therapy) between one and two years

Vocational interventions
Active w.p. – Active contact with the workplace during the period of sickness
Job training – job training or education
Adapted workplace

In order to examine whether the effect of a variable differs between countries, we also examine separate country equations. The results are discussed here and tables are available from the authors upon request. Separate equations are also estimated for work resumption, work ability and four measures of health. This enables us to see whether they are affected in a similar way by the various explanatory variables.

By the end of the first year, many had returned, and according to the multi-country-cohort equation this coincided with significant improvements in work ability and ADL scores. The coefficient of time in the work-resumption equation is less than unity, reflecting the fact that a larger percentage of those who were to resume work during the first year had already done so – or intended to do so within a month – when they answered the 90 day questionnaire.

Table 3.5.4 Work resumption. All country cohorts together

	Model 1	Model 2	Model 3
Intercept	-1.711***	-2.728***	-2.632***
	(0.051)	(0.803)	(0.782)
Time = 90 days		0	0
= 1 year		-1.206***	-0.854***
		(0.158)	(0.147)
= 2 years		1.562***	1.784***
		(0.128)	(0.123)
Work ability	0.404***	0.378***	
	(0.114)	(0.131)	
ADL	0.649***	0.681***	
	(0.111)	(0.128)	
Pain intensity	0.571***	0.528***	
	(0.093)	(0.103)	
Vitality	0.381***	0.385***	
	(0.108)	(0.127)	
Mental health	0.087	0.098	
	(0.096)	(0.107)	
Age/10		0.509	0.660**
		(0.349)	(0.341)
Age square/10		-1.125***	-1.391***
		(0.417)	(0.408)
Female		-0.365***	-0.454***
		(0.098)	(0.095)
Foreigner		-0.228***	-0.375***
		(0.139)	(0.136)
Education			
- Primary		0	0
- Secondary		-0.087	-0.040
		(0.114)	(0.111)
- Tertiary		-0.032	0.052
		(0.184)	(0.180)
- University		0.330*	0.477***
		(0.184)	(0.178)
Living alone		0.247*	-0.226
		(0.144)	(0.140)
Non-smoker		0.420***	0.419***
		(0.085)	(0.082)

	Model 1	Model 2	Model 3
Height/Weight index		0.286** (0.121)	0.276** (0.118)
Earnings		0.019** (0.009)	0.027*** (0.009)
Support Network		-0.122 (0.140)	0.099 (0.137)
Repetitive work		0.0009 (0.126)	-0.018 (0.122)
Heavy work		-0.295*** (0.116)	-0.381*** (0.112)
Sickness		-0.019*** (0.006)	-0.020*** (0.006)
Comorbidity		-0.498*** (0.134)	-0.634*** (0.132)
Proportion of years of work		2.1888** (0.934)	2.149** (0.898)
Work most important		-0.041 (0.094)	-0.094 (0.091)
Active w.p.		0.171** (0.092)	0.137 (0.088)
Active medical treatment, 90 days		-0.001 (0.092)	0.005 (0.089)
Active medical treatment, 1 year		-0.005 (0.127)	0.015 (0.124)
Active medical treatment, year 2		-0.399*** (0.145)	-0.528*** (0.141)
Job training		-0.287** (0.143)	-0.285** (0.138)
Adapted workplace		0.641*** (0.130)	0.736*** (0.128)
Log-likelihood	-2208.583	-1855.979	-1947.962
Uncensored spells	989	989	989
Censored spells	3460	3460	3460
Total spells	4449	4449	4449

Note: ***Significant at the 1 percent level. **Significant at the 5 percent level

323

Remarkably, individual country results indicate that significant improvements in pain scores were only noted for the cohort from the Netherlands, which is also indicated in a univariate analysis not reported here. As we have already discussed, the Dutch cohort had the best subjective work-resumption prognosis, and the results here confirm that many had already returned to work within the time period after 90 days, but before the questionnaire was answered.

Although the pain scores did not improve much, other health indicators did so by and large in most countries, as Table 3.5.5 shows. Only vitality showed an improvement for all countries together at two years, although the individual country results show continued significant improvement in work ability and ADL scores in the second year.

7.2 Gender and age

Women have worse odds than men for work resumption and improvements in the health scores, but not work ability. Interestingly, changes in health scores and work ability are not age-dependent, but returning to work is. Increasing age decreases the probability of work resumption.

7.3 Health, physical capacity and social functioning

The study includes many indicators of chronic health problems: smoking, low height-to-weight ratios, previous sickness history and comorbidity. Even living alone might be considered a health risk, in part because of a possible selection into this group of persons with more serious health histories and in part because living alone can be difficult even for persons without problematic health histories.

A social network is significant for perceived mental health, vitality and work ability, but not for ADL, pain and work resumption. With the exception of smoking in the mental health function, non-smoking and a good height-to-weight index have no significant correlation with health outcomes or work ability, but surprisingly enhance the prospects of return to work. Previous history of sickness with back pain in the past twelve months and the occurrence of another illness in addition to back pain reduce the odds for improving health scores, work ability and return to work.

8. Education, skills and knowledge

Improvements in perceived pain intensity; ADL and work-ability scores and work resumption are more likely for persons with higher education. Being born with another mother tongue, i.e. being a 'foreigner', can be classified as a skill and knowledge (cultural) disadvantage. This turns out to be the case for all health outcomes, work ability and return to work. The proportion of years of work since the age of 20 has a strong positive effect on work resumption, but also on ADL improvement. This indicates that persons with a stronger tie to the labor force are more likely to return to work. Higher earnings increase the odds for better mental health and vitality, and for returning to work.

8.1 Workplace characteristics

Heavy work is associated with reduced odds for improved pain intensity, work ability and work resumption. Repetitive work has no significant effect on outcomes. The combination of job demands and control over these – strain – was tested, but was not significant and was deleted.

8.2 Attitude towards work

Persons who do not report, 'Working is the most important thing in my life' have lower odds of improving their work ability, ADL and other health scores. This attitude does not significantly influence work resumption, however, according to these results.

8.3 Vocational rehabilitation

Accommodating the workplace to facilitate return to work increases the odds of work resumption, and for experiencing better mental health and less pain intensity. In the latter case it is not easy to say what the causal link is however, as less pain intensity might help people make the choice to return to an accommodated work situation. An active workplace has no significant effect on work resumption, but it does increase the odds for improving subjective vitality and mental health. Job training has a negative effect on work resumption.

Table 3.5.5 Work ability and health. All country cohorts together

	Work ability	ADL	Pain intensity	Vitality	Mental health
Intercept	-1.419	-1.367	-2.243***	-2.529***	-2.573***
	(0.901)	(0.906)	(0.747)	(0.843)	(0.755)
Time = 90 days	0	0	0	0	0
= 1 year	0.842***	0.691***	-0.489***	1.700***	0.473***
	(0.145)	(0.147)	(0.117)	(0.137)	(0.121)
= 2 years	0.470***	0.206	0.179	0.949***	0.137
	(0.165)	(0.170)	(0.139)	(0.165)	(0.144)
Age/10	-0.027	-0.192	0.326	-0.189	-0.064
	(0.398)	(0.396)	(0.326)	(0.368)	(0.328)
Age square/10	-0.580	-0.546	-0.667	-0.025	0.138
	(0.485)	(0.482)	(0.390)	(0.441)	(0.387)
Female	-016.6	-0.863***	-0.211**	-0.319***	-0.147*
	(0.112)	(0.119)	(0.091)	(0.105)	(0.091)
Foreigner	-0.466***	-0.677***	-0.532***	-0.795***	-0.633***
	(0.181)	(0.191)	(0.141)	(0.180)	(0.147)
Education					
- Primary	0	0	0	0	0
- Secondary	0.240*	0.525***	0.184*	0.470***	0.326***
	(0.147)	(0.154)	(0.110)	(0.129)	(0.109)
- Tertiary	0.743***	1.044***	0.347**	-0.122	0.030
	(0.207)	(0.218)	(0.168)	(0.231)	(0.177)
- University	1.102***	1.086***	0.741***	0.533***	0.042
	(0.199)	(0.218)	(0.170)	(0.209)	(0.187)
Living alone	0.173	0.029	0.027	0.089	0.122
	(0.154)	(0.159)	(0.126)	(0.146)	(0.126)
Non-smoker	-0.028	0.015	0.009	0.115	0.318***
	(0.098)	(0.099)	(0.080)	(0.091)	(0.080)
Height/weight index	-0.171	-0.011	0.130	0.007	0.076
	(0.140)	(0.145)	(0.111)	(0.130)	(0.112)
Earnings	0.016	0.019*	0.012	0.022**	0.065***
	(0.011)	(0.011)	(0.009)	(0.010)	(0.008)
Support network	0.649***	0.255	0.540	0.739***	0.737***
	(0.195)	(0.173)	(0.145)	(0.175)	(0.147)
Repetitive work	-0.122	0.021	0.046	-0.024	-0.072
	(0.139)	(0.143)	(0.119)	(0.132)	(0.117)
Heavy work	-0.481***	-0.180	-0.386***	-0.039	-0.092
	(0.121)	(0.131)	(0.105)	(0.129)	(0.113)
Sickness	-0.022***	-0.022***	-0.015***	-0.003***	0.003
	(0.009)	(0.008)	(0.006)	(0.006)	(0.005)
Comorbidity	-0.869***	-0.525***	-0.470***	-0.359***	-0.053
	(0.185)	(0.170)	(0.122)	(0.136)	(0.112)
Proportion of years of work	1.814	3.439***	0.812	0.162	-1.099
	(1.145)	(1.308)	(0.857)	(0.972)	(0.803)
Work most important	-0.218**	-0.274**	-0.238***	-0.422***	-0.371***
	(0.113)	(0.114)	(0.090)	(0.107)	(0.092)

	Work ability	ADL	Pain intensity	Vitality	Mental health
Active w.p.	0.133	0.174	0.164	-0.568***	0.284***
	(0.108)	(0.109)	(0.085)	(0.111)	(0.083)
Active medical treatment, 90 days	0.079	-0.009	0.028	0.214**	0.106
	(0.107)	(0.107)	(0.086)	(0.103)	(0.087)
Active medical treatment, 1 year	-0.044	0.203	-0.162	-0.105	0.021
	(0.139)	(0.143)	(0.120)	(0.121)	(0.125)
Active medical treatment, year 2	-0.680***	-0.797***	-0.201	0.050	-0.507***
	(0.240)	(0.265)	(0.189)	(0.192)	(0.204)
Job training	-0.234	-0.190	0.041	0.047	0.123
	(0.158)	(0.158)	(0.128)	(0.142)	(0.129)
Adapted workplace	0.214	-0.270	0.247**	0.161	0.234*
	(0.152)	(0.172)	(0.127)	(0.145)	(0.132)
Log-likelihood	-1531.208	-1493.788	-2100.363	-1667.663	-2019.830
Uncensored spells	538	531	897	696	903
Censored spells	4178	4164	3393	3793	3123
Total spells	4178	4164	3393	3793	3123

Note: ***Significant at the 1 percent level. **Significant at the 5 percent level

The workplace accommodations frequently used are adaptation of working hours and job redesign (Bergendorff and Gordon 2000). In the Netherlands, adaptation of working hours occurred in 62% of cases – and largely in the first year. Israel was close with 59%, and Denmark with 45% (and the US with 43%). Also noteworthy is that therapeutic work resumption occurred in 77% of the cases in the Netherlands – and within the first year. Sweden was second in this respect with therapeutic work resumption in 37% (32% in the first year) of cases. Adapting the work place occurred much less frequently than changing work hours or job redesign (in 20-30% of cases in Denmark, the Netherlands, Sweden and the US). In all countries but the United States, measures classified as 'adaptation of the workplace' have been essential in helping people to return to the work place. The effects are significant at the 1%

level in Denmark, Germany and Israel and at the 10% level in the Netherlands and Sweden. In all countries but the United States, this type of measure has been significant in helping people to return to the workplace. The effects are significant at the 1% level in Denmark, Germany and Israel and at the 10% level in the Netherlands and Sweden.

Table 3.5.6 Odds based on significant coefficients in the equations for all countries

	Work Resumption			Work ability	ADL	Pain intensity	Vitality	Mental health
	Model 1	Model 2	Model 3					
Intercept	0.181	0.065	0.072			0.106	0.080	0.076
Measuring time - 90 days								
- 1 year		0.299	0.426	2.321	1.996	0.613	5.474	1.605
- 2 years		4.768	5.954	1.600			2.583	
Work ability	1.498	1.459						
ADL	1.914	1.976						
Pain intensity	1.770	1.695						
Vitality	1.464	1.470						
Mental health								
Age/10			1.935					
Age square/10		0.325	0.249					
Female		0.694	0.635		0.422	0.810	0.727	0.863
Foreigner		0.796	0.687	0.628	0.508	0.587	0.452	0.531
Education - Primary								
- Secondary				1.271	1.690	1.202	1.600	1.385
- Tertiary				2.102	2.841	1.415		
- University	1.391		1.611	3.010	2.962	2.098	1.704	
Living alone		1.280						
Non-smoker		1.522	1.520					1.374
Height/Weight index		1.331	1.318					
Earnings		1.019	1.027		1.019		1.022	1.067

Job training and vocational education have a negative sign, and with the exception of a significant estimate at the 10% level in the Netherlands, are not significant factors. There are two possible explanations for this negative result. The first is the straightforward interpretation that those who receive these measures are not normally those who resume work within two years. It is possible that these are often used as the last option before granting disability. A more optimistic interpretation is that education and training programs take time. They do not get started until well into or after the first year and they may not be completed by the end of the observation period for the study. This means that we should simply interpret the negative result as indicating that the measure has not been completed, and that it is too early to resume work. Only a longer follow up can resolve which of these interpretations is the most plausible.

8.4 Medical interventions

Most of the medical treatment received by people in the study was received in the first three months (Hansson and Hansson 2000). Almost everyone received some form of active treatment, which makes it difficult to distinguish an effect compared to the absence of active treatment. Active medical treatment in the second year is associated with a reduction in the odds for improved mental health, ADL and work ability. This may simply mean that persons receiving active treatment at such a late date are simply the less successful patients.

9. Individual country-cohort results

Generally speaking, the time variables were significant in the country equations, but most of the other variables were only significant in a few of the countries. Why did so many variables turn out to be significant in the multi-country-cohort regressions? One answer is that they contain more degrees of freedom, and this may have helped, compared to the smaller number of observations in the country-cohort equations. Another answer is that the countries in which the effects are significant have even dominated the aggregate results. Adding more observations to those from a dominant country(ies) may have just strengthened results.

The following country results are worth noting (Table 3.5.6 and Table 3.5.7):

329

The time coefficients indicate that the Netherlands is the only country that shows improvements over both one and two years in both work ability and all four of the health indicators.

All countries but Denmark (there is no measurement for the US) show improvements in work ability in the first year, and this continues in the second year in the Netherlands and Sweden.

ADL improves in both the first and second years in Denmark, Israel, the Netherlands and Sweden, but not Germany.

Pain intensity improves in the Netherlands in both years, but the only other country where there is a significant change is in Germany in the second year.

Vitality increases in both years in Denmark, Israel, the Netherlands and Sweden, although it does not increase the second year in Germany. (It is not measured in the US.)

The mental health indicator improves in Germany, Israel and the Netherlands, but not in Denmark and Sweden.

Note that age is not a significant determinant of *work ability* in any of the country cohorts, and neither is gender, except apparently in the Netherlands. Low education decreases the odds of improving work ability in Sweden, while high education improves the odds in the Netherlands. Higher earnings contribute marginally to work ability in Germany and Israel, as does support in Germany. Heavy work is a negative factor in all countries, and significantly so at the 10% level in Germany, Sweden and the US. Note, however, the coefficient for repetitive work in Sweden is positive. Previous sick spells with back pain have a negative effect, but with high significance in the Netherlands, and to a lesser extent in Germany. Comorbidity is a strong negative factor in Sweden and Denmark.

The odds of improved *ADL* are significant and strong in both one and two years in Denmark, Israel, the Netherlands and Sweden, but not in Germany. Strangely, in Denmark, the relatively high odds of strongly improved ADL are not reflected in positive time responses for work ability or work resumption. Israel, the Netherlands and Sweden are much more consistent in this respect. In these countries, the odds of ADL improvement go hand and hand with the odds of improved work ability and work resumption.

As with work resumption, increasing age exerts a strong negative effect on ADL results at one and two years in Germany and Sweden. This reflects the large percentage of older workers in these two cohorts. Being a woman yields a significantly worse outcome for ADL in all countries but

Israel. Previous sickness has a small, significant negative effect in the Netherlands and Sweden and heavy work has a significant negative effect in Sweden. Note that active medical treatment has a positive sign in all countries, but is not significant at the 10% level. Remarkably, the odds of improvement on the *pain score* are significant in both years only in the Netherlands. Germany is the only other country in which there is improvement, and this is in the second year. The weak performance of this variable is especially surprising given that the ADL scores improved substantially in most countries.

Table 3.5.7 Relative odds for outcomes at different times

	Denmark	Ger-many	Israel	Nether-lands	Sweden	USA	All
Work resumption							
1 year	-	-	0.2	0.2	0.2	n.e.	0.4
2 years	-	1.9	8.3	18.5	26.5	n.e.	6.0
Work ability							
1 year	-	8.4	2.7	7.9	4.0	n.e.	2.3
2 years	-	-	-	6.3	2.9	n.e.	1.6
ADL							
1 year	4.0	-	2.9	5.0	3.0	n.e.	2.0
2 years	2.6	-	2.5	2.8	2.4	n.e.	-
Pain							
1 year	-	-	-	11.3	-	n.e.	0.6
2 years	-	2.7	-	8.4	-	n.e.	-
Vitality							
1 year	4.0	15.5	9.0	17.8	5.6	n.e.	5.4
2 years	3.2	-	8.2	10.9	.6	n.e.	2.6
Mental health							
1 year	-	4.2	4.4	4.5	-	n.e.	1.6
2 years	-	2.9	4.3	4.0	-	n.e.	-

It is important to ask why pain scores improved so dramatically in the Netherlands, whereas they did not in other countries. There are at least three possible explanations. The first is that medical treatment is more effective in the Netherlands. The second is that the Dutch cohort has a greater frequency of acute rather than *chronic* problems, and that these cases with acute (but passing) pain have been sick listed longer than in other countries – and account for the high rate of early work resumption. A third, and perhaps most likely, is that the Dutch system appears to provide more flexible possibilities, for example, part-time work, new work tasks, etc. Unfortunately, on the basis of the data in this study, it is not possible to discern which cause is the most likely. On the other hand, it is remarkable that pain scores have not improved across the board, given that the ADL scores have.

The negative coefficient for women suggests that their experience of pain differs from that of men. The coefficient is significant in Denmark and the Netherlands. Surprisingly, in four countries – Denmark, the Netherlands, Sweden and the US – higher education gives higher odds of improvement on the pain score. This may be a 'class' or life-style variable or proxy for the nature of work tasks for different educational levels. Another hypothesis is that persons with higher education improve because their conditions (either pain or situation otherwise) were not so poor from the outset. (In support of this is the fact that the education variable is not significant in Germany where the cohort's level of education was generally low.)

Previous absence from the workplace with back pain and comorbidity decrease the odds of improving on the pain score in Denmark. In Sweden comorbidity has a significant negative influence and in the US previous sick listing with back pain decreases the odds of improvement on the pain score.

Active medical treatment increases the odds of improving back pain in the US in the first 90 days, but only there. In fact there is a significant negative effect in Denmark in the initial 90-day period and in the Netherlands in both the first and second years. In Sweden returning to an adapted workplace is correlated with an improvement in back pain. It is difficult to distinguish in this case between cause and effect. It is possible that resuming work can have a positive effect on perceived pain.

In all countries where *vitality* is measured, the odds of increasing improve in both the first and second years. Generally, the improvement is greater in the first year, as the results for all countries indicate. In Denmark and Sweden, gender is important for perceived vitality, with the odds for women being lower than those for men.

One of the results of the analysis that is difficult to explain is the significant negative effect for Denmark, Israel and Sweden of active contact with the employer on vitality. This can be an indication that employer contacts are frequently focused on persons with worse health – since those with improved health tend to return anyway. On the other hand, this variable is not significant to the same extent in the other health outcome equations (although it is significant in Israel in the pain equation). Note that there is also a significant positive effect of job training and education on vitality in Denmark, but surprisingly, a negative correlation for Sweden.

In Germany, Israel and the Netherlands, time has a positive effect on improvement of *mental health*. It is noteworthy that in Denmark, the two age variables together indicate that the mental health of back-pain patients improves significantly as function of increasing age, rather than for all over time. This may reveal something about the Danish cohort, suggesting poor mental health for the younger persons in this group.

The support network variable is highly significant in Denmark, the Netherlands and Sweden. The proportion of years worked has a strong negative effect on the odds of improving mental health in Germany – which may reflect the fact that the German cohort is much older, and that the older patients also have poor mental health. In Sweden we find that the attitude variable 'work is the most important thing in my life' has a strong positive correlation with the odds of improving mental health.

In Denmark and the Netherlands active employer contact is correlated with improved mental health, but in Israel it is the other way around. In Sweden, active medical treatment in the first 90 days is associated with improved mental health.

10. Summing up

Country cohorts with good work-resumption results also have better odds for improvement in the work-ability and ADL outcomes. Whether this is a result of differences in the characteristics of cohorts or the success of interventions is difficult to say. Work resumption is the highest in Israel, the Netherlands, Sweden and the US. In the first three countries, where we were able to measure them, the time effects show strongly positive odds for improved work ability and ADL. Although ADL improvements also occurred in Denmark during the period of two years, the odds of returning to work did not.

333

Within continental Europe, Sweden and the Netherlands are noted for having more flexible labor contracts than Germany, which may be part of the explanation of why these cohorts are more successful in returning to work. (Although the German cohort is 'old', the Swedish cohort is also relatively old, but does better.) In Denmark, but also in Germany, work experience is the most important factor in improving the odds of work resumption.

Generally, workplace adaptation affected outcomes positively in Denmark, Germany, Israel, the Netherlands and Sweden. The Netherlands, on the other hand is the country that uses the whole battery (adapted workplace, flexible hours, new job tasks, etc) of workplace-accommodation measures extensively Bergendorff and Gordon (2000). General education, job training and vocational education do not yield positive results, perhaps because the follow up period was too short, but perhaps also because these are not effective measures.

Finally, it is not reasonable to pass judgment on health interventions on the basis of the results reported here. The ADL outcomes show that active health measures in the first year increase the odds of ADL improvement; however, the result is not significant at the 10% level. The nature of data collection for this study makes it difficult to discriminate between specific measures. To do this, it is important to work with randomized studies comparing specific techniques.

According to the multi-country-cohort results, changes in health scores and work ability are not age-dependent, but work resumption is. This suggests that the health of older workers can improve without leading to work resumption. Surprisingly, non-smoking and a good height-to-weight index have no significant effect on health variables or work ability, but enhance the prospects of return to work. Improvements over time in perceived pain, ADL scores and work resumption were more likely for persons with higher education, and heavy lifts reduce the odds for work resumption. Higher earnings are associated with better odds for mental health, vitality and returning to work. It appears then that there is some sort of selection mechanism that favors persons whose situation is relatively better to begin with.

Notes

[1] Bloch and Prins (2000) contains a detailed account of the characteristics of the country cohorts.

[2] This section draws on the summary of the country cohorts presented in Veerman and Palmer (2000).

[3] When this study was being performed, the results reported in Veerman and Palmer (2000), which include both univariate analyses and logit estimates of the probability of return to work at 1 and 2 years were known. The interested reader is referred to this study for these results.

References

Aarts, L. J. M. and de Jong, P. R. (1992). *Economic Aspects of Disability Behavior*. Amsterdam: Elsevier Science Pubishers.

Aarts, L. J .M. and de Jong, P. R. (1996). 'The Dutch disability program and how it grew' in *Curing the Dutch Disease. An International Perspective on Disability Reform* (eds. Aarts, L. J .M. de Jong, P. H. and Burkhauser, R.V.) Aldershot, England: Avebury.

Aarts, L. J. M., de Jong, P. H. and Burkhauser, R.V. (eds.) (1996). *Curing the Dutch Disease. An International Perspective on Disability Reform*. Aldershot, England: Avebury.

Bergendorff, S. and Gordon, D. (2000). 'Vocational and Other Non-Medical Interventions', Chapter 8 in *Who Returns to Work and Why? A Six-Country Study of Work Incapacity and Reintegration*. (eds. F. Bloch and R. Prins). Piscataway, New Jersey: Transaction Publishers Rutgers – The State University of New Jersey.

Berkowitz, E.D. and Burkhauser, R. V. (1996). 'A United States perspective on disability programs' in *Curing the Dutch Disease. An International Perspective on Disability Reform* (eds. Aarts L.J.M., De Jong P.H. and R.V. Burkhauser) Aldershot, England: Avebury.

Berkowitz, M. (ed.) (1988). *Measuring the Efficiency of Public Programs. Costs and Benefits in Rehabilitation*. Philadelphia: Temple University Press.

Bloch, F., Prins, R. and Veerman, T. (1993). *Core Design and Research Programme for the ISSA Cross-national Study on Work Incapacity and Reintegration*. Leiden: Arbeid en Sociale Zekerheid.

Bloch, F. and Prins, R. (eds.) (2000). *Who Returns to Work and Why? A Six-Country Study of Work Incapacity and Reintegration*. Piscataway, New Jersey: Transaction Publishers Rutgers – The State Univesity of New Jersey.

Butler, R.J. and Worall, J. D. (1985). 'Work Injury Compensation and the Duration of Non-work Spells.' The Economic Journal. 95.

Dean, D. H. and Dolan, R. C. (1991). 'Assessing the Role of Vocational Rehabilitation in Disability Policy.' *Journal of Political Analysis and Management*. Vol 10, no 4: 568-587.

Frick, B. and Sadowski, D. (1996). A German perspective on disability policy in *Curing the Dutch Disease. An International Perspective on Disability Reform* (eds. Aarts L .J. M., De Jong P. H. and Burkhauser, R. V.) Aldershot, England: Avebury.

Gruber, J. and Wise, D. (1999). Social Security and Retirement around the World. National Bureau of Economic Research Conference Report. Chicago and London: University of Chicago Press.

Hansson, T. and Hansson, E. (2000). 'The Role of Medical Interventions'. Chapter 7 in *Who Returns to Work and Why? A Six-Country Study of Work Incapacity and Reintegration.* (eds. F. Bloch and R. Prins). Piscataway, New Jersey: Transaction Publishers Rutgers – The State University of New Jersey.

Ilmarinen, J. (1999). *Ageing Workers in the European Union – Status and Promotion of work promotion of work ability, employ ability and employment.* Helsinki: Finnish Institute of Occupational Health.

Johnson, W. G., Baldwin, M. L. and Butler, R. J. (1998). 'Back Pain and Work Disability: The Need for a New Paradigm.' *Industrial Relations.* Vol. 37. No. 1.

Karasek, R. A. (1979). 'Job demands, job decision latitude and mental strain. Implications for job redesign.' ADM SCI Q 24:285-307.

Karasek, R. A. and Theorell, T. (1990). *Healthy work, stress, productivity and the reconstruction of working life.* Basic Books.

Meyer, B. and Viscusi, K. (1995). 'Workers Compensation and Injury Duration: Evidence from a Natural Experiment.' *American Economic Review.* Vol. 85. No. 3.

Palme, M. and Svensson, I. (2000). *Income Security Programs and Retirement in Sweden.* Mimeo, Stockholm School of Economics.

SBU, The Swedish Council on Technology in Health Care (2000). *Ont i ryggen och ont i nacken.* Stockholm: Statens beredning för medicinsk utvärdering.

Skoogman Thoursie, P. (1999). 'Disability and Work in Sweden.' Swedish Institute for Social Research. Discussion Series no. 39. Stockholm University.

Veerman, T. and Palmer, E. (2000). 'Work Resumption and the Role of Interventions'. Ch. 10 in *Who Returns to Work and Why? A Six-Country Study of Work Incapacity and Reintegration.* (eds. F. Bloch and R. Prins). Piscataway, New Jersey: Transaction Publishers Rutgers – The State University of New Jersey.

Wadensjö, E. and Palmer, E. (1996). 'Curing the Dutch disease from the Swedish Perspective' in *Curing the Dutch Disease. An International Perspective on Disability Reform* (eds. Aarts L.J.M., De Jong P.H. and R.V. Burkhauser) Aldershot, England: Avebury.

336

3.6 Demographic change and partial funding: is the Swedish pension reform a role model for Germany?

Jochen Jagob and Werner Sesselmeier[1]

1. Introduction

With the exception of Ireland most OECD countries can be described by a similar demographic development which forces the welfare states to reform their social security systems and especially their pension systems. The populations of all the member states are shrinking and getting older. This holds for Sweden and above all for Germany. Due to OECD figures the share of the ones 65 and over of the total population in West Germany has risen from 10.8 per cent in 1960 to 16.2 per cent in 1997 and it is assumed to double until 2040. In Sweden the rise was the same with 11.8 per cent in 1960 and 17.4 per cent in 1997. The forecasts are very similar to the German ones.

Consequently both countries have reacted on this challenges: Sweden with its pension reform act in 1994 and Germany with its pension reform act in 1999 which passed the parliament in 1997. This distinction is important because in 1998 the government changed and the new one immediately stayed the crucial part of the pension reform, the so-called demographic factor for two years. Instead of this the government discusses a fully-funded second pillar beside the pay-as-you-go system. Since the two main features of the Swedish reform are a generation-specific adjustment and a fully-funded component this chapter aims at assessing the relevance of the Swedish model for the German system.

Before we look at the pension systems in Sweden and Germany we discuss several ways of restructuring pension systems more generally.

2. Restructuring the old age security

In order to prepare a pension system for the demographic change that will arise within the next forty years several options are possible. These options for dealing with the demographic change can be divided in adjustments within a given pension system and reforms which change the system significantly (similar discussions can be found in Schmähl 1999 and Lindbeck 2000).

2.1 Reacting within a given pension system

Within a given system pay-as-you-go system there are three adjusting screws: the contribution rate, the age of retirement and the pension level.

Increasing the contributions. The easiest way to guarantee pension payments to the old in the future can be achieved by increasing the contribution rate. Though it is the easiest way and it follows the systematic of a pay-as-you-go financed pension system it is not desirable. The arguments against an increase of the contribution rate are by far too substantial and can not be ignored for economic reasons as well as for reasons of intergenerational fairness.

A further increase of the contribution rate will have the consequence of a significant shift of the burden on future generations. Jagob and Scholz (1998) have shown this for the German pension system by the method of Generational Accounting. If such a shift of the burden is considered as intergenerationally unfair an increase of the contribution will not be acceptable as an instrument of pension policy. Besides the pure reason of intergenerational justice as an argument against the policy of a rising contribution rate there are also economic reasons against increasing contribution rate. The most important one is that increasing contribution rates will lead to distortions on the labor market. As Thum and von Weizsäcker (1999) pointed out an increasing contribution rate due to the demographic change will have the effect of an increase of the implicit tax of the pension system. Firstly, this means that the spread between the amount paid into the pension system and the amount that the individual will receive when it retires will enlarge to the disadvantage of the individual.

Secondly, this will lead to a widening of the already large tax wedge between the production wage and the consumption wage. The consequences of this are a more aggressive behavior in the wage setting process and a decrease in the readiness of contribution payments (see Pigeau/Sesselmeier 2000). Since at least in Germany contributions to the pension system are a percentage rate on the wage such a development will create disincentives to take part in the regular labor market. Many workers will therefore decide to step into other kinds of employment like illicit work as one of the most drastic form. This effect which will even aggravate the financial situation of the pension system. Therefore an increase of the contribution rate is not desirable.

As we pointed out there are two kind of arguments against such a policy. One is that such a policy is intergenerationally unfair and the other is that it will create labor market distortions which will even worsen the situation.

Increasing the age of retirement. An increase of the regular age of retirement seems to be an appropriate way to deal with demographic change within any pension system. The increase of longevity over the last decades makes persisting on the current age of retirement implausible. Since people live longer in a quite good health it is more or less a consequence that they also can work a longer time of their live as they do now. This will have an effect on both the revenue and the expenditure side of the pension system. First of all on the revenue side: If people work a longer time of their live they also pay contributions for a longer time. Secondly on the expenditure side: Since people work longer they will receive less pensions. These two effects will improve the financial situation of the pension system. Note that the increase of the longevity has an effect on any pension system regardless if it is financed as a pay-as-you-go-system or as a fully funded one.

The increase of the regular age of retirement is a crucial point for many reasons. As Börsch-Supan/Schnabel (1999) investigated for Germany and Palme/Svensson (1999) for Sweden there is a tendency in pay-as-you-go financed pension systems towards early retirement, which can be found by an increasing average age of retirement and/or a decreasing labor market participation of the age cohorts over 60 years (see for an international comparison Jagob/Sesselmeier 2000a and for a different result for Finland Hakola 2000). Their labor market participation was decreasing over the time while their absolute number was not over the same time period and the average actual age of retirement is due to the investigations in both countries substantially lower than the age of retirement by law. Börsch-Supan/Schnabel (1999) took those results as an indicator for wrong incentives within the German pay-as-you-go system. They asserted that this is an argument for a complete transition towards a fully funded system. In fact the decreasing labor market participation of the age cohorts over 60 and as a consequence the decreasing average age of retirement was to a greater extent a result of the governments' labor market policy than of a voluntary choice of the individuals corresponding to any incentives of the pension system. It is doubtful if it is the adequate way to (ab-)use the pension system for labor market policy but at least it was one way to deal with the problem of unemployment especially in East Germany after reunification.

One attempt might be to increase the regular age of retirement as a guideline but keeping the possibility to retire earlier if it is needy or wanted. This flexible age of retirement must be connected with an actuarial fair adjustment as it is more or less already the case in the German system. The pension paid will therefore be lowered by the factor if an individual retires earlier than the regular age. This will leave the choice about retirement to a greater extent up to the individuals and will make the actual age of retirement much more flexible. As already stated an increase of the age of retirement is one way to improve the financial situation of the pension system as a consequence of the increasing life expectancy. Additionally a flexibilisation of the actual age of retirement connected with an actuarial fair factor could be useful in order to leave room for implicit contracts between the workers and the employers about early retirement.

Decreasing the pension level. The opposite of an increase of the contribution rate would be a decrease of the pension level. Since the contribution rate is determined by the expenditure side a decrease of the pension level will have a stabilizing effect on the contribution rate. A decrease of the pension level can be achieved in different ways. The easiest one is by determining it exogenously to a specified value. Another way is an endogenous adjustment of the pension level. This adjustment can be achieved by a demographic factor (see also Rürup 1998).

This factor works insofar as it decreases the pension level to a certain extent as the life expectancy rises. Such a factor may be shaped in two different ways. One way is to adjust the pension level by the overall life expectancy. The consequence of a such a factor would be that the costs of an increasing life expectancy would be distributed on both those who are already retired and those who still pay contributions. The other way would be a cohort specific adjustment. This means that every cohort that retires will have a different pension level according to their own life expectancy at the year when they retired. This is depicted graphically in the Figures 3.6.1 and 3.6.2.

The question which of those two possible ways is the appropriate depends on the consideration about what is regarded as fair. On the one hand it could be regarded as fair to spread the costs of an increasing life expectancy equally on every member of the (insured) society. This is especially the case if the pension system is regarded to a great extent as an important part of the social security system. On the other hand it could regarded as fair to impose the costs of an increasing life expectancy on those who cause the costs. This point of view follows more the insurance principle as it is practiced on private markets.

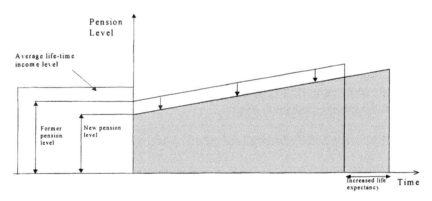

Figure 3.6.1   Cohort-specific adjustment and its effects on the amount of pensions

Source: Rürup 1998

341

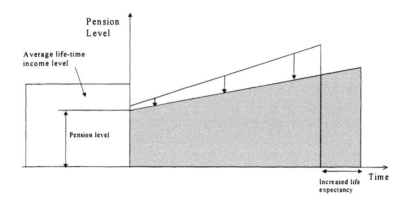

Figure 3.6.2   Overall adjustment and its effects on the amount of pensions

Source: Rürup 1998

So far we investigated three possibilities to stabilize a pension system. They all had in common that they were options which work within a given pay-as-you-go-system. But there are other options which need to be discussed. Most importantly a transition towards a mix between a fully funded and a pay-as-you-go system.

2.2 A mix between a fully funded and a pay-as-you-go system

Many economists favor a complete transition from a pay as you go system towards a fully funded system even though Breyer (1989) as well as Fenge (1997) have shown that a Pareto-efficient transition is impossible. Our point of view differs in this regard, too. We doubt that a complete transition towards a fully funded system is the perfect remedy for the pension systems in general, mainly because there are risks within a fully funded system itself as well. The most important reason against such a transition are the resulting burden for the working generations during the transition period. This burden is a result of the compensation needed for those who already did retire but do not get any or not enough benefits out of the new fully funded system. Even though for Germany most calculations are just based on the costs which are a direct result of the compensations, i.e. they neglect any distortions due to this kind of taxation and can thus barely be considered as a lower limit of the costs, the amount of the net present value of the compensation payments seems to be high enough. This tax which is levied for the compensation payments will have the effect that the disposable income of the individuals will be reduced. As a consequence the households may reduce their savings and the economy will therefore have lower overall savings.

The second reason why a complete fully funded system is not the right way to deal with the demographic problem is the widely spread misbelieve or myth, as Orszag and Stiglitz (1999) call it, that a fully funded system is not affected by the demographic change. In fact a fully funded system is not independent of the demographic change. On the one hand a continuously rising life expectancy will have an effect on the pensions as well if the retirement age stays on a fixed level and on the other hand the rates on returns will be reduced as well when the baby boomers will retire. The latter point has been pointed out by Heller (1998) and especially by Brooks (2000) in much more detail. The argument is pretty simple because the assets which are hold by the baby boomers have to be sold when they retire. Since the number of buyers is by far less then the number of sellers one can expect the prices to fall. As an effect the baby boomers will receive much less for their assets as usually assumed.

These are the most important reasons why a complete transition towards a fully funded system is not desirable. But there are good reasons to add fully funded elements to the mandatory pension system. These are mainly two. One is the lack of human capital in the future which is a result of the low fertility rates today (see Sinn (1999a, 1999b)). The second reason can be seen as a form of risk hedging. Since both systems have a different kind of risk structure both systems can complement each other. Furthermore each empirically given pension system is pathdependent not only in its economic consequences but also in generating socio-economic norms (see Bohn 1999 and Miles 2000 for elaborated studies on some kind of optimal mix of a pay-as-you-go system and a funded one).

343

3. Pension reform options: a comparison between Sweden and Germany

As everybody can easily imagine if the demographic change will occur as described a need for reforms is unavoidable both in Sweden and in Germany. In both countries different changes in the pension policy were discussed and resulted in two different reform approaches. The Swedish approach which to a great extent also got applied in Latvia (see Fox and Palmer 1999) is based on a cohort specific demographic adjustment of the pay as you go financed pension and an additional funded fraction. On the opposite the German Pension Reform Act of 1997 which got suspended by the current government intended an overall adjustment of the general pension level by the life expectancy of the elderly. In order to get a better understanding in the differences and the consequences of each of those approaches to deal with the demographic change the intention of both reforms will be explained in the following chapters.

3.1 The Swedish pension system

After World War II Sweden became a synonym for a modern Welfare State. It showed that a high level of social security does not conflict with the principles of a market economy. During the years of prosperity with both positive economic and population growth this approach proofed to be sustainable. As it comes to the pension system it can be seen in Figure 3.6.1 that since the 1980s the Swedish pension system had a rather high expenditure per GDP ratio. Approximately every tenth Swedish Krona was spent for the pension system.

As the years of prosperity came to an end the Swedish government realized quite early that a social policy on a high level like that could not be continued. In the year 1984 a commission was therefore founded by the Swedish Government in order to work out a reform plan for the Swedish Pension System (see also Persson 1998). This reform plan was presented to the Parliament in the year 1994. The need for a fundamental reform became more and more urgent since in the early 1990s a recession affected the Swedish economy. The result of it was besides a high unemployment and a substantial depreciation of the Swedish Krona that the conservative government under the Prime Minister Karl Bildt tightened their fiscal policy. One effect of this tighter fiscal policy can also be seen in Figure 3.6.3 by a small decline of the pension expenditure per GDP ratio. In order to demonstrate the effects of the Swedish pension reform we will first give a short insight into the Swedish Pension system before the Reform and afterwards we will investigate the Reform and its consequences in a greater detail.

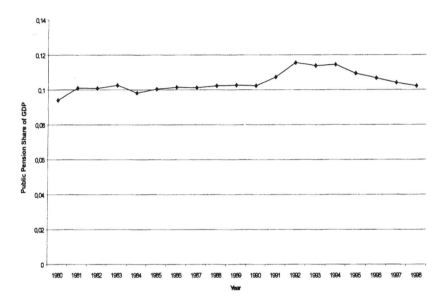

Figure 3.6.3   Public pension share of GDP in Sweden

The Pension System Before the Reform The Swedish Pension System before the reform was divided into two parts, the National basic Pension and the National supplementary pension (ATP). Both of them were financed at least to the main part as a pay-as-you-go-system. According to Ståhlberg (1995) the Swedish system was built on two principles. On the one hand there is the flat-rate National Basic Pension System which covers the basic needs after retirement. On the other hand there is also the National supplementary pension system which is a defined benefit system. Its benefits are based on the 15 years with the highest income during the working period which could be regarded as rather generous. Besides the general generosity of this system it has some bizarre effects for the redistribution and it sets wrong incentives for the retirement behavior. Both effects have an impact on the financiability of the system. In order to

345

analyze these effects and therefore to justify the need for a reform we have to look a little bit more carefully on these effects.

The effects of the pension system on the retirement behavior has been investigated by Palme and Svensson (1999) in a great detail. As in almost every European country the labor force participation of the people older than 60 was decreasing over the last decades. Though the regular age of retirement was at the age of 65. This tendency is an effect of the incentives given by the Swedish pension system. One of them is the dependency of the benefits on the 15 best earning years. This makes it attractive to retire earlier compared to a system where the pensions are related to the lifetime-income as in Germany. The reason for this is that in a system like in Sweden the loss due to a earlier retirement is much less or even nil compared to a system like in Germany. Since there is no loss due to early retirement it is not rational to stay in the labor force. Therefore it seemed to be necessary to connect the benefits in the Swedish pension system more to the lifetime-income and/or adjust the pension payments in so far as the pensioner does receive a lower pension when he retires before the regular age of retirement. Besides this incentive effect of the benefits the Swedish system was faced to a substantive demographic change which is to the main part a result of the increasing life expectancy of the 60 year old. The increasing life expectancy is a crucial element for the financiability of the Swedish system since it is already on high level compared to other OECD countries (Palmer 1999a). In order to get the pension system into an financial sound situation the system has to be reformed, where the main starting-points for a reform should be the handling of the increasing life expectancy and the actual age of retirement.

Another effect of the old system was regarding to Palmer (2000) that the pension system had rather undesired redistribution effects. The redistribution was insofar undesired because it was unfair which means that it transferred income from those with lower earnings to those with higher earnings. Finally the old system did not react appropriately to economic growth, i.e. high economic growth was not reflected in higher pensions at a nearly similar rate. As we can see there were several reasons why the public pension system had to be changed. In the next chapter we will look at the reform and investigate how it copes with these problems.

Since the Swedish Pension Reform, 'Averting the old age crisis' got published by the Worldbank (1994) the three pillar system became the key word whenever it came to a debate about pension policy. The Swedish pension reform is a shift towards a three pillar system. But opposite to the

Worldbank approach, it has a smaller capital-covered part. This is not the only difference the Swedish reform has compared to the Worldbank approach but it is the most important one. Similar reforms like the one in Sweden have also been introduced in countries like Latvia, Poland and Italy. But the Swedish reform is still a quite drastic change in social policy. Though a guarantee pension as the National Basic Pension was maintained but when it comes to the Supplementary Pension the direction of social policy moved much more towards the insurance system. This means that ex ante redistribution is completely left to the tax-/transfer-system, i.e. the government budget, while the supplementary pension system is now based on the actual contributions paid. In other words, the reform leads to a strict separation of the insurance system and the redistribution as a means of social policy. In this chapter we will therefore look at the reform in greater detail and show how the contribution and pension payments are determined.

One major change of the pension system is the switch from a defined benefit system to a defined contribution system. In the old system the benefits were related to the income of the 15 best earning years. The net replacement rate amounted to about 60% plus an additional 10% out of an occupational scheme. The yearly revenues of the system depended therefore on the expenditure in the same year. In contrast to this type of defined benefit system the new system after the reform will be a defined contribution system, i.e. a system with a fixed contribution rate at 18.5%. Besides that change the new system will be split into a pay as you go part and a fully funded part. Where 16% of the 18.5% contribution rate are for the pay as you go part and 2.5% are the fully funded part. This means that the new system is a hybrid system with a fully funded and pay as you go part and it has a contribution rate which is fixed at 18.5% of the income. Additionally to the mandatory Public pension system many employees are also covered by an occupational pension scheme that is providing a coverage up to a rate of approximately 2% of their working income (see Figure 3.6.4). The relevant question which has to be answered now is, how are the benefits calculated?

First of all the pension payments in the new system will depend on the age of retirement. The reform made it possible for the workers to chose their own retirement age within the range from 61 to 65. This means that the regular age of retirement is not as rigid as it was or as it more or less still is in Germany. But there is an incentive to postpone retirement insofar as the pension depends on a so called divisor which reflects the life

347

expectancy of an individual at the age when she retires. At least for the pay as you go financed pillar the individual pension can be calculated as follows. Every worker pays a contribution of 16% on a notional account. Notional means that the money the employee paid on the account will not be invested on the capital market but paid out immediately to the pensioners as it is usual for every Pay as you go system. But the pension the employee will receive after he retires is based on these contribution payments which are on the account. They get adjusted by the general growth rate of the wages. At the end there is an accumulated and growth adjusted amount which gets divided by the divisor. The divisor reflects the life expectancy of every cohort, that retires at the age of 65. The demographic adjustment is therefore in contrast to the German one not an overall adjustment but a cohort- specific one. The divisor is according to Palmer (1999b) given as:

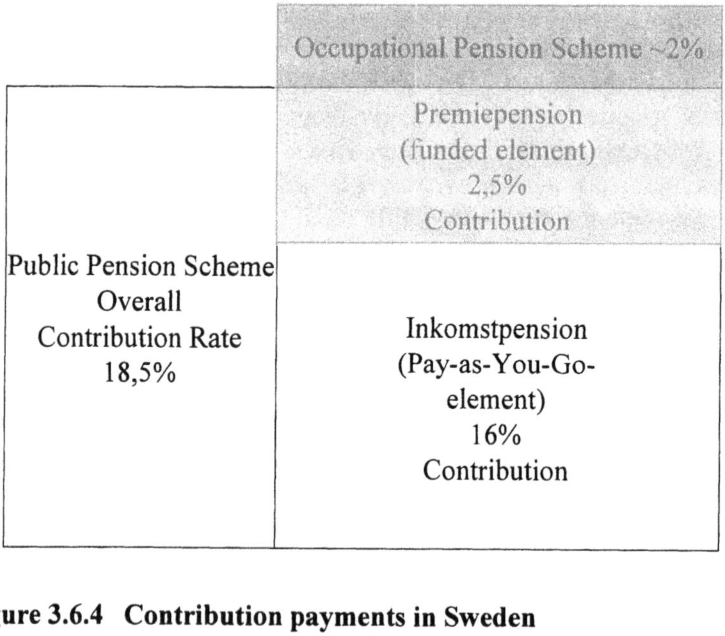

	Occupational Pension Scheme ~2%
Public Pension Scheme Overall Contribution Rate 18,5%	Premiepension (funded element) 2,5% Contribution
	Inkomstpension (Pay-as-You-Go-element) 16% Contribution

Figure 3.6.4 Contribution payments in Sweden

(1) $\qquad G_{i,r} = \dfrac{\displaystyle\sum_{t=i}^{N}(1+r)^{-(N-i)}lx_i}{lx_i},$

348

where r is the real rate of return and lx is an expression for the survival probability of a person in a certain age. The G-value can be obtain if we are summing over all lx-values for which people are presently alive, N, and by dividing it with the lx-value for the age cohort under consideration (see Palmer (1999b)). The annuity, A, for every individual retiring is than calculated by dividing the amount accumulated on the notional account over the time, C, with the divisor G:

$$(2) \qquad A_{i,r} = \frac{C_i}{G_{i,r}}$$

Since the factor G reflects the remaining life expectancy of an individual belonging to a special age cohort exactly at the age of retirement it can easily be seen that an earlier retirement reduces the annuity of the individual. The effect of a system like this will be that there is a incentive for the individual to postpone retirement until the regular limit at the age of 65. The annuity that an individual receives calculated as in equation (2) gives the pay as you go pension. But the individual receives additionally a funded pension which consists of the 2% of her income she is paying into a private fund during her working period plus interest.

As far as our investigation goes, we can summarize that there are four substantial changes of the Swedish pension system which are of economic relevance. First there is a switch from a defined benefit system to a notional defined contribution system. Secondly the pay as you go pension system gets enlarged by an additional funded system. Thirdly the age of retirement is flexible insofar as the individual can choose within a range between 61 and 65. And last but not least the individual level of a pension for a member of a special age cohort will depend on the average life expectancy of his age cohort. This will have two effects. On the one hand there is an automatic stabilizer of the system and on the other hand there is an incentive to postpone retirement.

4. The German pension system

The Pension System before the Reform A statutory old age insurance system can be organized in very different ways and according to different principles. It can be financed through the tax system or from contributions, it can be conceived as a 'benefit' system or as a 'provision' system which serves to alleviate poverty or it can have a living standard security function as a security aim, and it can be in the form of compulsory insurance or be organized subject to compulsory insurance. There is no one 'system' – in the sense of an universal design – of statutory old age insurance in Germany. Rather, there is a large number of very different historically founded old age insurance facilities – in respect of organization, class of insured, benefit and financing – which – with the exception of farmers' old age insurance which only represents basic insurance – have in common the fact that they have the aim of providing living standard security, in the sense that a certain income level during the working life should be maintained in retirement.

Table 3.6.1 The share of the old age security systems of the legal provision for old age (measured according to volume of benefits)

Old age security system	Pensions in DM billion 1998	Share
Statutory pension insurance	353.0	86.8%
Civil servant provision	34.5	8.5%
Additional provision for public servants	11.0	2.7%
Farmers old age insurance	5.2	1.3%
Occupational provisions	3.0	0.7%
Total	406.7	100.0%

The most important old age security system in Germany – from which about 70% of all old age income originate – is the Statutory Pension Insurance. Statutory Pension Insurance is a pay-as-you-go provision system organized as statutory compulsory insurance in which pension-scheme entitlements are based on the amount of the insured income, i.e. it depends on contributions made. The members, subject to compulsory insurance, of this insurance scheme are basically all salaried employees, with the exception of civil servants, judges as well as temporary and professional soldiers. Since entering into compulsory insurance is connected to the employment situation, the self-employed are on principle not subject to compulsory insurance.

The contributions – currently 19.3% – which must be paid equally by the employer and the employee are charged on the wages of the members up to the income limit (~ double the employee income). The number of members of compulsory insurance is currently just short of 28 million people. Out of these, approximately 27 million are in employment subject to compulsory insurance and 160.000 are mandatorily insured self-employed. The payments of the Statutory Pension Insurance and the Social Miners' and Mine-employees' Insurance can fundamentally be split into pension payments (incl. of payments for health insurance for pensioners of about DM 350 billion in 1998) and rehabilitation payments (1998: approx. DM 7.6 billion); that will, however, not be examined in the following.

It can be seen in Figure 3.6.5 in the 1970s there was a strong increase in the expenditures of the pension system. Measured as per GDP ratio it rose for nearly 3%. During the 1980s it was rather stable and since the beginning of the 1990s it is continually climbing up to nearly 8% again for West Germany and nearly 9% for Germany as a whole. Especially in Eastern Germany this is due to a labor market orientated policy of early retirement.

In comparison with this development in Sweden one can see that the relative costs of the public pension system is lower in Germany but that it is steadily rising in the last ten years whereas in Sweden it is continually falling.

Legislature differentiates between old age, disability and surviving dependents' pensions. The *old age pension* may be divided as follows:

Normal old age pension. The pre-condition for the entitlement to this pension is simply to reach the normal old age pension age of 65 years and to fulfil the general qualifying period of 5 years.

Old age pension for long-term insured. The insured may take an old age pension before reaching their 65th year if they have reached the age of 62 years and have fulfilled the qualifying period of 35 years.

Old age pension for the severely handicapped. The insured are entitled to this pension from their 63rd birthday – after a qualifying period of 35 years - if they are recognized as being severely handicapped.

The amount of the monthly pension to be paid is calculated according to the annual benefits accrued by the contributions during the life of the insured. In addition, account is taken of the time of entry into the pension scheme and of the type of pension.

In accordance with these various grounds for the payment of a pension, the amount of the pension is calculated based on the following *pension formula*, which is valid since 1992:

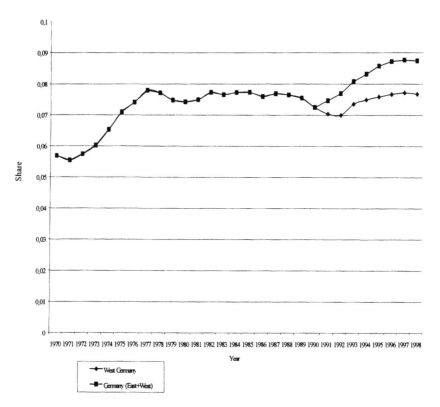

Figure 3.6.5   Public pension share of GDP in Germany

The *income index* is determined on the basis of the relationship between the personal benefit achieved in a calendar year and the benefit of all insured. It therefore takes into account individual contributions made and the length of insurance. The insurance period is usually longer than the period in which contributions were made. Thus, for example, contribution-free periods would be taken into account if they serve to compensate for times it was not possible for the insured to work subject to compulsory insurance. One makes a differentiation between fictitious qualifying periods (e.g. military and civilian service), credit periods (e.g. disablement, rehabilitation, bringing up of children, occupational training periods) and attribution periods (in respect of inability to work and inability to follow one's occupation pensions). There are extremely varied regulations in

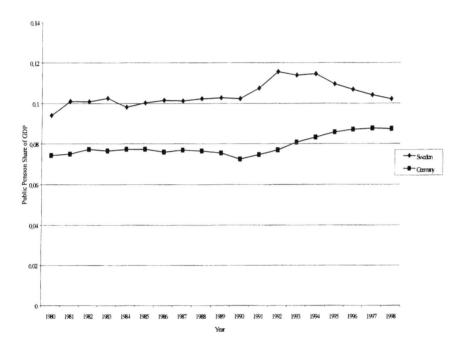

Figure 3.6.6   Comparison of GDP ratios between Germany and Sweden

respect of the compensation and valuation of contribution-free periods. In addition to the contribution-free times there are also allowance periods (bringing up of children and caring) and contribution reducing periods. Periods of unemployment belong to both the contribution reducing and the contribution-free periods.

The *access factor* is set according to the time of the insured's receipt of the pension. It reduces the pension in respect of early retirees and increases it in respect of late retirees. In respect of a claim to an early old age pension, the pension is reduced by an entrance factor of 0.003 in respect of each month earlier than the relevant, definitive age limit. This corresponds to a reduction in the pension of 0.3% (3.6% p. a.) for each month of early pension payment. Pension reduction first becomes of importance with the commencement of the raising of the early retirement old age pension age limit from 2000.

Pension Formula:

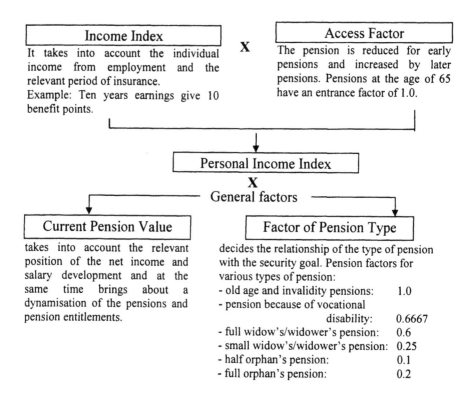

Income Index		Access Factor
It takes into account the individual income from employment and the relevant period of insurance. Example: Ten years earnings give 10 benefit points.	**X**	The pension is reduced for early pensions and increased by later pensions. Pensions at the age of 65 have an entrance factor of 1.0.

Personal Income Index

X

General factors

Current Pension Value	Factor of Pension Type
takes into account the relevant position of the net income and salary development and at the same time brings about a dynamisation of the pensions and pension entitlements.	decides the relationship of the type of pension with the security goal. Pension factors for various types of pension: - old age and invalidity pensions: 1.0 - pension because of vocational disability: 0.6667 - full widow's/widower's pension: 0.6 - small widow's/widower's pension: 0.25 - half orphan's pension: 0.1 - full orphan's pension: 0.2

The personal income index, made up of the income index and the access factor, represent the individual part of the pension formula. In addition to this, there are also two general factors: the pension type factor and the actual pension value.

The *pension type factor* has the task of giving various weights, according to the security aim, to the individual pensions. Pensions with full income replacement functions have a higher weight than pensions with income supplement functions or with maintenance functions.

The *actual pension value* creates a connection with overall economic benefit developments.

The standard pension (or benchmark pension) which is used to establish living standards security is a pension that an insured person with a period of insurance of 45 years at the average wage has attained. This so-called benchmark pensioner has thereby made 45 benefit points. The pension type factor amounts to 1.0. Together with the actual pension value of 48.29 for West and 42.01 for East Germany a gross monthly pension of about DM 2,144 (West) and DM 1,839 (East) is calculated. After the deduction of the contributory share for health and nursing insurance one receives a net standard pension (at the amount of DM 2,007.90 for West and DM 1,741.11 for East Germany). The net standard pension is related to the net employed income of all insured and from this the net benchmark level of 70% is arrived at.

The possible pension system after Reform I. The Federal government, which lost power in 1998, wanted to reduce the cost of the system only by a reform within the pay as you go system and especially by introducing a demographic factor. The intention of the demographic factor was relating the reduction of the pension level to the development of the life expectancy.

Except the demographic factor DF_t the Pension formula is the same as described before. It consists of the Income Index IP_a, the Access Factor AF, the current Pension Value cPV_t and the Factor of Pensions Type PT. The only difference is that the individual monthly pension will be adjusted by an overall demographic factor DF_t which takes account of the development of the average life expectancy LE :

$$(3) \qquad R(t) = \sum_{a=0}^{A} IP_a \cdot AF \cdot cPV_t \cdot PT \cdot DF_t ,$$

$$\text{where} \quad DF_t = \left(\frac{LE_{t-2}}{LE_{t-1}} - 1 \right) \cdot \frac{1}{2} + 1$$

Contrary to the cohort-specific adjustment in the Swedish reform the Pension Reform Act scheduled for an overall adjustment concerning both pensions in payment and pensions newly awarded. Both methods have different effects on the amount of pensions. If we look at the sum of the present discounted value of the pensions an average individual is expected to receive in the Swedish system the amount will be distributed on the remaining lifetime while the same amount will be reduced in the German system.

Furthermore the Pension Reform Act scheduled that the adjustment of pension by the higher life expectancy is only effected by half. Contribution payers and the recipients of a pension should have the same burden of these additional costs of the higher life expectancy. Besides a certain kind of just impression there is only one politico-economic reason for this division: Without it the pension level would decline from 71% to about 62% of the net earnings (Rürup 1998, 290) which seemed not to be acceptable for the former government.

The second crucial measure of the Pension Reform Act is a kind of actuarial fairness as reaction to the costs of early retirement. Although the incentives for early retirement were not as high as in the Swedish pension system there was a huge fraction of workers retiring before the normal age of 65 (see Jagob/Sesselmeier 2000b). As mentioned in the pension formula this actuarial fairness reduces the pension in respect of early retirees and increases it in respect of late retirees. In respect of a claim to an early old age pension, the pension is reduced by an entrance factor of 0.003 in respect of each month earlier than the relevant, definitive age limit. This corresponds to a reduction in the pension of 0.3% (3.6% p. a.) for each month of early pension payment.

This one and other measures of the Pension Reform Act of 1999 (for an overview see Götz et al. 1998) are still effective whereas the demographic factor is temporarily cancelled by the federal government.

The possible pension system after Reform II. The present Federal government replaced the demographic factor through a two-stage pension increase not according to wage development as foreseen but only according to the rate of inflation, i.e. of 0.6% in 2000 and (so far) 1.3% in 2001. The consequences of this inflation targeting is a rather fast decline of the pension level from 71% in 1999 down to under 68% in 2001 and then staying slightly over 68% over the next thirty years. Therefore the pension would remain on a higher level as regarding to the demographic factor which would have led to about 64%.

Additionally a capital covered provision is discussed which should supplement the pay-as-you-go system with its then reduced benefits. Due to the government this should be a compulsory saving; a certain amount of the

356

(gross) wage should – up to the income threshold – be invested into a portfolio of different investment kinds which has to fulfil certain minimum requirements, i.e. has to secure a long-life income, to secure and make calculable the future benefits and to return the paid contributions (see Greisler 1999).

The obligation of a private capital covered provision is required if the state wants to secure the standard of living despite the necessary reduction of the pay-as-you-go system. As, for information economic reasons, a statutory compulsory (pension) insurance is useful (see e.g. Wellisch 2000, 251-255) in order to counter the problem of adverse selection and thus to achieve a better situation for all persons, a compulsory insurance is - at least - also necessary for a capital covered additional provision, if the state is no longer able and willing to maintain the standard of living during the old age by the Statutory Pension Insurance alone but adheres to the objective of a state secured standard of living. The overall standard of living provision for the target group can be effected only by means of an obligatory percentage. The development of the capital covered self-provision does, consequently, not primarily mean a price reduction for the pay-as-you-go system but rather the reach of the welfare state's protection. If the state does not want to accept provision gaps it must make the additional provision, i.e. the old age provision saving mandatory. If these funds are saved on a voluntary basis, the securing of the standard of living is no longer left to the state but, as the case may be, to other preferences of the individual person.

Besides this, an obligatory percentage (a certain percentage of the gross wage) will, during the implementation period and a net wage orientation of the pensions, have a sedative effect on the pensions development and thus the contributions. As the pensions will (with the exception of the years 2000 and 2001) be oriented according to the net wage development of the preceding year, pension increases would be lower without having to lower the net pension level. This way, the pensioners would contribute to the financing of the capital covered provision's development.

Due to the obligatory percentage the contribution rate's increase which is inevitable because of the demographic development will be maintained at a low level.

The possible pension system after Reform III The echo coming from the media and the opposition about this mandatory second pillar was so

357

negative that the federal government launched a new pension reform. This third reform again is a combination of the statutory pension insurance constituting the first pillar and a second fully-funded pillar. The crucial difference between the current plan and the former one is that the second pillar is now merely voluntary instead of being mandatory.

Starting in 2001 people are supposed to pay into fully-funded saving plans starting with a rate of 0.5% of gross wage which is getting increased year by year by 0.5% up to 4% in 2008. Because it is not mandatory the government has to provide some other incentives to make the people join this program. First both wage earners and salaried employees will be entitled to receive a saving subsidy up to DM 400 a year, provided their yearly taxable income did not exceed DM 35,000 for single earners and DM 70,000 for married couples. Only those saving plans would be subsidized which assured a sustained income in old age and which guaranteed the return of at least the sum which was invested. The second incentive is much stronger because the reform plan also envisages a reduction in the level of future retirement entitlements paid by the statutory pension insurance. This reduction is necessary to hold the contribution rate constant at about 20% in 2020 and 22% in 2030. Technically the reduction works through an additional so called 'balancing factor' by which the pension formula will be multiplied.

This balancing factor (BF) combines the pension out of the PAYG system (PP) with the pension resulting of the fully-funded pillar (CP) in the following way:

$$BF = (PP - 0.5\ CP) / PP$$

    where $CP = CP\,(i, t)$
    with i = interest rate
         t = period until getting a pension.

The consequences of this balancing factor on the pension level out of the statutory pension insurance and on the pension level on the whole depend crucially on the estimated interest rate and on the period t between the start of a private savings backed plan and retirement. The longer the investment period and the higher the interest rate, the lower the level of the statutory pension benefit and the higher the overall pension level. Starting from a pension level of 70% of the net wage in 2000 an interest rate of 4% will lead to a PAYG pension level of 64% respectively an overall pension level of 72.5% of the net wage in 2030 or to 60% respectively 77% in 2050. Taking an interest rate of 5.5% the levels amount 62% respectively 74% in 2030 or 54% respectively 82% in 2050 (see Figure 3.6.7).

What has changed dramatically is the role of the government for securing individuals' standard of living. In this latest variety of the pension reform the responsibility for it changes. Now the individual person itself is responsible for securing its standard of living. For more than the last 20 years people were used to a pension level out of the statutory pension insurance of 70% of the net wage or more (see Figure 3.6.8).

A more serious problem results from the construction of the statutory pension insurance. As already mentioned it is wage-related and aimed to secure the standard of living, but there is no minimum pension. Thus low-wage-earners who are not able or not willing to invest in private saving plans run the risk of getting a pension below the subsistence level. Therefore they have to ask for additional social assistance – a possibility which is not very well-known.

The possible pension system after Reform IV. Again their was huge critique focussing on the benefit level out of the pay-as-you-go pillar in 2050. Therefore the government changed the reform plans one more time. Most important they cut the interrelationship between the two pillars via the balancing factor. Now the pension level of the first pillar should fall to 64% in 2030. From 2011 on the benefit level of the new retirees should fall on a yearly rate of 0.3%. This could have the effect that many will try to retire in 2010. Another effect will be that people within the same cohort will receive different pension payments whether they will early retire or not, without looking at mechanisms due to actuarial fairness. Additionally a modified pension formula due to a new defined net wage should be introduced in 2002. Payments for the second pillar should not belong to the net wage anymore with the consequence that the net wage is shrinking by definition and so the foundation for the yearly adjustment of the pension level. Starting in 2001 people again are supposed to pay voluntarily into fully-funded saving plans starting with a rate of 0.5% of gross wage which is getting increased year by year by 0.5% up to 4% in 2008.

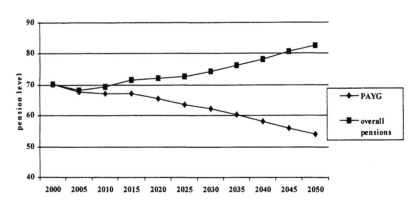

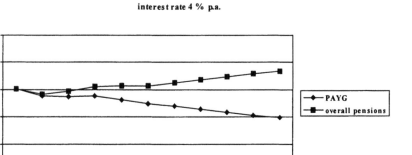

Figure 3.6.7   Estimation development of pension levels 2000-2050

The main difference to the former reform plan is that the state now is responsible for securing the standard of living again. We do not want to discuss whether 64% of a former net wage are enough to secure the standard of living or not. But if the government think that it is enough why should it subsidise an additional and voluntary funded pillar?

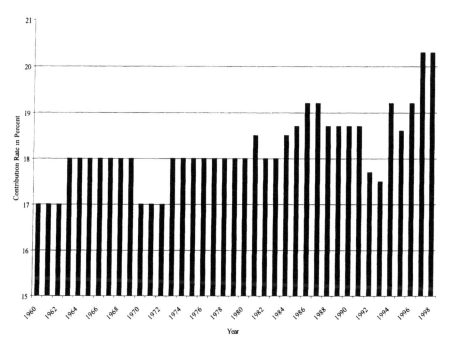

Figure 3.6.8   Pension level in percent of the net wage 1957-1997

5. Concluding remarks

The Swedish reform approach is of major relevance in the political debate in Germany. The reason why it is so appealing to many countries are various. Most importantly the mix between a funded and a pay-as-you-go system should be mentioned. Besides this the Swedish approach managed it to find a way how to deal with the demographic problem of a continuously rising average life expectancy of the elderly and simultaneously creating an incentive to postpone retirement by reducing the benefits according to the age of retirement.

The relevance of this approach can be seen to the main part in the partial funding. As in every country where pensions are financed by a pay-as-you-go system the demographic change in Sweden and Germany does affect the sustainability of pension policy. Undoubted reforms became necessary in both countries. The interesting point about the Swedish pension reform is that they managed it to get such a mandatory partly funded system started. Even though the rate of 2.5% is rather arbitrary – as

361

any other rate would be – the system will give a certain level of security. Organizing this additional fully funded part in a mandatory way becomes the only solution if the aim of social policy is to guarantee the individuals a similar standard of living as they had before.

The second very interesting feature of the Swedish pension reform is its demographic factor. A comparison between this factor and the one which was intended to be installed by the former government, shows a major difference. The German factor affects every retired person. It is an overall adjustment of the pension level and the costs on a higher life expectancy is spread on every pensioner. The Swedish factor affects only those cohorts who are retiring, i.e. every cohort has a different pension level which will not be changed until they die. The Swedish system does insofar impose the costs of a higher life expectancy directly on those who cause the costs. A second positive effect of the Swedish factor in connection with the flexible retirement age is its incentive to postpone retirement. The advantage of the Swedish system is the wider range for early retirement and therefore the greater scope for labour market policy.

What can we learn for the German discussion?

First of all we have to decide whether we want a reform only within the pay-as-you-go pillar or a reform via a complementary fully funded pillar. It seems that the German government will choose the second option.

Secondly, because a fully funded pension system is negatively effected by the demographic change too, reforming the pay as you go pillar is also necessary. To postpone the age of retirement, which actually is 59, seems to be the most relevant task.

Thirdly, we have to ask who should be responsible for securing the standard of living. If we want a mixed system and if we want the state to secure the living standard, then we need a mandatory second pillar.

Note

1 For helpful comments we thank Barbara Wolfe and the participants of the 7th International Research Seminar on 'issues in Social Security' of Foundation International Studies on Social Security in Sigtuna 17th – 20th June 2000.

References

Bohn, Henning, 1999, Social Security and Demographic Uncertainty: The Risk Sharing Properties of Alternative Policies, NBER Working Paper 7030, Cambridge/Mass.

Börsch-Supan, Axel, Reinhold Schnabel, 1999, Social Security and Retirement in Germany, in J. Gruber and D. Wise (eds.): *Social Security and Retirement around the world*, Chicago, 135-180.

Breyer, Friedrich, 1989, On the Intergenerational Pareto Efficiency of Pay-As-You-Go Financed Pension Systems, *Journal of Institutional and Theoretical Economics*, 145, 643-658.

Brooks, Robin, 2000, What will happen to Financial Markets when the Baby Boomers retire?, IMF Working Paper 00/18.

Fenge, Robert, 1997, Effizienz der Alterssicherung, Wirtschaftswissenschaftliche Beiträge, Band 149, Physica Verlag, Heidelberg.

Fox, Louise, Edward Palmer, 1999, Latvian Pension Reform, Social Protection Discussion Paper No. 9922, Washington D.C., World Bank.

Götz, Marion, Helmut Stahl, Frank Wollschläger, Neuregelungen bei den Altersrenten, Deutsche Rentenversicherung 1-2/1998, 2-9.

Greisler, Peter, 1999, Mittel- und langfristige Entwicklung der privaten Vorsorge, in: Cramer, J. et al. (eds.), *Handbuch Altersvorsorge*, Frankfurt am Main, 1011-1023.

Hakola, Tuulia, 2000, In transit-labour market transitions of the aged in Finland, paper presented at the 7th International Research Seminar on 'Issues in Social Security' at FISS in Sigtuna 17th-20th June 2000.

Heller, Peter S., 1998, Rethinking Public Pension Reform Initiatives, IMF Working Paper 98/61.

Jagob, Jochen, Oliver Scholz, 1998, Reforming the German Pension System: Who wins and Who loses? A Generational Accounting Perspective, Discussion Paper in German Studies IGS98/12, Institute for German Studies, University of Birmingham.

Jagob, Jochen and Werner Sesselmeier, 2000a, The Interaction of the Labour Market and Pension Systems – An International Comparison, in: Jun Young Kim/Per Gunnar Svensson (eds.): *Domain Linkages and Privatization in Social Security*, Ashgate.

Jagob, Jochen, Werner Sesselmeier, 2000b, Vorruhestand versus Altersteilzeit als strategische Optionen betrieblicher Restrukturierungsprozesse, in: Rainer George, Olaf Struck (eds.), *Generationenaustausch im Unternehmen*, München und Mering, 123-140.

Lindbeck, Assar, 2000, Pensions and Contemporary Socioeconomic Change, NBER Working Paper 7770, Cambridge/Mass.

Miles, David, 2000, Funded and Unfunded Pension Schemes: Risk, Return and Welfare, CESifo Working Paper Series No. 239, Munich.

Orszag, Peter R., Joseph E. Stiglitz, 1999, Rethinking Pension Reform: Ten Myths about Social Security Systems, Paper presented at the conference on 'New Ideas About Old Age Security', The World Bank, Washington D.C., September 14-15,1999.

Palme, Mårten, Ingemar Svensson, 1999, Social Security, Occupational Pensions, and Retirement in Sweden, in J. Gruber and D. A. Wise (eds.): *Social Security and Retirement around the world*, Chicago, 355-402.

Palmer, Edward, 1999a, Exit from the Labor Force for Older Workers: Can the NDC Pension System Help?, The Geneva Papers on Risk and Insurance, 24, 461-472.

Palmer, Edward, 1999b, The Swedish Pension Reform Model – Framework and Issues – mimeo.

Palmer, Edward, 2000, Swedish Pension Reform – How did it evolve and what does it mean for the future, Paper presented at the NBER Kiel Institute Conference 'Coping with the Pension Crisis – Where does Europe stand'.

Persson, Mats, 1998, Reforming Social Security in Sweden, in Horst Siebert (ed.): *Redesigning Social Security*, Institut für Weltwirtschaft an der Universität Kiel, Mohr Siebeck, Tübingen

Pigeau, Manon and Werner Sesselmeier, 2000, Consequences of the European Monetary Union on Social Security Systems, Discussion Paper No. IGS 00/4, Institute for German Studies, University of Birmingham.

Rürup, Bert, 1998, Zur Berücksichtigung der Lebenserwartung in der gesetzlichen Rentenversicherung, Deutsche Rentenversicherung 5/1998, 281-291.

Schmähl, Winfried, 1999, Steigende Lebenserwartung und soziale Sicherung – Tendenzen, Auswirkungen und Reaktionen, ZeS Arbeitspapier Nr. 4/1999, Universität Bremen.

Sinn, Hans-Werner (1999a), The Crisis of Germany's Pension Insurance System and How It can be Resolved, CESifo Working Paper Series No. 191, Munich.

Sinn, Hans-Werner (1999b), Pension reform and Demographic Crisis: Why a Funded System is Needed and Why It is not Needed, CESifo München, paper presented at the 55th IIPF Congress in Moscow.

Ståhlberg, Ann-Charlotte, 1995, Pension Reform in Sweden, *Scandinavian Journal of Social Welfare*, 4, 267-273.

Thum, Marcel and Jakob von Weizsäcker, 1999, Implizite Einkommensteuer als Messlatte für die aktuellen Rentenreformvorschläge ifo Discussion Paper No. 64.

Wellisch, Dietmar, 2000, Finanzwissenschaft I: Rechtfertigung der Staatstätigkeit, München

World Bank, 1994, *Averting the Old Age Crisis: Policies to Protect the Old and Promote Growth*, Oxford University Press: Oxford.

List of contributors

Esther N. Bergsma
Researcher at the Social Security Supervisory Board (Ctsv) in the Netherlands

Jonathan Bradshaw
Professor of Social Policy, Department of Social Policy and Social Work, University of York, United Kingdom

Jasper C. van den Brink
Researcher at the Social Security Supervisory Board (Ctsv) in the Netherlands

Bea Cantillon
Professor of Social Policy Studies, Centre for Social Policy, University of Antwerp, Belgium

Andreas Cebulla
Centre for Research in Social Policy, Loughborough University, United Kingdom

Rudi van Dam
Centre for Social Policy, University of Antwerp, Belgium

Joris Ghysels
Centre for Social Policy, University of Antwerp, Belgium

Robert H. Haveman
Department of Economics and Lafoyette Institute of Public Policy, University of Wisconsin–Madison, Wisconsin, U.S.A.

Jochen Jagob
> Department of Economics and Public Finance, Darmstadt University of Technology, Germany

Melissa Mullikin
> Department of Economics, University of Wisconsin–Madison, Wisconsin, U.S.A.

Ninke Mussche
> Centre for Social Policy, University of Antwerp, Belgium

Edward Palmer
> University of Uppsala and National Insurance Institute, Stockholm, Sweden

Maneerat Pinyopusarerk
> Senior Welfare Services Economist, Australian Institute of Health and Welfare, Canberra, Australia

Simon Roberts
> Centre for Research in Social Policy, Department of Social Sciences, Loughborough University, Loughborough, United Kingdom

Martin T.W. Rosenfeld
> Institute for Economic Research Halle (IWH), Saale, Germany

Peter Saunders
> Director, Social Policy Research Centre, University of New South Wales, Sydney, Australia

Erik Schokkaert
> Catholic University of Leuven, Belgium

Werner Sesselmeier
> Department of Economics and Public Finance, Darmstadt University of Technology, Germany

Ali Tasiran
School of Economics and Law, Satisticle Institute and Faculty of Public Health, University of Göteborg, Sweden

Lotta Westerhäll
School of Economics and Law, University of Göteborg, Sweden

Barbara L. Wolfe
Departments of Economics and Preventive Medicine, University of Wisconsin–Madison, Wisconsin, U.S.A

www.ingramcontent.com/pod-product-compliance
Ingram Content Group UK Ltd.
Pitfield, Milton Keynes, MK11 3LW, UK
UKHW020402010325
455677UK00021B/578